Hollywood Musicals

YEAR BY YEAR

THIRD EDITION

Also by Stanley Green

The World of Musical Comedy

The Great Clowns of Broadway

Encyclopedia of the Musical Theatre

Encyclopedia of the Musical Film

Broadway Musicals of the 1930s (Ring Bells! Sing Songs!)

Starring Fred Astaire

The Rodgers and Hammerstein Story

Broadway Musicals Show by Show

Hollywood Musicals

YEAR BY YEAR
THIRD EDITION

BY STANLEY GREEN
REVISED AND UPDATED
BY BARRY MONUSH

APPLAUSE
THEATRE & CINEMA BOOKS

An Imprint of Hal Leonard Corporation
NEW YORK

Third edition published in 2010 by Applause Theatre & Cinema Books
An Imprint of Hal Leonard Corporation
7777 West Bluemound Road
Milwaukee, WI 53213

Trade Book Division Editorial Offices
19 West 21st Street, New York, NY 10010

Printed in the United States of America

Book composition by Kristina Rolander

The Library of Congress has catalogued the first edition as follows:

Green, Stanley.
    Hollywood Musicals year by year / Stanley Green.
cm.
    Includes indexes.
    ISBN 0-88188-610-6 (pbk.) : $16.95
Musical films—United States—History and criticism.
I   Title.
PN1995.9M86G74   1990
791.43 ' 657—dc20

                                                          90-53537

                                                          CIP

ISBN 978-1-4234-8903-0

www.applausepub.com

JUN 1 - 2010

CONTENTS

(For a complete alphabetical listing of the
movies included in this book, see page 360.)

Contents

Contents

Contents

Contents

Contents

Indexes

PREFACE

TO THE THIRD EDITION

"Without a song or a dance what are we?
So, I say thank you for the music,
For giving it to me."

—From the score of *Mamma Mia!*

When I was invited by my publisher to update this book, I had a mixed reaction. On one hand I found it daunting to be asked to take someone else's work (in this instance, the late Stanley Green, whom I had never met) and carry it on, as if it was my own property or a project I had been involved with from the start. But then I figured if someone was going to do it, I certainly felt qualified, as musicals are something I live for and long for, especially at the movies, where they aren't exactly in abundance. If you've collected the annual reference book that I edit, *Screen World* (and I certainly hope you do), over the past several years you might have noticed that I try my best to ensure there is room on the cover for a musical or two. They are that significant to me.

I am always on the lookout for official, bona fide musicals, or anything even vaguely resembling a staged musical number in a movie, no matter what the genre. As far as I'm concerned, a song or dance can make a motion picture that much better. The already enjoyable *Ferris Bueller's Day Off* went up a notch or two in my estimation when Matthew Broderick led a group of Chicago parade spectators through a rendition of "Twist and Shout"; the undisputed highlight of *Come Blow Your Horn* was Frank Sinatra belting the title tune to Tony Bill while squiring him around New York in what was otherwise a straightforward comedy; and how delightful it was to see Joseph Gordon-Levitt start dancing through the park as a celebration of his romantic happiness in *(500) Days of Summer.* Many a film could have benefited from a tune or two, if you ask me, including several animated features that were otherwise drowning in snarky sarcasm, or such live-action fantasies as *The Flintstones,* which didn't seem to have much reason to exist if Fred and Barney weren't going to break into some fancy footwork or chime in on some, uh…"rock" music.

There are times when I believe that those of us who truly embrace all things musical are, as someone dear to me likes to call us, "a teeny, tiny band," as the term *musicals* scares away select moviegoers who usually condemn them for the same tired reasons you've heard for eons. "They're not realistic" (this usually stated by people who then gladly pay money to see *Transformers* or *The Lord of the Rings,* which, as we all know, are just chock full of "real" situations that happen to us all on a daily basis); "They're sentimental" (an assessment by those who can't stand to see stark emotionalism of any kind, especially when sung); "The concept only works in older movies" (a declaration of defeat, if you ask me, or a weird idealization of all things past being better because they are over, dead and gone); "They have no relevance for today's audience" (this from complainers who don't understand that musicals need not be operettas set in the style and manner of the early 20th century but can encompass everything from pop to show music to hip-hop to rock to country and so on). Frankly, I've always felt that people who dismiss screen musicals are missing out on one of the best ways to tell a story, something unique and divertingly out of the ordinary. And considering how clichéd and routine so many films can be, why wouldn't you want to see something that shakes up conventions with a bit of warbling or perhaps some dancing?

Fortunately, unexpectedly, and happily, there seems to have been a slight turn in the tide since the new century began. When audiences didn't shy away from Baz Luhrmann's kinetic *Moulin Rouge!* this was definitely a sign of progress. But what really helped put the genre back on top was the tremendously favorable reaction to the 2002 film adaptation of *Chicago.* Not only was there a consensus that this stage property had been excitingly reimagined for cinema, but even those people who had stayed away from musicals showed up in huge numbers, turning this into a blockbuster moneymaker that ended up winning the Academy Award for Best Picture. Because of *Chicago,* all sorts of musicals that had been proposed over the years suddenly got the green light. Ultimately, there were varying degrees of success (commercial or artistic) for each, but it no longer seemed risky to back a project that involved actors singing onscreen. How nice to have had an entire decade in which you could look forward to an occasional musical showing up on the year's film schedule, which was a hell of a lot more interesting than a calendar filled with horror schlock, unnecessary remakes, extensions of former television series, and sequels, sequels, sequels.

Of the 40 new entries I've added (think of it, at least 40 films qualified as musicals since 1999; nothing to sneeze at, really), I had already seen a majority on theater screens when they were released (often, more than once) but had no problem revisiting them in order to keep a fresh perspective. As I see it, whether they are great or good or just passable or flat-out misfires, musicals are already miles ahead of the pack because they took the risk of blending cinema with song. The musical is often described as the hardest genre to execute, but it is more often than not the most fulfilling one. I can only hope that as long as the film industry survives, more musicals will be dancing our way and that, should we update this book in another 10 years, there will be many additional pages to fill.

Barry Monush
New York City
January 2010

PREFACE
TO THE SECOND EDITION

I was fortunate enough to be the editor for the original edition of *Hollywood Musicals Year by Year*, Stanley Green's last book. Stanley's easy and scrupulous grasp of voluminous facts, his wit, and his pithy prose were quite an education for a young editor. He was an old pro in every sense. Amazingly, he did the layout of this book himself, writing exactly to the length needed in each entry. (The same was true for *Broadway Musicals: Show by Show.*) He also did his own photo research. The man rarely ever made a mistake of any kind, even in juggling thousands of details in a book such as this. That kind of professionalism was impressive to me then. In retrospect, I value and respect it even more.

Stanley Green, who died in December of 1990, was the most prominent American musical theatre historian of the twentieth century, publishing at least eight books on the subject. He was one of the first writers to take a field considered to be popular entertainment and treat it as legitimate history. However, his writing is anything but dull. Even in presenting facts, what he *really* thinks is almost always there. Just read between the lines carefully and you'll find his dry wit. Stanley's expertise and enthusiasm extended to musical film, which he addressed in two books beyond this volume: *Starring Fred Astaire*, and *Encyclopaedia of the Musical Film*.

With Kay Green's blesing, we undertook an update to *Hollywood Musicals Year by Year* with writer Elaine Schmidt, adding ten years of movies from the 1990s. Stanley, I hope we did you justice.

Rick Walters, Editor
Milwaukee, Wisconsin
August, 1999

PREFACE
TO THE FIRST EDITION

Something of a companion volume to my previous *Broadway Musicals Show by Show*, *Hollywood Musicals Year by Year* is a combination history, guide, fact book, and photograph album of some 300 of the screen's major musical productions from the *The Jazz Singer* in 1927 to *The Little Mermaid* (1989). Not falling under the scope of the survey, however, are documentaries, operas, westerns with singing cowboys, foreign-language musicals, short subjects, or silent films, even those with accompanying scores. My admittedly loose criteria for selection have been box office popularity, quality of the songs, talent of the performers, staging of the musical sequences, seminal influence, uniqueness of subject matter and approach, size of the production budget, and personal taste.

Under the film's credits, I have – wherever known – included names in parentheses of writers, directors, or choreographers who, for whatever reason, failed to receive official credit for their efforts. Cast lists generally include only major actors except in cases in which well-known personalities may have had bit parts. To save space, only the names by which actors are best known are listed, even though they may have used different names during their early careers.

In the text, references have been made to movies with the highest theatre rentals in the United States and Canada during each decade; i.e. the portion of box office ticket sales grosses paid by the exhibitors to the film's distributor. Information was gleaned from the surveys of "All-Time Film Rental Champs" that appear annually in the trade paper *Variety*.

Following the text are listed soundtrack LP and CD albums (ST) and video cassettes (VC), as well as studio-made LPs and CDs featuring the movie's star. In all cases, I have indicated the names of the companies that currently hold the release rights.

Among reference books consulted were *The World of Entertainment* by Hugh Fordin (Doubleday), *The Melody Lingers On* by Roy Hemming (Newmarket), *The Film Encyclopaedia* by Ephraim Katz (Crowell), *The Films of Jeanette MacDonald and Nelson Eddy* by Eleanor Knowles (Arlington), *The Movie Musical* edited by Miles Kreuger (Dover), *The Disney Films* by Leonard Maltin (Crown), *The American Movies Reference Book* edited by Paul Michael (Prentice-Hall), *The Fox Girls* by James Robert Parish (Arlington), *Reel Facts* by Cobbett Steinberg (Vintage), and *The Hollywood Musical* by John Russell Taylor and Arthur Jackson (McGraw-Hill).

Those who were generous in supplying information and making suggestions include Ted Chapin, Saul Cooper, Terry Driscoll, Bert Fink, Nicole Friedman, Roy Hemming, Mary Henderson, Edward Jablonski, Ephraim Katz, Don Koll, Dan Langan, Irv Lichtman, Bob Lissauer, and Alfred Simon. I am especially indebted to Mr. Hemming for photographs from this collection and to Joe Savage for rare video tapes. Others who supplied tapes and discs were Sue Procko and Cinde Clarke of MGM/UA Home Video, Louise Alaimo of Nelson Entertainment, and Dan Rivard of CBS Special Products. In addition Jane Aker of MCA Home Video, Angela Chicorel of CBS/Fox Video, Pamela Dill of Turner Home Entertainment, and Michael Finnegan of Warner Bros. Video all responded to my requests for aid, and Mary Corliss and Terry Gesken of the Museum of Modern Art Film Stills Archives were also of great assistance.

Rick Walters, my editor at Hal Leonard, as well as Glenda Herro, my previous editor, were particularly cooperative and enthusiastic, and I also appreciate the support I received from Keith Mardak and Mary Bultman.

My wife, Kay, was always available to peruse the manuscript and to offer indispensable advice, and daughter Susan and son Rudy could be counted on to provide input whenever needed.

Stanley Green
Brooklyn, New York
September, 1990

INTRODUCTION

In 1927, when the Warner brothers wanted a suitable vehicle with which to demonstrate their Vitaphone sound system, they chose a story that had the one ingredient impossible to communicate in a silent film – the songs. *The Jazz Singer*, therefore, was not only a pioneer sound film, it also inaugurated the movie musical.

Potenially, so much was possible by combining camera, soundtrack, and song. Because movies were unrestricted by a theater's proscenium, they could take full advantage of cinematic techniques that allowed musical sequences to be staged alongside real trains, atop real airplanes, high up on real mountains, all over crowded cities, up in the clouds, under the water, and over the rainbow. They could offer spectacular production numbers that created their own fantasy world in defiance of space, gravity, and logic. They could even show actors mouthing songs while the actual singing emanated from someone else's throat. Any they didn't have to be restricted to stories about human beings since an artist's skill and imagination could bring cartoon characters to vividly animated life.

The Depression years of the 1930s and the war years of the 1940s were periods in which the desire for escapist entertainment nurtured the flowering of the screen musical. Each of the major studios was distinguished by its own special style – or styles. Warner Bros. (as the company has always been billed on the screen) offered backstage musicals with Ruby Keeler and Dick Powell embellished by spectacularBusby Berkeley production numbers. Metro-Goldwyn-Mayer offered lush operettas with underwater musicals with Esther Williams and "backyard" musicals with Mickey Rooney and Judy Garland. RKO Radio offered elegant, stylized dancing musicals with Fred Astaire and Ginger Rogers. 20th Century-Fox offered kiddie musicals with Shirley Temple, period musicals and picture post-cart musicals with Alice Faye and Betty Grable, and skating musicals with Sonja Henie. Paramount offered collegiate musicals with Bing Crosby and self-kidding "Road" shows with Crosby, Bob Hope and Dorothy Lamour. Universal offered teenage musicals with Deanna Durbin. Walt Disney offered cartoon fantasies. The post-war years were dominated by the productions of the prolific Arthur Freed whose Freed Unit at MGM was responsible for what many believe was the apotheosis of the movie musical, with films featuring such stars as Gene Kelly, Fred Astaire, Mickey Rooney, Judy Garland, Cyd Charisse, Leslie Caron, Frank Sinatra, June Allyson, Howard Keel, and Red Skelton.

The screen has always depended on the Broadway theatre both for its movie version of stage hits and also as a source of subject matter for backstage stories. *The Jazz Singer* was based on a popular play and *42nd Street*, the film most responsible for ushering in the golden age of screen musicals, was an original Hollywood creation all about the trials of putting on a Broadway show. The first operetta transferred to the sound screen was *The Desert Song* in 1929, though Rio Rita, released the same year, was a far bigger hit as well as the precursor of stage-to-screen musicals that have continues thus far, up to *Evita*. On the other hand, screen-to-stage musicals, once rare, have suddenly become fashionable: *Big*, *Saturday Night Fever*, *Footloose*, *Meet Me in St. Louis*, *State Fair*, *Sunset Boulevard*, etc.

It is no secret that musicals in the traditional mould are no longer part of the mainstream of screen entertainment. Since the seventies, we have had either an occasional trickle of remade Broadway shows or movies that are preoccupied with the seamier aspects of contemporary life, e.g. *Saturday Night Fever*, *The Rose*,

Pennies from Heaven, and *Flashdance*. This is regrettable but understandable. At their best, musicals of old overflowed with freshness and charm and romance. They celebrated the joy of living. We cheerfully overlooked the frequently inane plots to relish the glorious music by master songwriters that were sung and danced by stars who justly deserved the adjective legendary. In our current bluejearns world, with its permissive behavior and percussive music, there seems to be little room for the kind of entertainment that once lifted hearts and set feet tapping.

But all is not completely lost. Disney, almost solely on its own, has kept the musical film alive in recent years in animation. If there appears of be no future for the live action musical film as we once knew it, past achievements can always be savored through the medium of home video. At the touch of a button, Busby's girls are still performing their kaleidoscopic patters, Jeannette and nelson are still singing their Indian love call, Fred is still twirling Ginger or Rita or Cyd around the dancefloor, Jimmy is still giving his regards to Broadway, Judy is still pouring her heart out to Mr. Gable and yearning to fly over the rainbow, Bing is still bounding down the roads with Bob and Dorothy, Gene is still splashing his way through a rain-drenced street, Barbra is still warning everyone not to rain on her parade, and Julie is still making us believe that the hills will always be alive with the sound of music.

Stanley Green
1990

Hollywood Musicals

YEAR BY YEAR

THIRD EDITION

The Jazz Singer. Al Jolson belting out "Toot, Toot, Tootsie!" in a San Francisco nightspot.

THE JAZZ SINGER

Screenplay: Alfred A. Cohen
Titles: Jack Jarmuth
Produced by: Darryl F. Zanuck for Warner Bros.
Directed by: Alan Crosland
Photography: Hal Mohr
Cast: Al Jolson, May McAvoy, Warner Oland, Eugenie Besserer, Otto Lederer, Bobby Gordon, Roscoe Karns, Cantor Josef Rosenblatt, William Demarest, Myrna Loy
Songs: "Kol Nidre" (trad.); "Dirty Hands, Dirty Face" (James Monaco-Edgar Leslie, Grant Clarke); "Toot, Toot, Tootsie!" (Ted Fiorito, Robert King-Gus Kahn); "Yahrzeit" (trad.); "Blue Skies" (Irving Berlin); "Mother of Mine, I Still Have You" (Louis Silvers-Clarke); "My Mammy" (Walter Donaldson-Sam Lewis, Joe Young)
Released: October 1927; 89 minutes

"Wait a minute! Wait a minute! You ain't heard nothin' yet . . . " The first words spoken in a feature-length motion picture were uttered by an exuberant Al Jolson in *The Jazz Singer* just before launching into "Toot, Toot, Tootsie! " in a San Francisco nightclub. Thus the film—even though only its musical sequences and a few bits of dialogue were wired for sound—gets the credit as not only the first "talkie" but also the first screen musical. Since music is the one element impossible to convey in silent movies, it was both inevitable and logical that when the screen found its voice it would also burst into song.

The historic premiere of *The Jazz Singer* took place on October 6, 1927, at the Warner Theatre in New York. Its genesis occurred five years earlier as a short story, "The Day of Atonement" by Samson Raphaelson, who had modeled the central character on Al Jolson. The author subsequently adapted the story into a play, first called *Prayboy* then *The Jazz Singer,* with Jolson himself set for the leading role. But a disagreement between star and playwright brought about Jolson's replacement by George Jessel. Opening on Broadway in the fall of 1925, the play enjoyed a run of over 300 performances.

In 1926, Warner Bros., after purchasing the Vitaphone sound-on-disc process from Western Electric, released a silent movie, *Don Juan,* which was the first full-length dramatic film with a background score. The studio had already secured the screen rights to *The Jazz Singer* for $50,000, with Jessel signed to repeat his part, when Sam Warner decided to add audible musical sequences. When Jessel broke his contract because he felt the addition of sound entitled him to more money, the studio turned to Jolson to play Jakie Rabinowitz, the cantor's son, who, much to the distress of his parents, runs away from home to become jazz singer Jack Robin. After his father dies, however, Jakie gives up his big chance to star in a Broadway revue to assume the cantor's duties for the Yom Kippur services.

Though its emphasis on mother love makes it unduly maudlin, the film follows the general design of the stage production, except for a tacked-on ending that shows Jack Robin, some years later, belting out "My Mammy" in blackface to his own beaming mammy in the audience at a Broadway revue. The film's only spoken dialogue occurs earlier when Jackie unexpectedly returns home, sings "Blue Skies" for his mother, and then interrupts the song to tell her of all the wonderful things he is now able to do for her. Even the practice of voice dubbing began with *The Jazz Singer,* since the singing of Warner Oland, as the cantor, actually emanated from the soundtrack voice of Joseph Deskay.

In 1945, Warners planned a remake of *The Jazz Singer,* but shelved it because of Columbia's imminent production of *The Jolson Story.* The studio did release an updated version in 1952, with Danny Thomas in the title role (renamed Jerry Golding), Peggy Lee, and Eduard Franz as the cantor. A third variation, in 1980, co-starred Neil Diamond (now Jess Robin né Rabinovitch), Laurence Olivier as his improbable procreator, and Lucie Arnaz as the love interest, and reset the story in the milieu of the pop-rock world. In both remakes, not only does the father live but he becomes an enthusiastic booster of his son's career.
Sountrak ST. MGM/UA VC.

THE SINGING FOOL

Music: Ray Henderson, etc.
Lyrics: B. G. DeSylva & Lew Brown, etc.
Screenplay: C. Graham Baker
Titles: Joseph Jackson
Produced by: Darryl F. Zanuck for Warner Bros.
Directed by: Lloyd Bacon
Choreography: Larry Ceballos
Photography: Byron Haskin
Cast: Al Jolson, Betty Bronson, Josephine Dunn, Davey Lee
Songs: "It All Depends on You"; "I'm Sitting on Top of the World";
"There's a Rainbow 'Round My Shoulder" (Dave Dreyer-Billy Rose-
Al Jolson); "Golden Gate" (Joseph Meyer-Dreyer-Rose-Jolson);
"Sonny Boy" (with Jolson).
Released: September 1928; 101 minutes

Though it was still only a part-talkie, *The Singing Fool* became the first sound film to gross $4 million in U.S. and Canadian theatre rentals—and it would not be outgrossed until ten years later when it was overtaken by *Snow White and the Seven Dwarfs*. In this sentimental tale, Al Jolson plays a singing waiter who rises in show business, then hits the skids when his wife leaves him. There's further grief when his three-year-old son (Davey Lee) dies, but he bounces back with the aid of a good woman. The movie was the first with sound to show the screen's potential for launching song hits, since it was responsible for introducing "There's a Rainbow 'Round My Shoulder" and "Sonny Boy" (which its creators, DeSylva, Brown and Henderson, had written half-jokingly to see how many mawkish clichés they could pack into one lyric).

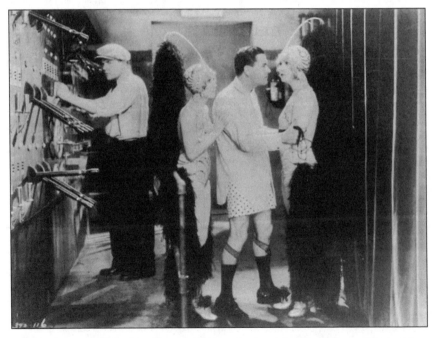

The Broadway Melody. A backstage confrontation involving Bessie Love, Charles King, and Anita Page.

THE BROADWAY MELODY

Music: Nacio Herb Brown
Lyrics: Arthur Freed
Screenplay: Sarah Y. Mason, Norman Houston, James Gleason, Edmund
      Goulding
Titles: Earl Baldwin
Produced by: Irving Thalberg for MGM
Directed by: Harry Beaumont
Choreography: George Cunningham
Photography: John Arnold (part Technicolor)
Cast: Charles King, Anita Page, Bessie Love, Jed Prouty, Kenneth
      Thomson, Mary Doran, Eddie Kane, James Gleason, James Burrows,
      Nacio Herb Brown, Biltmore Trio
Songs: "Broadway Melody"; "Broadway Babies"; "You Were Meant for Me";
      "Truthful Parson Brown" (Willard Robison); "The Wedding of the Painted
      Doll"; "The Boy Friend"
Released: February 1929; 104 minutes

A milestone in the development of the screen musical, *The Broadway Melody* was the progenitor of the rash of backstage sagas that have long been so much a part of Hollywood's musical output. Though originally conceived as a part-sound, part-silent production, after viewing some early sound rushes producer Irving Thalberg decided to make it MGM's first all-talkie—or, as the ads proclaimed, the first "ALL TALKING! ALL SINGING! ALL DANCING!" release. It also claimed to have the first original screenplay written for a musical, the first with an original score (songwriters Nacio Herb Brown and Arthur Freed, later to become MGM's top producer of musicals, won the assignment over Fred Fisher and Billy Rose), the first to utilize songs as part of the plot, the first to prerecord the musical numbers, the first to make use of large sound stages; and the first musical film to include a sequence in two-color Technicolor ("The Wedding of the Painted Doll" number, which had a chorus of 60 and was added after shooting had been completed). Moreover, it was the first all-talkie film seen by most of the country since a majority of exhibitors chose it as their premiere attraction with sound. (The studio, however, took the precaution of also releasing a silent version just in case the public was still not ready for an entire movie musical with sound.)

In the triangular plot, singer-hoofer-songwriter Eddie Kerns (Charles King) is engaged to "Hank" Mahoney (Bessie Love), but ditches her when he falls in love with, and eventually marries, her kid sister and vaudeville partner, Queenie (Anita Page). All three are involved in the latest Francis Zanfield (sic) musical extravaganza, *The Broadway Melody,* in which Eddie scores a hit by strutting across the stage in top hat and tails singing, in the title song, the praises of the Great White Way. Full of backstage wisecracks and cross talk, the film was said to have been inspired by the career of Vivian and Rosetta Duncan, a vaudeville sister act, who were originally slated for the leading roles, but instead were cast in a similar backstage musical, *It's a Great Life.*

The success of *The Broadway Melody* resulted in the plethora of musicals that clogged the screen for the next two years (there were almost 50 in 1929 alone), and it also provided the rubric for three subsequent MGM backstage sagas, in 1936, 1938, and 1940. (A fifth, in 1943, was to have starred Eleanor Powell and Gene Kelly, but it was never made.) The basic plot of the first *Broadway Melody,* however, was reused in 1940 for Metro's *Two Girls on Broadway,* starring Lana Turner, Joan Blondell, and George Murphy, though the ambiance was switched to that of a glitzy nightclub.
MGM/UA VC.

ON WITH THE SHOW

Music: Harry Akst
Lyrics: Grant Clarke
Screenplay: Robert Lord
Produced by: Darryl F. Zanuck for Warner Bros.
Directed by: Alan Crosland
Choreography: Larry Ceballos
Photography: Tony Gaudio (Technicolor)
Cast: Betty Compson, Arthur Lake, Sally O'Neil, Joe E. Brown, Louise Fazenda, Ethel Waters, William Bakewell, Fairbanks Twins, Sam Hardy, Henry Fink, Josephine Houston
Songs: "Welcome Home"; "Let Me Have My Dreams"; "Am I Blue?"; "In the Land of Let's Pretend"; "Birmingham Bertha"
Released: May 1929; 101 minutes

The first talkie shot completely in two-color Technicolor, *On With the Show* was a backstage-onstage musical whose special distinction was that it created, as closely as possible, the ambiance of a Broadway-bound musical of 1929. It was also the first of a long line of screen musicals in which an inexperienced newcomer (here Sally O'Neil) takes over from an ailing star (Betty Compson), and it presents excerpts from the show being performed in such a manner that audiences can easily follow the story (this technique wouldn't be repeated until 24 years later with the film version of *Kiss Me, Kate*). Moreover, the running time of the film—as in the subsequent *George White's Scandals* (1934 edition), *Wonder Bar*, and *Murder at the Vanities*—takes exactly the same length as the story being told. The locale is the Wallace Theatre (city unspecified) and the film begins with arrival of the audience, then goes through a series of improbable melodramatic and comic situations, and ends with the company—including the stage hands!—taking curtain calls. The movie's musical highlight is the appearance of Ethel Waters, as a plantation worker in a scene from the show, introducing "Am I Blue?"

THE HOLLYWOOD REVUE OF 1929

Music: Gus Edwards*; Nacio Herb Brown**, etc.
Lyrics: Joe Goodwin*; Arthur Freed**, etc.
Dialogue: Al Boasberg, Robert Hopkins, Joe Farnham
Produced by: Harry Rapf for MGM
Directed by: Charles F. Reisner
Choreography: Sammy Lee, Albertina Rasch, Natacha Natova
Photography: John Arnold, Irving Reis, Maximilian Fabian (part Technicolor)
Cast: Marion Davies, John Gilbert, Norma Shearer, William Haines, Joan
        Crawford, Buster Keaton, Bessie Love, Charles King, Conrad Nagel,
        Marie Dressler, Jack Benny, Gus Edwards, Laurel & Hardy, Cliff
        Edwards, Anita Page, Polly Moran, Lionel Barrymore, Nils Asther,
        Brox Sisters, Ann Dvorak
Songs: "Got a Feelin' for You" (Louis Alter-Jo Trent); "Your Mother and
        Mine"*; "You Were Meant for Me"**; "Nobody but You"*; "Tom-
        my Atkins on Parade"**; "Singin' in the Rain"**; "Orange
        Blossom Time"*
Released: June 1929; 130 minutes

During the early days of the talkies, the major studios offered revue-type feature films intended to show off the speaking and singing ability of their roster of players. MGM led the way with *The Hollywood Revue of 1929*, with Jack Benny and Conrad Nagel as masters of ceremony. Apart from "Singin' in the Rain," introduced by Cliff Edwards and chorus all wearing slickers while being pelted with rain, other pleasures include Nagel singing (with Charles King's voice) *The Broadway Melody* hit "You Were Meant for Me," Joan Crawford flappering energetically through "Got a Feelin' for You," and the balcony scene from *Romeo and Juliet* (renamed *The Neckers),* with Norma Shearer and John Gilbert, directed by Lionel Barrymore.

GOLD DIGGERS OF BROADWAY

Music: Joe Burke
Lyrics: Al Dubin
Screenplay: Robert Lord
Produced by: (uncredited) for Warner Bros.
Directed by: Roy Del Ruth
Choreography: Larry Ceballos
Photography: Barney McGill, Ray Rennahan (Technicolor)
Cast: Nancy Welford, Conway Tearle, Winnie Lightner, Ann Pennington,
        Lilyan Tashman, William Bakewell, Nick Lucas
Songs: "Tip Toe Through the Tulips With Me"; "Painting the Clouds With
        Sunshine"; "And They Still Fall in Love"; "What Will I Do Without You?"
Released: August 1929; 98 minutes

Based on *The Gold Diggers,* a 1919 play by Avery Hopwood featuring Ina Claire, and *Gold Diggers,* the 1923 silent screen version, the first musical treatment lengthened the title to *Gold Diggers of Broadway* presumably to avoid giving the impression that the movie was about the California gold rush. The well-used story concerns a worldly chorus girl (Nancy Welford) who tries to convince a stuffy Boston Brahmin (Conway Tearle) that his nephew's sweetheart, another chorus girl, is not just after the lad's money. After the worldly one does her best to embarrass the stuffy one, the two appear headed for matrimony. Lilyan Tashman was the only member of the original Broadway cast to appear in the movie.

In all, there were five Warner musicals bearing the *Gold Diggers* rubric. The plot of the first two in the series also served as the model for Warners' 1951 musical, *Painting the Clouds With Sunshine* (the title of the hit song of the 1929 version), with the setting switched from New York to Las Vegas. Tom Conroy, Virginia Mayo, and Dennis Morgan were in the cast.

SUNNY SIDE UP

Music: Ray Henderson
Lyrics: B. G. DeSylva & Lew Brown
Screenplay: B. G. DeSylva, Lew Brown & Ray Henderson
Produced by: B. G. DeSylva for Fox
Directed by: David Butler
Choreography: Seymour Felix
Photography: Ernest Palmer, John Schmitz (part Multicolor)
Cast: Janet Gaynor, Charles Farrell, El Brendel, Marjorie White, Frank
          Richardson, Sharon Lynn, Mary Forbes, Jackie Cooper
Songs: "I'm a Dreamer, Aren't We All?"; "Sunny Side Up"; "You Find the Time,
          I'll Find the Place"; "Turn on the Heat";   "If Had a Talking Picture of You"
Released: October 1929; 115 minutes

The steady outpouring of musical films in 1929 prompted a steady stream of Hollywood-bound Broadway songwriters. Three early arrivals were B. G. DeSylva, Lew Brown and Ray Henderson who provided both songs and screenplay for *Sunny Side Up* (also written *Sunnyside Up*), which they fashioned along the familiar Cinderella lines that had long provided librettos for stage musicals. In this case, it's poor Molly Carr (Janet Gaynor), from New York's Yorkville, who manages to meet rich playboy Jack Cromwell (Charles Farrell) from Southampton, and so impresses him with her singing of "Sunny Side Up" ("If you meet with gloom, don't fall down and go boom") that he invites her to appear in a lavish charity show to be presented on his family's estate. In the show, they express their romantic feelings in "If I Had a Talking Picture of You" and Miss Gaynor does a solo turn to the wistful "I'm a Dreamer, Aren't We All?" The movie also offers the first purely cinematic production number in "Turn on the Heat." The scene opens in the frozen North where chorus girls emerge from igloos wearing heavy furs, then disrobe to brief tops and bottoms as the snow melts, grass grows, palm trees sprout, steam rises from the ground, and even a fire breaks out. When last seen, the girls escape the conflagration by diving into a lagoon.

RIO RITA

Music: Harry Tierney
Lyrics: Joseph McCarthy
Screenplay: Russell Mack, Luther Reed
Produced by: William LeBaron for RKO Radio
Directed by: Luther Reed
Choreography: Pearl Eaton
Photography: Robert Kurrle (part Technicolor)
Cast: Bebe Daniels, John Boles, Bert Wheeler, Robert Woolsey, Dorothy Lee, Don Alvarado, George Renavent, Eva Rosita
Songs: "The Kinkajou"; "River Song"; "Rio Rita"; "The Rangers' Song"; "You're Always in My Arms"; "If You're in Love You'll Waltz"; "Poor Fool"; "Sweetheart, We Need Each Other"
Released: October 1929; 140 minutes

Hollywood has always been dependent upon Broadway to supply sources for its musicals. Even in the silent years, such stage musicals as *Little Johnny Jones, The Merry Widow, Poppy* (renamed *Sally of the Sawdust), The Student Prince, Oh, Kay!* and *Rose-Marie* made their inaudible way to the silver screen. *Show Boat* (1928) did fairly well as a part-talkie, but *The Desert Song,* the first all-talkie adaptation of a stage musical, was a disaster. It remained for *Rio Rita,* RKO Radio's initial musical release, to hold the distinction of being the first Broadway success to also become a Hollywood success. With Bert Wheeler and Robert Woolsey recreating their original comic roles and the Harry Tierney-Joseph McCarthy score almost intact, the story is a faithful adaptation of Ziegfeld's 1927 hit—even structured like a two-act play, with the second half in color.

In the plot, Capt. James Stewart (John Boles) and his Texas Rangers pursue the bandit known as the Kinkajou across the Rio Grande, but the captain soon finds himself pursuing the suspected outlaw's sister, Rita Ferguson (Bebe Daniels). Eventually, the real bandit, none other than the villainous General Ravenoff, is apprehended during a barge party on the river. (Echoes of the plot would be later found in the 1936 MGM film, *Rose Marie,* in which James Stewart played the errant brother who impedes the romance between sister Jeanette MacDonald and Canadian Mountie Nelson Eddy.) In 1942, MGM made its own *Rio Rita,* which bore scant relationship to the original. Kathryn Grayson, John Carroll, and Abbott & Costello were in it.

Rio Rita. John Boles and Bebe Daniels menaced by George Renavent.

The Love Parade. Maurice Chevalier singing "My Love Parade" to Jeanette MacDonald.

THE LOVE PARADE

Music: Victor Schertzinger
Lyrics: Clifford Grey
Screenplay: Ernest Vajda & Guy Bolton
Producer-director: Ernst Lubitsch for Paramount
Photography: Victor Milner
Cast: Maurice Chevalier, Jeanette MacDonald, Lupino Lane, Lillian Roth, Edgar Norton, Lionel Belmore, Eugene Pallette, Virginia Bruce, Ben Turpin, Jean Harlow
Songs: "Paris, Stay the Same"; "Dream Lover"; "My Love Parade"; "March of the Grenadiers"; "Nobody's Using It Now"
Released: November 1929; 110 minutes

Though adapted from a French play, *Le Prince Consort, The Love Parade* is something of a spinoff of the Viennese operetta, *The Merry Widow,* in its tale of a diplomatic aide stationed in Paris who is summoned home to the mythical country of Sylvania because the Queen is upset at his many scandalous affairs. Count Alfred Renard and Queen Louise—or Maurice Chevalier and Jeanette MacDonald—soon fall in love, marry, and spend the rest of the time trying to find something for Alfred to do beside fulfilling the Queen's amorous needs. In his airy, satirical approach to sex, Ernst Lubitsch, directing his first talkie, established a very personal, stylized tone that set the standard for continental froth on the Hollywood screen. And in roguish Chevalier and demure MacDonald (who appeared together in three Lubitsch films, plus Rouben Mamoulian's *Love Me Tonight),* the screen found its first major musical team.

THE SHOW OF SHOWS

Produced by: Darryl F. Zanuck for Warner Bros.
Directed by: John Adolfi
Choreography: Jack Haskell, Larry Ceballos
Photography: Bernard McGill (Technicolor)
Cast: John Barrymore, Richard Barthelmess, Noah Beery, Sally Blane, Irene Bordoni, Georges Carpentier, Betty Compson, Chester Conklin, Dolores Costello, Sally Eilers, Douglas Fairbanks Jr., Frank Fay, Louise Fazenda, Alexander Grey, Lupino Lane, Ted Lewis Orch., Winnie Lightner, Beatrice Lillie, Myrna Loy, Nick Lucas, Patsy Ruth Miller, Chester Morris, Carmel Myers, Rin-Tin-Tin, Bert Roach, Sid Silvers, Ann Sothern, Ben Turpin, H. B. Warner, Alice White, Loretta Young
Songs: "If I Could Learn to Love" (Herman Ruby-M. K. Jerome); "The Only Song I Know" (Ray Perkins-J. Keirn Brennan); "Singin' in the Bathtub" (Michael Cleary-Ned Washington, Herb Magidson); "You Were Meant for Me" (Nacio Herb Brown-Arthur Freed); "Just an Hour of Love" (Al Bryan-Ed Ward); "Lady Luck" (Perkins)
Released: November 1929; 99 minutes

The film opens on a chilling scene during the French Revolution in which an aristocrat is about to be guillotined. He asks to speak but the executioner denies him the privilege. "Death to the tyrant," the executioner proclaims after the aristocrat is beheaded. Then—breaking into a wide grin—he announces, "And on with The Show of Shows!" So begins Warners' hodge-podge of songs, sketches, gags, and production numbers which—like MGM's *Hollywood Revue of 1929* before it and Paramount's *Paramount on Parade* that followed—was a showcase for most of the stellar names in the studio's roster of players. It includes a comic recreation of the Florodora Sextette, some embarrassing comedy involving Frank Fay and Beatrice Lillie, an offbeat "international" number featuring eight pairs of sisters, a song borrowed from MGM's *Hollywood Revue* ("You Were Meant for Me"), Myrna Loy as a Chinese dancing girl, John Barrymore reciting a speech from Shakespeare's *Henry VI, Part 3,* and an interminable "Lady Luck" finale involving about half the population of California.

KING OF JAZZ

Music: Milton Ager, etc.
Lyrics: Jack Yellen, etc.
Sketches: John Murray Anderson, Harry Ruskin
Produced by: Carl Laemmle Jr. for Universal
Directed by: John Murray Anderson
Choreography: Russell Markert
Photography: Hal Mohr, Jerome Ash, Ray Rennahan (Technicolor)
Cast: Paul Whiteman Orch., Bing Crosby, Joe Venuti, Eddie Lang, Jeanie Lang, Grace Hayes, William Kent, Jeanette Loff, Stanley Smith, Laura La Plante, Al Rinker, Harry Barris, John Boles, Frankie Trumbauer, Brox Sisters, Slim Summerville, Walter Brennan
Songs: "Rhapsody in Blue" (George Gershwin); "So the Bluebirds and the Blackbirds Got Together" (Harry Barris-Billy Moll); "Mississippi Mud" (Barris-James Cavanaugh); "It Happened in Monterey"(Mabel Wayne-Billy Rose); "Ragamuffin Romeo" (Wayne-Harry DeCosta); "Happy Feet"; "Song of the Dawn"; "A Bench in the Park"
Released: March 1930; 101 minutes

Universal's entry into the revue-type genre concentrated not on the studio's stable of stars but on the orchestra of Paul Whiteman, then the most prestigious band in the country. In the film Whiteman leads his musicians through more than 70 pieces, many featuring one of his vocalists, Bing Crosby, in his screen debut. The selections begin with Gershwin's *Rhapsody in Blue* (Whiteman's signature which finds the entire orchestra seated inside a 40-foot piano) and contains an international pot-pourri representing eight countries under the title "The Melting Pot of Music."
MCA VC.

PARAMOUNT ON PARADE

Produced by: Albert S. Kaufman for Paramount
Directed by: Dorothy Arzner, Otto Brower, Edmund Goulding, Victor Heerman, Edwin Knopf, Rowland Lee, Ernst Lubitsch, Lothar Mendes, Victor Schertzinger, A. Edward Sutherland, Frank Tuttle
Choreography: David Bennett, Marion Morgan
Photography: Harry Fischbeck, Victor Milner (part Technicolor)
Cast: Richard Arlen, Jean Arthur, Mischa Auer, George Bancroft, Clara Bow, Evelyn Brent, Mary Brian, Clive Brook, Virginia Bruce, Nancy Carroll, Ruth Chatterton, Maurice Chevalier, Gary Cooper, Leon Errol, Stuart Erwin, Kay Francis, Skeets Gallagher, Mitzi Green, Phillips Holmes, Helen Kane, Dennis King, Abe Lyman Orch., Fredric March, Nino Martini, Mitzi Mayfair, Jack Oakie, Warner Oland, Zelma O'Neal, Eugene Pallette, William Powell, Charles Buddy" Rogers, Lillian Roth, Fay Wray
Songs: "Any Time's the Time to Fall in Love" (Jack King-Elsie Janis); "My Marine" (Richard Whiting-Ray Egan); "All I Want Is Just One" (Whiting-Robin); "Let's Drink to the Girl of My Dreams" (Abel Baer-L. Wolfe Gilbert); "I'm True to the Navy Now" (King-Janis); "Sweeping the Clouds Away" (Sam Coslow)
Released: April 1930; 102 minutes

Following *The Hollywood Revue of 1929* and *The Show of Shows, Paramount on Parade* offers a variety show parading the studio's most lustrous stars. Capitalizing on their screen images, William Powell is seen as detective Philo Vance, Warner Oland as Fu Manchu, Maurice Chevalier (directed by Ernst Lubitsch) doing an Apache dance with Evelyn Brent, Clara Bow in a nautical number, Helen Kane as a Boop-Boop-a-Dooping school teacher, Ruth Chatterton as a teary Montmartre street walker, and Chevalier leading a chorus of chimney sweeps across the roofs of Paris and eventually up on a rainbow. Paramount utilized no less than 11 directors on this project, which was also released in French and Spanish versions with Jeanette MacDonald as mistress of ceremonies.

MONTE CARLO

Music: Richard Whiting & W. Franke Harling
Lyrics: Leo Robin
Screenplay: Ernest Vajda & Vincent Lawrence
Producer-director: Ernst Lubitsch for Paramount
Photography: Victor Milner
Cast: Jack Buchanan, Jeanette MacDonald, ZaSu Pitts, Claud Allister, Tyler
Brooke, Lionel Belmore, Donald Novis, Frances Dee, John Carroll
Songs: "Beyond the Blue Horizon"; "Give Me a Moment, Please"; "Trimming the
Women"; "Whatever It Is, It's Grand"; "Always in All Ways"
Released: August 1930; 90 minutes

The second of Ernst Lubitsch's bubbly continental musicals, *Monte Carlo* pairs Jeanette MacDonald with Britain's debonair song-and-dance man Jack Buchanan (who would wait 23 years before appearing in his other Hollywood musical, *The Band Wagon*).The saucy tale offers Miss MacDonald as impoverished Countess Helene Mara, who leaves her wimpish — but titled — husband-to-be at the altar to hop aboard the Blue Express—as she sings "Beyond the Blue Horizon" to the accompaniment of locomotive wheels—that takes her to Monte Carlo. There she meets a more attractive nobleman, Count Rudolph Farriere (Buchanan), masquerading as a hairdresser, and shows her skill at the gambling table. Eventually, class distinction melts away—particularly when it affects a rich aristocrat in disguise. Adapted from a German play, *Die Blaue Kuste (The Blue Coast),* with an "opera" sequence taken from Booth Tarkington's play *Monsieur Beaucaire,* the film shows an advance over *The Love Parade* in its cinematic fluidity and the way it utilizes its musical sequences for maximum effect within the context of the story.

WHOOPEE!

Music: Walter Donaldson
Lyrics: Gus Kahn
Screenplay: William Conselman
Produced by: Samuel Goldwyn, Florenz Ziegfeld (released by United Artists)
Directed by: Thornton Freeland
Choreography: Busby Berkeley
Photography: Lee Garmes, Ray Rennahan, Gregg Toland (Technicolor)
Cast: Eddie Cantor, Eleanor Hunt, Paul Gregory, Ethel Shutta, John Rutherford, Spencer Charters, Chief Caupolican, Albert Hackett, Marian Marsh, Betty Grable, Virginia Bruce, George Olsen Orch.
Songs: "I'll Still Belong to You" (Nacio Herb Brown-Edward Eliscu); "Makin' Whoopee"; "A Girl Friend of a Boy Friend of Mine"; "Stetson"; "My Baby Just Cares for Me"; "Song of the Setting Sun"
Released: September 1930; 93 minutes

Ziegfeld's 1928 Broadway musical was one of Eddie Cantor's biggest hits, but its run was terminated when Samuel Goldwyn bought the screen rights and made immediate plans to film it with Cantor again in the lead (his first starring part in a feature-length movie). With six other stage performers recreating their roles (plus George Olsen's orchestra heard on the soundtrack), the show moved virtually intact from stage to screen—even though only three of the original 13 songs were retained. Goldwyn's first musical, for which Ziegfeld served as advisor, made good use of the two-color Technicolor process and it was also the film that introduced the talents of choreographer Busby Berkeley to the screen. The story (a variation on Owen Davis's 1923 play, *The Nervous Wreck*, in which Otto Kruger had played the lead) tells of hypochondriac Henry Williams (Cantor) who goes to California for his health. There he unwittingly gets involved with a rancher's daughter (Eleanor Hunt) who, aided by Henry, runs away from the sheriff to whom she affianced, and ends in the arms of the half-breed Indian (Paul Gregory) whom she loves. Danny Kaye's role in Goldwyn's *Up in Arms* (1944) was credited with being modeled on the character in *The Nervous Wreck*, though the only similarity was that he too was a hypochondriac.
Nelson VC.

Whoopee! Eddie Cantor singing "Makin' Whoopee."

THE SMILING LIEUTENANT

Music: Oscar Straus
Lyrics: Clifford Grey
Screenplay: Ernest Vajda, Samson Raphaelson, Ernst Lubitsch
Producer-director: Ernst Lubitsch for Paramount
Photography: George Folsey
Cast: Maurice Chevalier, Claudette Colbert, Miriam Hopkins, Charlie Ruggles, George Barbier, Hugh O'Connell, Elizabeth Patterson
Songs: "While Hearts Are Singing"; "Breakfast Table Love"; "One More Hour of Love"; "Jazz Up Your Lingerie"
Released: March 1931; 89 minutes

By 1931, the proliferation of musical films—there had been over 60 in 1930—became such a glut on the market that the public soon tired of them and no more than 15 were released during the year. Still, the Ernst Lubitsch—Maurice Chevalier formula continued to enjoy popularity, possibly because it broke so distinctively with the usual backstage fare and, during the dark days of the Depression, could be accepted as the purest kind of escapism. The spry and sprightly *Smiling Lieutenant* was based on a 1907 Oscar Straus Viennese operetta, *Ein Walzertraum (A Waltz Dream)*, which had already been filmed as a German silent movie in 1925 with Mady Christians and Willy Fritsch. The story tells of flirtatious Lieutenant Niki (Chevalier) who so catches the eye and heart of drab, lovelorn Princess Anna (Miriam Hopkins) that—shades of *The Love Parade*—she chooses him for her prince consort. Although Niki has been having an affair with the vivacious Franzi (Claudette Colbert), the leader of an all-girl orchestra at an outdoor restaurant, she is well aware that their romance cannot last and even teaches Anna some of the tricks of love to keep Niki from smiling at anyone else. The film, which was shot at Paramount's Astoria, Long Island, studio, was also released in a French version called *Le Lieutenant Souriant.*

ONE HOUR WITH YOU

Music: Oscar Straus*; Richard Whiting**
Lyrics: Leo Robin
Screenplay: Samson Raphaelson
Produced by: Ernst Lubitsch for Paramount
Directed by: Ernst Lubitsch, George Cukor
Photography: Victor Milner
Cast: Maurice Chevalier, Jeanette MacDonald, Genevieve Tobin, Roland Young, Charlie Ruggles, George Barbier, Josephine Dunn, Richard Carle, Donald Novis
Songs: "We Will Always Be Sweethearts"*; "Three Times a Day"***; "One Hour With You" **; "Oh, That Mitzi!" *; "What Would You Do?"**
Released: March 1932; 80 minutes

There were even fewer screen musicals in 1932 than in 1931, but again the dominant personality was Maurice Chevalier. Once more teamed with Jeanette MacDonald (in a role originally intended for Carole Lombard) and directed by Ernst Lubitsch, he was starred in an airy souffle adapted from the director's 1924 silent film, *The Marriage Circle* (with Monte Blue, Florence Vidor, and Adolphe Menjou). The story is concerned with Andre Pertier, a successful, happily married doctor whose wife Colette—with more than a little good reason—suspects him of having an affair with Mitzi Olivier, her best friend (Genevieve Tobin). Though originally Lubitsch planned to direct the movie, he had not yet completed another film and turned the assignment over to George Cukor, but then replaced him after two weeks. A French version —called *Une Heure pres de Toi*—was also shot with Chevalier and MacDonald.

Love Me Tonight. Tailor Maurice Chevalier sets out to deal with a money-owing customer.

Love Me Tonight. Charlie Ruggles, Myrna Loy, and C. Aubrey Smith.

LOVE ME TONIGHT

Music: Richard Rodgers
Lyrics: Lorenz Hart
Screenplay: Samuel Hoffenstein, Waldemar Young, George Marion Jr.
Producer-director: Rouben Mamoulian for Paramount
Photography: Victor Milner
Cast: Maurice Chevalier, Jeanette MacDonald, Charlie Ruggles, Charles Butterworth, Myrna Loy, C. Aubrey Smith, Elizabeth Patterson, Ethel Griffies, Blanche Friderici, Joseph Cawthorn, Robert Greig, Bert Roach, George "Gabby" Hayes, Tyler Brooke, Herbert Mundin, Cecil Cunningham, Marion "Peanuts" Byron, Rolfe Sedan, Edgar Norton, Rita Owin, Mel Calish
Songs: "That's the Song of Paree"; "Isn't It Romantic?"; "Lover"; "Mimi"; "A Woman Needs Something Like That"; "The Deer Hunt" (instrumental); "The Poor Apache"; "Love Me Tonight"; "The Son of a Gun Is Nothing but a Tailor"
Released: August 1932; 96 minutes

With a title as dull as the picture itself was adventurous, *Love Me Tonight* was a seminal production in the evolution of a purely cinematic form of musical comedy. Through its close interweaving of plot, songs, background scoring, its imaginative camera work, and its skillful editing (by William Shea), it remains a timeless and constantly inventive creation. With Maurice Chevalier and Jeanette MacDonald in the leading roles, it is full of the deft, imaginative touches usually associated with the films of Ernst Lubitsch—only this time the director was, surprisingly, Rouben Mamoulian, whose work here contrasts strikingly with the melodramatic offerings (*Applause, Dr. Jekyll and Mr. Hyde*) with which he had previously been associated.

Mamoulian and Broadway songwriters Richard Rodgers and Lorenz Hart (who had written their first original Hollywood score in 1931 for *The Hot Heiress)* worked closely together to achieve the properly stylized blending of a fairytale story that was actually told through music. This they achieved through a number of remarkably staged sequences— the early morning opening scene showing Paris waking up to the sounds of the city (a concept the director borrowed from his own staging of the 1927 play *Porgy* and which would also be borrowed by director Otto Preminger for the 1959 film version of *Porgy and Bess);* the use of one song, "Isn't It Romantic?," to move the action from Maurice's tailor shop in Paris to Princess Jeanette's chateau in the French countryside; a deer hunt ballet in slow motion; a split-screen image of Chevalier and MacDonald who, though alone, seem to be singing the title song to each other; and the quick cutting to various parts of the chateau as the inhabitants register shock upon discovering that Chevalier, who has been masquerading as a baron, is nothing but a tailor. Another memorable scene shows the leading characters' first meeting on a country road (after Jeanette has sung "Lover" to her horse) in which Maurice expresses his confused romantic feelings in "Mimi".

Though Lubitsch was the obvious choice to direct *Love Me Tonight,* he was then working on *Trouble in Paradise* and Paramount studio head Adolph Zukor approached a reluctant Rouben Mamoulian to find a suitable vehicle for Chevalier and MacDonald. At the suggestion of playwright Leopold Marchand, he found the property in a play called *Tailor in the Chateau,* which Marchand had co-authored. One line from the film has since become a classic. After the lovelorn Princess Jeanette has had a fainting spell, Charlie Ruggles asks Myrna Loy, as the man-hungry Countess Valentine, if she could go for a doctor. "Certainly," she replies, "bring him right in."

THE PHANTOM PRESIDENT

Music: Richard Rodgers
Lyrics: Lorenz Hart
Screenplay: Walter DeLeon & Harlan Thompson
Produced by: (uncredited) for Paramount
Directed by: Norman Taurog
Photography: David Abel
Cast: George M. Cohan, Claudette Colbert, Jimmy Durante, George Barbier, Sidney Toler, Alan Mowbray
Songs: "The Country Needs a Man"; "Somebody Ought to Wave a Flag"; "Give Her a Kiss"; "The Convention"
Released: September 1932; 80 minutes

Broadway's legendary Yankee Doodle Boy, George M. Cohan, was a prolific songwriter as well as an actor, but his only appearance in a screen musical was in a political satire with a score by Richard Rodgers and Lorenz Hart. *The Phantom President* involves a singing and dancing medicine showman who, because he is a deadringer for a stuffy banker (also Cohan), the choice of his party for President of the United States, is substituted as the candidate for the duration of the campaign. But the showman falls in love with the banker's fiancée (Claudene Colbert) and—once the real candidate has been exiled to the North Pole—ends up in the White House. Rodgers and Hart's major contribution was the presidential convention in which the entire sequence—including speeches and delegates' reactions—is set to music. Though Cohan and the song writers did not get along, five years later they were reunited on Broadway for another political spoof, *I'd Rather Be Right,* which found Cohan playing President Franklin D. Roosevelt.

THE BIG BROADCAST

Screenplay: George Marion Jr.
Produced by: (uncredited) for Paramount
Directed by: Frank Tuttle
Photography: George Folsey
Cast: Stuart Erwin, Bing Crosby, Leila Hyams, Sharon Lynne, George Burns, Gracie Allen, George Barbier, Eddie Lang, Kate Smith Boswell Sisters, Cab Calloway Orch., Mills Brothers, Arthur Tracy, Vincent Lopez Orch., Donald Novis
Songs: "Dinah" (Harry Akst-Sam Lewis, Joe Young); "Here Lies Love" (Ralph Rainger-Leo Robin); "Please" (Rainger-Robin); "Tiger Rag" (Nick La Rocca); "Trees" (Oscar Rasbach-Joyce Kilmer); "Crazy People" (James Monaco-Edgar Leslie); "It Was So Beautiful" (Harry Barris-Arthur Freed); "Kickin' the Gong Around" (Harold Arlen-Ted Koehler)
Released: October 1932; 78 minutes

The first of Paramount's four *Big Broadcast* movies set the pattern for the series by using a slim plot about broadcasting as an excuse to present an all-star lineup of musical talent. Thus we are offered the Mills Brothers harmonizing to "Tiger Rag", Cab Calloway gyrating through "Kickin' the Gong Around", Donald Novis singing his trademark "Trees", and Kate Smith filling both the screen and the soundtrack with "It Was So Beautiful". The tale, enlivened by some cinematic sight gags, is concerned with the rivalry between radio crooner Bing Crosby (his name in the picture) and wealthy Texan Stuart Erwin for the affection of Leila Hyams (Erwin gets her), and the problems arising when Crosby fails to show up on time for the Big Broadcast (though he does get to reprise "Please" for the finale). The movie credits a 1932 Broadway play, *Wild Waves,* as its source, but the only similarity was that it too was about a singer on a radio station.
Sountrak ST.

Hallelujah, I'm a Bum. The law closes in on Edgar Connor, Al Jolson, and Harry Langdon.

HALLELUJAH, I'M A BUM

Music: Richard Rodgers
Lyrics: Lorenz Hart
Screenplay: S. N. Behrman
Produced by: Joseph M. Schenck for United Artists
Directed by: Lewis Milestone
Photography: Lucien Andriot
Cast: Al Jolson, Madge Evans, Frank Morgan, Harry Langdon, Chester Conklin, Tyler Brooke, Bert Roach, Edgar Connor, Richard Rodgers, Lorenz Hart
Songs: "I Gotta Get Back To New York"; "My Pal Bumper"; "Hallelujah, I'm a Bum"; "Dear June"; "Bumper Found a Grand"; "What Do You Want With Money?"; "You Are Too Beautiful"
Released: January 1933; 82 minutes

Based on a story by Ben Hecht, *Hallelujah, I'm a Bum* was a somewhat daring musical since it dealt directly with a social issue caused by the Great Depression—the plight of homeless men forced to live in New York's Central Park (which scenes, ironically, were shot at the Riviera Country Club in Pacific Palisades). Bumper (Al Jolson), the leader of these men, is a friend of dapper Mayor John Hastings (Frank Morgan), whose relationship with his fiancée June Archer (Madge Evans) is not going too smoothly. (When late for a luncheon appointment with June, the Mayor explains, "I was laying a cornerstone." To which the dubious lady responds, "A cornerstone?") After they break up over a misunderstanding, June is rescued by Bumper from a suicide attempt which causes her amnesia. Bumper falls in love with June, but once she regains her memory she's back in Hastings' arms and Bumper is back in Central Park.

In the movie, Rodgers and Hart extended further their use of rhythmic dialogue, an innovation they had experimented with in *Love Me Tonight* and *The Phantom President,* in which rhymed conversation, with musical accompaniment, is used to affect a smoother transition to actual song and also to give the story a firmer musical structure. Both men are seen briefly in the film: Rodgers as a photographer's assistant and Hart as a bank teller. In Britain, the film was retitled *Hallelujah, I'm a Tramp.*

This was actually the second screen treatment of the story to star Jolson. The recently completed first version, titled *Happy Go Lucky,* was directed by Chester Erskine, had songs by Irving Caesar, and featured Roland Young as the mayor. It was so bad all the prints were destroyed and the entire film had to be remade.

42ND STREET

Music: Harry Warren
Lyrics: Al Dubin
Screenplay: James Seymour, Rian James
Produced by: Darryl F. Zanuck for Warner Bros.
Directed by: Lloyd Bacon (Mervyn LeRoy uncredited)
Choreography: Busby Berkeley
Photography: Sol Polito
Cast: Warner Baxter, Bebe Daniels, George Brent, Ruby Keeler, Dick Powell, Ginger Rogers, Una Merkel, Guy Kibbee, Ned Sparks, George E. Stone, Allen Jenkins, Eddie Nugent, Henry B. Walthall, Clarence Nordstrom, Harry Warren, Al Dubin, Harry Akst, Jack LaRue, Louise Beavers, Toby Wing, Dave O'Brien
Songs: "You're Getting to Be A Habit With Me"; "Shuffle Off to Buffalo"; "Young and Healthy"; "Forty-Second Street"
Released: February 1933; 89 minutes

After only 11 film musicals released in 1932, there were well over 30 the following year. Just as the surge in 1929 could be credited to the success of the backstage musical *The Broadway Melody,* so the surge in 1933 could be credited to another backstage musical, the even more successful *42nd Street.* The movie's assets are its variety of characters, memorable songs, authentic backstage atmosphere, and wisecrack-peppered dialogue that is crisp and funny ("She only said no once, and then she didn't hear the question"). But its most notable innovations are the Busby Berkeley kaleidoscopic routines which made such imaginative use of the camera that they created their own fantasy world, one that would be impossible to achieve in any other entertainment medium.

Though the film was adapted from a novel by Bradford Ropes, there are marked variations in the story line and the characters. In the book, hard-driving director Julian Marsh is a wealthy homosexual who lives with juvenile lead Tommy Lawler, and Dorothy Brock, the aging star of Marsh's show *Pretty Lady,* is two-timed by her lover, Pat Denning. After Dorothy, while drunk, falls down a flight of stairs, Tommy recommends that Peggy Sawyer, a fresh-faced chorus girl from Maine, be given the chance to replace her. Overnight, Peggy becomes a first-magnitude star and a first-class bitch. On the screen, Marsh (Warner Baxter) is still hard-driving but now he's an ailing, chain-smoking loner who has been wiped out by the Wall Street crash. Dorothy (Bebe Daniels) and Pat (George Brent) are devoted to each other, and Tommy (Dick Powell) is smitten by blank-faced chorine Peggy (Ruby Keeler), just off the bus from Sioux City, Iowa. When Dorothy gets drunk and breaks her ankle, the show's backer (Guy Kibbee) wants "Anytime Annie" Lowell (Ginger Rogers) to replace her, but Annie nobly recommends Peggy. On the opening night of the Philadelphia tryout (despite the movie's title, we never see the New York premiere), Marsh takes Peggy aside to give her a pep talk ending with classic line, "Sawyer, you're going out a youngster but you've got to come back a star." *Pretty Lady,* of course, is a smash (at least in Philadelphia).

The most elaborate Berkeley creations in the somewhat disjointed stage show are "Shuffle Off to Buffalo," in which a bridal couple takes a musical train ride, and the melodramatic "Forty-Second Street" finale, a panorama of the area with assorted types depicting the frantic, violent nature of that "naughty, bawdy, gaudy, sporty" locale. The film marked the screen debut of Ruby Keeler, who would be teamed with Dick Powell in six other Warners musicals.

In 1968, the Off-Broadway musical *Dames at Sea* was a partial spoof of the movie, as were two films, *The Boy Friend* (1971) and the *Baxter's Beauties* half of the two-part parody that made up *Movie, Movie* (1978). *42nd Street* itself was adapted in 1980 as a Broadway musical. It featured Tammy Grimes and Jerry Orbach and ran almost eight and one-half years.
MGM/UA VC.

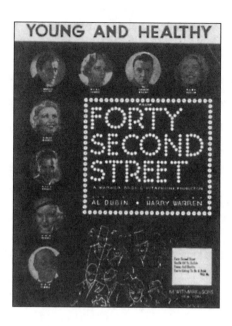

42nd Street. Director Warner Baxter has stern words for chorine Ruby Keeler. Looking on are Una Merkel, George E. Stone, and Ginger Rogers.

SHE DONE HIM WRONG

Screenplay: Harvey Thew & John Bright, Mae West
Produced by: William LeBaron for Paramount
Directed by: Lowell Sherman
Photography: Charles Lang
Cast: Mae West, Cary Grant, Owen Moore, Gilbert Roland, Noah Beery,
        Rochelle Hudson, Fuzzy Knight, Grace LaRue, Louise Beavers
Songs: "Silver Threads Among the Gold" (Hart Danks-Eben Rexford);
        "Masie, My Pretty Daisy" (Ralph Rainger); "Easy Rider" (Shelton
        Brooks); "I Like a Guy What Takes His Time" (Rainger); "Frankie and
        Johnny" (trad.)
Released: February 1933; 66 minutes

Mae West's first starring vehicle was an adaptation of her own play, *Diamond Lil,* a Broadway success of 1928. Though Paramount was not optimistic about the film's prospects, it turned out to be one of the year's blockbusters with a domestic gross of over $2 million. The movie, which took only 18 days to shoot and runs for little over an hour, is set in New York's Bowery in the late 1890's. In the tale, saloon singer Lady Lou (changed from the original Lil) is involved in various shady dealings, including white slave traffic. She must also contend with a former lover who has just escaped from prison and a new love (Cary Grant), a federal agent disguised as a Salvation Army officer. The film was full of Miss West's characteristic one-liners (to an acquaintance who calls her a fine woman, she replies, "One of the finest women who ever walked the streets"), and also included the famous invitation to Grant, "Why don't you come up sometime 'n see me?"
MCA VC.

INTERNATIONAL HOUSE

Music: Ralph Rainger
Lyrics: Leo Robin
Screenplay: Francis Martin, Walter DeLeon
Produced by: (uncredited) for Paramount
Directed by: A. Edward Sutherland
Photography: Ernest Haller
Cast: Peggy Hopkins Joyce, W.C. Fields, Stuart Erwin, Sari Maritza,
        George Burns, Gracie Allen, Bela Lugosi, Franklin Pangborn,
        Sterling Holloway, Rudy Vallee, Stoopnagle & Budd, Cab Calloway
        Orch., Baby Rose Marie
Songs: "Tea Cup"(lyric: Rainger); "Thank Heaven For You"; "My
        Bluebirds are Singing the Blues"; "Reefer Man"(J. Russel
        Robinson-Andy Razaf)
Released: May 1933; 70 minutes

Originally, *International House* was not supposed to have any songs, but by the time it was finished it could easily qualify for inclusion in Paramount's series of *Big Broadcast* musicals. In fact, it was somewhat of a pioneering effort since it was about the invention of television, here called radioscope, and it used specialty acts (Rudy Vallee, Stoopnagle and Budd, Cab Calloway and his Orchestra, and Baby Rose Marie) for the demonstrations. Because the radioscope inventor is Chinese, representatives from various countries gather at International House in Wu-Hu, China, to bid for the rights to market the invention. Making a mad plot even madder, W. C. Fields (as Prof. Henry R. Quail) enters the scene by landing his autogiro on the hotel roof, and demanding to know where he is. When hotel manager Franklin Pangborn petulantly calls, "Wu-Hu," Fields removes the large flower from his lapel and snarls, "Don't let the posy fool ya." He then proceeds to disrupt the place with a variety of Fieldsian gags and props (including a miniature automobile he drives through halls, onto fire escapes, and into an elevator).

GOLD DIGGERS OF 1933

Music: Harry Warren
Lyrics: Al Dubin
Screenplay: Erwin Gelsey, James Seymour, David Boehm, Ben Markson
Produced by: Hal B. Wallis for Warner Bros.
Directed by: Mervyn LeRoy
Choreography: Busby Berkeley
Photography: Sol Polito
Cast: Warren William, Joan Blondell, Aline MacMahon, Ruby Keeler, Dick Powell, Ginger Rogers, Ned Sparks, Guy Kibbee, Clarence Nordstrom, Sterling Holloway, Ferdinand Gottschalk, Etta Moten, Billy Barty, Busby Berkeley, Dennis O'Keefe
Songs: "We're in the Money"; "Shadow Waltz"; "I've Got to Sing a Torch Song"; "Pettin' in the Park"; "Remember My Forgotten Man"
Released: May 1933; 96 minutes

So confident were the Warner brothers in the future of backstage musicals that preliminary work on *Gold Diggers of 1933* had begun even before *42nd Street* was in general release. The new film was based on the same play (about a Boston Brahmin who falls in love with a chorus girl even though he suspects her of being a fortune hunter) that had led to previous *Gold Diggers* films in 1923 and 1929. Since the second, titled *Gold Diggers of Broadway,* also had songs, the studio found itself releasing two musicals within the space of four years that were both based on the same source.

In other respects, *Gold Diggers of 1933* was strongly linked to *42nd Street*. It retained the previous film's cast members Dick Powell, Ruby Keeler, Ginger Rogers, Ned Sparks, Guy Kibbee, and Clarence Nordstrom (George Brent was originally to play the Bostonian but he was replaced by Warren William), and it kept the same songwriters (Al Dubin had also written the lyrics for *Gold Diggers of Broadway*), co-author (James Seymour), costume designer (Orry-Kelly), music director (Leo Forbstein), and choreographer. That was the ubiquitous Busby Berkeley, who devised dazzling routines for such numbers as "Shadow Waltz" (girls in blonde wigs and white gowns appearing to play white electrified violins), "Pettin' in the Park" (almost a Freudian vision of New York's Central Park), and "Remember My Forgotten Man" (a panorama of post-war disillusionment). Also as in *42nd Street*—and as in *On With the Show* before that and in many a backstage musical to follow—an untried newcomer gets the chance to take over from a featured performer (in this case it's tyro songwriter Powell who replaces juvenile Nordstrom when he gets an attack of lumbago).

Possibly the element that distinguishes the 1933 *Gold Diggers* from other backstage sagas of the period is that it is the only one showing the influence of the Depression. In addition to the grim "Remember My Forgotten Man" sequence, the movie not only deals with the problems of raising money to produce a show, but also with the daily financial concerns of aspiring actresses Keeler, Rogers, Joan Blondell, and Aline MacMahon. *MGM/UA VC.*

Gold Diggers of 1933. Aline MacMahon, Joan Blondell, and Ruby Keeler react to the news that Dick Powell is backing their new show.

FOOTLIGHT PARADE

Music: Harry Warren*; Sammy Fain**
Lyrics: Al Dubin*; Irving Kahal**
Screenplay: Manuel Seff & James Seymour
Produced by: Hal B. Wallis for Warner Bros.
Directed by: Lloyd Bacon
Choreography: Busby Berkeley
Photography: George Barnes
Cast: James Cagney, Joan Blondell, Ruby Keeler, Dick Powell, Guy Kibbee, Frank McHugh, Ruth Donnelly, Claire Dodd, Hugh Herbert, Herman Bing, Billy Barty, Gracie Barrie, Hobart Cavanaugh, Dave O'Brien, Jimmy Conlin, Billy Taft
Songs: "Ah, the Moon Is Here"**; "Sittin' on a Backyard Fence"**; "Honeymoooon Hotel"*; "By a Waterfall"**; "Shanghai Lil"*
Released: September 1933; 104 minutes

During 1933 Warner Bros. managed to turn out three legendary backstage musicals, *42nd Street, Gold Diggers of 1933,* and *Footlight Parade.* As in the previous two, *Footlight Parade* again featured Dick Powell and Ruby Keeler as the ingenuous juveniles and its cast again included character actor Guy Kibbee. Also associated with all three films were co-author James Seymour, songwriters Harry Warren and Al Dubin (though this assignment was shared with Sammy Fain and Irving Kahal), music director Leo Forbstein, costume designer Orry-Kelly, and, of course, choreographer Busby Berkeley. It shared the same director (Lloyd Bacon) as *42nd Street,* and the same producer (Hal Wallis), art director (Anton Grot), editor (George Amy), and leading lady (Joan Blondell) as *Gold Diggers of 1933.*

But it was dynamic James Cagney, in his first film musical, who gave the *Footlight Parade* its special distinction. Cagney plays Chester Kent, a fast-talking, fast-moving dance director whose character seems to have been not only modeled on Berkeley himself but was also something of a forerunner of Bob Fosse's alter ego in the 1979 movie, *All That Jazz.* Unlike most backstage musicals of the day, the plot does not revolve around the crises inherent in staging a Broadway extravaganza but around the crises inherent in staging touring stage productions, known as "prologues," which accompanied feature films in major motion-picture houses during the early days of the talkies.

In his search for fresh ideas, the Cagney character gets the novel notion of staging complete miniature musicals instead of just a series of variety acts, and he is given the opportunity to audition three such spectacles at three different movie theatres in New York. Because of this plot construction, the film's production numbers are all offered within the last half hour. These are the narrative "Honeymoon Hotel," an apparent sequel to *42nd Street*'s "Shuffle Off to Buffalo," even though the hotel is located in Jersey City; "By a Waterfall," an aquatic dream sequence which takes place both by a waterfall and also in and around a mammoth swimming pool (Cagney's inspiration had been the sight of black children in the street cavorting under the spray of an open fire hydrant); and "Shanghai Lil," in which Cagney (as an accidental last-minute substitution for a drunken actor) appears as a sailor searching for his oriental inamorata in a Shanghai saloon and opium den. The sailor gets into a brawl, finds his Lil (Ruby Keeler)and tap dances with her on top of a bar. After some spectacular drill formations and a card display of the American flag and the image of President Roosevelt, he returns to his ship accompanied by the tenacious girl, now disguised as a sailor.
MGM/UA VC.

Footlight Parade. James Cagney and Ruby Keeler in the "Shanghai Lil" number.

DANCING LADY

Music: Jimmy McHugh*; Burton Lane**
Lyrics: Dorothy Fields*; Harold Adamson**
Screenplay: Allen Rivkin & P. J. Wolfson
Produced by: David O. Selznick for MGM
Directed by: Robert Z. Leonard
Choreography: Sammy Lee, Eddie Prinz (Fred Astaire uncredited)
Photography: Oliver T. Marsh
Cast: Joan Crawford, Clark Gable, Franchot Tone, May Robson, Winnie Lightner, Fred Astaire, Robert Benchely, Ted Healy, Three Stooges, Art Jarrett, Gloria Foy, Grant Mitchell, Nelson Eddy, Sterling Holloway, Eve Arden, Lynn Bari
Songs: "Hey, Young Fella" *; "Everything I Have Is Yours" **; "My Dancing Lady""*; "Heigh-Ho, the Gangs All Here"**; "Let's Go Bavarian""**; "That's the Rhythm of the Day" (Richard Rodgers-Lorenz Hart)
Released: November 1933; 90 minutes

After originating the backstage musical with *The Broadway Melody,* MGM waited until the form was revived four years later by Warner Bros. before filming another of the genre. Though based on a novel by James Warner Bellah supposedly inspired by the early years of dancer Claire Luce, *Dancing Lady* is little more than a variation on *42nd Street.* Like its predecessor, the film tells the story of a Broadway-bound production—called *Dancing Lady*—from its inception to opening night. Here again is the ruthless director (Clark Gable), the wide-eyed chorus girl (Joan Crawford) who takes over the top spot from the show's aging star, and the wealthy backer (Franchot Tone) infatuated with the leading lady. In addition it also had a final production number ("That's the Rhythm of the Day," sung by top-hatted Nelson Eddy) dealing with the frantic pace of big-city life. *Dancing Lady* marked the first screen appearance of Fred Astaire, who danced with Miss Crawford in two incongruously linked numbers, "Heigh-Ho, the Gang's All Here" and "Let's Go Bavarian." *MGM/UA VC.*

Dancing Lady. "Heigh-Ho, the Gang's All Here," Fred Astaire's first production number on the screen, paired the dancer with Joan Crawford.

Roman Scandals. Gloria Stuart and Eddie Cantor.

ROMAN SCANDALS

Music: Harry Warren
Lyrics: Al Dubin
Screenplay: William Anthony McGuire, George Oppenheimer,
     Arthur Sheekman, Nat Perrin
Produced by: Samuel Goldwyn (released by United Artists)
Directed by: Frank Tuttle
Choreography: Busby Berkeley
Photography: Gregg Toland
Cast: Eddie Cantor, Ruth Etting, Gloria Stuart, David Manners, Veree
     Teasdale, Edward Arnold, Alan Mowbray, Jane Darwell,
     Billy Barty, Lucille Ball
Songs: "Build a Little Home"; "No More Love"; "Keep Young and
     Beautiful"; "Put a Tax on Love" (lyric with L. Wolfe Gilbert)
Released: December 1933; 85 minutes

The fourth (of six) musicals Eddie Cantor made for Samuel Goldwyn was his most opulent production. As in the previous three films, it was again choreographed by Busby Berkeley. It was also the only one with a score written by Harry Warren and Al Dubin. Originally, Goldwyn had wanted playwrights George S. Kaufman and Robert E. Sherwood (who were eventually replaced) to come up with a script suggested by the Androcles legend. The story was soon changed, however, to one about a citizen of West Rome, Oklahoma, who is upset about the corruption in his town and dreams that he is back in ancient Rome, where he finds the corruption even more rampant. One of the movies's memorable scenes is the slave market, where a bevy of Goldwyn Girls (including Lucille Ball) are clad only in modesty preserving long blond wigs.
Nelson VC.

FLYING DOWN TO RIO

Music: Vincent Youmans
Lyrics: Edward Eliscu & Gus Kahn
Screenplay: Cyril Hume, H. W. Hanemann, Erwin Gelsey
Produced by: Louis Brock for RKO Radio
Directed by: Thornton Freeland
Choreography: Dave Gould, Hermes Pan (Fred Astaire uncredited)
Photography: J. Roy Hunt
Cast: Dolores Del Rio, Gene Raymond, Raul Roulien, Ginger Rogers, Fred Astaire, Blanche Friderici, Franklin Pangborn, Eric Blore, Etta Moten, Betty Furness, Mary Kornman
Songs: "Music Makes Me"; "The Carioca"; "Orchids in the Moonlight"; "Flying Down to Rio"
Released: December 1933; 89 minutes

Though initially Fred Astaire's dancing partner in *Flying Down to Rio* was to have been Dorothy Jordan (wife of studio executive Merian C. Cooper), the film marked the first joint appearance of Astaire with Ginger Rogers (they did ten movies in all), whose dance to "The Carioca" established the team. Created as a star vehicle for Dolores Del Rio, who was paired with Gene Raymond, the story is concerned with the daughter of a Rio de Janeiro hotel owner and the bandleader-songwriter-aviator who flies down to Rio to win her away from countryman Raul Roulien. As a climax, the film offers a spectacular aerial floorshow in which scantily clad chorus girls perform constricted dance maneuvers while strapped to the wings of airplanes. (The scene was later parodied in "The Riviera" sequence of Ken Russell's 1971 spoof, *The Boy Friend*.) The movie's most eyebrow-raising line (said by Mary Korman as a jealous North American friend of Miss Del Rio): "What have these South Americans got below the equator that we haven't?"
Classic Intl. ST   Turner VC.

Flying Down to Rio. Fred Astaire and Ginger Rogers play it cool after Fred has been thrown out of a Rio de Janeiro restaurant.

GOING HOLLYWOOD

Music: Nacio Herb Brown
Lyrics: Arthur Freed
Screenplay: Donald Ogden Stewart
Produced by: Walter Wanger for MGM
Directed by: Raoul Walsh
Choreography: Albertina Rasch
Photography: George Folsey
Cast: Marion Davies, Bing Crosby, Fifi D'Orsay, Patsy Kelly, Stuart Erwin, Ned Sparks, Bobby Watson, Radio Rogues, Sterling Holloway
Songs: "Our Big Love Scene"; "Beautiful Girl"; "Going Hollywood"; "We'll Make Hay While the Sun Shines"; "After Sundown"; "Temptation"
Released: December 1933; 80 minutes

Financed by William Randolph Hearst's Cosmopolitan Productions to show off the talents of Hearst's close friend Marion Davies, *Going Hollywood* was a variation on the theme of the newcomer who successfully takes over a role from the production's star and the alcoholic problems of one who cannot cope with early fame. It was also one of the first uses of Hollywood as the setting for a movie musical. Bing Crosby was loaned by Paramount at Miss Davies' request, even though Hearst was not one of his admirers. Crosby's appearance in the film, considered a boost to his career, allowed him to introduce six songs by MGM's resident team of Nacio Herb Brown and Arthur Freed. Among the numbers was the durable "Temptation," performed in a seedy saloon as the inebriated Crosby sings of his inability to resist temptress Fifi D'Orsay.
Columbia (Crosby LP).

THE CAT AND THE FIDDLE

Music: Jerome Kern
Lyrics: Otto Harbach
Screenplay: Bella & Samuel Spewack
Produced by: Bernard Hyman for MGM
Directed by: William K. Howard
Choreography: Albertina Rasch
Photography: Harold Rosson, Charles Clarke (part Technicolor)
Cast: Ramon Novarro, Jeanette MacDonald, Frank Morgan, Charles Butterworth, Jean Hersholt, Vivienne Segal, Joseph Cawthorn, Frank Conroy, Henry Armetta, Herman Bing, Sterling Holloway, Leonid Kinskey; Irene Franklin; Earl Oxford; Christian Rub
Songs: "The Night Was Made for Love"; "One Moment Alone"; "She Didn't Say 'Yes' "; "Don't Ask Us Not to Sing"; "I Watch the Love Parade"; "A New Love Is Old"; "Try to Forget"
Released: February 1934; 92 minutes

The Cat and the Fiddle was a rarity for its day in that every song in the original 1931 Jerome Kern-Otto Harbach stage production was retained for the movie version. Having gone this far, it is curious that the story should have been so altered. It's still the tale of American composer Shirley Sheridan (Jeanette MacDonald) who succumbs to the ardor of impetuous Rumanian composer Victor Flouescu (Ramon Novarro), a fellow student at the music conservatory in Brussels who has written an operetta. But on the screen most of the action is set in Paris and the new story is about the conflict that arises because Victor is unhappy being supported by Shirley, who has struck it rich by writing a hit song, "The Night Was Made for Love." (Victor had collaborated on the music but somehow he is not cut in on the royalties!) The film's climax, almost a satire on this sort of screen musical, has Shirley taking over the leading role in the operetta after Victor's patron and prima donna (Vivienne Segal) has left—even though Shirley has had nothing whatever to do with the production before opening night. Apart from the score, *The Cat and the Fiddle* was notable for its use of three-color Technicolor for the final scenes of Victor's show.
H'wood Soundstage ST.

WONDER BAR

Music: Harry Warren
Lyrics: Al Dubin
Screenplay: Earl Baldwin
Produced by: Robert Lord for Warner Bros.
Directed by: Lloyd Bacon
Choreography: Busby Berkeley
Photography: Sol Polito
Cast: Al Jolson, Dolores Del Rio, Ricardo Cortez, Kay Francis, Dick Powell, Guy Kibbee, Hugh Herbert, Ruth Donnelly, Louise Fazenda, Fifi D'Orsay, Henry O'Neill, Jane Darwell, Hobart Cavanaugh, Spencer Charters, Dennis O'Keefe, Hal LeRoy
Songs: "Vive la France"; "Wonder Bar"; "Why Do I Dream Those Dreams?"; "Don't Say Goodnight"; "Going to Heaven on a Mule"
Released: February 1934; 84 minutes

Adapted from a Berlin and London stage hit, in which Al Jolson had appeared on Broadway in 1931, *Wonder Bar* was another star-crammed Warners extravaganza with songs by Warren and Dubin, direction by Lloyd Bacon, and choreography by Busby Berkeley. Here the setting is a lavish Paris cabaret and the melodramatic doings involve Wonder Bar proprietor Al Jolson (as Al Wonder) and singer-songwriter Dick Powell, who both pine for featured dancer Dolores Del Rio. Del Rio, however, is infatuated with her caddish dancing partner, Ricardo Cortez, whom she stabs to death because of his affair with wealthy and married Kay Francis. The entire action of the film takes place during a single evening, with the movie's duration—as in *On With the Show* (1929), *George White's Scandals* (1934), and *Murder at the Vanities* (1934)— covering the same time frame as the story being told. *H'wood Soundstage ST.*

WE'RE NOT DRESSING

Music: Harry Revel
Lyrics: Mack Gordon
Screenplay: Horace Jackson, Francis Martin, George Marion Jr.
Produced by: Benjamin Glazer for Paramount
Directed by: Norman Taurog
Photography: Charles Lang
Cast: Bing Crosby, Carole Lombard, George Burns, Gracie Allen, Ethel Merman, Leon Errol, Ray Milland
Songs: "It's Just a New Spanish Custom"; "I Positively Refuse to Sing"; "May I?"; "She Reminds Me of You"; "Goodnight Lovely Little Lady"; "Love Thy Neighbor"; "Once in a Blue Moon"
Released: April 1934; 63 minutes

Vaguely based on James M. Barrie's turn-of-the-century play, *The Admirable Crichton*, *We're Not Dressing* offers the tale of sailor Bing Crosby aboard a yacht owned by spoiled heiress Carole Lombard. After a shipwreck on Pacific island (uninhabited except for scientists Burns and Allen), the sailor assumes command in helping the survivors cope with the primitive surroundings. Running a mere 63 minutes, the lighthearted film was well suited to Crosby's easygoing style, while also providing the singer with such sentiments as "Love Thy Neighbor," performed as he builds a hut, and "Once in a Blue Moon," as he strolls with Miss Lombard on the beach. The movie also teamed Ethel Merman and Leon Errol to offer "It's Just a New Spanish Custom," but left Miss Merman's big number, "It's the Animal in Me," on the cutting-room floor (though it was later inserted in *The Big Broadcast of 1936*). *Decca (Crosby LP).*

Evergreen. The banquet in the 1909 prologue honoring the affianced couple, Jessie Matthews and Ivor McLaren.

EVERGREEN

Music: Richard Rodgers*; Harry Woods**
Lyrics: Lorenz Hart*; Harry Woods**
Screenplay: Marjorie Gaffney & Emlyn Williams
Produced by: Michael Balcon for Gaumont-British
Directed by: Victor Saville
Choreography: Buddy Bradley
Photography: Glen MacWilliams
Cast: Jessie Matthews, Sonnie Hale, Betty Balfour, Barry Mackay, Ivor MacLaren, Hartley Power
Songs: "Daddy Wouldn't Buy Me a Bow-Wow" (Joseph Tabrar); "When You've Got a Little Springtime in Your Heart"**; "If I Give in to You "*; "Tinkle Tinkle Tinkle"**; " Dear, Dear" *; "Dancing on the Ceiling"*; "Just by Your Example"**; "Over My Shoulder"**
Released: June 1934; 90 minutes

The reigning international queen of British film musicals in the Thirties was lithesome Jessie Matthews, who scored her greatest success in *Evergreen*. In this adaptation of Miss Matthews' 1930 London stage hit (written *Ever Green),* Harriet Green, the daughter of an Edwardian music-hall singer who had disappeared, becomes a sensation by posing as her own miraculously preserved mother. Eventually, she confesses the deception and wins the sympathy of the public. In the stage production, Miss Matthews had, with more logic, passed herself off as her own grandmother, and Sonnie Hale, here playing an explosive director, had been the romantic lead. Only three of the original 15 Rodgers and Hart songs (including the gossamer hit, "Dancing on the Ceiling") were retained for the film, which added four new numbers by Harry Woods.
Video Yesteryear VC.

ONE NIGHT OF LOVE

Screenplay: S. K. Lauren, James Gow, Edmund North
Produced by: Everett Riskin for Columbia
Directed by: Victor Schertzinger
Photography: Joseph Walker
Cast: Grace Moore, Tullio Carminati, Lyle Talbot, Mona Barrie, Jessie Ralph, Jane Darwell, Henry Armetta, Herman Bing
Songs & arias: "One Night of Love" (Victor Schertzinger-Gus Kahn); "Sempre libera" (Verdi); "Sextet" (Donizetti); "Ciribiribin". (Albert Pestalozza); "'Tis the Last Rose of Summer" (Thomas Moore); "Habañera" (Bizet); "Un bel di" (Puccini); "None but the Lonely Heart" (Tschaikowsky); "Indian Love Call" (Rudolf Friml-Otto Harbach, Oscar Hammerstein II)
Released: June 1934; 80 minutes

After being turned down for the co-starring role in MGM's remake of *The Merry Widow* (the part went to Jeanette MacDonald), Grace Moore was signed by Columbia to appear in *One Night of Love,* thus becoming the first opera diva to win Hollywood acclaim. In the somewhat autobiographical film, Miss Moore plays an American soprano who studies in Italy and eventually makes her debut at the Metropolitan Opera. The non-too demanding acting chore allows the singer ample opportunities to offer a variety of arias as well as the popular title song (whose melody was based on the love duet from *Madame Butterfly).* As a result of the movie's success, other divas, notably Lily Pons and Gladys Swarthout, were lured to Hollywood but none achieved Miss Moore's screen popularity. In 1953, Miss Moore was the subject of a fictitious screen biography, *So This Is Love,* in which she was portrayed by Kathryn Grayson.
RCA/Columbia VC.

DAMES

Music: Harry Warren, etc.
Lyrics: Al Dubin, etc.
Screenplay: Delmer Daves
Produced by: Darryl F. Zanuck for Warner Bros.
Directed by: Ray Enright
Choreography: Busby Berkeley
Photography: Sid Hickox, George Barnes
Cast: Joan Blondell, Dick Powell, Ruby Keeler, ZaSu Pitts, Guy Kibbee, Hugh Herbert, Phil Regan, Sammy Fain
Songs: "When You Were a Smile on Your Mother's Lips" (Sammy Fain-Irving Kahal); "I Only Have Eyes for You"; "Try to See It My Way" (Allie Wrubel-Mort Dixon); "The Girl at the Ironing Board"; "Dames"
Released: August 15, 1934; 90 minutes

Continuing the Warner Bros. parade of backstage musicals, *Dames* was a reworking of the ingredients that had proved so successful in the past. On hand to provide the link were the ingenuous twosome, Dick Powell and Ruby Keeler, songwriters Warren and Dubin, and choreographer Busby Berkeley. The plot also includes the by-now expected situation of a last-minute cast switch—in this case it's Joan Blondell going on for Miss Keeler because of the latter's inability to get to the theatre on time. The story of *Dames* (which could just as easily have been titled *Gold Diggers of 1934*) has to do with the desire of wealthy bluenose Hugh Herbert to give away a fortune to morally deserving individuals, and the way Joan Blondell blackmails Herbert's cousin Guy Kibbee into backing Powell's show. The hit song "I Only Have Eyes for You" is performed twice: first by Powell singing to Keeler on a ferryboat (her reaction: "Gee, Jimmy, that's swell"), then in a Berkeley extravaganza set in a New York subway where Ruby's face shows up on all the advertising cards and which later turns into a dream with all the chorus girls sashaying about as Ruby Keeler doubles. *MGM/UA VC.*

Dames. One of Busby Berkeley's overhead patterns in the title-song production number.

THE MERRY WIDOW

Music: Franz Lehar
Lyrics: Lorenz Hart
Screenplay: Ernest Vajda & Samson Raphaelson
Produced by: Irving Thalberg for MGM
Directed by: Ernst Lubitsch
Choreography: Albertina Rasch
Photography: Oliver T. Marsh
Cast: Maurice Chevalier, Jeanette MacDonald, Edward Everett Horton, Una Merkel, George Barbier, Minna Gombell, Sterling Holloway, Donald Meek, Herman Bing, Henry Armetta, Akim Tamiroff, Shirley Ross, Leonid Kinskey, Richard Carle, Billy Gilbert, Virginia Field, Ferdinand Munier, Rolfe Sedan
Songs: "Girls, Girls, Girls"; "Vilia"; "Tonight Will Teach Me to Forget" (lyric: Gus Kahn); "Maxim's"; "Melody of Laughter"; "The Merry Widow Waltz"; "If Widows Are Rich"
Released: September 1934; 110 minutes

After director Ernst Lubitsch and his star attraction Maurice Chevalier had worked together on such operetta bonbons as *The Love Parade* and *The Smiling Lieutenant,* both at Paramount, it was almost inevitable that they would become involved in the first sound version of the most celebrated of all Viennese operettas, Franz Lehar's *The Merry Widow.* But since it was MGM, not Paramount, that held the rights, it was at that studio that the two men were brought together for their fifth and final association. Since he had already appeared in three films with Jeanette MacDonald, Chevalier wanted a change in his leading lady and fought to get the part for Grace Moore. Lubitsch, however, held out for Miss MacDonald. The movie also marks the only stage or screen assignment in which lyricist Lorenz Hart's words are not mated to the music of Richard Rodgers. (For contractural reasons, however, Rodgers received screen credit as co-lyricist.)

Based on a French play, *L'Attaché d'Ambassade,* the durable work had its premiere in 1905 (as *Die Lustige Witwe),* caused a sensation in London and New York two years later, and was screened twice in the U.S. as a silent—a 1912 two-reeler with Wallace Reid and Alma Rubens, and a much-altered Erich Von Stroheim feature-length adaptation in 1925 with John Gilbert and Mae Murray. For the 1934 *Merry Widow,* the action was set back from 1905 to the 1880s, the mythical kingdom's name was changed from Marsovia to Marshovia, Danilo was demoted from prince to count, widow Sonia Sadoya had lost her last name, and Marshovian Ambassador Popoff (Edward Everett Horton) no longer had an unfaithful wife. Most of the action takes place in Paris, where the dashing Danilo is on assignment from his government to woo and wed the wealthy widow to prevent her from marrying a foreigner. After mistaking Sonia for a cabaret girl at Maxim's (where another girl proudly exhibits a garter from Danilo inscribed "Many Happy Returns"), Danilo and Sonia meet again at the Marshovian Embassy ball. There, to the strains of the mesmeric "Merry Widow Waltz," they lead hundreds of waltzing couples as they airily glide through elegantly mirrored halls. Because Danilo's pride is hurt that Sonia considers him a fortune hunter, he refuses to fulfil his matrimonial mission and is tried and convicted in his homeland. Sonia then sets him free in the only way possible—she marries him.

A French version, *La Veuve Joyeuse,* shot by Lubitsch at the same time, also co-starred Chevalier and MacDonald. The third MGM remake of *The Merry Widow* was filmed in Technicolor in 1952 with non-singing Lana Turner (as Crystal Radek) and Ferdinand Lamas (as Count Danilo). Una Merkel, who played the queen in 1934, now showed up as Lana's best friend. To avoid confusion with this version, the 1934 *Merry Widow* has been given the meaningless title *The Lady Dances* when shown on television.
H'wood Soundstage ST. MGM/UA VC.

The Merry Widow. "The Merry Widow Waltz" performed by Maurice Chevalier and Jeanette MacDonald at the Marshovian Embassy in Paris.

THE GAY DIVORCEE

Screenplay: George Marion Jr., Dorothy Yost, Edward Kaufman
Produced by: Pandro S. Berman for RKO Radio
Directed by: Mark Sandrich
Choreography: Dave Gould, Hermes Pan (Fred Astaire uncredited)
Photography: David Abel
Cast: Fred Astaire, Ginger Rogers, Alice Brady, Edward Everett Horton,
Erik Rhodes, Eric Blore, Betty Grable, Lillian Miles, E.E. Clive
Songs: "Don't Let It Bother You" (Harry Revel-Mack Gordon); "A Needle
in a Haystack" (Con Conrad-Herb Magidson); "Let's K-nock K-nees"
(Revel-Gordon); "Night and Day" (Cole Porter); "The Continental"
(Conrad-Magidson)
Released: October 1934; 107 minutes

Because the Hays office decreed that a divorce could never be gay but that a divorcee
could, the title of the 1932 Broadway musical *Gay Divorce* had to be changed to *The Gay
Divorcee* when RKO made the screen version with Fred Astaire (who had been in the
original) and Ginger Rogers. The team's first starring vehicle, it also brought them together
with director Mark Sandrich (who helmed five of their movies) and producer Pandro S.
Berman (who was in charge of seven). Of Cole Porter's original stage score, the only song
retained was "Night and Day," which served to introduce audiences to the sight of formally
clad Astaire and Rogers performing the first of their romantic dance routines. Their skills
on the dancefloor were further demonstrated through their introduction of the daring new
dance sensation, "The Continental," in a sequence lasting 17 minutes.

In the story, dancer Guy Holden (Astaire) is mistakenly believed by divorce-seeking
Mimi Glossop (Miss Rogers) to be the professional corespondent with whom she must
spend the night at a fashionable English resort. Further complications arise when the real
corespondent, Rodolfo Tonetti (Erik Rhodes repeating his stage role), shows up, but
matters are pretty much straightened out by the next morning's breakfast.
Turner VC.

The Gay Divorcee. Betty Grable singing "Let's K-nock K-nees" to Edward
Everett Horton.

KID MILLIONS

Music: Walter Donaldson*; Burton Lane**
Lyrics: Gus Kahn *; Harold Adamson **
Screenplay: Arthur Sheekman, Nat Perrin, Nunnally Johnson
Produced by: Samuel Goldwyn (released by United Artists)
Directed by: Roy Del Ruth
Choreography: Seymour Felix
Photography: Ray June (part Technicolor)
Cast: Eddie Cantor, Ann Sothern, Ethel Merman, George Murphy, Jesse
         Block, Eve Sully, Nicholas Brothers, Lucille Ball, Paulette Goddard
Songs: "An Earful of Music" *; "When My Ship Comes In" *; "Your Head
         on My Shoulder"**; "I Want to Be a Minstrel Man"**; "Mandy"
         (Irving Berlin); "Okay Toots"*; "Ice Cream Fantasy"*
Released: October 1934; 90 minutes

Eddie Cantor's fifth and penultimate musical for Samuel Goldwyn had a trifling plot (about con artists trying to fleece our hero out of his inheritance) embellished by elaborate production numbers. In the attractive supporting cast were Ann Sothern and George Murphy (his first film) as the love interest and Ethel Merman posing as Cantor's long-lost mother (she was then 25 to his 42). Among the musical bright spots was a spangly minstrel show staged aboard a ship heading for Egypt which offered the Nicholas Brothers doing "I Want to Be a Minstrel Man" (whose music would be reused for Fred Astaire's "You're All the World to Me" number in *Royal Wedding)* and Cantor (in blackface) singing "Mandy." *Classic Intl. ST. Nelson VC.*

Music in the Air. Meeting in the office of Munich music publisher Reginald Owen, are June Lang, Douglass Montgomery, Al Shean, Joseph Cawthorn, John Boles, and Gloria Swanson.

Sweet Adeline. Irene Dunne singing "Why Was I Born?" accompanied by Donald Woods.

MUSIC IN THE AIR

Music: Jerome Kern
Lyrics: Oscar Hammerstein II
Screenplay: Howard Young & Billy Wilder
Produced by: Erich Pommer for Fox
Directed by: Joe May
Choreography: Jack Donohue
Photography: Ernest Palmer
Cast: Gloria Swanson, John Boles, Douglass Montgomery, Reginald
Owen, Al Shean, June Lang, Joseph Cawthorn, Jed Prouty, Fuzzy
Knight, Marjorie Main, Christian Rub
Songs: "I've Told Ev'ry Little Star"; "There's a Hill Beyond a Hill"; "I Am
So Eager"; "I'm Alone"; "One More Dance" ("Night Flies By");
"We Belong Together"
Released: December 1934; 85 minutes

Following a sweeping panorama of the Alps (foreshadowing the opening of *The Sound of Music*), *Music in the Air* was turned into a fairly close reproduction of the Kern-Hammerstein Broadway success of 1932—except for the omission of four songs including the hit ballad "The Song Is You." The tale unfolds the sad experience of Sieglinde Lessing (June Lang), a simple Bavarian mountain maid who takes over the starring role in a Munich operetta, *The Love Call* (called *Tingle-Tangle* on the stage), after temperamental Frieda Hatzfeld (Gloria Swanson in her only musical) has walked out following a spat with her lover, librettist Bruno Mahler (John Boles). Boldly bucking the cherished Hollywood tradition, however, the girl proves totally inadequate and Bruno and his colleagues are happy to welcome Frieda back. Al Shean, as Sieglinde's composer father, and Marjorie Main, as Frieda's maid, were the only Broadway actors to repeat their roles on the screen.

SWEET ADELINE

Music: Jerome Kern
Lyrics: Oscar Hammerstein II
Screenplay: Erwin Gelsey
Produced by: Edward Chodorov for Warner Bros.
Directed by: Mervyn LeRoy
Choreography: Bobby Connolly
Photography: Sol Polito
Cast: Irene Dunne, Donald Woods, Hugh Herbert, Ned Sparks, Joseph
Cawthorn, Wini Shaw, Louis Calhern, Nydia Westman, Phil Regan,
Dorothy Dare, Noah Beery
Songs: "Play Us a Polka, Dot"; "Here Am I"; "We Were So Young"; "Why Was I
Born?"; "Mollie
O'Donahue"; "Lonely Feet"; "'Twas Not So Long Ago"; "Don't
Ever Leave Me"
Released: January 1935; 87 minutes

The 1929 Jerome Kern-Oscar Hammerstein Broadway musical (starring Helen Morgan) was transferred to the screen with a reasonable amount of fidelity, retaining eight of the original 17 songs, adding two, "We Were So Young" and "Lonely Feet" (first sung in the London musical *Three Sisters),* and not doing too much damage to the story. It was also the first of five Kern screen musicals to star Irene Dunne. The nostalgic, atmospheric tale, set during the Spanish-American War, relates how Addie Schmidt, the daughter of a Hoboken beer garden owner, gets her chance to star on Broadway in two shows—an indescribable hodge-podge called *The Love Song* (whose run is terminated when Addie suffers a near-fatal accident caused by a jealous actress, who also happens to be a Spanish spy) and *The Belle of Hoboken* (which turns out to be the story of her life).

Roberta. Ginger Rogers and Fred Astaire dancing to "Smoke Gets in Your Eyes."

ROBERTA

Music: Jerome Kern
Lyrics: Otto Harbach*; Dorothy Fields **
Screenplay: Jane Murfin, Sam Mintz, Glen Tryon, Allan Scott
Produced by: Pandro S. Berman for RKO Radio
Directed by: William A. Seiter
Choreography: Hermes Pan (Fred Astaire uncredited)
Photography: Edward Cronjager
Cast: Irene Dunne, Fred Astaire, Ginger Rogers, Randolph Scott, Helen Westley, Victor Varconi, Claire Dodd, Lucille Ball, Candy Candido, Gene Sheldon
Songs: "Let's Begin"*; "I'll Be Hard to Handle" (lyric: Bernard Dougall); "Yesterdays"*; "I Won't Dance"** (lyric with Oscar Hammerstein II); "Smoke Gets In Your Eyes"*; "Lovely to Look At"**
Released: February 1935; 105 minutes

Kern and Harbach's *Roberta* gave RKO the opportunity to star the established Irene Dunne with the popular new team of Fred Astaire and Ginger Rogers. The movie was adapted from a 1933 Broadway musical that had been based on Alice Duer Miller's novel *Gowns by Roberta*, but it made sure to build up the Astaire and Rogers parts and it added two pieces, "I Won't Dance" (for a dazzling Astaire solo) and "Lovely to Look At" (the theme of the fashion show that concludes the film), to the four songs retained from the stage production. The story relates what happens when former All-American halfback John Kent (Randolph Scott) inherits his Aunt Minnie's Parisian haute couture establishment, Roberta's, and falls in love with his aunt's assistant, exiled Russian Princess Stephanie (Miss Dunne). The new secondary plot concerns John's friend Huck Haines (Astaire), band-leader of the Wabash Indianians, and his rather casual romance with hometown girlfriend Lizzie Gatz (Miss Rogers), now singing at the Cafe Russe under the name of Countess Tanka Scharwenka. This, of course, is just an excuse for the team to light up the screen with their dances to "I'll Be Hard to Handle" and "Smoke Gets in Your Eyes." A second screen version of *Roberta*, called *Lovely to Look At,* was released in 1952 (see page 172).
Classic Intl. ST.   MGM/UA VC.

Folies Bergere de Paris. Maurice Chevalier imitating a baron in the "Au Revoir, L'Amour" number performed in the revue.

FOLIES BERGERE DE PARIS

Music: Jack Stern, etc.
Lyrics: Jack Meskill, etc.
Screenplay: Bess Meredyth & Hal Long
Produced by: Darryl F. Zanuck for 20th Century (released by United Artists)
Directed by: Roy Del Ruth
Choreography: Dave Gould
Photography: Barney McGill, J. Peverell Marley
Cast: Maurice Chevalier, Merle Oberon, Ann Sothern, Walter Byron, Eric Blore
Songs: "Valentine" (Albert Willemetz-André Christine); "Rhythm of the Rain"; "You Took the Words Right Out of My Mouth" (Burton Lane-Harold Adamson); "I Was Lucky"; "Singing a Happy Song"
Released: February 1935; 84 minutes

An entertainer who is a dead ringer for a titled financier-playboy impersonates him on stage and is hired to take his place at a social function while the gentleman is out of town. The performer fools everyone except the man's wife. But the playboy comes back to town after the guests have departed. He changes places with the impersonator and spends the night with his wife. His dilemma is that he is unsure whether his wife is faithful by being aware of the switch or whether she is unfaithful by assuming she has been with the double. This basic story, originally the plot of a play by Rudolph Lothar and Hans Adler, was made into three 20th Century musicals: *Folies Bergere de Paris* (1935), *That Night in Rio* (1941), and *On the Riviera* (1951). In the first, with Maurice Chevalier in the dual role (after it had been turned down by Charles Boyer), the celebrated Parisian music hall provides the setting for most of the numbers, including "Rhythm of the Rain," a pluvial extravaganza with Chevalier and Ann Sothern leading the chorus in twirling umbrellas and splashing down the street.

GOLD DIGGERS OF 1935

Music: Harry Warren
Lyrics: Al Dubin
Screenplay: Manuel Seff & Peter Milne
Produced by: Robert Lord for Warner Bros.
Director-choreographer: Busby Berkeley
Photography: George Barnes
Cast: Dick Powell, Adolphe Menjou, Gloria Stuart, Alice Brady, Glenda
Farrell, Frank McHugh, Hugh Herbert, Joseph Cawthorn, Grant
Mitchell, Wini Shaw, Virginia Grey
Songs: "I'm Going Shopping With You"; "The Words Are in My Heart";
"Lullaby of Broadway"
Released: March 1935; 95 minutes

The first musical for which Busby Berkeley served as director as well as choreographer, *Gold Diggers of 1935* is distinguished primarily for two production numbers, "The Words Are in My Heart," featuring 56 girls supposedly playing 56 pianos, and especially "Lullaby of Broadway," a mini-morality musical. The latter, taking place in New York during a 24-hour dawn-to-dawn period, focuses on the hedonistic life of a girl-about-town (Wini Shaw), who sleeps all day and plays all night, and her playboy escort (Dick Powell). These two, it seems, are the only guests at a mammoth high-in-the-sky night spot where they are entertained by hundreds of frantically tapping dancers and where the girl is accidentally pushed to her death from a balcony. The film's chief gold digger is temperamental director Adolphe Menjou and the romance involves poor medical student Powell and rich non-singing, non-dancing Gloria Stuart.
MGM/UA VC.

Gold Diggers of 1935. The "Lullaby of Broadway" sequence with Wini Shaw and Dick Powell at the upper right.

GO INTO YOUR DANCE

Music: Harry Warren
Lyrics: Al Dubin
Screenplay: Earl Baldwin
Produced by: Samuel Bischoff for Warner Bros.
Directed by: Archie Mayo
Choreography: Bobby Connolly
Photography: Tony Gaudio, Sol Polito
Cast: Al Jolson, Ruby Keeler, Helen Morgan, Glenda Farrell, Patsy Kelly, Phil Regan, Benny Rubin, Barton MacLane, Akim Tamiroff, Arthur Treacher, Harry Warren, Al Dubin
Songs: "A Good Old-Fashioned Cocktail"; "Mammy, I'll Sing About You"; "About a Quarter to Nine"; "The Little Things You Used to Do"; "She's a Latin from Manhattan"; "Go Into Your Dance"
Released: March 1935; 90 minutes

Except for a brief joint appearance in *Show Girl in Hollywood* (1930), Al Jolson and Ruby Keeler (then Mr. and Mrs.) were seen on the screen together only in *Go Into Your Dance*. In the backstage story, Jolson plays an irresponsible Broadway entertainer who successfully teams with Keeler in Chicago. There are all sorts of melodramatic goings-on—involving a false murder rap and an attempted underworld assassination—before the couple can enjoy a triumphant opening night at their glitzy new New York nightclub. The film profited from the curiosity value in pairing the dynamic "Mammy" singer and the blank-faced, clod-hopping ingenue. But for Jolson it was the solo spotlight or nothing and he refused the studio's entreaties to costar with his wife in another movie. Of more lasting value than the picture is the varied, attractive score by Harry Warren and Al Dubin. The movie was called *Casino de Paree* in Great Britain.
H'wood Soundstage ST.

Naughty Marietta. Jeanette MacDonald and Nelson Eddy.

NAUGHTY MARIETTA

Music: Victor Herbert
Lyrics: Rida Johnson Young
Screenplay: John Lee Mahin, Frances Goodrich, Albert Hackett
Produced by: Hunt Stromberg for MGM
Directed by: W. S. Van Dyke
Photography: William Daniels
Cast: Jeanette MacDonald, Nelson Eddy, Frank Morgan, Elsa Lanchester, Douglass Dumbrille, Joseph Cawthorn, Cecilia Parker, Akim Tamiroff, Edward Brophy, Marjorie Main, Walter Kingsford
Songs: "Chansonette" (lyric: Gus Kahn); "Tramp, Tramp, Tramp"; " 'Neath the Southern Moon"; "Italian Street Song"; "I'm Falling in Love With Someone"; "Ah! Sweet Mystery of Life"
Released: March 1935; 106 minutes

Naughty Marietta inaugurated the series of eight operettas co-starring Jeanette MacDonald and Nelson Eddy, which would fill the screen with the lush melodies of Victor Herbert, Rudolf Friml, Herbert Stothart, Sigmund Romberg, Noel Coward, and Richard Rodgers. Adapted from a 1910 stage production, *Naughty Marietta* kept the same locale and time period (New Orleans in the late 1700s), but underwent a number of changes. The heroine, formerly a Neapolitan named Marietta D'Altena, is now a French princess, Marie de Namours de la Bonfain. Marie avoids a loveless marriage by sailing to the New World—as Marietta Frannini—with a shipload of casquette girls sent to provide wives for Louisiana planters and trappers. Though on stage stalwart Capt. Dick Warrington spent most of his time pursuing a notorious pirate, on screen Capt. Dick and his band of tramp, tramp, tramping men conveniently overcome the pirate gang early in the story so that most of the footage is devoted to Marietta's efforts to conceal her true identity, Capt. Dick's efforts to keep the lady from sailing back to France, and the couple's realization that they are in love when they suddenly find words to "Ah! Sweet Mystery of Life."

In 1940, MacDonald and Eddy co-starred in *New Moon*, based on Romberg and Hammerstein's 1928 operetta, which was set in the same locale at about the same time as *Naughty Marietta.* Here, however, the situation is reversed, with Eddy as a French duke in disguise who has been brought to New Orleans as a bondsman to work on MacDonald's plantation. Both films made the same historic error: at the time New Orleans belonged to Spain, not to France.
H'wood Soundstage ST. MGM/UA VC.

MISSISSIPPI

Music: Richard Rodgers
Lyrics: Lorenz Hart
Screenplay: Francis Martin & Jack Cunningham
Produced by: Arthur Hornblow Jr. for Paramount
Directed by: A. Edward Sutherland
Photography: Charles Lang
Cast: Bing Crosby, W. C. Fields, Joan Bennett, Queenie Smith, Gail
          Patrick, Claude Gillingwater, John Miljan, Ann Sheridan, Dennis
          O'Keefe, King Baggott, Paul Hurst
Songs: "Roll Mississippi"; "Soon"; "Down by the River"; "It's Easy to
          Remember"; "Old Folks at Home" (Stephen Foster)
Released: April 1935; 73 minutes

Hollywood's second costume musical about a Mississippi showboat was based on Booth
Tarkington's 1923 play, *Magnolia* (which had been filmed twice as a silent). It offers Bing
Crosby as Tom Grayson, a peace-loving Philadelphian who refuses to follow the South's
code of honor by fighting a duel over his fiancee (Gail Patrick). Branded a coward, Tom becomes a singer on a showboat run by Capt. Orlando Jackson (W. C. Fields), who publicizes
him as "The Notorious Col. Steele." Eventually, Tom redeems his honor and ends in the
arms of his former fiancee's sister (Joan Bennett). *Mississippi* had already begun shooting
when leading man Lanny Ross was replaced by Crosby, who wanted another song. Since
Rodgers and Hart had already returned to New York, they wrote the film's biggest hit, "It's
Easy to Remember," while in the East, then sent a demo record to the producer. It is in this
movie that Fields, relating the tale of his battle against the savage Indian, mutters the
deathless line, "I unsheathed my Bowie knife and cut a path through this wa-a-all of human
flesh dragging my canoe behind me."
Decca (Crosby LP).

Mississippi. Bing Crosby, King Baggott, W.C. Fields, and Paul Hurst.

TOP HAT

Music & lyrics: Irving Berlin
Screenplay: Dwight Taylor & Allan Scott
Produced by: Pandro S. Berman for RKO Radio
Directed by: Mark Sandrich
Choreography: Hermes Pan (Fred Astaire uncredited)
Photography: David Abel
Cast: Fred Astaire, Ginger Rogers, Edward Everett Horton, Helen
Broderick, Erik Rhodes, Eric Blore, Lucille Ball, Leonard Mudie,
Edgar Norton
Songs: "No Strings"; "Isn't This a Lovely Day?"; "Top Hat, White Tie and
Tails"; "Cheek to Cheek"; "The Piccolino"
Released: August 1935; 101 minutes

Since *The Gay Divorcee* had proved to be such an auspicious vehicle for Fred Astaire and Ginger Rogers in 1934, RKO used the same general formula the following year with *Top Hat,* a film that in style, plot, characterizations, and casting was so close to the previous movie that it amounted almost to self-plagiarism. The settings are again London and a fashionable resort (this time it's the Lido), and the wildly improbable tale of mistaken identity again finds Astaire as an American dancer falling in love at first sight with Rogers as another visiting American. The high points once more occur when the formally clad twosome appear on the dance floor both to reveal their love through a dance ("Cheek to Cheek," succeeding the previous film's "Night and Day") and to take part in an outdoor production number introducing a new melody ("The Piccolino" succeeding "The Continental"). The three male character comedians in *The Gay Divorcee*—Edward Everett Horton, Erik Rhodes, and Eric Blore—are again on hand to play, respectively, Astaire's prissy friend, Astaire's volatile rival, and Horton's bumptious valet. *Top Hat* also shared the same producer, director, choreographers, cameraman, art director (Van Nest Polglase), music director (Max Steiner), and editor (William Hamilton).

Generally regarded as the quintessential Astaire-Rogers musical, the film is further enhanced by a score by Irving Berlin (his first major Hollywood effort) consisting of five numbers all tied to situations in the plot. This is true even of Astaire's tailor-made "Top Hat, White Tie and Tails," which, though seen as part of a London stage production, is performed in a way that makes the song's "invitation through the mails" refer to a telegram Horton had received from his wife (Helen Broderick) in the previous scene. (The number's climax with Astaire shooting down chorus boys with his cane was based on a routine the dancer had performed in the 1930 stage musical, *Smiles.*) One logic-stretching period covers a single night at the Lido resort that includes the cheek-to-cheek dance, a marital misunderstanding, a phony wedding, a threatened duel, a gondola drifting out to sea, and the elaborate "Piccolino" finale (which presumably takes place at dawn).

Director Mark Sandrich began work on *Top Hat* in December 1934, some four months before actual shooting, and Astaire devoted at least five weeks to blocking out and rehearsing the dance numbers. Making a brief appearance in a flowershop scene was Lucille Ball who, in 1958, would take control of the RKO Radio studio for her own television company, Desilu Productions. The chief mishap that occurred during filming involved the gown Ginger Rogers wore in the "Cheek to Cheek" sequence. The dress was covered with thousands of feathers and as Ginger began to dance the feathers began to molt. Dozens of takes were required before the dance was finally completed without any of the flying tufts visible on the screen. This scene was used again as the climax to Woody Allen's 1985 film *The Purple Rose of Cairo.*
Columbia (Astaire CD); Sountrak ST. Turner VC.

Top Hat. Fred Astaire and male chorus in the "Top Hat, White Tie and Tails" number.

BROADWAY MELODY OF 1936

Music: Nacio Herb Brown
Lyrics: Arthur Freed
Screenplay: Jack McGowan, Sid Silvers, Harry Conn
Produced by: John Considine Jr. for MGM
Directed by: Roy Del Ruth
Choreography: Dave Gould, Albertina Rasch
Photography: Charles Rosher
Cast: Jack Benny, Eleanor Powell, Robert Taylor, Una Merkel, Frances Langford, Sid Silvers, Buddy Ebsen, June Knight, Vilma Ebsen, Harry Stockwell, Nick Long Jr., Robert Wildhack
Songs: "Broadway Melody"; "You Are My Lucky Star"; "I've Got a Feelin' You're Foolin'"; "Sing Before Breakfast"; "All I Do Is Dream of You"; "Broadway Rhythm"
Released: August 1935; 110 minutes

No doubt spurred by the success of the Warner Bros. *Gold Diggers* series, MGM dusted off the *Broadway Melody* title after six years for a film designed to show off the tapping talent of its new contractee, Eleanor Powell. The story concerns a feud between producer-songwriter Robert Taylor and gossip columnist Jack Benny, and Benny's attempt to embarrass Taylor by publicizing an imaginary French actress known as La Belle Aulette. After Taylor decides to star her, sight unseen, in *Broadway Rhythm*, it's the unknown Miss Powell, of course, who passes herself off as the blonde foreign attraction and scores a huge success. Songwriters Brown and Freed added a "Broadway Rhythm" to their "Broadway Melody" and also came up with a new hit, "You Are My Lucky Star."

THE BIG BROADCAST OF 1936

Music: Ralph Rainger & Richard Whiting, etc.
Lyrics: Leo Robin, etc.
Screenplay: Walter DeLeon, Francis Martin, Ralph Spence
Produced by: Benjamin Glazer for Paramount
Directed by: Norman Taurog
Choreography: LeRoy Prinz
Photography: Leo Tover
Cast: Jack Oakie, Lyda Roberti, George Burns, Gracie Allen, Wendy Barrie, Akim Tamiroff, Henry Wadsworth, Nicholas Brothers, Ray Noble Orch., Bill Robinson, Bing Crosby, Benny Baker, Ina Ray Hutton Orch., Vienna Choir Boys, Ethel Merman, Amos 'n Andy, Mary Boland, Charlie Ruggles
Songs: "Miss Brown to You"; "Why Dream?"; "I Wished on the Moon" (lyric: Dorothy Parker); "Double Trouble"; "Tales from the Vienna Woods" (Johann Strauss); "It's the Animal in Me." (Harry Revel-Mack Gordon); "The Very Thought of You" (Ray Noble)
Released: September 1935; 97 minutes

With Warners' *Gold Diggers* series and MGM's *Broadway Melody* series taking care of backstage musicals, Paramount chose to reuse its 1932 *Big Broadcast* rubric for a series about radio. Like *International House*, the 1936 edition (filmed in 1935) focuses its attention on early television—here called "radio eye"—through which is seen such specialty acts as the Nicholas Brothers scat singing and tapping to "Miss Brown to You" (heard and danced to by Bill Robinson on a Harlem street); Bing Crosby crooning "I Wished on the Moon"; and Ethel Merman, accompanied by a jungle chorus and "dancing" elephants, belting out "It's the Animal in Me" (the scene had been filmed for—but never used in—*We're Not Dressing).* The zany plot has something to do with Jack Oakie as a radio singing heartthrob known as Lochinvar, whose vocals are dubbed by Henry Wadsworth (whose vocals were dubbed by Kenny Baker), and the romantic complications that ensue on a Caribbean island owned by Lyda Roberti.

THANKS A MILLION

Music: Arthur Johnston
Lyrics: Gus Kahn
Screenplay: Nunnally Johnson
Produced by: Darryl F. Zanuck for 20th Century-Fox
Directed by: Roy Del Ruth
Photography: J. Peverell Marley
Cast: Dick Powell, Fred Allen, Ann Dvorak, Patsy Kelly, Paul Whiteman
Orch., Ramona, Raymond Walburn, Rubinoff, Yacht Club Boys,
Benny Baker, Alan Dinehart, Andrew Tombes, Lynn Bari
Songs: "Thanks a Million"; "Pocketful of Sunshine"; "Sugarplum"; "I'm
Sittin' High on a Hilltop"; "New O'leans"
Released: October 1935; 87 minutes

Darryl Zanuck's first production following the merger of 20th Century and Fox was *Metropolitan*; his second—which he claimed was responsible for launching the company as a major studio—was *Thanks a Million*. As did *The Phantom President*, the movie offers the once outlandish notion that an entertainer could be more successful at running for public office than a stuffy politician. In this case, it's vaudevillian Dick Powell (in a part originally intended for Bing Crosby) who is substituted for the hapless Raymond Walburn as the candidate for the governership of an unnamed state. Powell wins the election by singing a song or two at political rallies, making a speech denouncing crooked party bosses, and urging people not to vote for him. A surprise boxoffice hit, the film marked the first screen appearance of deadpan radio comic Fred Allen. In 1946, a remake, *If I'm Lucky*, put Perry Como in the Powell role.

Thanks a Million. Dick Powell singing the title song at a political rally.

KING OF BURLESQUE

Music: Jimmy McHugh
Lyrics: Ted Koehler
Screenplay: Gene Markey & Harry Tugend
Produced by: Darryl F. Zanuck & Kenneth MacGowan for 20th Century-Fox
Directed by: Sidney Lanfield
Choreography: Sammy Lee
Photography: J. Peverell Marley
Cast: Warner Baxter, Alice Faye, Jack Oakie, Mona Barrie, Arline Judge, Dixie Dunbar, Gregory Ratoff, Herbert Mundin, Fats Waller, Nick Long Jr., Kenny Baker, Keye Luke, Andrew Tombes, Gareth Joplin
Songs: "Whose Big Baby Are You?"; "I'm Shooting High"; "I Love to Ride the Horses" (Lew Pollack-Jack Yellen); "Lovely Lady"; "I've Got My Fingers Crossed"; "'Spreading Rhythm Around"
Released: December 1935; 88 minutes

Again cast in the role of a Broadway director, which he had played in *42nd Street,* Warner Baxter shows up initially as the impresario of a rowdier form of entertainment in *King of Burlesque.* Craving respectability, he leads cohorts Alice Faye and Jack Oakie uptown to the more legitimate theatrical area where they succeed with a series of high-stepping revues. Baxter marries socialite Mona Barrie, who is down to her last tiara, thus causing lovelorn Alice to flee to London where she becomes a stellar attraction. After Baxter stages a pretentious flop Mona ditches him and he takes to the bottle. But Alice returns to make everything end happily by secretly backing Baxter's lavish theatre restaurant, in which she appears with Dixie Dunbar, Kenny Baker, Fats Waller, Gareth Joplin, and Nick Long Jr. (If the plot seems familiar, it turned up eight years later in *Hello, Frisco, Hello* with Miss Faye and Mr. Oakie playing similar roles.)

Rose Marie. Fugitive James Stewart is apprehended by Mountie Nelson Eddy much to Jeanette MacDonald's distress.

ROSE MARIE

Music: Rudolf Friml*, Herbert Stothart #
Lyrics: Otto Harbach & Oscar Hammerstein II, etc.
Screenplay: Frances Goodrich, Albert Hackett, Alice Duer Miller
Produced by: Hunt Stromberg for MGM
Directed by: W. S. Van Dyke
Choreography: Chester Hale
Photography: William Daniels
Cast: Jeanette MacDonald, Nelson Eddy, James Stewart, Reginald Owen, Allan Jones, Una O'Connor, Alan Mowbray, David Niven, Herman Bing, Gilda Gray, George Regas, Robert Greig, Jimmy Conlin, Lucien Littlefield, Halliwell Hobbes, Edgar Dearing, Rolfe Sedan; Russell Hicks
Songs: "Pardon Me, Madame" # (lyric: Gus Kahn); "The Mounties" * #; "Dinah" (Harry Akst-Sam Lewis, Joe Young); "Some of These Days" (Shelton Brooks); "Rose Marie" *; "Totem Tom-Tom" * #; "Just For You"* (lyric: Kahn); "Indian Love Call"*
Released: January 1936; 110 minutes

Derived from the 1924 Broadway production, *Rose Marie* was rewritten for the screen even more drastically than the first Jeanette MacDonald-Nelson Eddy opus, *Naughty Marietta*. On stage, the Otto Harbach-Oscar Hammerstein plot dealt with the romance between French-Canadian Rose-Marie La Flamme and gold prospector Jim Kenyon. After Jim is falsely accused of murder, he manages to clear his name with the help of, among others, Sergeant Malone of the Northwest Mounted Police. In the 1936 movie version, Marie de Flor (Miss MacDonald) is a Canadian opera star who takes the name of Rose Marie after journeying to the Canadian Rockies in search of her brother, John Flower (James Stewart in his second film), a murderer who has escaped from prison. This brings Rose Marie in contact with the Mounties' Sergeant Bruce (Eddy) and they fall in love singing the "Indian Love Call." They have a tearful—but temporary—parting, however, after the officer must do his duty and arrest young Flower. (In the 1929 movie, *Rio Rita,* Capt. James Stewart of the Texas Rangers fell in love with the titular heroine but almost lost her because he suspected her brother of being a bank robber.)

The music for *Rose Marie* was changed almost as much as the plot. Only four songs were retained from the 14 heard on Broadway (divided equally between composers Rudolf Friml and Herbert Stothart), with the score augmented by selections from Gounod's *Roméo et Juliette* and Puccini's *Tosca* (or *La Tosca,* according to a billboard outside a Montreal theatre), with Allan Jones singing opposite Miss MacDonald in the opera sequences. Also included were two pop standards and two new songs created for the film. Most of the people responsible for putting *Naughty Marietta* on the screen were assigned to *Rose Marie:* producer Stromberg, director Van Dyke, writers Goodrich and Hackett, lyricist Kahn, cameraman Daniels, music director and adapter Stothart, art director Cedric Gibbons, and editor Blanche Sewell. Originally, the movie's female star was to have been Grace Moore, but she proved to be unavailable when shooting began and had to be replaced by Miss MacDonald.

MGM made two other versions of *Rose-Marie* (the hyphenated name was always used on Broadway). The first was a silent in 1928 directed by Lucien Hubbard, featuring Joan Crawford and James Murray; the second, in 1954, co-starring Ann Blyth, Fernando Lamas, and Howard Keel, was directed by Mervyn LeRoy. (See page 183.) To avoid confusion with this version, the 1936 *Rose Marie* has been retitled *Indian Love Call* when shown on television.

H'wood Soundstage ST. MGM/UA VC.

Anything Goes. Bing Crosby, Ethel Merman, and Charlie Ruggles.

ANYTHING GOES

Music & lyrics: Cole Porter, etc.
Screenplay: Howard Lindsay, Russel Crouse, Guy Bolton
Produced by: Benjamin Glazer for Paramount
Directed by: Lewis Milestone
Photography: Karl Struss
Cast: Bing Crosby, Ethel Merman, Charlie Ruggles, Ida Lupino, Arthur
Treacher, Grace Bradley, Richard Carle, Margaret Dumont, Philip
Ahn, Keye Luke, Dennis O'Keefe, Chill Wills
Songs: "Anything Goes"; "I Get a Kick Out of You"; "There'll Always Be a
Lady Fair"; "Sailor Beware" (Richard Whiting-Leo Robin);
"Moonburn" (Hoagy Carmichael-Edward Heyman); "My Heart and I
(Frederick Hollander-Robin)"; "You're the Top"; "Shanghai-Di-Ho"
(Hollander-Robin)
Released: February 1936; 92 minutes

On Broadway, where it opened in 1934, *Anything Goes* was one of the decade's merriest
and most successful musicals. The movie version enlisted three of the four original writers,
kept four of the original 12 Cole Porter songs (though there were changes in the lyric to
"You're the Top"), and retained Ethel Merman to repeat her role of Reno Sweeney, a
nightclub singer sailing on an ocean liner from New York to Southampton. Otherwise, four
new numbers were added (including "Moonburn," Hoagy Carmichael's first movie song),
energetic William Gaxton was replaced by easygoing Bing Crosby and bumbling Victor
Moore by bumbling Charlie Ruggles (who took over from W. C. Fields). In the story, Billy
Crocker (Crosby), a friend of Reno's, stows aboard the ship to be near Hope Harcourt (Ida
Lupino), the heiress he loves, and Public Enemy No. 13 (Ruggles) masquerades as the
Rev. Dr. Moon. Eventually, Reno snares a titled Englishman (Arthur Treacher), Billy gets
his Hope, and Dr. Moon is officially declared harmless.

In 1956, Paramount released a second film titled *Anything Goes,* but it bore scant
relationship to the first except that Crosby was also in it and five of the original Porter songs
were used (James Van Heusen and Sammy Cahn came up with three new ones).
Jeanmaire, Mitzi Gaynor, and Donald O'Connor were co-starred. For its showings on
television, the original *Anything Goes has* been given the awkward title *Tops Is the Limit.
Decca (Crosby LP).*

FOLLOW THE FLEET

Music & lyrics: Irving Berlin
Screenplay: Dwight Taylor & Allan Scott
Produced by: Pandro S. Berman for RKO Radio
Directed by: Mark Sandrich
Choreography: Hermes Pan (Fred Astaire uncredited)
Photography: David Abel
Cast: Fred Astaire, Ginger Rogers, Randolph Scott, Harriet Hilliard, Astrid Allwyn, Lucille Ball, Betty Grable, Joy Hodges, Tony Martin, Frank Jenks, Ray Mayer, Russell Hicks, Harry Beresford, Addison Randall, Herbert Rawlinson
Songs: "We Saw the Sea"; "Let Yourself Go"; "Get Thee Behind Me, Satan"; "I'd Rather Lead a Band"; "But Where Are You?"; "I'm Putting All My Eggs in One Basket"; "Let's Face the Music and Dance"
Released: February 1936; 110 minutes

After putting Fred Astaire and Ginger Rogers in the elegant surroundings of *The Gay Divorcee, Roberta,* and *Top Hat,* producer Pandro Berman felt that it was time to lower their social standing. To achieve this, he cast them in a musical loosely based on a 1922 Broadway play, *Shore Leave* by Hubert Osborne, which was about Connie Martin, a New England dressmaker, who becomes so smitten with Bilge Smith, a marriage-shy sailor, that she has a ship salvaged for him after his discharge. Berman, of course, was well aware that the play, which was filmed in 1925, had also served as the basis for a 1927 musical comedy, *Hit the Deck* (score by Vincent Youmans, Clifford Grey, and Leo Robin), which RKO turned into a movie three years later with Jack Oakie and Polly Walker. This time, however, the producer wanted an entirely new approach. Thus, in *Follow the Fleet,* with Randolph Scott as Bilge and Harriet Hilliard as Connie, their story became secondary to one involving two newly created characters: sailor Bake Baker, Bilge's shipmate, and dancehall singer Sherry Martin, Connie's sister, a former vaudeville team who meet again at the Paradise Ballroom in San Francisco. For the score, though the RKO brass favored Harry Warren and Al Dubin, Berman insisted on retaining Irving Berlin, whose songs had proved so important to the success of *Top Hat,* the last Fred and Ginger vehicle.

As Bake and Sherry, Astaire and Rogers provided a contrasting comic romance just as they had previously done in *Roberta* (in which Scott had also played Astaire's friend), thereby replacing the customary character comedians who had given such valuable support in all previous Astaire-Rogers movies. The film's main locales were the dancehall (where the partners let themselves go dancing to "Let Yourself Go"), the deck of a battleship (where Astaire leads the tapping sailors in "I'd Rather Lead a Band"), and the deck of a reconstructed steam schooner (where Fred and Ginger clown around rehearsing "I'm Putting All My Eggs in One Basket" and later perform the compelling "Let's Face the Music and Dance" as part of a benefit show). In 1981, the last sequence was inserted in Herbert Ross's film, *Pennies from Heaven.* Two Berlin songs, "Moonlight Maneuvers" and "With a Smile on My Face," though written for *Follow the Fleet,* were never used in the movie.

Seen briefly in *Follow the Fleet* were sailor Tony Martin (in his film debut), backup singer Betty Grable, and Lucille Ball as one of the Paradise girls. (After a burly, gravel-voiced sailor makes a pass at her, Lucille deadpans, "Tell me, little boy, did you get a whistle or a baseball bat with that suit?")

Matching the popularity of the previous year's *Roberta* and *Top Hat, Follow the Fleet* turned out to be one of the biggest box office winners of 1936.
Columbia (Astaire CD); H'wood Soundstage ST. Turner VC.

THE GREAT ZIEGFELD

Music: Walter Donaldson, etc.
Lyrics: Harold Adamson, etc.
Screenplay: William Anthony McGuire
Produced by: Hunt Stromberg for MGM
Directed by: Robert Z. Leonard
Choreography: Seymour Felix
Photography: Oliver T. Marsh, George Folsey, Karl Freund, Ray June
Cast: William Powell, Myrna Loy, Luise Rainer, Frank Morgan, Fanny Brice, Virginia Bruce, Reginald Owen, Ray Bolger, Ernest Cossart, Joseph Cawthorn, Nat Pendleton, Harriet Hoctor, Herman Bing, Raymond Walburn, William Demarest, Dennis Morgan, Virginia Grey, Jean Chatburn, A.A. Trimble, Buddy Doyle, Esther Muir, Robert Greig, Charles Judels
Songs: "Won't You Come and Play With Me?" (Anna Held); "It's Delightful to Be Married" (Vincent Scotto-Held); "If You Knew Susie" (Joseph Meyer-B.G. DeSylva); "Shine on Harvest Moon" (Nora Bayes-Jack Norworth); "A Pretty Girl Is Like a Melody" (Irving Berlin); "You Gotta Pull Strings"; "She's a Follies Girl"; "You"; "You Never Looked So Beautiful"; "Queen of the Jungle"; "My Man" (Maurice Yvain-Channing Pollock); "A Circus Must Be Different in a Ziegfeld Show" (Con Conrad-Herb Magidson)
Released: April 1936; 176 minutes

Broadway's legendary showman, Florenz Ziegfeld, produced 52 musicals between 1896 and 1931, including 21 editions of the opulent *Ziegfeld Follies,* plus such book shows as *Sally, Rio Rita, Show Boat, Rosalie, The Three Musketeers,* and *Whoopee. The Great Ziegfeld,* the first of a number of elaborate show-business screen biographies, purports to trace Ziegfeld's career from the days he managed Sandow the Strong Man at the Chicago World's Fair of 1893, through his stage successes, financial reverses, relationships with his two wives (the temperamental Anna Held and the more indulgent Billie Burke), and death at the age of 65. William Powell portrays the craggy, bilious impresario as a witty, urbane charmer but it is Luise Rainer as Anna who has the film's most memorable dramatic scene in which she makes an hysterical telephone call to her former husband congratulating him on his new marriage.

The most memorable musical scene, supposedly taking place during the first *Ziegfeld Follies,* was built around the song "A Pretty Girl Is Like a Melody" (which Irving Berlin had written for the 13th annual edition in 1919). Added as an afterthought and costing a record $220,000, the scene features a towering volute, 70 feet in diameter, with 175 spiral steps and weighing 100 tons. As the structure revolves, Dennis Morgan (unaccountably dubbed by Allan Jones) sings the theme song, with some 82 singers, dancers, and musicians performing selections ranging from *Pagliacci* to the *Rhapsody in Blue.* The sequence ends with the sight of Virginia Bruce, as the Spirit of the *Follies,* perched atop the volute as a satin curtain descends in folds all around it.

Ziegfeld's associates, librettist William Anthony McGuire, had first sold the idea of a biographical film to Universal, but the studio abandoned the project after a year, and MGM secured the rights. At first the cast was to have included such Ziegfeld luminaries as Marilyn Miller, Irving Berlin, Gilda Grey, Ann Pennington, and Leon Errol, but they either refused to appear in the movie or were left on the cutting-room floor. Two discoveries, Eddie Cantor and Will Rogers, were impersonated by, respectively, Buddy Doyle and A. A. Trimble. The movie did, however feature two authentic Ziegfeld attractions: comedienne Fanny Brice (whose specialty, "My Man," was unconscionably abridged) and contortionistic ballet dancer Harriet Hoctor. One alleged discovery, Ray Bolger, had never been in a Ziegfeld show. Ziegfeld was again played by Powell in the 1946 film, *Ziegfeld Follies*; others who portrayed him on the screen were Paul Henreid in *Deep in My Heart* (1954) and Walter Pidgeon in *Funny Girl* (1968).
Classic Intl. ST. MGM/UA VC.

The Great Ziegfeld. The "Pretty Girl Is Like a Melody" number, with Virginia Bruce atop the volute.

Show Boat. The obviously smitten Irene Dunne and Allan Jones get differing reactions from Charles Winninger and Helen Westley.

SHOW BOAT

Music: Jerome Kern
Lyrics & screenplay: Oscar Hammerstein II
Produced by: Carl Laemmle Jr. for Universal
Directed by: James Whale
Choreography: LeRoy Prinz
Photography: John Mescall, John Fulton
Cast: Irene Dunne, Allan Jones, Charles Winninger, Paul Robeson, Helen Morgan, Helen Westley, Donald Cook, Sammy White, Queenie Smith, Hattie McDaniel, Harry Barris, LeRoy Prinz, Eddie "Rochester"Anderson, Francis X. Mahoney, Sunnie O'Dea, Clarence Muse, Barbara Pepper, E.E. Clive
Songs: "Cotton Blossom"; "Where's the Mate for Me?"; "Make Believe"; "Ol' Man River"; "Can't Help Lovin' Dat Man"; "I Have the Room Above Her"; "Gallivantin' Around"; "You Are Love"; "Ah Still Suits Me"; "Bill" (lyric with P. G. Wodehouse); "Goodbye, My Lady Love" (Joe Howard); "After the Ball" (Charles K. Harris)
Released: April 1936; 113 minutes

Opening under the Ziegfeld banner in 1927, *Show Boat* was soon recognized as both a stage classic and a highly influential work in the development of the American musical theatre. The first screen version was adapted directly from the Edna Ferber novel on which the Kern-Hammerstein musical had been based. It was produced by Carly Laemmle for Universal in 1929,with Laura La Plante and Joseph Schildkraut in the leads. Though filmed as a silent, the movie was then reshot with some audible dialogue and songs, plus an 18-minute prologue featuring selections from the play sung by original cast members Helen Morgan, Jules Bledsoe, and Tess Gardella.

The 1936 screen version, produced by Laemmle's son, Carl Jr., was closer in spirit and design to the stage musical, with Hammerstein himself responsible for the adaptation. Nine of the original 16 songs were retained (incredibly, the duet, "Why Do I Love You?" was left on the cutting room floor), with three new ones— "I Have the Room Above," "Gallivantin' Around," and "Ah Still Suits Me"—written specially for the film. Heading the cast were Irene Dunne, who had played Magnolia Hawks in the original touring company, and Allan Jones, who had played Gaylord Ravenal in summer stock (though Laemmle's first choice had been Nelson Eddy). Helen Morgan (as the mulatto Julie LaVerne), Charles Winniger (as Magnolia's father and showboat owner, Captain Andy Hawks), and Sammy White (as hoofer Frank Schultz) were all veterans of the 1927 New York production. Paul Robeson, for whom the song "Ol' Man River" had been written, was in the London company in 1928 and on Broadway in the 1932 revival.

The episodic story covers the period from the mid-1880s to the present, and is concerned with the fortunes of the impressionable Magnolia Hawks and the ne'er-do-well riverboat gambler Gaylord Ravenal, who fall in love even before the first chorus of their first duet, "Make Believe." They become leading actors on the Mississippi showboat *Cotton Palace* (it had been *Cotton Blossom* on Broadway), get married, then take off for the high life in Chicago where their daughter Kim is born. Gaylord, however, soon loses his money and deserts his family. After Magnolia gets the chance to sing at the Trocadero nightclub on New Year's Eve (because the featured attraction, her old friend Julie, has obligingly walked out after singing "Bill" at a rehearsal), she has a tearful reunion with her father who helps her overcome her nervousness while singing "After the Ball." Eventually, both she and Kim become musical-comedy stars in New York. In the stage version, Magnolia and Gaylord are separated for 20 years and are reunited aboard the *Cotton Blossom;* in the 1936 film the reunion takes place not on the Mississippi, where it rightfully belongs, but in a Broadway theatre, where Ravenal is the backstage doorman, during the opening night of Kim's latest success. For the 1951 screen version of *Show Boat*, see page 164. *MGM/UA VC.*

POOR LITTLE RICH GIRL

Music: Harry Revel
Lyrics: Mack Gordon
Screenplay: Sam Hellman, Gladys Lehman, Harry Tugend
Produced by: Darryl F. Zanuck & B. G. DeSylva for 20th Century-Fox
Directed by: Irving Cummings
Choreography: Jack Haskell, Ralph Cooper
Photography: John Seitz
Cast: Shirley Temple, Alice Faye, Gloria Stuart, Jack Haley, Michael Whalen, Jane Darwell, Claude Gillingwater, Henry Armetta, Tony Martin
Songs: "Oh, My Goodness"; "When I'm With You"; "But Definitely", "You Gotta Eat Your Spinach, Baby"; "Military Man"
Released: June 1936; 72 minutes

By the time of her 18th movie, *Poor Little Rich Girl,* eight-year-old Shirley Temple was in her second year as the country's leading box office star (a position she would continue to hold for the next two years). Celebrated for her Bright Eyes, her Curly Top, and her Dimples, Shirley held the affection of the Depression-weary nation because of her ability to conquer adversity through determination, unflagging optimism, and a cheery song and dance. In this representative offering (vaguely based on Eleanor Gates' children's story that had once been adapted as a silent vehicle for Mary Pickford), rich, motherless, lonely Shirley runs away and is befriended by a married vaudeville team (Alice Faye and Jack Haley). They lose no time in putting her in their act, which—with such numbers as "When I'm With You", "You Gotta Eat Your Spinach, Baby," and "Military Man"—easily becomes a popular radio attraction.
Casablanca ST. Playhouse VC.

Poor Little Rich Girl. Shirley Temple performing "Military Man" during a radio broadcast.

San Francisco. Jack Holt, Clark Gable, and Jeanette MacDonald.

SAN FRANCISCO

Screenplay: Anita Loos & Robert Hopkins
Produced by: John Emerson & Bernard Hyman for MGM
Directed by: W. S. Van Dyke
Choreography: Val Raset
Photography: Oliver T. Marsh
Cast: Clark Gable, Jeanette MacDonald, Spencer Tracy, Jack Holt, Ted Healy, Jessie Ralph, Margaret Irving, Shirley Ross, Al Shean, Richard Carle, Charles Judels, Bert Roach, Edgar Kennedy, Vince Barnett, Dennis O'Keefe
Songs & arias: "San Francisco" (Bronislau Kaper-Gus Kahn); "A Heart That's Free" (Alfred Robyn-T. Reilley); "Would You?" (Nacio Herb Brown-Arthur Freed); "Air des bijoux" (Gounod); "Sempre libera" (Verdi)
Released: June 1936; 115 minutes

To prove that she was a major screen personality in her own right without Nelson Eddy as costar, Jeanette MacDonald got MGM to cast her opposite Clark Gable in a disaster epic that Anita Loos and Robert Hopkins wrote as a tribute to the brawling, courageous spirit of their native city. With the leading male character based on their friend, gambler and raconteur Wilson Mizner, the writers dreamed up a melodramatic tale, set in 1906, about Barbary Coast cabaret owner Blackie Norton (Gable) and his love for prim prima donna Mary Blake (MacDonald). Mary spends most of her time alternately singing rousing numbers (such as the titular theme song) at Blackie's Paradise Café and grand opera at the Tivoli Opera House. At the film's end, she manages to survive the spectacularly reconstructed 20-minute San Francisco earthquake along with Blackie and their friend Father Tim Mullin (Spencer Tracy).

Fox's Darryl Zanuck was so impressed (the film was one of the top moneymaking releases of 1935-36) that he tried to borrow Gable and Jean Harlow from MGM for his own disaster epic, *In Old Chicago,* which would culminate in the fire of 1871. When Miss Harlow's death put an end to the negotiations, the producer filmed his saga the following year with Fox contractees Tyrone Power, Alice Faye, and Don Ameche.
MGM/UA VC.

Swing Time. Ginger Rogers and Fred Astaire dancing to the "Waltz in Swing Time."

SWING TIME

Music: Jerome Kern
Lyrics: Dorothy Fields
Screenplay: Howard Lindsay & Allan Scott
Produced by: Pandro S. Berman for RKO Radio
Directed by: George Stevens
Choreography: Hermes Pan (Fred Astaire uncredited)
Photography: David Abel
Cast: Fred Astaire, Ginger Rogers, Victor Moore, Helen Broderick, Eric
    Blore, Betty Furness, George Metaxa, Landers Stevens, Frank Jenks,
    Ferdinand Munier, John Harrington, Pierre Watkin, Gerald Hamer,
    Edgar Dearing
Songs: "Pick Yourself Up"; "The Way You Look Tonight"; "Waltz in Swing
    Time" (instrumental); "A Fine Romance"; "Bojangles of Harlem"; "Never
    Gonna Dance"
Released: August 1936; 103 minutes

Just as *Follow the Fleet* had previously lowered their social standing by making Fred Astaire a sailor and Ginger Rogers a dime-a-dance ballroom singer, so *Swing Time* (based on Erwin Gelsey's story, "Portrait of John Garnett") continued the process by making Fred a vaudeville hoofer and gambler and Ginger a dance instructress. It was the only Astaire-Rogers film directed by George Stevens (whose father, Landers Stevens, played Betty Furness's father in the movie), and it was their only one with a complete score by Jerome Kern and Dorothy Fields (though they had written two songs together for *Roberta)*. The movie also gave the screen's premier male dancer the chance to perform some uncharacteristic routines: he was an inept dance pupil (but only as a joke, of course) at the beginning of "Pick Yourself Up," he wore blackface for the only time in his career in the "Bojangles of Harlem" number, and his wooing technique on the dancefloor failed to win over Ginger during their emotional performance of "Never Gonna Dance." Astaire even sang the chief romantic expression, "The Way You Look Tonight," in Ginger's hotel room while the object of his admiration was in the bathroom shampooing her hair.

Swing Time traces the rise of dancers Lucky Garnett and Penny Carrol at two elegant New York night clubs while at the same time dealing with romantic roadblocks caused by a society band leader (Georges Metaxa) in love with Penny and a small-town socialite (Betty Furness) to whom Lucky is engaged. The movie had its share of mind-boggling plot devices found in almost every Astaire-Rogers film, such as the one, early in the story, in which Lucky is persuaded by the members of his vaudeville dance act that, according to the latest fashion, he couldn't possibly get married wearing cuffless striped trousers with a cutaway. And then there is the scene at the Club Raymond where Lucky and Penny dance the "Waltz in Swing Time" as an audition for the Silver Sandal without anyone from the latter night club bothering to show up.

Swing Time also welcomed back the supporting comic characters that had been in two earlier Fred and Ginger vehicles, *The Gay Divorcee* and *Top Hat*, but had been dropped from *Follow the Fleet:* Helen Broderick as Penny's best friend, Victor Moore as Lucky's best friend, and Eric Blore in the truncated role of an officious dance-studio manager. Initially called *I Won't Dance*, then *Never Gonna Dance*, the movie scrapped such negative appellations in favor of the more upbeat *Swing Time,* even though the story had nothing to do with big bands or jitterbugs.
Columbia (Astaire CD); Sountrak ST. Turner VC.

THE BIG BROADCAST OF 1937

Music: Ralph Rainger, etc.
Lyrics: Leo Robin, etc.
Screenplay: Walter DeLeon & Francis Martin
Produced by: Lewis Gensler for Paramount
Directed by: Mitchell Leisen
Choreography: LeRoy Prinz
Photography: Theodore Sparkuhl
Cast: Jack Benny, George Burns, Gracie Allen, Bob Burns, Martha Raye, Shirley Ross, Ray Milland, Frank Forrest, Eleanore Whitney, Virginia Weidler, Ernest Cossart, Benny Fields, Sam Hearn, Benny Goodman Orch. (incl. Gene Krupa), Larry Adler, Leopold Stokowski's Symphony Orchestra, Frank Jenks, Leonid Kinskey, Ellen Drew
Songs: "La Bomba", "You Came to My Rescue", "Here's Love in Your Eye"; "Bugle Call Rag" (Elmer Schoebel, Billy Meyers); "Talking Through My Heart"; "Fugue in G Minor" (Bach); "Vote for Mr. Rhythm"
Released: October 1936; 102 minutes

The third in Paramount's series of musicals about radio concerns Jack Benny, the troubled manager of the National Networks Broadcasting Co., who gets Burns and Allen (veterans of the two previous *Big Broadcast* movies) to sponsor a Big Broadcast featuring Benny Goodman's Orchestra swinging through "Bugle Call Rag," Shirley Ross singing "Talking Through My Heart," Leopold Stokowski leading his Philharmonic Symphonic Orchestra (sic) in Bach's "Fugue in g," and Martha Raye belting "Vote for Mr. Rhythm." The film's romantic interest is provided by Miss Ross (in her first major screen role) and Ray Milland.

Born to Dance. "Hey, Babe, Hey" performed at the Lonely Hearts Club by Frances Langford, Buddy Ebsen, Eleanor Powell, James Stewart, Una Merkel, and Sid Silvers.

BORN TO DANCE

Music & lyrics: Cole Porter
Screenplay: Jack McGowan & Sid Silvers
Produced by: Jack Cummings for MGM
Directed by: Roy Del Ruth
Choreography: Dave Gould
Photography: Ray June
Cast: Eleanor Powell, James Stewart, Virginia Bruce, Una Merkel, Sid Silvers, Frances Langford, Raymond Walburn, Alan Dinehart, Buddy Ebsen, Juanita Quigley, Georges & Jalna, Reginald Gardiner, Barnett Parker, The Foursome, Helen Troy, Dennis O'Keefe, Roger Edens
Songs: "Rolling Home"; "Rap Tap on Wood"; "Hey, Babe, Hey"; "Entrance of Lucy James"; "Love Me Love My Pekinese"; "Easy to Love"; "I've Got You Under My Skin"; "Swingin' the Jinx Away"
Released: November 1936; 105 minutes

Cole Porter went to Hollywood late in 1935 under contract to MGM to write his first screen score. After tossing ideas around for two months, writers Jack McGowan and Sid Silvers came up with a story, originally called *Great Guns!*, about three sailors (to be played by Allan Jones, Buddy Ebsen, and Silvers) on assignment in New York who become romantically involved with three hostesses (Eleanor Powell, Judy Garland, and Una Merkel) at the Lonely Hearts Club. For conflict, a bored socialite (Frances Langford) was added to try to win Jones away from Powell. As the work progressed, Jones was replaced by James Stewart (who thereby got to introduce "Easy to Love," performed in a Central Park setting), Miss Garland by Miss Langford, and Miss Langford by Virginia Bruce, whose role was changed to that of a tempestuous musical-comedy star. Along the way, three numbers were dropped: "Goodbye, Little Dream, Goodbye," "It's De-Lovely," and "Who but You?"

In the tradition of backstage movies, the inexperienced Miss Powell gets to replace Miss Bruce in a new Broadway show, even through one is a tall, leggy, dark-haired dancer and the other a slim, delicate featured blonde singer. Sonja Henie was to have made her screen debut in *Born to Dance* but her fee of $100,000 for two minutes of figure skating was considered a bit too much. Therefore, instead of Jimmy taking Virginia to an ice-skating rink, they go to the more formal Club Continental to see Georges and Jalna dance to "I've Got You Under My Skin" (later sung by Miss Bruce to Stewart on a mammoth penthouse terrace).

The movie's spectacular climax, "Swingin' the Jinx Away," was performed as the finale of a nautical revue during its opening night on Broadway. The scene is the forward portion of a battleship on which Captain Eleanor, wearing shako, black cape and spangled tights, taps and turns cartwheels in front of a crew of thousands of dancing sailors and a blaring military band.

Released the year between two *Broadway Melody* musicals, *Born to Dance* was really *Broadway Melody of 1937* under another name. All three movies have the same female tapping star, along with the same comic dancer (Ebsen), director (Roy Del Ruth), writers (McGowan and Silvers), choreographer (Dave Gould), orchestrator (Roger Edens), art director (Cedric Gibbons), costume designer (Adrian), and editor (Blanche Sewell). And all three were concerned with what it takes for an inexperienced dancer to win the leading role in her very first Broadway musical.
Classic Intl. ST.   MGM/UA VC.

GOLD DIGGERS OF 1937

Music: Harry Warren*; Harold Arlen**
Lyrics: Al Dubin*; E. Y. Harburg**
Screenplay: Warren Duff
Produced by: Hal B. Wallis for Warner Bros.
Directed by: Lloyd Bacon
Choreography: Busby Berkeley
Photography: Arthur Edeson
Cast: Dick Powell, Joan Blondell, Victor Moore, Glenda Farrell, Osgood
Perkins, Lee Dixon, Jane Wyman
Songs: "With Plenty of Money and You" *; "Speaking of the Weather" **;
"Let's Put Our Heads Together" **; "All's Fair in Love and War"*
Released: December 1936; 100 minutes

The fourth and penultimate *Gold Diggers* movie from Warners (the ultimate was *Gold Diggers in Paris*) offers something of a twist on the formula by casting Dick Powell as an insurance salesman who gets ailing Broadway producer Victor Moore to take out a $1 million life-insurance policy. The scheme, concocted by Moore's unscrupulous aides, is to make sure they'll have enough money to put on a show after Moore dies. But Moore recovers, somehow gets the money himself and puts on the *J. J. Hobart Revue* with a cast headed by Powell, Joan Blondell, and Lee Dixon. The Busby Berkeley finale, "All's Fair in Love and War," is a lighthearted battle-of-the-sexes spectacle in which Miss Blondell leads a company of 70 white-helmeted girls carrying flags, beating drums, and tooting bugles as they go through all sorts of military drills. Because of budget restrictions, Berkeley staged the number before a backdrop consisting only of shiny black surfacing.

ONE IN A MILLION

Music: Sidney Mitchell
Lyrics: Lew Pollack
Screenplay: Leonard Praskins, Mark Kelly
Produced by: Darryl F. Zanuck & Raymond Griffith for 20th Century-Fox
Directed by: Sidney Lanfield
Choreography: Jack Haskell, Nick Castle
Photography: Edward Cronjager
Cast: Sonja Henie, Don Ameche, Adolphe Menjou, Jean Hersholt, Ned
Sparks, Ritz Brothers, Arline Judge, Dixie Dunbar, Borrah
Minevitch, Leah Ray, Montagu Love
Songs: "One in a Million"; "We're Back in Circulation Again"; "Who's Afraid
of Love?"; "The Moonlight Waltz"
Released: December 1936; 95 minutes

Though her international fame had been won as a champion ice skater and her acting experience had been limited to a single silent film made in her native Norway, blonde, twinkly Sonja Henie was signed—without an audition—by Darryl Zanuck to a lucrative contract for a series of Fox musicals. In *One in a Million,* the first of nine she made for the studio, Miss Henie was cast as the daughter of a Swiss innkeeper (Jean Hersholt) who trains her for the Olympics. Not only does she win the competition (after doubts have been raised about her amateur standing), she also finds romance with brash American reporter Don Ameche, appears in a nightclub show with Adolphe Menjou's all-girl orchestra, and ends up heading a spectacular ice show at New York's Madison Square Garden. Much to everyone's surprise, Zanuck's gamble paid off: *One in a Million* turned out to be one of the biggest money-makers of 1937.

ON THE AVENUE

Music & lyrics: Irving Berlin
Screenplay: Gene Markey & William Conselman
Produced by: Darryl F. Zanuck & Gene Markey for 20th Century-Fox
Directed by: Roy Del Ruth
Choreography: Seymour Felix
Photography: Lucien Andriot
Cast: Dick Powell, Madeleine Carroll, Alice Faye, Ritz Brothers, George Barbier, Alan Mowbray, Cora Witherspoon, Walter Catlett, Joan Davis, Stepin Fetchit, Sig Rumann, Billy Gilbert, Lynn Bari, Marjorie Weaver, E. E. Clive
Songs: "He Ain't Got Rhythm"; "The Girl on the Police Gazette"; "You're Laughing at Me"; "This Year's Kisses"; "I've Got My Love to Keep Me Warm"; "Slumming on Park Avenue"
Released: February 1937; 89 minutes

As something of a variation on the usual backstage musicals dealing with the vicissitudes of getting a Broadway show ready for its inevitably successful opening night, *On the Avenue* is about a show—called *On the Avenue*—that is just beginning a lengthy run on Broadway. Here the problem has to do with the efforts of Mimi Caraway (Madeleine Carroll), the richest girl in the world, to stop Gary Blake (Dick Powell), the show's star and author, from lampooning her and her family so maliciously in one of the revue's sketches. Mimi and Gary, of course, fall in love and manage to surmount the attempts of Gary's jilted sweetheart and costar, Mona Merrick (Alice Faye), to drive a wedge between the couple. Except for "You're Laughing at Me," sung by Powell to Miss Carroll in Central Park, all the Irving Berlin songs are introduced in scenes in the revue—including Miss Faye's torchy "This Year's Kisses" and Powell's jaunty "I've Got My Love to Keep Me Warm."

On the Avenue was directly linked to the 1933 Broadway musical, *As Thousands Cheer*, which also had a Berlin score and in which the line, "On the avenue," was sung in the song "Easter Parade." That was a satirical revue, created in the form of a newspaper, with all the scenes commenting on newsworthy people and events. In effect, the movie's plot tells what might have happened had one of the targets objected to the way he or she was depicted in the show.
H'wood Soundstage ST.

On the Avenue. Alice Faye "Slumming on Park Avenue."

MAYTIME

Screenplay: Noel Langley
Produced by: Hunt Stromberg for MGM
Directed by: Robert Z. Leonard
Photography: Oliver T. Marsh
Cast: Jeanette MacDonald, Nelson Eddy, John Barrymore, Herman Bing, Tom Brown, Lynne Carver, Sig Rumann, Harry Davenport, Billy Gilbert, Leonid Kinskey, Walter Kingsford, Ivan Lebedeff, Don Cossack Choir, Rafaela Ottiano, Charles Judels, Paul Porcasi, Edgar Norton, Guy Bates Post, Ian Wolfe
Songs & arias: "Will You Remember?" (Sigmund Romberg-Rida Johnson Young); "Les Filles de Cadix" (Delibes); "Le Regiment de Sambre et Meuse" (Planquette); "Plantons la Vigne" (trad.); "Vive l'Opera" (trad.-Robert Wright, George Forrest); "Ham and Eggs" (Herbert Stothart-Wright-Forrest); "Carry Me Back to Old Virginny" (James Bland); "Nobles Seigneurs, Salut" (Meyerbeer); "Chi Me Frena" (Donizetti); "Une Dame Noble et Sage" (Meyerbeer); "Czaritza" excerpts (Tschaikowsky, arr. Wright & Forrest)
Released: March 1937; 132 minutes

The 1917 Broadway operetta, *Maytime,* had a score by Sigmund Romberg and Rida Johnson Young and a story, set in Washington Square, New York, about two lovers whose romance is doomed but whose grandchildren finally find happiness together. The 1929 London and Broadway operetta, *Bitter Sweet,* had a score by Noel Coward and a story, set in London and Vienna, about an aging English duchess who gives romantic advice to a young girl by telling her, in flashback, of her blissful but brief marriage to an Austrian café singer who was killed in a duel. This is enough to convince the girl that marrying for love is preferable to marrying for position.

For the movie operetta called *Maytime,* MGM retained the title and just one song from the 1917 production and changed the story into a variation on the 1929 production. Now it is about an aging woman (Jeanette MacDonald) in a small American town on May Day 1905 who gives romantic advice to a young girl, Barbara Roberts (Lynne Carver), by telling her, in flashback, of her days in Paris as opera singer Marcia Mornay, and her brief but blissful romance with opera singer Paul Allison (Nelson Eddy). Marcia, however, sacrifices love for a career, weds her Svengali-like manager Nicolai Nazaroff (John Barrymore), and wins international acclaim. When Paul comes back into her life during an engagement at New York's Metropolitan Opera, Nazaroff is so tortured by jealousy that he kills Paul. Returning to 1905, this revelation is enough to convince Barbara that marrying for love is preferable to an opera career. Then recalling the ending of Sigmund Romberg and Oscar Hammerstein's 1930 screen operetta, *Viennese Nights,* with Vivienne Segal and Alexander Gray—Marcia shares one last duet (to "Will You Remember?") with Paul's materialized spirit.

The third film co-starring MacDonald and Eddy, *Maytime* was originally to have been produced by MGM's production chief, Irving Thalberg, and directed by Edmund Goulding. When Thalberg died during the filming, Hunt Stromberg and Robert Z. Leonard, the new producer and director, scrapped the original screenplay—which had nothing to do with the Romberg-Johnson operetta either—and came up with the altered version of the Coward operetta. Three years later, MacDonald and Eddy did, in fact, star in their own version of *Bitter Sweet.* To avoid comparison with *Maytime,* this one omitted the modern-day opening and closing but otherwise stuck fairly close to the original plot outline.
MGM/UA VC.

Maytime. Nelson Eddy and Jeanette MacDonald singing "Santa Lucia" (accompanied by gypsy guitarist L. Comarchio) at the May Day Festival in St. Cloud.

WAKE UP AND LIVE

Music: Harry Revel
Lyrics: Mack Gordon
Screenplay: Harry Tugend & Jack Yellen
Produced by: Darryl F. Zanuck & Kenneth MacGowan for 20th Century-Fox
Directed by: Sidney Lanfield
Choreography: Jack Haskell
Photography: Edward Cronjager
Cast: Walter Winchell, Ben Bernie, Alice Faye, Patsy Kelly, Ned Sparks, Jack Haley, Grace Bradley, Walter Catlett, Joan Davis, Leah Ray, Condos Brothers, William Demarest, George Givot, Barnett Parker, Etienne Girardot, Eddie "Rochester" Anderson
Songs: "It's Swell of You"; "I'm Bubbling Over"; "Wake Up and Live"; "Never in a Million Years"; "I Love You Much Too Much, Muchacha"; "There's a Lull in My Life"
Released: April 1937; 91 minutes

Radio's ability to create instant romantic singing idols—such as Rudy Vallee, Bing Crosby, and Russ Columbo—was satirized in *Wake Up and Live* (as it had been in *Twenty Million Sweethearts* and *The Big Broadcast of 1937*). Here the story deals with singer Jack Haley, whose career is severely hampered by his mike fright. He is helped by Alice Faye—the radio station's "Wake Up and Live" girl—and one night, through an accident, his voice (actually Buddy Clark's) goes over the air during a broadcast by Ben Bernie's Orchestra. Haley creates such a sensation that Bernie takes credit for having discovered this "Phantom Troubadour," but he is exposed by columnist Walter Winchell (he and Bernie were then engaged in a well-publicized "feud," which also figured in *Love and Hisses* later the same year). The generally upbeat score contains one torch balad, "There's a Lull in My Life," which turned out to be Miss Faye's only best-selling record.
H'wood Soundstage ST.

Shall We Dance. Fred Astaire and Ginger Rogers' roller-skating dance to "Let's Call the Whole Thing Off."

SHALL WE DANCE

Music: George Gershwin
Lyrics: Ira Gershwin
Screenplay: Allan Scott & Ernest Pagano
Produced by: Pandro S. Berman for RKO Radio
Directed by: Mark Sandrich
Choreography: Hermes Pan, Harry Losee (Fred Astaire uncredited)
Photography: David Abel
Cast: Fred Astaire, Ginger Rogers, Edward Everett Horton, Eric Blore, Jerome Cowan, Ketti Gallian, Harriet Hoctor, Ann Shoemaker, Ben Alexander, William Brisbane, Marek Windheim, Rolfe Sedan, Emma Young
Songs: "(I've Got) Beginner's Luck"; "Slap That Bass"; "Walking the Dog" (instrumental); "They All Laughed"; "Let's Call the Whole Thing Off"; "They Can't Take That Away from Me"; "Shall We Dance"
Released: April 1937;116 minutes

While in Hollywood, Richard Rodgers and Lorenz Hart wrote a scenario for Fred Astaire in which they cast him as a dancer anxious to combine classical ballet with modern jazz. Astaire, however, rejected the idea since he felt his fans would not accept him in a role that gave him no opportunity to wear his trademark attire of top hat, white tie and tails. When the songwriters returned to New York they turned the story into a Broadway musical called *On Your Toes,* which became such a hit that it made Astaire change his mind. Producer Pandro Berman tried to secure the screen rights for an Astaire-Rogers vehicle, but lost out to Warner Bros., which incongruously teamed Eddie Albert and Vera Zorina. Nothing daunted, Berman went ahead with his own plans and came up with a story based on Lee Loeb and Harold Buchman's scenario called *Watch Your Step* that would also deal with the world of ballet.

In *Shall We Dance* (without the question mark), Astaire plays the part of Pete Peters, an American ballet dancer know as Petrov, who dreams of uniting classical movement with tap and ballroom dancing. While in Paris, Pete becomes smitten with American musical-comedy star Linda Keene (Miss Rogers) and pursues and woos her (to "Beginner's Luck") on a palatial ocean liner heading for New York. Somehow the rumor gets around that they are secretly married, which prompts all sorts of naive misunderstandings and ludicrous plot complications after they land. Pete even gets the bright idea that, to put an end to speculation, they really do get married in order to get a divorce. (When Pete asks the officiating New Jersey judge what the grounds for divorce are in his state, the judge rasps the single word, "Marriage.") At the film's end—during an engagement at a swank rooftop nightclub—Pete fulfills his ambition to combine modern dancing with ballet, and, to no one's surprise, is also happily reunited with Linda.

The only Astaire-Rogers movie with a score by George and Ira Gershwin, *Shall We Dance* was the last of the team's vehicles to surround them with the kind of unrealistic luxury with which they were identified. It also surrounded them with their two most faithful supporting comedians, Edward Everett Horton as a fussy ballet impresario and Eric Blore as an unctuous hotel manager. Among the movie's highlights is the totally irrelevant musical logomachy, "Let's Call the Whole Thing Off," sung by Astaire and Rogers in Central Park, then danced to on roller skates. The number required four days of shooting and took less than two-and-one-half minutes on the screen.

At various times during its preparation, *Shall We Dance* was known as *Stepping Toes, Stepping Stones, Stepping High,* and *Watch Your Step.*
Columbia (Astaire CD); Sountrak ST. Turner VC.

A DAY AT THE RACES

Music: Bronislau Kaper & Walter Jurmann
Lyrics: Gus Kahn
Screenplay: George Seaton, Robert Pirosh, George Oppenheimer
Produced by: Irving Thalberg, Sam Wood for MGM
Directed by: Sam Wood
Choreography: Dave Gould
Photography: Joseph Ruttenberg
Cast: The Marx Brothers, Allan Jones, Maureen O'Sullivan, Margaret
        Dumont, Sig Rumann, Esther Muir, Ivie Anderson, Carole Landis
Songs: "A Message from the Man in the Moon"; "On Blue Venetian
        Waters"; "Tomorrow Is Another Day"; "All God's Chillun Got
        Rhythm"
Released: June 1937; 109 minutes

The second of the five films made at MGM by the raucous, riotous Marx Brothers, *A Day at the Races* was something of a successor to *A Night at the Opera*. It was also more of a musical since it had four new songs compared to its predecessor's two. In one number, "All God's Chillun Got Rhythm," Harpo appears as a flute-playing Pied Piper who attracts a horde of shanty-town blacks thinking he's Gabriel. *A Day at the Races* finds the familiar characters—the leering, conniving Groucho, the simple-minded, mute Harpo, and the thick-headed foil Chico—engaged in helping Maureen O'Sullivan and Allan Jones raise enough money to save their sanitorium, which is accomplished when Harpo rides Jones' racehorse to victory.
MGM/UA VC.

HIGH, WIDE AND HANDSOME

Music: Jerome Kern
Lyrics & screenplay: Oscar Hammerstein II
Produced by: Arthur Hornblow Jr. for Paramount
Directed by: Rouben Mamoulian
Choreography: LeRoy Prinz
Photography: Victor Milner, Theodore Sparkuhl
Cast: Irene Dunne, Randolph Scott, Dorothy Lamour, Raymond Walburn,
        Akim Tamiroff, Charles Bickford, Ben Blue, Elizabeth Patterson,
        William Frawley, Alan Hale, Lucien Littlefield, Rolfe Sedan
Songs: "High, Wide and Handsome"; "Can I Forget You?"; "Will You
        Marry Me Tomorrow, Maria?"; "The Folks Who Live on the Hill";
        "The Things I Want"; "Allegheny Al"
Released: July 1937; 112 minutes

The only original screen musical Kern and Hammerstein ever wrote together, *High, Wide and Handsome* was an earthier, folksier companion piece to their *Show Boat*. For this lively chunk of Americana, the film focuses on the romance between singer Sally Waterson (Irene Dunne) and farmer Peter Cortlandt (Randolph Scott) set against the discovery of oil in western Pennsylvania in 1859. Problems arise when a railroad robber baron (Alan Hale) tries to take over the land, and there is a spectacular climax when the robber baron's men attempt to prevent Peter's men from laying a pipeline to the refinery, an undertaking in which the farmers are aided by an entire circus troupe, elephants and all. The *Show Boat* connection is particularly marked in the characters and in the casting. Sally Waterson is a variation on the previous film's Magnolia Hawks (also played by Miss Dunne), while such characters as the tragic Molly (Dorothy Lamour), Sally's blustery father (Raymond Walburn), and Peter's bossy grandmother (Elizabeth Patterson) are reminiscent of *Show Boat's* Julie La Verne, Captain Andy, and Parthy Hawks. In Britain, *High, Wide, and Handsome* was known as *Black Gold*.

High, Wide and Handsome. Dorothy Lamour pouring for Alan Hale, Lucien Littlefield, and James Burke.

High, Wide and Handsome. Irene Dunne singing "Can I Forget You?" in a carnival.

DOUBLE OR NOTHING

Music: Arthur Johnston, etc.
Lyrics: Johnny Burke, etc.
Screenplay: Charles Lederer, Erwin Gelsey, John Moffitt, Duke Atterberry
Produced by: Benjamin Glazer for Paramount
Directed by: Theodore Reed
Photography: Karl Struss
Cast: Bing Crosby, Martha Raye, Mary Carlisle, Andy Devine, William Frawley, Samuel S. Hinds, Frances Faye, Benny Baker, Harry Barris
Songs: "Smarty" (Burton Lane-Ralph Freed); "All You Want to Do Is Dance"; "It's the Natural Thing to Do"; "It's On It's Off" (Al Siegel-Sam Coslow); "The Moon Got in My Eyes"; "After You" (Siegel-Coslow)
Released: August 1937; 95 minutes

Believing most people to be both honest and intelligent, a recently deceased millionaire has left a will calling for the random citywide dispersion of wallets each containing $500. The honest souls who return the money then get the opportunity to win $5000, which they keep only if they double their investments within a month. The lucky ones are Bing Crosby, Martha Raye, Andy Devine, and William Frawley, but only Crosby is successful by opening—what else?—a nightclub. Almost every musical number in this unpretentious and offbeat musical is staged in a novel manner—operatic counterpoint for "Smarty," an automobile radio to provide music for sidewalk dancing for "All You Want to Do Is Dance," Crosby's hands making shadowy wall silhouettes to accompany "It's the Natural Thing to Do." Even the orchestra at Bing's nightspot dispenses with musical instruments in favor of imitating them vocally in "The Moon Got in My Eyes."
Decca (Crosby LP).

VARSITY SHOW

Music: Richard Whiting
Lyrics: Johnny Mercer
Screenplay: Jerry Wald, Richard Macaulay, Sig Herzig, Warren Duff
Produced by: Louis Edelman for Warner Bros.
Directed by: William Keighley
Choreography: Busby Berkeley
Photography: Sol Polito, George Barnes
Cast: Dick Powell, Fred Waring Orch., Ted Healy, Rosemary Lane, Priscilla Lane, Walter Catlett, Johnny Davis, Mabel Todd, Lee Dixon, Sterling Holloway, Buck & Bubbles, Edward Brophy, Roy Atwell
Songs: "We're Working Our Way Through College"; "On With the Dance"; "You've Got Something There"; "Moonlight on the Campus"; "Have You Got Any Castles, Baby?"; "Love Is on the Air Tonight"
Released: August 1937; 121 minutes

Varsity Show provided Rosemary Lane and Priscilla Lane with their first movie roles, presumably because the cast also featured Fred Waring and His Pennsylvanians, the band with which the sisters had previously sung. In the story, Broadway producer-director Dick Powell returns to his alma mater, Winfield College, to stage the Varsity Show. Opposition from the stuffy members of the faculty, however, sends him back to New York—only to have the students follow him and put on the show on Broadway. The Busby Berkeley finale, seen as part of the show, offers a salute to the country's major colleges and universities, complete with hundreds of marching boys and girls, flying footballs, and the chorus singing appropriate school songs while forming appropriate school initials. Though lasting two hours when first released, *Varsity Show* was subsequently cut by 40 minutes.

BROADWAY MELODY OF 1938

Music: Nacio Herb Brown, etc.
Lyrics: Arthur Freed, etc.
Screenplay: Jack McGowan & Sid Silvers
Produced by: Jack Cummings for MGM
Directed by: Roy Del Ruth
Choreography: Dave Gould
Photography: William Daniels
Cast: Robert Taylor, Eleanor Powell, George Murphy, Buddy Ebsen, Sophie Tucker, Judy Garland, Binnie Barnes, Charles Igor Gorin, Robert Benchley, Billy Gilbert, Willie Howard, Raymond Walburn, Charley Grapewin, Barnett Parker, Robert Wildhack, Helen Troy, Carole Landis
Songs: "Toreador Song" (Bizet); "Follow in My Footsteps"; "Yours and Mine"; "Everybody Sing"; "Some of These Days" (Shelton Brooks); "I'm Feelin' Like a Million"; "Largo al Factotum" (Rossini); "Dear Mr. Gable (You Made Me Love You)" (James Monaco-Joseph McCarthy; Roger Edens); "Your Broadway and My Broadway"
Released: August 1937; 110 minutes

Broadway Melody of 1938 is basically a revised version of *Broadway Melody of 1936*. Again Robert Taylor is the producer-songwriter of a new musical revue (here called *Broadway Melody*), again it's newcomer Eleanor Powell whom he wants for the leading role, and again he is having difficulty raising the necessary money. This time, Miss Powell comes to his rescue when her opera-loving horse, Stargazer, wins a race after hearing Charles Igor Gorin sing "Largo al Factotum." Songwriters Brown and Freed came up with a new "Broadway" song—"Your Broadway and My Broadway"—for the splashy finale, but the movie is best remembered for the out-of-left-field scene in which 15-year-old Judy Garland (incongruously cast as Sophie Tucker's daughter) sings the pop standard "You Made Me Love You," while penning a fan letter to her idol, Clark Gable.
MGM/UA VC.

THE FIREFLY

Music: Rudolf Friml
Lyrics: Robert Wright & George Forrest, etc.
Screenplay: Frances Goodrich & Albert Hackett
Produced by: Hunt Stromberg for MGM
Directed by: Robert Z. Leonard
Choreography: Albertina Rasch
Photography: Oliver T. Marsh
Cast: Jeanette MacDonald, Allan Jones, Warren William, Douglass Dumbrille, Billy Gilbert, Henry Daniell, George Zucco, Alan Curtis, Dennis O'Keefe, Ian Wolfe, Rolfe Sedan
Songs: "Love Is Like a Firefly"; "The Donkey Serenade" (music with Herbert Stothart); "Giannina Mia" (lyric: Otto Harbach), "He Who Loves and Runs Away" (lyric: Gus Kahn); "Sympathy" (lyric: Harbach, Kahn); "When a Maid Comes Knocking at Your Heart" (lyric with Harbach)
Released: September 1937; 138 minutes

Since the first three MacDonald-Eddy musicals had proved so successful at the boxoffice, the MGM hierarchs got the idea that splitting up the team—at least temporarily—might yield two hits instead of one. And so Jeanette went into *The Firefly* (her first solo starring movie) opposite Allan Jones and Nelson went into *Rosalie* opposite Eleanor Powell.

Apart from the change in leading men, in all other respects *The Firefly* was a typical MacDonald-Eddy operation. It was produced by Hunt Stromberg (responsible for five of the team's releases) and directed by Robert Z. Leonard (he had helmed *Maytime*). And while it retained five of the 16 Rudolf Friml songs from the 1912 Broadway musical of the same name, script writers Frances Goodrich and Albert Hackett (they also adapted *Naughty Marietta* and *Rose Marie)* completely ignored the original plot. Set in Spain during Napoleon's invasion, *The Firefly* offers Miss MacDonald as a Spanish secret agent who saves the life of King Ferdinand VII and sings duets with a French officer. "The Donkey Serenade," warbled by Allan Jones to Miss MacDonald as she rides in a mule-drawn coach over the Pyrenees, was based on a 1920 piano piece "Chanson."

ONE HUNDRED MEN AND A GIRL

Screenplay: Bruce Manning, Charles Kenyon, James Mulhauser
Produced by: Charles Rogers & Joe Pasternak for Universal
Directed by: Henry Koster
Photography: Joseph Valentine
Cast: Deanna Durbin, Leopold Stokowski, Adolphe Menjou, Alice Brady, Eugene Pallette, Mischa Auer, Billy Gilbert, J. Scott Smart, Jed Prouty, Leonid Kinskey, Frank Jenks
Music: "Symphony No. 5, 4th Movement" (Tschaikowsky); "It's Raining Sunbeams" (Frederick Hollander-Sam Coslow); "A Heart That's Free" (Alfred Robyn-T. Reilly); *"Lohengrin* Prelude" (Wagner); "Alleluja" (Mozart); "2nd Hungarian Rhapsody" (Liszt); "Libiamo ne' lieti calici" (Verdi)
Released: September 1937; 84 minutes

At the age of 14, Deanna Durbin made her feature film debut in the 1936 release, *Three Smart Girls,* in which the actress displayed her ingenuous charm and classically trained voice. Her second and even more successful film, *One Hundred Men and a Girl,* expanded the musical content by including concert works conducted by Leopold Stokowski. In the movie, Miss Durbin appears as the daughter of an unemployed trombonist (Adolphe Menjou), and the Cinderella tale is concerned with her efforts to find a patron for a symphony orchestra which will provide employment for her father and his fellow jobless musicians. At the concert that crowns her efforts, Miss Durbin is unexpectedly called on to sing. When Stokowski asks her what selection she has chosen, the young lady furnishes the only information that is apparently needed: *"Traviata."* During her 13-year stay in Hollywood, Deanna Durbin appeared in 21 films, the first ten of which were produced by Joe Pasternak.

A Damsel in Distress. Jan Dugan and Mary Dean are not amused at Fred Astaire's antics during their choral group's singing of "Nice Work If You Can Get It."

A DAMSEL IN DISTRESS

Music: George Gershwin
Lyrics: Ira Gershwin
Screenplay: P. G. Wodehouse, Ernest Pagano, S. K. Lauren
Produced by: Pandro S. Berman for RKO Radio
Directed by: George Stevens
Choreography: Hermes Pan (Fred Astaire uncredited)
Photography: Joseph August
Cast: Fred Astaire, George Burns, Gracie Allen, Joan Fontaine, Reginald Gardiner, Ray Noble, Constance Collier, Montagu Love
Songs: "I Can't Be Bothered Now"; "The Jolly Tar and the Milkmaid"; "Stiff Upper Lip"; "Things Are Looking Up"; "A Foggy Day"; "Nice Work If You Can Get It"
Released: November 1937; 100 minutes

Fred Astaire's only Gingerless movie during his stay at RKO uses a plot based on a 1919 P. G. Wodehouse novel which Wodehouse and Ian Hay had converted into a London play nine years later. With the author collaborating on the screenplay, *A Damsel in Distress* deals with an American dancer in London (shades of *The Gay Divorcee* and *Top Hat)* who goes to the romantic rescue of a titled English lady living in a castle (shades of *Love Me Tonight).* Supporting comic characters are played by Burns and Allen (as Astaire's press agent and secretary), Reginald Gardiner (as a scheming butler), and Ray Noble (as a silly-ass nobleman). For Astaire's leading lady, producer Pandro Berman first considered Ruby Keeler, then tried getting British dancing star Jessie Matthews, but settled for Joan Fontaine who, though she couldn't sing or dance, was at least convincingly aristocratic. The George and Ira Gershwin score contains such superior numbers as "Nice Work If You Can Get It," "A Foggy Day" (sung not in London town but on the grounds of the castle), and "Stiff Upper Lip." The last finds Astaire with Burns and Allen merrily prancing all over an elaborate amusement park fun house complete with treadmills, a spinning disk, a revolving barrel, and distorted mirrors.
Columbia (Astaire CD); Curtain Calls ST. Turner VC.

SNOW WHITE AND THE SEVEN DWARFS

Music: Frank Churchill
Lyrics: Larry Morey
Screenplay: Ted Sears, Otto Englander, Earl Hurd, Dorothy Ann Blank,
    Richard Creedon,Dick Richard, Merrill de Maris, Webb Smith
Produced by: Walt Disney (released by RKO Radio)
Directed by: David Hand, Perce Pearce, Larry Morey, William Cottrell,
    Wilfred Jackson, Ben Sharpsteen (Technicolor)
Voices: Andriana Caselotti, Harry Stockwell, Lucille LaVerne, Roy Atwell,
    Pinto Colvig, Otis Harlan, Billy Gilbert, Scott Mattraw, Moroni Olsen
Songs: "I'm Wishing"; "One Song"; "With a Smile and a Song"; "Whistle
    While You Work"; "Heigh-Ho"; "Isn't This a Silly Song?"; "Some Day
    My Prince Will Come"
Released: December 1937; 83 minutes

It took a staff of over 750 artists working almost three years to create *Snow White and the Seven Dwarfs,* the screen's first feature-length cartoon. Walt Disney's trailblazing achievement also marked the first time human figures were animated (Marge Champion was the model for Snow White), but even more memorable was the humanizing and individualizing of the dwarfs (Doc, Grumpy, Happy, Sleepy, Sneezy, Bashful, and Dopey) and the vivid scenic designs, especially of the forest sequences, enhanced by Disney's initial use of three-color Technicolor and the special "multiplane" camera which gave the scenes a three-dimensional look.

Little Snow White, the fairy tale by Jacob and Wilhelm Grimm, underwent a number of changes on its way to the screen. In the movie, Snow White is considerably older than in the original story when the jealous Queen first tries to have her poisoned (in the book she had also tried strangling and paralyzing). In addition, Snow White is now brought back to life when the Prince kisses her (instead of when a poisoned apple is removed from her throat), and the Queen, disguised as a witch, now falls to her death in a ravine during a rainstorm (instead of dancing to her death in a pair of red-hot iron slippers at the wedding reception of Snow White and the Prince).

With a ticket sale of $6.7 million on its first release, *Snow White and the Seven Dwarfs* overtook the previous record of $4 million set by Al Jolson's *The Singing Fool* ten years earlier. In 1944, the RCA Victor recording of the *Snow White* score became the first soundtrack album of a motion picture. The film has been so successfully revived through the years that, as of 1989, it had grossed almost $62 million in U.S. and Canadian rentals and over $330 million worldwide. On July 17, 1987, in honor of the movie's 50th anniversary the film was rereleased throughout the world. With 4,000 prints projected simultaneously in the United States and in 57 different countries, it was the biggest opening day in screen history.

Walt Disney began his career as a Hollywood film animator in 1923, but it was not until four years later that he created his most famous character, Mickey Mouse (known as Steamboat Willie in his first short subject with sound). Other popular animal cartoon characters conceived by Disney were Mickey's mate Minnie Mouse, Donald Duck, Goofy, Pluto the Pup, and the Three Little Pigs. Disney's only serious rivals at the time were Paramount's Dave and Max Fleischer, the inventors of Betty Boop, who, in 1939, released their own full-length cartoon feature based on Jonathan Swift's *Gulliver's Travels.*

The overwhelming success of *Snow White and the Seven Dwarfs* prompted Disney to make two other animated cartoons based on popular fairy tales, *Cinderella* (1950) and *The Sleeping Beauty* (1959), both of which have been periodically rereleased. A fourth fairy-tale cartoon feature, *The Little Mermaid,* was made by the Disney studio in 1989. The following year, an animated sequel to *Snow White* called *Happily Ever After,* was released by Filmation.

RCA ST; Disneyland ST.

ROSALIE

Music & lyrics: Cole Porter
Screenplay: William Anthony McGuire
Produced by: William Anthony McGuire for MGM
Directed by: W. S. Van Dyke
Choreography: Albertina Rasch
Photography: Oliver T. Marsh
Cast: Nelson Eddy, Eleanor Powell, Ray Bolger, Frank Morgan, Ilona Massey, Edna May Oliver, Billy Gilbert, Reginald Owen, George Zucco, Virginia Grey, William Demarest, Jerry Colonna, Al Shean, Janet Beecher, Pierre Watkin
Songs: "Who Knows?"; "I've a Strange New Rhythm in My Heart"; "Rosalie"; "In the Still of the Night"; "Spring Love Is in the Air"
Released: December 1937; 122 minutes

In 1928, librettist William Anthony McGuire took two recent events, Lindbergh's solo flight to Paris and the visit to the United States of Rumania's Queen Marie and her daughter, as his "inspiration" for a Broadway musical called *Rosalie*. Under Ziegfeld's sponsorship, it was turned into a sumptuously mounted vehicle for Marilyn Miller and became one of the successes of the season. For the screen version, MGM reversed its usual procedure: it retained the original story (McGuire was hired to write the screenplay and to produce the film) but scrapped the original score (divided between George Gershwin and Sigmund Romberg) in favor of a new one by Cole Porter. The result was a stupefying art-deco fantasy with a cast of literally thousands which managed to become one of the year's top moneymakers thanks to the odd pairing of its popular stars, Nelson Eddy and Eleanor Powell. It even produced two song hits, "Rosalie" (which the composer never liked) and the throbbing ballad, "In the Still of the Night." Frank Morgan, as the King of Romanza, was the only member of the cast who had been in the stage production.
MGM/UA VC.

Rosalie. Eleanor Powell, surrounded by a chorus of thousands, dancing to the title song.

HOLLYWOOD HOTEL

Music: Richard Whiting
Lyrics: Johnny Mercer
Screenplay: Jerry Wald, Maurice Leo, Richard Macaulay
Produced by: Hal B. Wallis for Warner Bros.
Director-choreographer: Busby Berkeley
Photography: Charles Rosher, George Barnes
Cast: Dick Powell, Rosemary Lane, Hugh Herbert, Ted Healy, Benny
Goodman Orch., Louella Parsons, Glenda Farrell, Lola Lane,
Johnny Davis, Alan Mowbray, Frances Langford, Jerry Cooper,
Raymond Paige Orch., Mabel Todd, Allyn Joslyn, Edgar Kennedy,
Ronald Reagan
Songs: "Hooray for Hollywood"; "I'm Like a Fish Out of Water";
"Silhoueted in the Moonlight"; "Let That Be a Lesson to You";
"I've Hitched My Wagon to a Star"; "Sing, You Son of a Gun"
Released: December 1937; 109 minutes

Though it was entirely different in subject matter and setting, Warners' *Hollywood Hotel*
(which took its title from a popular radio program) contained elements linking it with the
same studio's previous release, *Varsity Show*. Again the cast featured Dick Powell,
Rosemary Lane, Ted Healy, Johnny "Scat" Davis, and Mabel Todd, plus a popular dance
band (in this case Benny Goodman's) and it also had the same songwriting team, script
writers, and choreographer. In this lighthearted spoof of Hollywood deception, the writers
capitalized on the resemblance between sisters Rosemary and Lola Lane, and came up
with a tale about the former, an aspiring actress, who manages to pass for the latter, a
temperamental star. It is even something of a forerunner of *Singin' in the Rain* by having
Powell's voice dubbed in a movie for that of ham actor Alan Mowbray. Despite the jubilant,
tongue-in-cheek opening number, "Hooray for Hollywood," the movie is less concerned
with film making than with the entertainment provided at the mythical Hollywood Hotel. The
film marked the fourth screen appearance of Ronald Reagan, seen here as a radio
announcer interviewing celebrities attending a movie premiere.
H'wood Soundstage ST.

Hollywood Hotel. The finale with Jerry Cooper, Frances Langford, Johnny Davis, Lola
Lane, Dick Powell, Rosemary Lane, Raymond Paige, Louella Parsons, Ken Niles, Mabel
Todd, and Ted Healy.

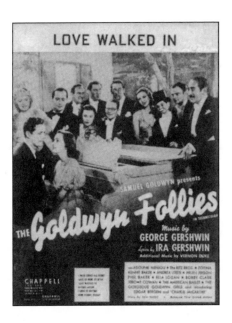

THE GOLDWYN FOLLIES

Music: George Gershwin
Lyrics: Ira Gershwin
Screenplay: Ben Hecht
Produced by: Samuel Goldwyn (released by United Artists)
Directed by: George Marshall
Choreography: George Balanchine
Photography: Gregg Toland (Technicolor)
Cast: Adolphe Menjou, Ritz Brothers, Edgar Bergen, Vera Zorina,
Kenny Baker, Andrea Leeds, Helen Jepson, Phil Baker, Ella Logan,
Bobby Clark, Jerome Cowan, Charles Kullman, Alan Ladd
Songs: "Love Walked In"; "Love Is Here to Stay"; "I Love to Rhyme";
"I Was Doing All Right"; "Spring Again" (music: Vernon Duke)
Released: January 1938; 120 minutes

After the death of Broadway impresario Florenz Ziegfeld in 1932, Hollywood impresario Samuel Goldwyn announced that he would carry on the *Ziegfeld Follies* tradition by producing his own annual *Goldwyn Follies.* Over the years at least nine successive writers were hired to work on what was to be the first in the series until, in 1937, Ben Hecht came up with something the producer liked. But despite such creative talents as the songwriting Gershwin brothers and choreographer George Balanchine, no one seemed to know what to do with a heterogeneous cast that included opera diva Helen Jepson, ballerina Vera Zorina, ventriloquist Edgar Bergen, and the Ritz Brothers (though partly because of its early use of three-color Technicolor, the picture showed up among the year's biggest boxoffice hits). One of the innovations planned but never filmed was the screen's first full-length ballet, which was to have been choreographed to Gershwin's "An American in Paris." Because the composer died midway through the shooting (his last song was "Love Is Here to Stay"), Vernon Duke was assigned to write whatever additional music was needed. *Nelson VC.*

THE BIG BROADCAST OF 1938

Music: Ralph Rainger
Lyrics: Leo Robin
Screenplay: Walter DeLeon, Francis Martin, Ken Englund
Produced by: Harlan Thompson for Paramount
Directed by: Mitchell Leisen
Choreography: LeRoy Prinz
Photography: Harry Fishbeck, Gordon Jennings
Cast: W. C. Fields, Bob Hope, Dorothy Lamour, Shirley Ross, Martha Raye, Lynne Overman, Leif Erickson, Ben Blue, Grace Bradley, Patricia Wilder, Shep Fields Orch., Tito Guizar, Kirsten Flagstad
Songs: "You Took the Words Right Out of My Heart"; "Brunnhilde's Battle Cry" (Wagner); "Thanks for the Memory"; "Mama, That Moon Is Here Again"; "The Waltz Lives On"
Released: February 1938; 90 minutes

The fourth and final movie in Paramount's series celebrating radio entertainment benefited from the appearance of W.C. Fields (in the dual role of shipping magnate T. Frothingwell Bellows and his twin brother S. B. Bellows), who performed his classic routines on the golf course and at the billiard table. It also marked the feature film debut of a glib comedian named Bob Hope (who won the role after it had been turned down by Jack Benny). The movie, somewhat more elaborate than its predecessors, has a plot concerning a transatlantic race between two mammoth ocean liners, the *Gigantic* (where most of the action takes place) and the *Colossal.* To justify the movie's title—and the inclusion in the cast of such diverse talents as Shep Fields and His Rippling Rhythm, Mexican crooner Tito Guizar, and Wagnerian soprano Kirsten Flagstad—the *Gigantic* provides daily broadcasts presided over by Bob Hope. But the most memorable musical scene occurs at the ship's bar where Hope and Shirley Ross, as a still-in-love divorced couple, ruefully reminisce—in "Thanks for the Memory"—about the varied experiences they once shared.

The Big Broadcast of 1938. Bob Hope and Shirley Ross at the railing of the *Gigantic.*

Joy of Living. Irene Dunne singing "What's Good About Goodbye?"

JOY OF LIVING

Music: Jerome Kern
Lyrics: Dorothy Fields
Screenplay: Gene Towne, Graham Baker, Allan Scott
Produced by: Felix Young for RKO Radio
Directed by: Tay Garnett
Photography: Joseph Walker
Cast: Irene Dunne, Douglas Fairbanks Jr., Alice Brady, Lucille Ball, Guy Kibbee, Mischa Auer, Jean Dixon, Eric Blore, Billy Gilbert, Franklin Pangborn, Fuzzy Knight, Spencer Charters
Songs: "You Couldn't Be Cuter"; "Just Let Me Look at You"; "What's Good About Goodnight?"; "Heavenly Party"
Released: March 1938; 90 minutes

Based on a story by Herbert and Dorothy Fields originally titled *The Joy of Loving,* the screwball comedy is about a musical-comedy star (Irene Dunne), her sponging family (including Alice Brady, Lucille Ball, and Guy Kibbee), and the roguish, wealthy globetrotter (Douglas Fairbanks Jr.) who teaches her how to enjoy life—by visiting a beer hall, a record-your-voice studio, and a skating rink—and then spirits her off to a South Pacific island. *Joy of Living* was the last of five films in which Miss Dunne sang the songs of Jerome Kern (the other four: *Sweet Adeline, Roberta, Show Boat,* and *High, Wide and Handsome).* Among the selections were the chipper "You Couldn't Be Cuter" (sung to put two nieces to sleep) and the languid "Just Let Me Look at You" (supposedly a song going into a Broadway show *after* its opening).
Turner VC.

Alexander's Ragtime Band. Jack Haley, Alice Faye, Don Ameche, Tyrone Power, and Wally Vernon.

ALEXANDER'S RAGTIME BAND

Music & lyrics: Irving Berlin
Screenplay: Kathryn Scola & Lamar Trotti
Produced by: Darryl F. Zanuck & Harry Joe Brown for 20th Century-Fox
Directed by: Henry King
Choreography: Seymour Felix
Photography: J. Peverell Marley
Cast: Tyrone Power, Alice Faye, Don Ameche, Ethel Merman, Jack Haley, Helen Westley, Jean Hersholt, John Carradine, Wally Vernon, Ruth Terry, Dixie Dunbar, Grady Sutton, Chick Chandler, Tyler Brooke, Lon Chaney Jr., Robert Gleckler, Paul Hurst, Douglas Fowley, Cully Richards, Eddie Collins
Songs: "Alexander's Ragtime Band"; "Ragtime Violin"; "That International Rag"; "Everybody's Doin' It"; "Now It Can Be Told"; "This Is The Life"; "When the Midnight Choo-Choo Leaves for Alabam' "; "For Your Country and My Country"; "I Can Always Find a Little Sunshine in the YMCA"; "Oh, How I Hate to Get Up in the Morning"; "We're on Our Way to France"; "Say It With Music"; "A Pretty Girl Is Like a Melody"; "Blue Skies"; "Pack Up Your Sins and Go to the Devil"; "What'll I Do?"; "My Walking Stick"; "Remember"; "Everybody Step"; "All Alone"; "Easter Parade"; "Heat Wave"
Released: May 1938; 105 minutes

Alexander's Ragtime Band was the first of a spate of movie musicals that sought to evoke nostalgia for the past through the songs of the past. In this case, all the songs were the creation of one man, Irving Berlin, with the story line merely a peg on which to hang 20 of his most familiar standards (plus two, "Now It Can Be Told" and "My Walking Stick," that were written specially for the film). Possibly because the leading character in the picture, like Berlin, was in charge of staging a revue during the first World War, there has been a mistaken belief that the movie is a biography of the songwriter. It is, in fact, a purely fictitious account covering the fortunes of a bandleader known as Alexander (Tyrone Power), his best friend Charlie Dwyer (Don Ameche), a pianist-composer, and singer Stella Kirby (Alice Faye), from their first meeting in a San Francisco honky tonk in 1911 (the year "Alexander's Ragtime Band" was written), through a variety of professional and personal ups and downs culminating in a glittering Carnegie Hall Concert in 1937 (doubtlessly prompted by Benny Goodman's concert the same year). Incredibly, not one of the characters ages a day during the 27-year period. The great appeal of the movie is in its ability of the familiar, changing rhythms of the songs—mostly sung by Miss Faye and Ethel Merman—to recreate the sense of time and atmosphere of the varying periods that are being covered in the episodic story.

The film, which cost over $2 million, required 85 sets, and was in preparation for over a year, had the same stars and director as another big-budget effort, *In Old Chicago,* which Fox had released earlier in 1938. It also inaugurated a period— roughly to the end of World War II—when the studio, under Darryl Zanuck, churned out a seemingly endless stream of costume musicals, biographical musicals, and picture-postcard musicals almost invariably featuring at least one of Fox's stellar lineup of Alice Faye, Betty Grable, Sonja Henie, and Carmen Miranda.

The first of the Irving Berlin anthological surveys, *Alexander's Ragtime Band* led the way to Paramount's *Blue Skies* (1946), MGM's *Easter Parade* (1948), Paramount's *White Christmas* (1954), and 20th Century-Fox's *There's No Business Like Show Business* (1954).

H'wood Soundstage ST.

SING YOU SINNERS

Music: James Monaco
Lyrics: Johnny Burke
Screenplay: Claude Binyon
Producer-director: Wesley Ruggles for Paramount
Photography: Karl Struss
Cast: Bing Crosby, Fred MacMurray, Donald O'Connor, Elizabeth
Patterson, Ellen Drew, Harry Barris
Songs: "I've Got a Pocketful of Dreams"; "Don't Let the Moon Get Away";
"Laugh and Call It Love"; "Small Fry" (Hoagy Carmichael-Frank
Loesser)
Released: August 1938; 88 minutes

Sing You Sinners concerns three brothers, hardworking Fred MacMurray, penniless dreamer Bing Crosby, and youngest sibling Donald O'Connor. After Bing makes a pass at Ellen Drew, Fred's fiancee, he leaves home to play the horses and does so well that he is able to open a "swap shop" in Los Angeles. He even buys a horse, Uncle Gus, which Donald rides to victory despite the efforts of some unscrupulous types. Curiously, the title song (the only justification for the film's title) isn't sung in the movie, which still offers the pleasures of Bing, Fred, and Donald swinging though "I've Got a Pocketful of Dreams," and the trio's routine about "Small Fry," with Bing in top hat and whiskers, Fred in drag puffing on a corncob pipe, and Donald, as Small Fry, in patched overalls.
Decca (Crosby LP).

CAREFREE

Music & lyrics: Irving Berlin
Screenplay: Ernest Pagano & Allan Scott
Produced by: Pandro S. Berman for RKO Radio
Directed by: Mark Sandrich
Choreography: Hermes Pan (Fred Astaire uncredited)
Photography: Robert de Grasse
Cast: Fred Astaire, Ginger Rogers, Ralph Bellamy, Luella Gear, Jack
Carson, Clarence Kolb, Franklin Pangborn, Hattie McDaniel, Walter
Kingsford, Kay Sutton
Songs: "I Used to Be Color Blind"; "The Yam"; "Change Partners"
Released: August 1938; 83 minutes

Fred Astaire and Ginger Rogers' reunion movie found them surrounded by the trappings of believable affluence rather than by the implausible luxury of most of their previous vehicles. The first film in which Astaire did not play a dancer or a musician, *Carefree* cast him as a psychiatrist ("I wanted to be a dancer but psychiatry showed me I was wrong") whose dream-inducing treatment reveals that Miss Rogers is in love with him rather than with fiancé Ralph Bellamy. Surprisingly, considering that Irving Berlin wrote the songs, only three numbers are sung, with two others ("Since They Turned Loch Lomond Into Swing" and "The Night Is Filled with Music") played as orchestral accompaniment. The languorous "I Used to Be Color Blind" (written for a dream sequence originally planned in Technicolor) and the lively ballroom dance step "The Yam" (demonstrated at the exclusive Medwick Country Club) were the major Fred-and-Ginger dance routines. Astaire's golf dance, however, was his most original and difficult, combining harmonica playing, tap dancing, and golf-club swinging. To prepare for it, the dancer had to hit almost 1,000 balls during a ten-day rehearsal period that took two-and-one-half days to film. Total time on the screen: less than three minutes.
Classic Intl. ST.; Columbia (Astaire CD); Turner VC.

THE GREAT WALTZ

Music: Johann Strauss Jr.
Lyrics: Oscar Hammerstein II
Screenplay: Samuel Hoffenstein & Walter Reisch
Produced by: Bernard Hyman for MGM
Directed by: Julien Duvivier (Victor Fleming, Josef Von Sternberg uncredited)
Choreography: Albertina Rasch
Photography: Joseph Ruttenberg
Cast: Luise Rainer, Fernand Gravet, Miliza Korjus, Hugh Herbert, Lionel Atwill, Curt Bois, Leonid Kinskey, Al Shean, Minna Gombell, George Houston, Bert Roach, Herman Bing, Henry Hull, Sig Rumann, Christian Rub
Songs: "An Artist's Life"; "I'm in Love With Vienna"; "There'll Come a Time"; "Tales from the Vienna Woods"; "One Day When We Were Young"; "Only You"; "The Blue Danube"
Released: November 1938; 102 minutes

Although it bore the same title as a 1934 Broadway production, *The Great Waltz* had nothing to do with that biographical musical except to retain the best-known Johann Strauss waltzes. It had nothing to do with the life of Johann Strauss either, even though that is the name of the principal character. The film, which begins in Vienna in 1845, loses no time in showing the Waltz King (Fernand Gravet) winning fame at Dommeyer's Restaurant, then spends most of the footage on the composer's infatuation with a coloratura soprano (Miliza Korjus) that almost wrecks his marriage. Famed French director Julien Duvivier, who spoke little English, returned to Paris during the shooting, which was completed by Victor Fleming and Josef Von Sternberg. The Great Waltz marked Miss Korjus's only screen appearance and it gave Luise Rainer (as Frau Strauss) the chance to repeat her laughing-through-tears specialty first displayed in *The Great Ziegfeld*. The movie's most celebrated occasion is the early morning scene in which Strauss rides with the diva in a carriage through the Vienna Woods. As he hears birds chirping, horses' hoofs beating, a shepherd fluting, and a coachman blowing his horn, he is so exultantly inspired that he composes "Tales from the Vienna Woods" on the spot. Johann Strauss has been portrayed in at least eight other movies, including one, in 1972, also called *The Great Waltz*. Horst Buchholst played the composer.
Sountrak ST.

The Great Waltz. Minna Gombell, Fernand Gravet, Hugh Herbert, and Luise Rainer.

SWEETHEARTS

Music: Victor Herbert
Lyrics: Robert Wright & George Forrest
Screenplay: Dorothy Parker & Alan Campbell (Noel Langley uncredited)
Produced by: Hunt Stromberg for MGM
Directed by: W. S. Van Dyke
Choreography: Albertina Rasch
Photography: Oliver T. Marsh, Allen Davey (Technicolor)
Cast: Jeanette MacDonald, Nelson Eddy, Frank Morgan, Ray Bolger, Florence
Rice, Mischa Auer, Terry Kilburn, Betty Jaynes, Douglas McPhail,
Reginald Gardiner, Herman Bing, Allyn Joslyn, Raymond Walburn,
George Barbier, Kathleen Lockhart, Gene Lockhart, Lucile Watson
Songs: "Wooden Shoes"; "Every Lover Must Meet His Fate"; "Sweethearts";
"Pretty as a Picture"; "Summer Serenade"; "On Parade"
Released: December 1938; 114 minutes

After a temporary split-up, Jeanette MacDonald and Nelson Eddy resumed their partnership in *The Girl of the Golden West* and *Sweethearts,* both released in 1938. The most
lighthearted of their movies, *Sweethearts,* marked the first time that the team gave up period
costumes or uniforms, and it was also MGM's first use of three-color Technicolor. In most
other respects, however, the film abides by the usual formula of offering selections from a
celebrated operetta score (this one by Victor Herbert) while ignoring the original lyrics and
story (about a prince and princess in disguise that dated back to 1913). In the film,
MacDonald and Eddy appeared as costars of *Sweethearts,* a Broadway hit still running after
six years, who break up over a misunderstanding but eventually get back together for what
looks like at least another six years. The couple made three more pictures together—*New
Moon, Bitter Sweet,* and *I Married an Angel*—but none was as popular as their earlier efforts.
MGM/UA VC.

THE STORY OF VERNON AND IRENE CASTLE

Screenplay: Richard Sherman
Produced by: George Haight for RKO Radio
Directed by: H. C. Potter
Choreography: Hermes Pan (Fred Astaire uncredited)
Photography: Robert de Grasse
Cast: Fred Astaire, Ginger Rogers, Edna May Oliver, Walter Brennan,
Lew Fields, Janet Beecher, Leonid Kinskey, Clarence Derwent,
Victor Varconi, Donald MacBride, Marge Champion, Rolfe Sedan
Songs: "Yama-Yama Man" (Karl Hoschna-Collin Davis); "Only When You're
in My Arms" (Harry Ruby, Con Conrad-Bert Kalmar); "Waiting for the
Robert E. Lee" (Lewis Muir-L. Wolfe Gilbert); "Too Much Mustard"
(Cecil Macklin); "Hello, Hello, Who's Your Lady Friend?" (Bert Lee-
Worton David)
Released: March 1939; 90 minutes

Vernon and Irene Castle were the dancing sensations of pre-World War I America just as
Fred Astaire and Ginger Rogers were the dancing sensations of pre-World War II America.
Thus, there was a certain artistic logic in the second team portraying the first team in their
ninth and last RKO assignment. The movie, which ably recaptures a bygone era not only
in its story but in its use of authentic songs and dances, takes the couple—with a number
of historic rearrangements— from their meeting in New Rochelle in 1910, through their
marriage and early setbacks, their first success in Paris introducing the Castle Walk, their
sensational American tour, Vernon's enlistment in the Royal Air Corps, and ends with his
death when, as a flight instructor, he crashes his plane to avoid hitting a student pilot. As
a coda, Vernon's spirit appears for one last waltz with Irene, much as in *Maytime,* Nelson
Eddy's spirit had returned for one last duet with Jeanette MacDonald. Adding an authentic touch, the movie includes a scene with Lew Fields, with whom Vernon—before his
dancing days— had appeared as a comic stooge in five musicals. Historic note: In 1915,
the Castles themselves had appeared in a biographical film called *The Whirl of Life.*
Turner VC.

SECOND FIDDLE

Music & lyrics: Irving Berlin
Screenplay: Harry Tugend
Produced by: Gene Markey for 20th Century-Fox
Directed by: Sidney Lanfield
Choreography: Harry Losee
Photography: Leon Shamroy
Cast: Sonja Henie, Tyrone Power, Rudy Vallee, Edna May Oliver, Mary
Healy, Lyle Talbot, Alan Dinehart, Minna Gombell, Spencer Charters
Songs: "An Old Fashioned Tune Always Is New"; "Song of the
Metronome"; "Back to Back"; "When Winter Comes"; "I Poured
My Heart into a Song"; "I'm Sorry for Myself"
Released: July 1939; 86 minutes

Second Fiddle combines a spoof of the lengthy search for an actress to play Scarlett O'Hara in Gone With the Wind with a takeoff on Cyrano de Bergerac. After a three-year hunt, Consolidated Pictures signs the 436th applicant to be tested for the lead in the movie version of the best-seller Girl of the North. She turns out to be Sonja Henie, playing a schoolteacher and skating instructor in Bergen, Minnesota, for whom studio publicist Tyrone Power concocts a headlines-grabbing romance with actor Rudy Vallee. To aid in the wooing, Power even writes poems and a song ("I Poured My Heart Into a Song") for the inarticulate Vallee. Learning of the deception, Miss Henie rushes back to Bergen and Power rushes right after her. Of the six songs Irving Berlin wrote for the film, four are concerned in one way or another with the subject of music.

Second Fiddle. Edna May Oliver, Rudy Vallee, Sonja Henie, and Tyrone Power dancing "Back to Back."

THE WIZARD OF OZ

Music: Harold Arlen
Lyrics: E. Y. Harburg
Screenplay: Noel Langley, Florence Ryerson, Edgar Allan Woolf (John Lee Mahin uncredited)
Produced by: Mervyn LeRoy for MGM
Directed by: Victor Fleming (King Vidor uncredited)
Choreography: Bobby Connolly
Photography: Harold Rosson, Allen Darby (Technicolor)
Cast: Judy Garland, Frank Morgan, Ray Bolger, Bert Lahr, Jack Haley, Billie Burke, Margaret Hamilton, Charley Grapewin, Clara Blandick
Songs: "Over the Rainbow"; "Ding-Dong! The Witch Is Dead"; "We're Off to See the Wizard"; "Follow the Yellow Brick Road"; "If I Only Had a Brain"; "The Merry Old Land of Oz"; "If I Were King of the Forest"
Released: August 1939; 101 minutes

The huge success scored by Walt Disney's *Snow White and the Seven Dwarfs* inevitably prompted Hollywood's leading studios to search for other children's fantasies. A logical choice was L. Frank Baum's classic *The Wonderful Wizard of Oz*, written in 1900, which had been adapted as a Broadway musical in 1903 (with the title minus the word "Wonderful"), starring Dave Montgomery and Fred Stone as the Tin Woodman and the Scarecrow. Samuel Goldwyn acquired the screen rights in 1933 and sold them to MGM five years later. Mervyn LeRoy, who had just joined MGM as a producer, and Arthur Freed, who wanted to be a producer, both claimed that he was the one who had persuaded studio boss Louis B. Mayer to make the purchase. Mayer appointed LeRoy as producer and Freed as his assistant.

Three directors, Richard Thorpe, George Cukor, and Lewis Milestone, were assigned before LeRoy settled on Victor Fleming, though the final three weeks of shooting were taken over by King Vidor when Fleming had to report for work on *Gone With the Wind*. (Vidor directed the pivotal "Over the Rainbow" scene, which was almost cut from the film.) The movie made a star of 16-year-old Judy Garland, who played Dorothy, after Mayer was unsuccessful in borrowing Shirley Temple from Fox. Others in the cast were Ray Bolger as the Scarecrow (though the part had originally been given to Buddy Ebsen), Jack Haley as the Tin Woodman (after Ebsen, switched to this part, was hospitalized when the aluminum dust sprayed on his face had gotten into his lungs), Frank Morgan as the Wizard (after the part had been turned down by W. C. Fields and Ed Wynn), and Margaret Hamilton as the Wicked Witch of the West (though LeRoy had initially wanted Gale Sondergaard). Bert Lahr as the Cowardly Lion, was everyone's choice from the start.

In the screen treatment, Dorothy Gale, unhappy on her drab, sepia-tinted Kansas farm, is knocked out during a tornado (actually a 35-foot windsock made of muslin) and dreams that she is over the rainbow in the colorful land of Oz. There she meets the adorable Munchkins (played by 124 midgets) and goes off on the Yellow Brick Road to see the all-powerful Wizard in the Emerald City. Despite the machinations of the Wicked Witch of the West, Dorothy and her new friends, the Scarecrow, the Tin Woodman, and the Cowardly Lion, complete the journey only to discover that the Wizard is a fraud. He does, however, convince the little girl's companions that they already possess the desired brains, heart, and courage, and Dorothy wakes up from her dream convinced that there's no place like home.

A cartoon variation, *Journey Back to Oz*, was shown in 1974 (though completed in 1962) with well-known actors doing voice-overs, including Miss Garland's daughter, Liza Minnelli, as Dorothy. An urbanized all-black stage version, *The Wiz*, which opened on Broadway in 1975, was brought to the screen three years later with a cast headed by Diana Ross, Michael Jackson, Nipsey Russell, Ted Ross, Richard Pryor, and Lena Horne. In 1985, a Disney production, *Return to Oz*, combined live actors with assorted animated creatures.
MCA ST; CSP ST. MGM/UA VC.

The Wizard of Oz. The Tin Woodman (Jack Haley), the Cowardly Lion (Bert Lahr), Dorothy (Judy Garland), and the Scarecrow (Ray Bolger) are met at the Emerald City by the Gate Keeper (Frank Morgan).

BABES IN ARMS

Screenplay: Jack McGowan & Kay Van Riper (Noel Langley uncredited)
Produced by: Arthur Freed for MGM
Director-choreographer: Busby Berkeley
Photography: Ray June
Cast: Mickey Rooney, Judy Garland, Charles Winninger, Guy Kibbee, June Preisser, Grace Hayes, Betty Jaynes, Douglas McPhail, Rand Brooks, John Sheffield, Henry Hull, Barnett Parker, Ann Shoemaker, Margaret Hamilton, Charles Smith
Songs: "Good Morning" (Nacio Herb Brown-Arthur Freed); "You Are My Lucky Star" (Brown-Freed); "Broadway Rhythm" (Brown-Freed); " Babes in Arms" (Richard Rodgers-Lorenz Hart); "Where or When" (Rodgers-Hart); "I Cried for You" (Gus Arnheim, Abe Lyman-Freed); "Daddy Was a Minstrel Man" (Roger Edens); "I'm Just Wild About Harry" (Eubie Blake-Noble Sissle); "God's Country" (Harold Arlen-E. Y. Harburg)
Released: October 1939; 97 minutes

On Broadway, where it opened in 1937, *Babes in Arms* was a small-scale musical comedy which showed how some talented teenagers, the children of former vaudevillians, manage to avoid being sent to a work school by staging their own show. Though the screen version retained the general outline of the plot, it kept only two of the original 11 Rodgers and Hart songs (among the casualties: "My Funny Valentine" and "The Lady Is a Tramp"), changed the names of the characters, used a minstrel show as the highlight of the revue, and added a romantic and professional complication in the person of a Shirley Temple-type movie star, played by tumbling June Preisser. It was also the first picture to costar Mickey Rooney (who sang, danced, played piano and cello, and imitated Clark Gable and Lionel Barrymore) and Judy Garland (whose "I Cried for You" echoed her previous "Dear Mr. Gable"), and the first product of the celebrated Freed Unit at MGM. Under the direction of Busby Berkeley (his first at Metro), *Babes in Arms* succeeded so well—distributors voted Rooney the most popular actor of the year—that it spawned three other Mickey-Judy movies of the "Why-don't-us-kids-put-on-our-own-show" genre: *Strike Up The Band, Babes on Broadway,* and *Girl Crazy*. It also begat such low-budget clones as MGM's *Born to Sing* (1942) with Ray McDonald and Virginia Weidler (and a finale directed by Busby Berkeley) and Universal's *Babes on Swing Street* (1944), with Peggy Ryan, Ann Blyth, and even June Preisser. *Curtain Calls ST. MGM/UA VC.*

Babes in Arms. As Mickey Rooney slaps the cello, Judy Garland and Betty Jaynes sing their contrapuntal "Broadway Rhythm" and "You Are My Lucky Star."

Pinocchio. Gepetto and Pinocchio.

PINOCCHIO

Music: Leigh Harline
Lyrics: Ned Washington
Screenplay: Ted Sears, Otto Englander, Webb Smith, William Cottrell,
 Joseph Sabo, Erdman Penner, Aurelius Battaglia
Produced by: Walt Disney (released by RKO Radio)
Directed by: Ben Sharpsteen, Hamilton Luske, Bill Roberts, Norman
 Ferguson, Jack Kenney, Wilfred Jackson, T. Hee (Technicolor)
Voices: Dickie Jones, Christian Rub, Cliff Edwards, Evelyn Venable, Walter
 Catlett, Charles Judels, Frankie Darro
Songs: "When You Wish Upon a Star", "Give a Little Whistle", "Turn on
 the Old Music Box"; "Hi-Diddle-Dee-Dee (An Actor's Life for Me)";
 "I've Got No Strings"
Released: February 1940; 88 minutes

Snow White and the Seven Dwarfs proved conclusively to Walt Disney that feature-length cartoons based on juvenile classics could be highly profitable. For his second, Disney went back to *Pinocchio: the Story of a Puppet,* written by Carlo Collodi in 1880. The film begins with Jiminy Cricket (an original Disney creation) urging everyone to wish upon a star as he spins the tale of Gepetto, a wood-carving Pygmalion, who creates a boy that comes to life with the aid of the Blue Fairy. He is called Pinocchio, and soon he is running off to join a marionette troupe where his lying makes his nose grow longer and longer, and even sprout branches. But as soon as the Blue Fairy gives him a second chance, he gets into bad company on Pleasure Island where he almost turns into a donkey. In his last adventure, Pinocchio manages to rescue Gepetto from the belly of Monstro the whale, an act that persuades the Blue Fairy to turn Pinocchio into a real boy.

 The character of Jiminy Cricket (with Cliff Edwards' voice), who serves as Pinocchio's conscience, became so popular that he turned up again in a 1947 Disney feature, *Fun and Fancy Free.* As she had been for Snow White, Marge Champion was the model for the Blue Fairy in *Pinocchio.* In 1987, another animated film "inspired" by the same story, *Pinocchio and the Emperor of the Night,* was released by Filmation.
Disneyland ST. Disney VC.

BROADWAY MELODY OF 1940

Music & lyrics: Cole Porter
Screenplay: Leon Gordon & George Oppenheimer
Produced by: Jack Cummings for MGM
Directed by: Norman Taurog
Choreography: Bobby Connolly (Fred Astaire uncredited)
Photography: Oliver T. Marsh, Joseph Ruttenberg
Cast: Fred Astaire, Eleanor Powell, George Murphy, Frank Morgan, Ian
Hunter, Florence Rice, Lynne Carver, Douglas McPhail, Herman
Bing, Vera Vague, Joe Yule
Songs: "Please Don't Monkey With Broadway"; "Between You and Me"';
"I've Got My Eyes on You"; "I Concentrate on You"; "Begin the
Beguine"
Release date: February 1940;102 minutes

After completing *The Story of Vernon and Irene Castle*, his tenth film for RKO, Fred Astaire left the studio to begin his association with MGM (where he also made ten films, though not consecutively). For Astaire's first post-Ginger Rogers picture, *Broadway Melody of 1940*, the dancer was paired with Eleanor Powell, the screen's most celebrated female tap dancer, and the movie gave them both unlimited opportunities in which to perform both individually and together. It also gave Astaire George Murphy as his first male dancing partner. Though, as the title indicates, this is still another backstage yarn, it has less to do with the usual problems of putting on a show than it has with the dilemma posed when Murphy, Astaire's song-and-dance partner, is mistakenly chosen as Eleanor's leading man instead of Fred. But not to worry. Cole Porter contributed four new songs to the picture (his first assignment for an Astaire film), but the terpsichorean highlight—and the movie's finale—is the marathon tapping to the composer's five-year-old standard, "Begin the Beguine" (though the sequence's most dazzling moments occur when Astaire and Powell dance without any musical accompaniment). *Broadway Melody of 1940,* the third in the series to star Eleanor Powell, was the fourth and last of the MGM show-business sagas to bear the "Broadway Melody" rubric.
Classic Intl. ST. MGM/UA VC.

Broadway Melody of 1940. Eleanor Powell and Fred Astaire performing their "Jukebox Dance."

Road to Singapore. Dorothy Lamour, Bing Crosby, and Bob Hope in the "Sweet Potato Piper" number.

ROAD TO SINGAPORE

Music: Victor Schertzinger*; James Monaco**
Lyrics: Johnny Burke
Screenplay: Frank Butler & Don Hartman
Produced by: Harlan Thompson for Paramount
Directed by: Victor Schertzinger
Choreography: LeRoy Prinz
Photography: William Mellor
Cast: Bing Crosby, Dorothy Lamour, Bob Hope, Charles Coburn, Anthony
 Quinn, Jerry Colonna, Judith Barrett
Songs: "Captain Custard" *; "The Moon and the Willow Tree" *; "Sweet
 Potato Piper"**; "Too Romantic"**
Released: February 1940; 84 minutes

The special appeal of the seven "Road" pictures was their self-kidding "we-knowthis-is-all-nonsense" approach which had Bing Crosby and Bob Hope speaking directly to the audience, ad-libbing topical gags, and poking fun at movie-making in general. Originally, Paramount planned to team Fred MacMurray and Jack Oakie in a comic adventure film to be called *Road to Mandalay*. But since Crosby and Hope were then conducting a friendly feud on their radio shows, the studio decided that casting them in the picture would be more commercial. Dorothy Lamour was given the female lead, the destination was rerouted to Singapore, and the "Road" trips were on their way. These pictures were among the most profitable series in Hollywood history, with each of the first six never failing to place high on the annual lists of the top theatre rental films in the U.S. and Canada.

Road to Singapore sets the basic tone for the series. Crosby plays the son of a shipping magnate, Hope is his penniless buddy, and together they take off for the South Seas where they meet and fall for Miss Lamour (she's partial to Bing), help her out of danger, and escape from various scrapes by distracting their adversaries with their "patty-cake" routine. In subsequent adventures, the boys were shown as itinerant hustlers—with Bing the scheming con man and Bob the patsy—who also happen to be song-and-dance men and/or sideshow performers.

After Singapore the trio traveled to Zanzibar (1941), Morocco (1942), Utopia (really the Klondike) (1945), Rio (1947), Bali (1952), and Hong Kong (1962). James Van Heusen wrote music for all but the first (the combined work of Victor Schertzinger, the film's director, and James Monaco) and Johnny Burke wrote lyrics for all but the last (the work of Sammy Cahn). "Moonlight Becomes You" was the series' biggest song hit, with other popular numbers being "Too Romantic," "Constantly," "Personality," "But Beautiful," and "You Don't Have to Know the Language."

Dorothy Lamour played a princess in both *Morocco* and *Bali,* and Anthony Quinn was the villain in both *Singapore* and *Morocco*. Though Lamour preferred Crosby over Hope in all the pictures, they were never seen as a wedded couple— yet she did marry Hope in *Rio* and *Utopia*. *Zanzibar, Rio,* and *Hong Kong* all opened with Crosby forcing Hope to perform a death-defying stunt that, in the first two, was responsible for starting a fire (the third one landed Hope in a hospital). *Bali* was the only one in Technicolor and *Hong Kong* the only one with a definite article in the title. For *Hong Kong,* Crosby and Hope (both then 59) dropped 48-year-old Lamour as the female lead in favor of 29-year-old Joan Collins (though Lamour did show up in a small role as herself). In 1944, Paramount released a spinoff of the series called *Rainbow Island* with Lamour, Eddie Bracken, and Gil Lamb. In 1987, *Ishtar* (reputed to have cost a record $51 million) offered Warren Beatty and Dustin Hoffman in an updated variation on the *Road* pictures.

For credits for the other films in the series, see pages 101*(Zanzibar),* 116 *(Morocco),* 134 *(Utopia),* 144 *(Rio),* 174 *(Bali)* and 226 *(Hong Kong).*
Decca (Crosby LPs); MCA (Crosby CD, Morocco*); Liberty ST (*Hong Kong*). Utopia MCA VC* (Utopia); *RCA/Columbia VC* (Rio); *Unicorn VC (*Bali*).*

LILLIAN RUSSELL

Screenplay: William Anthony McGuire
Produced by: Darryl F. Zanuck & Gene Markey for 20th Century-Fox
Directed by: Irving Cummings
Choreography: Seymour Felix
Photography: Leon Shamroy
Cast: Alice Faye, Don Ameche, Henry Fonda, Edward Arnold, Warren William, Leo Carrillo, Helen Westley, Ernest Truex, Lynn Bari, Nigel Bruce, Claud Allister, Joe Weber, Lew Fields, Eddie Foy Jr., Joseph Cawthorn
Songs: "Comin' Thro' the Rye" (trad.-Robert Burns); "The Band Played On" (Charles Ward-John Palmer); "Come Down, Ma Evenin' Star" (John Stromberg-Edgar Smith); "Ma Blushin' Rosie" (Stromberg-Smith), "After the Ball" (Charles Harris), "Blue Lovebird" (Bronislau Kaper-Gus Kahn)
Released: May 1940; 127 minutes

Lillian Russell was a flamboyant, well-proportioned singing actress who was the queen of comic opera in the two decades before the turn of the century, then became a featured attraction in six rowdy Weber and Fields revues, and was celebrated throughout the land as the personification of womanly beauty. Beloved by Diamond Jim Brady, she married composer Edward Solomon (her second husband), who was responsible for several of her early hits, and newspaper publisher Alexander Moore, (her fourth and last husband). Though the costly, plodding film biography was one of the biggest box office hits of the year, the woman's vivid personality and influence were never quite captured in the script. Moreover, the movie divided the number of her husbands in half, with Solomon (Don Ameche) depicted as merely her accompanist (and a surly one at that), while Moore (Henry Fonda) was turned into a rather colorless character. Among the film's virtues were the historical accuracy of the costumes and furnishings, and Edward Arnold's Brady, a part he had first played in Universal's *Diamond Jim*. Adding a further touch of authenticity was the appearance of Joe Weber and Lew Fields, who came out of retirement to perform their "casina-casina" comic routine.

STRIKE UP THE BAND

Music & lyrics: Roger Edens, etc.
Screenplay: John Monks Jr. & Fred Finklehoffe
Produced by: Arthur Freed for MGM
Director-choreographer: Busby Berkeley
Photography: Ray June
Cast: Mickey Rooney, Judy Garland, Paul Whiteman & Orch., June Preisser, William Tracy, Larry Nunn, Ann Shoemaker
Songs: "Our Love Affair" (lyric: Arthur Freed); "Do the La Conga"; "Nobody"; "The Drummer Boy"; "Strike Up the Band" (George Gershwin-Ira Gershwin)
Released: September 1940; 120 minutes

MGM's second Mickey-Judy musical directed by Busby Berkeley for producer Arthur Freed could just as well have been called *Babes on the Bandstand*. In this one, instead of putting on a show, Mickey puts together a high school orchestra featuring Judy as vocalist and lots of his own drumming. After several melodramatic hurdles—plus the distraction of cuddlesome June Preisser and some sanctimonious moralizing—Mickey and his band win Whiteman's national radio contest and perform the rousing title song (the movie's only connection with the Gershwins' 1930 Broadway musical). It was in *Strike Up the Band* that Mickey explains to Judy—in a scene suggested by Vincente Minnelli—how he'd like to orchestrate a song ("Our Love Affair") using animated fruit on a dining-room table to represent members of a symphony orchestra.
Curtain Calls ST. MGM/UA VC.

DOWN ARGENTINE WAY

Music: Harry Warren, etc.
Lyrics: Mack Gordon, etc.
Screenplay: Karl Tunberg & Darrel Ware
Produced by: Darryl F. Zanuck & Harry Joe Brown for 20th Century-Fox
Directed by: Irving Cummings
Choreography: Nick Castle
Photography: Ray Rennahan, Leon Shamroy (Technicolor)
Cast: Don Ameche, Betty Grable, Carmen Miranda, Charlotte Greenwood, Henry Stephenson, Nicholas Brothers, Leonid Kinskey, J. Carrol Naish
Songs: "South American Way" (Jimmy McHugh-Al Dubin); "Down Argentina Way"; "Two Dreams Met"; "Mama Yo Quiero" (Jaraca Paiva); "Sing to Your Senorita"
Released: October 1940; 94 minutes

After appearing in 31 movies since 1930, Betty Grable finally won stardom in a major musical when, because of the illness of Alice Faye, she was substituted in the leading female role in *Down Argentine Way*. (The movie also marked the first screen appearance of Carmen Miranda, though she only performed specialty numbers filmed in New York.) Miss Grable's cuddly good looks and spirited dancing quickly made her a box office draw equal to Miss Faye, and the picture's success prompted Fox studio head Darryl F. Zanuck to follow it up by alternating the actresses (usually in the company of Miss Miranda) in a string of Technicolor musicals featuring glamorous locales—*That Night In Rio* (Faye, Miranda), *Moon Over Miami* (Grable), *Weekend in Havana* (Faye, Miranda), *Song of the Islands* (Grable), and *Springtime in the Rockies* (Grable, Miranda). As for the plot of *Down Argentine Way,* it had something to do with Miss Grable going to Argentina to buy a horse from Don Ameche and their inevitable falling in love. What conflict there was had to do with Ameche's father, Henry Stephenson, the old grouch, who has been feuding with Grable's family.
H'wood Soundstage ST. Key VC.

Down Argentine Way. Betty Grable dancing to "Down Argentina Way" in a New York nightclub.

One Night in the Tropics. Robert Cummings
cornered by Peggy Moran in a telephone booth.

ONE NIGHT IN THE TROPICS

Music: Jerome Kern
Lyrics: Dorothy Fields
Screenplay: Kathryn Scola & Francis Martin
Produced by: Leonard Spigelgass for Universal
Directed by: A. Edward Sutherland
Choreography: Larry Ceballos
Photography: Joseph Valentine
Cast: Allan Jones, Nancy Kelly, Robert Cummings, Bud Abbott & Lou
Costello, Leo Carrillo, Mary Boland, Peggy Moran, William Frawley,
Barnett Parker, Richard Carle
Songs: "Remind Me"; "You and Your Kiss"; "Your Dream (Is the Same
as My Dream)" (lyric: Otto Harbach, Oscar Hammerstein II);
"The Farandola"
Released: November 1940; 82 minutes

In serious financial trouble in 1940, Universal decided that its best chance for survival would
be a moderately elaborate musical. For the story, producer Leonard Spigelgass chose Earl
Derr Biggers' novel *Love Insurance* (which had been filmed in 1919 as a silent) and for the
songs he went back four years to a Jerome Kern-Dorothy Fields score written for an
unproduced movie called *Riviera*. Set mostly on the fictitious Caribbean island of San
Marcos, *One Night in the Tropics* spins a gossamer yarn about an insurance salesman
(Allan Jones) who sells his playboy friend (Robert Cummings) a policy to make sure he
weds his fiancee (Nancy Kelly), but then falls in love with her himself. While the film did
nothing to reverse Universal's fortunes, it did provide Abbott and Costello with their screen
debut, thus beginning a series of 28 comedies the team made for the studio that, more
than anything else, kept the company solvent.

FANTASIA

Produced by: Walt Disney (released by RKO Radio)
Directed by: Samuel Armstrong, James Algar, Bill Roberts, Paul Satterfield,
Hamilton Luske, Jim Handley, Ford Beebe, T. Hee, Norman
Ferguson, Wilfred Jackson (Technicolor; Fantasound)
Cast: Deems Taylor, Leopold Stokowski & the Philadelphia Orch.
Music: "Toccata & Fugue in d" (Bach); "The Nutcracker Suite"
(Tschaikowsky); "The Sorcerer's Apprentice" (Dukas); "The Rite
of Spring" (Stravinsky); "Pastoral Symphony" (Beethoven); "Dance
of the Hours" (Ponchielli); "Night on Bald Mountain" (Mussorgsky);
"Ave Maria" (Schubert)
Released: November 1940; 120 minutes

Combining animation with live characters, Walt Disney's third feature-length film was a unique, even controversial attempt to visualize eight concert pieces through the use of cartoons. It originated as an animated short based on Dukas' "The Sorcerer's Apprentice," in which Mickey Mouse was seen in the title role and for which Leopold Stokowski and a local pickup orchestra furnished the soundtrack accompaniment. At Stokowski's suggestion, Disney expanded the short into a feature-length attraction by adding seven other classical works, with musicologist Deems Taylor as narrator and Stokowski conducting the Philadelphia Orchestra. The various interpretive approaches include abstract (Bach's "Toccata and Fugue"), narrative ("The Sorcerer's Apprentice"), terpsichorean ("The Nutcracker Suite" and "Dance of the Hours"), primeval ("The Rite of Spring"), comically mythological ("Pastoral Symphony"), wildly ritualistic ("Night on Bald Mountain"), and serenely spiritual ("Ave Maria"). In 1982, because of the deterioration in the quality of the original soundtrack, *Fantasia* was rereleased in Dolby Sound with the soundtrack orchestra conducted by Irwin Kostal.
Buena Vista ST.

TOO MANY GIRLS

Music: Richard Rodgers
Lyrics: Lorenz Hart
Screenplay: John Twist
Producer-director: George Abbott for RKO Radio
Choreography: LeRoy Prinz
Photography: Frank Redman
Cast: Lucille Ball, Richard Carlson, Ann Miller, Eddie Bracken, Frances
Langford, Desi Arnaz, Hal LeRoy, Van Johnson, Grady Sutton
Songs: "Heroes in the Fall"; "Pottawatomie"; "You're Nearer"; "I Didn't Know
What Time It Was"; "Spic and Spanish"; "Love Never Went to
College"; " 'Cause We Got Cake"
Released: November 1940; 85 minutes

With George Abbott, the producer-director of the original 1939 stage production, serving in the same capacities, it was hardly surprising that *Too Many Girls* emerged as an unusually faithful cinematic reincarnation. Retained were seven of the original 14 Rodgers and Hart songs (plus the addition of "You're Nearer"), such members of the Broadway cast as Hal LeRoy, Eddie Bracken, Desi Arnaz, and Van Johnson (the last three making their screen debuts), and vocal arranger Hugh Martin. To keep Lucille Ball away from fortune hunters, her millionaire father sends her to his faraway alma mater, Pottawatomie College in Stop Gap, New Mexico. As an added precaution, he hires four former All-American football players—LeRoy, Bracken, and Arnaz, plus Richard Carlson—to enroll in the school and to serve, without daughter's knowledge, as her bodyguards. Lucille falls for Carlson and there are the customary misunderstandings and reconciliations in tales of this sort. The basic plot was reused in Elvis Presley's 1965 film, *Girl Happy*.
Turner VC.

TIN PAN ALLEY

Screenplay: Robert Ellis & Helen Logan
Produced by: Darryl F. Zanuck & Kenneth MacGowan for 20th Century-Fox
Directed by: Walter Lang
Choreography: Seymour Felix
Photography: Leon Shamroy
Cast: Alice Faye, Betty Grable, Jack Oakie, John Payne, Allen Jenkins, Esther Ralston, Nicholas Brothers, John Loder, Billy Gilbert, Elisha Cook Jr.
Songs: "You Say the Sweetest Things, Baby" (Harry Warren-Mack Gordon); "Moonlight Bay" (Percy Wenrich-Edward Madden); "Honeysuckle Rose" (Fats Waller-Andy Razaf); "America, I Love You" (Archie Gottler-Edgar Leslie); "Goodbye, Broadway, Hello France" (Billy Baskette-Francis Reisner, Benny Davis); "The Sheik of Araby" (Ted Snyder-Harry B. Smith); "K-K-K-Katie" (Geoffrey O' Hara)
Released: November 1940; 94 minutes

Betty Grable's second major assignment found the dancing kewpie doll costarred with Alice Faye, the actress whom she had replaced in *Down Argentine Way*. The only film Fox's two leading musical stars made together—though Miss Grable's role was decidedly secondary—is a nostalgic tale about the rise of a pair of singing sisters and the rise of a pair of music publishers (John Payne and Jack Oakie) during the years between 1915 and the end of World War I. Something of a follow-up to *Alexander's Ragtime Band* (it had originally been scheduled for Faye, Tyrone Power, and Don Ameche), *Tin Pan Alley* unfortunately lacked an authentic musical sound since only about half of its songs had been written during the specified period. In 1950, Jean Haver, William Lundigan, Gloria DeHaven, and Dennis Day appeared in an updated variation called *I'll Get By*.
Sountrak ST.

Tin Pan Alley. Betty Grable and Alice Faye.

THAT NIGHT IN RIO

Music: Harry Warren
Lyrics: Mack Gordon
Screenplay: George Seaton, Bess Meredyth, Hal Long
Produced by: Fred Kohlmar for 20th Century-Fox
Directed by: Irving Cummings
Choreography: Hermes Pan
Photography: Leon Shamroy, Ray Rennahan (Technicolor)
Cast: Alice Faye, Don Ameche, Carmen Miranda, S.Z. Sakall, J. Carrol Naish, Curt Bois, Leonid Kinskey, Maria Montez, Banda da Lua, George Renavent, Flores Brothers
Songs: "Chica Chica Boom Chic"; "They Met in Rio"; "Cae Cae" (Roberto Martins-Pedro Berrios); "I, Yi, Yi, Yi, Yi (I Like You Very Much)"; "Boa Noite"
Released: March 1941; 90 minutes

The success of *Down Argentine Way* spurred Fox's production chief Darryl Zanuck to come up with another brightly Technicolored musical set in South America— though *That Night in Rio* offered nothing more indigenous to the locale than Brazilian entertainer Carmen Miranda. The same composer, lyricist, director, cameraman, and art director (Richard Day) who had worked on *Argentine* were assigned to the film as well as four of the leading actors. As for the story, Zanuck reached back six years to *Folies Bergere de Paris* and hired its screenwriters to do a remake of the same basic plot, the one about an entertainer who doubles for a rich playboy. Replacing *Folies* stars Maurice Chevalier, Merle Oberon, and Ann Sothern were Don Ameche, Alice Faye (in their sixth and final movie together), and Miss Miranda (in her first acting part). A variation on the same theme, *On the Riviera,* came along 10 years later and involved Danny Kaye, Gene Tierney, and Corinne Calvert. *Curtain Calls ST.*

ROAD TO ZANZIBAR

Music: James Van Heusen
Lyrics: Johnny Burke
Screenplay: Frank Butler & Don Hartman
Produced by: Paul Jones for Paramount
Directed by: Victor Schertzinger
Choreography: LeRoy Prinz
Photography: Ted Tetzlaff
Cast: Bing Crosby, Bob Hope, Dorothy Lamour, Una Merkel, Eric Blore, Douglass Dumbrille, Joan Marsh, Iris Adrian, Leo Gorcey, George Renavent, Ken Carpenter, Norma Varden
Songs: "Birds of a Feather"; "You Lucky People You"; "Road to Zanzibar"; "You're Dangerous"; "It's Always You"
Released: April 1941; 92 minutes

(See page 95.)

ZIEGFELD GIRL

Screenplay: Marguerite Roberts & Sonya Levien
Produced by: Pandro S. Berman for MGM
Directed by: Robert Z. Leonard
Choreography: Busby Berkeley
Photography: Ray June
Cast: James Stewart, Judy Garland, Hedy Lamarr, Lana Turner, Tony
Martin, Jackie Cooper, Ian Hunter, Charles Winninger, Edward
Everett Horton, Philip Dorn, Paul Kelly, Dan Dailey, Eve Arden,
Rosario & Antonio, Al Shean, Felix Bressart, Rose Hobart, Leslie
Brooks, Georgia Carroll
Songs: "You Stepped Out of a Dream" (Nacio Herb Brown-Gus Kahn);
"I'm Always Chasing Rainbows" (Harry Carroll-Joseph McCarthy);
"Minnie from Trinidad" (Roger Edens); "Mr. Gallagher & Mr.
Shean" (Ed Gallagher-Al Shean); "You Never Looked So Beautiful"
(Walter Donaldson-Harold Adamson)
Released: April 1941; 131 minutes

Of MGM's three "Ziegfeld" movies, *The Great Ziegfeld, Ziegfeld Girl,* and *Ziegfeld Follies,*
the second was the only one in which the legendary producer did not appear. Because the
film was concerned with the way *Follies* showgirls were chosen, this was a curious omission
since Ziegfeld always personally selected the decorative ladies who adorned the 21
editions of his celebrated revue. The movie focuses on three such girls: vaudevillian Judy
Garland, who goes on to become a featured attraction; Hedy Lamarr, who gives up show
business to rejoin Philip Dorn, her estranged concert violinist husband; and Lana Turner,
who ditches boyfriend James Stewart in favor of being a kept woman and must, of course,
pay the price. The picture ends with a recreation of the giant volute seen in *The Great
Ziegfeld,* with girls dancing on the steps and Judy Garland perched on top like a wedding
cake decoration.
Classic Intl. ST. MGM/UA VC.

Ziegfeld Girl. Lana Turner, Hedy Lamarr, Tony Martin, and Judy Garland
in the "You Stepped Out of a Dream" sequence.

Moon Over Miami. Betty Grable and Hermes Pan dancing to "Kindergarten Conga."

MOON OVER MIAMI

Music: Ralph Rainger
Lyrics: Leo Robin
Screenplay: Vincent Lawrence & Brown Tolmes
Produced by: Harry Joe Brown for 20th Century-Fox
Directed by: Walter Lang
Choreography: Hermes Pan (Jack Cole uncredited)
Photography: Leon Shamroy, Allen Davey, J. Peverell Marley (Technicolor)
Cast: Don Ameche, Betty Grable, Robert Cummings, Carole Landis, Charlotte Greenwood, Jack Haley, Cobina Wright Jr., Condos Brothers, Hermes Pan, Jack Cole, Spencer Charters
Songs: "Oh Me, Oh Mi-ami"; "You Started Something"; "I've Got You All to Myself"; "Is That Good?"; "Loveliness and Love"; "Kindergarten Conga"
Released: June 1941; 91 minutes

Fox's series of vividly hued musicals supposedly taking place in glamorous locales continued with *Moon Over Miami* which, as in *Down Argentine Way,* had a cast headed by Don Ameche, Betty Grable, and Charlotte Greenwood. In this tale, Miss Grable, as a fortune hunter trying to snare a well-heeled husband at a Miami resort, poses as a wealthy socialite with sister Carole Landis as her secretary and Aunt Charlotte as her maid. She does find herself a rich playboy (Robert Cummings) but ditches him in favor of a poor playboy (Ameche). Though the cameras went on location to film background scenes at such Florida attractions as the Everglades, surprisingly there wasn't one shot of anyone on a beach. The movie was adapted from the same London play that would later serve as the foundation for another Fox musical, *Three Little Girls in Blue* (see page 138). *Key VC.*

SUN VALLEY SERENADE

Music: Harry Warren
Lyrics: Mack Gordon
Screenplay: Robert Ellis & Helen Logan
Produced by: Milton Sperling for 20th Century-Fox
Directed by: H. Bruce Humberstone
Choreography: Hermes Pan
Photography: Edward Cronjager
Cast: Sonja Henie, John Payne, Glenn Miller Orch. (incl. Ray Anthony, Billy May, Hal McIntyre, Tex Beneke, Paula Kelly, The Modernaires), Milton Berle, Lynn Bari, Joan Davis, Nicholas Brothers, Dorothy Dandridge, Martha Tilton
Songs: "It Happened in Sun Valley"; "I Know Why (and So Do You)"; "In the Mood" (Joe Garland); "Chattanooga Choo-Choo"; "The Kiss Polka"
Released: July 1941; 86 minutes

After starring in six films in four years, Sonja Henie took a two-year hiatus from the screen, then returned in a film that had the added box office draw of the Glenn Miller Orchestra at the height of its popularity. Based on an idea that Darryl Zanuck had dreamed up while vacationing in Sun Valley, Idaho, the story is about a Norwegian wartime refugee who is sponsored by the Miller orchestra, and who then follows the band to the Sun Valley Lodge where she falls in love with Miller's pianist-arranger, John Payne (Chummy MacGregor did the playing). The standout number, "Chattanooga Choo-Choo," is performed during a band rehearsal, which features Dorothy Dandridge and the Nicholas Brothers, all in costume, singing and dancing on a stage with a painted backdrop of the choo-choo itself. *Mercury ST.*

BIRTH OF THE BLUES

Screenplay: Harry Tugend & Walter DeLeon
Produced by: B.G. DeSylva & Monta Bell for Paramount
Directed by: Victor Schertzinger
Photography: William Mellor
Cast: Bing Crosby, Mary Martin, Brian Donlevy, Eddie "Rochester" Anderson, Jack Teagarden, J. Carrol Naish, Carolyn Lee, Ruby Elzy, Harry Barris
Songs: "The Birth of the Blues" (Ray Henderson-B.G. DeSylva, Lew Brown); "By the Light of the Silvery Moon" (Gus Edwards-Edward Madden); "Cuddle Up a Little Closer" (Karl Hoschna-Otto Harbach); "Wait 'til the Sun Shines, Nellie" (Harry Von Tilzer-Andrew Sterling); "My Melancholy Baby" (Ernie Burnett); "The Waiter and the Porter and the Upstairs Maid" (Johnny Mercer); "St. Louis Blues" (W.C. Handy)
Released: September 1941; 85 minutes

Birth of the Blues was Hollywood's initial effort to deal with the world of jazz, specifically with the creation of the first all-white band (here called the Basin Street Hot Shots but actually modeled on the Original Dixieland Jazz Band). More of an easygoing Bing Crosby vehicle than a history lesson, the movie traces the efforts of the musicians to win favor in New Orleans which, of course, they eventually do. Among the numbers was Johnny Mercer's "The Waiter and the Porter and the Upstairs Maid," performed by Crosby, Mary Martin, and Jack Teagarden, which relates the story of a guest at a stuffy party who sneaks into the kitchen and has himself a ball with the hired help. Two other jazz-inspired movies came out soon after *Birth of the Blues*—Warners' *Blues in the Night* and RKO's *Syncopation*. Decca (Crosby LP).

WEEK-END IN HAVANA

Music: Harry Warren
Lyrics: Mack Gordon
Screenplay: Karl Tunberg & Darrel Ware
Produced by: William LeBaron for 20th Century-Fox
Directed by: Walter Lang
Choreography: Hermes Pan
Photography: Ernest Palmer (Technicolor)
Cast: Alice Faye, John Payne, Carmen Miranda, Cesar Romero, Cobina
        Wright Jr., Leonid Kinskey, George Barbier, Sheldon Leonard, Billy
        Gilbert
Songs: "A Week-End in Havana"; "When I Love I Love"; "Tropical Magic";
        "Romance and Rumba" (music: James Monaco); "The Nango"
Released: September 1941; 80 minutes

After making good-neighborly visits below the border to Argentina and Rio de Janeiro (if only in the movies' titles), Fox decided it was time for a weekend in Havana—and even showed a montage of the city's major attractions to prove it. In this one, Alice Faye, a salesgirl at Macy's on a vacation cruise to Cuba, is given a free trip to the Cuban capital to persuade her to sign a waiver clearing the steamship company of any responsibility for the ship hitting a reef off the coast of Florida. Her escort is shipping executive John Payne, who takes her to the Casino Madrilena to hear the highly animated Carmen Miranda (and to provide a setting for Miss Faye to sing the languid "Tropical Magic"). Despite the advances of fortune hunter Cesar Romero ("I am not Cuban. I was born in Brooklyn as a child"), who also happens to be Miss Miranda's lover, matters manage to get straightened out in time for the big finale.
Curtain Calls ST.

Week-End in Havana. Alice Faye and John Payne singing "Tropical Magic" on the back of a donkey cart.

YOU'LL NEVER GET RICH

Music & lyrics: Cole Porter
Screenplay: Michael Fessier & Ernest Pagano
Produced by: Samuel Bischoff for Columbia
Directed by: Sidney Lanfield
Choreography: Robert Alton (Fred Astaire uncredited)
Photography: Philip Tanura
Cast: Fred Astaire, Rita Hayworth, Robert Benchley, John Hubbard, Osa Massen, Frieda Inescort, Donald MacBride, Cliff Nazarro, Ann Shoemaker, Marjorie Gateson, Martha Tilton, Delta Rhythm Boys, Chico Hamilton, Donald Saddler
Songs: "Shootin' the Works for Uncle Sam"; "Since I Kissed My Baby Goodbye"; "So Near and Yet So Far"; "Wedding Cake Walk"
Released: September 1941; 88 minutes

Columbia's most lavish musical to date was an important boost to the career of its contractee, Rita Hayworth, who was at last given the chance to display her dancing ability in a major production. To make sure that she would have the best of everything, she was costarred with the screen's premier dancer, Fred Astaire (who was then 42 to her 22), and the songs were written by one of the masters, Cole Porter. The film, which was released just three months before the attack on Pearl Harbor, was also the first big-budget musical to be concerned with rookie life at a basic-training camp. Astaire plays a Broadway dance director who falls for Miss Hayworth, one of the girls in the show, gets drafted into the army, spends most of his time in the guardhouse (obviously an ideal place to perform two spectacular tap routines), and is reunited with Rita when she turns up to appear in a servicemen's show. In the show, Fred, in formal attire, woos Rita in song and dance to the compelling "So Near and Yet So Far," then appears with her in the joyous "Wedding Cake Walk" finale in which, along with a chorus of 80 boys and girls, they dance all over a huge wedding cake with a rather menacing army tank perched on top.
H'wood Soundstage ST. RCA/Columbia VC.

BLUES IN THE NIGHT

Music: Harold Arlen
Lyrics: Johnny Mercer
Screenplay: Robert Rossen
Produced by: Hal B. Wallis for Warner Bros.
Directed by: Anatole Litvak
Photography: Ernest Haller
Cast: Priscilla Lane, Betty Field, Richard Whorf, Lloyd Nolan, Jack Carson, Wallace Ford, Elia Kazan, Peter Whitney, Billy Halop, Jimmie Lunceford Orch., Will Osborne Orch., William Gillespie
Songs: "This Time the Dream's on Me"; "Says Who, Says You, Says I!"; "Blues in the Night"; "Hang on to Your Lids, Kids"
Released: October 1941; 88 minutes

For a jailhouse scene in a movie to be called *Hot Nocturne,* Harold Arlen and Johnny Mercer were obliged to come up with a wailing, authentic-sounding blues number for William Gillespie. The piece they wrote, "Blues in the Night," made such a deep impression that Warner Bros. promptly changed the movie's title to that of the song. The offbeat film is a reasonably serious attempt to offer an honest view of the dilemma of jazz musicians who must choose between playing the kind of music they believe in or making money by going commercial. In the melodramatic script, Richard Whorf is the band's pianist and leader, Elia Kazan its clarinetist, and Jack Carson its trumpeter. Whorf becomes involved with two-faced, worrisome Betty Field, who distracts him from his goals but conveniently is killed in a suicidal car crash.

Babes on Broadway. Mickey Rooney doing his Carmen Miranda routine.

BABES ON BROADWAY

Music: Burton Lane, etc.
Lyrics: Ralph Freed, etc.
Screenplay: Fred Finklehoffe & Elaine Ryan
Produced by: Arthur Freed for MGM
Director-choreographer: Busby Berkeley
Photography: Lester White
Cast: Mickey Rooney, Judy Garland, Fay Bainter, Virginia Weidler, Ray McDonald, Richard Quine, Alexander Woollcott, Donald Meek, James Gleason, Emma Dunn, Six Hits and a Miss, Donna Reed, Joe Yule, Ava Gardner, Margaret O'Brien
Songs: "Babes on Broadway"; "Anything Can Happen in New York" (lyric: E.Y. Harburg); "How About You?"; "Hoe Down" (music: Roger Edens); "Chin Up! Cheerio! Carry On!" (lyric: Harburg); "Mama Yo Quiero" (Vincente Paiva-Jararaca); "F.D.R. Jones" (Harold Rome); "Waiting for the Robert E. Lee" (Lewis Muir-L. Wolfe Gilbert)
Released: December 1941; 118 minutes

As the title indicates, *Babes on Broadway* was the closest to *Babes in Arms* in the series of four musicals involving Mickey Rooney, Judy Garland, director Busby Berkeley, and producer Arthur Freed. In this one, Mickey, a member of a struggling song-and-dance act, "The Three Balls of Fire," gets the bright notion that the only way beginners can get a break on Broadway is to put on— that's right—their own show (this time for the benefit of a settlement house). It even copied *Babes in Arms* by repeating the format of a minstrel show as the finale. Among the highlights are Mickey and Judy singing "How About You?" and doing imitations in a deserted theatre (Mickey does takeoffs on Richard Mansfield as Cyrano, George M. Cohan, and Harry Lauder, and Judy does Blanche Ring, Fay Templeton, and Sarah Bernhardt). The biggest howls, however, were reserved for Rooney's uninhibited impression of Carmen Miranda gyrating through "Mama Yo Quiero." *Curtain Call ST. MGM/UA VC.*

THE FLEET'S IN

Music: Victor Schertzinger
Lyrics: Johnny Mercer
Screenplay: Walter DeLeon & Sid Silvers
Produced by: Paul Jones for Paramount
Directed by: Victor Schertzinger
Choreography: Jack Donohue
Photography: William Mellor
Cast: Dorothy Lamour, William Holden, Betty Hutton, Eddie Bracken, Leif Erickson, Jimmy Dorsey Orch., Helen O'Connell, Bob Eberle, Cass Daley, Barbara Brittan, Betty Jane Rhodes, Gil Lamb, Rod Cameron, Harry Barris
Songs: "The Fleet's In"; "Tangerine"; "Not Mine"; "I Remember You"; "If You Build a Better Mousetrap"; "Arthur Murray Taught Me Dancing in a Hurry"
Released: January 1942; 93 minutes

Like the Astaire-Rogers film *Follow the Fleet, The Fleet's In* tells the tale of two sailors who become romantically involved with two girls they meet in a San Francisco dance hall. The resemblance ended there, however, since the plot of the Paramount film, based on a 1933 Broadway play, *Sailor, Beware!*, by Kenyon Nicholson and Charles Robinson, is about a shy sailor (William Holden) who is mistakenly thought to be so irresistible to women that his shipmates bet that he can get the icy Countess (Dorothy Lamour), a singer at the Swingland dance hall, to kiss him in public. This she eventually does, but only after they are married. The movie was another one of the growing number of musicals at that time to feature popular dance bands, in this case Jimmy Dorsey's, and it provided the orchestra with such closely identified songs as "Tangerine" and "I Remember You." These numbers, plus "Arthur Murray Taught Me Dancing in a Hurry," sung by Betty Hutton in her film debut, were written by the film's director, Victor Schertzinger. *The Fleet's In* was remade in 1951 as a vehicle for Dean Martin and Jerry Lewis under the title *Sailor Beware.*
H'wood Soundstage ST.

MY GAL SAL

Music: Paul Dresser*; Ralph Rainger**
Lyrics: Paul Dresser*; Leo Robin**
Screenplay: Seton I. Miller, Darrel Ware, Karl Tunberg
Produced by: Robert Bassler for 20th Century-Fox
Directed by: Irving Cummings
Choreography: Hermes Pan, Val Raset
Photography: Ernest Palmer (Technicolor)
Cast: Rita Hayworth, Victor Mature, Carole Landis, John Sutton, James Gleason, Phil Silvers, Walter Catlett, Curt Bois, Andrew Tombes, Hermes Pan, Terry Moore
Songs: "Liza Jane"*; "Come Tell Me"*; "On the Gay White Way"**; "Oh, the Pity of It All"**; "Here You Are"**; The Convict and the Bird"*; "On the Banks of the Wabash"*; "Me and My Fella"**; "Mr. Volunteer"*; "My Gal Sal"*
Released: April 1942; 103 minutes

The success of *Lillian Russell* made it almost mandatory that Fox would schedule another quasi-biographical show-business musical starring Alice Faye. But Miss Faye was pregnant and though attempts were made to secure either Irene Dunne, Betty Grable, or even Mae West for *My Gal Sal,* the studio borrowed Columbia's Rita Hayworth (who could dance but whose singing had to be dubbed by Nan Wynn) to play a fictitious turn-of-the-century musical-comedy star. The film, however, is not about her life but about the life of the 19th century songwriter Paul Dresser ("On the Banks of the Wabash," "My Gal Sal"), whose brother, novelist Theodore Dreiser, had supplied the original story. Regrettably, the saga not only plays hobs with Dresser's life (as expected), it uses only six Dresser songs with four new ones supplied by the studio team of Ralph Rainger and Leo Robin. In the tale, Dresser (Victor Mature) rises from humble beginnings as a medicine-show entertainer (which he was) to his emergence as a successful Broadway songwriter (which he wasn't), and is concerned with his tempestuous romance with his gal Sal (actually Dresser had a miserable marriage and died in poverty).

Yankee Doodle Dandy. James Cagney leading Jeanne Cagney, Joan Leslie, Walter Huston, Rosemary DeCamp, and chorus in "You're a Grand Old Flag."

YANKEE DOODLE DANDY

Music & lyrics: George M. Cohan
Screenplay: Robert Bruckner & Edmund Joseph (Julius & Philip
      Epstein, uncredited)
Produced by: Hal B. Wallis for Warner Bros.
Directed by: Michael Curtiz
Choreography: LeRoy Prinz, Seymour Felix, John Boyle
Photography: James Wong Howe
Cast: James Cagney, Joan Leslie, Walter Huston, Richard Whorf, Irene
          Manning, George Tobias, Rosemary DeCamp, Jeanne Cagney,
          Frances Langford, George Barbier, S.Z. Sakall, Walter Catlett, Eddie
          Foy Jr., Odette Myrtil, Charles Smith, Georgia Carroll, Leslie Brooks,
          Spencer Charters
Songs: "I Was Born in Virginia"; "Harrigan"; "The Yankee Doodle Boy";
          "Give My Regards to Broadway"; "Oh, You Wonderful Girl"; "I'll Be
          True to You"; "Belle of the Barbers' Ball"; "Mary's a Grand Old
          Name"; "Forty-Five Minutes from Broadway"; "So Long, Mary";
          "You're a Grand Old Flag"; "Over There"
Released: May 1942; 126 minutes

As composer, lyricist, librettist, director, producer, playwright, actor, singer and dancer, George M. Cohan (1878-1942) was the most versatile talent in the history of the Broadway stage. He wrote 21 musicals and acted in ten of them, and 22 plays and acted in 12 of *them*. Cohan was the embodiment of American brashness, self-confidence, and naivity, and his fast-moving, flag-waving shows gave him ample opportunity to display his multiple gifts.

Despite its sentimentality and wartime jingoism, *Yankee Doodle Dandy* is a superior show-business saga thanks largely to James Cagney's dynamic portrayal of the cocky song-and-dance man. Told in flashback as Cohan supposedly relates his life story to an uncommonly patient and conveniently undisturbed President Roosevelt, the saga begins with Cohan's birth (on the Fourth of July!), covers his barnstorming vaudeville days with his father (Walter Huston), mother (Rosemary DeCamp, who was 14 years younger than Cagney), and sister (Cagney's sister Jeanne), and goes on to successes and failures on Broadway. Following a period of crotchety retirement, the actor triumphantly returns to the boards at the age of 59 in Rodgers and Hart's *I'd Rather Be Right* (which offered the triple image of Cagney impersonating Cohan impersonating President Roosevelt), and receives a Congressional Medal of Honor for his patriotic songs, "You're a Grand Old Flag" and "Over There." (Far from being mysteriously summoned by Roosevelt for the presentation, as in the film, Cohan had actually waited four years to pick up the medal.) The movie's most memorable sequence is the 11-minute recreation of two scenes from Cohan's first hit, *Little Johnny Jones,* which finds Cagney strutting, hopping, tapping, sprinting, and scaling proscenium walls while dancing to "The Yankee Doodle Boy" and "Give My Regards to Broadway."

Cohan had long resisted his story being told on the screen but he finally gave his approval—for which he took $125,000 plus 10% of the picture's gross— because the script of *Yankee Doodle Dandy* emphasized his songs and professional career rather than his personal life. (For one thing, Cohan was married twice, to stage star Ethel Levey and dancer Agnes Nolan, though the movie showed him wedded to only one wife, and her name—as in the song—was Mary.) Cagney, however, found the Cohan-approved script too somber and insisted that uncredited writers Julius and Philip Epstein be called in to liven things up.

In a career spanning 62 films, Cagney danced in only four besides *Yankee Doodle Dandy*. One of them, *The Seven Little Foys,* with Bob Hope as vaudevillian Eddie Foy, found Cagney doing a guest bit as Cohan. The first screen biography of a Broadway composer, *Yankee Doodle Dandy* took in the six highest theatre rental fees of all the musicals of the Forties. In 1968, Joel Gray starred on Broadway as Cohan in *George M!,* but it was not an adaptation of the movie.
Curtain Calls ST.   MGM/UA VC.

HOLIDAY INN

Music & lyrics: Irving Berlin
Screenplay: Claude Binyon
Producer-director: Mark Sandrich
Choreography: Danny Dare (Fred Astaire uncredited)
Photography: David Abel
Cast: Bing Crosby, Fred Astaire, Marjorie Reynolds, Virginia Dare, Walter Abel, Louise Beavers, Harry Barris, Bob Crosby's Bob Cats, Leon Belasco, Marek Windheim, Irving Bacon, James Bell
Songs: "I'll Capture Your Heart Singing"; "Lazy"; "You're Easy to Dance With"; "White Christmas"; "Happy Holiday"; "Holiday Inn"; "Let's Start the New Year Right"; "Abraham"; "Be Careful, It's My Heart"; "I Can't Tell a Lie"; "Easter Parade"; "Song of Freedom"; "Let's Say It with Firecrackers"; "Plenty to Be Thankful For"
Released: June 1942; 100 minutes

In 1933, Irving Berlin and sketch writer Moss Hart collaborated on a Broadway revue, *As Thousands Cheer,* in which every scene was based on either a news story or a feature in a newspaper. For the first-act finale, the rotogravure section found the cast in monochromatic brown going back fifty years to an old-fashioned Fifth Avenue Easter Parade, set to the strains of the now-familiar Berlin ballad. That scene gave Berlin and Hart the idea for an entire revue based on American holidays but they were never able to develop it. Then in 1941 Berlin offered the concept to Mark Sandrich, who had directed five Astaire-Rogers films at RKO and was now a producer-director at Paramount, and together they worked up an outline for a Bing Crosby vehicle. In the scenario, which begins on Christmas Eve and ends on New Year's Eve two years later, a member of a song-and-dance act quits show business to become a farmer in Connecticut. When, after a year, he realizes that farming isn't for him, he decides to renovate the farmhouse as a cabaret and open it only on holidays. Complications develop when he and his former partner vie for the affection of the same girl, but matters do get straightened out in time for the final festivities on New Year's Eve.

To play Crosby's former partner and romatic rival, Berlin and Sandrich held out for Fred Astaire, thus bringing together Hollywood's leading male singer and Hollywood's leading male dancer. For the first time since becoming a major screen attraction, Astaire appears in a somewhat unsympathetic role and also, for the first time, loses the girl (played by Marjorie Reynolds singing with Martha Mears' dubbed voice). Astaire did, however, get the chance to dance with three partners—Miss Reynolds, Virginia Dare, and firecrackers (in a scene that had to be shot 38 times before the dancer was satisfied).

Unquestionably, the special appeal of *Holiday Inn* is the nine songs Irving Berlin contributed to tie in with the eight featured holidays—Christmas, New Year's Eve, Lincoln's Birthday, Valentine's Day, Washington's Birthday, Easter, the Fourth of July (which got two numbers), and Thanksgiving. Of these, "Easter Parade" was the only one not written specifically for the film, and "White Christmas" was not only the most popular song in the movie, it would go on to become far and away the most popular secular Christmas song of all time. One song, "It's a Great Country," which was written for the movie, was not used.

Holiday Inn (among the biggest moneymakers of the year) was followed four years later by another Crosby-Astaire-Berlin film, *Blue Skies*, also from Paramount, but director Sandrich's death forced his replacement by Stuart Heisler.
MCA (Crosby, Astaire CD); Sountrak ST. MCA VC.

Holiday Inn. While Bing Crosby sings "Be Careful It's My Heart," Marjorie Reynolds dances with Fred Astaire.

ORCHESTRA WIVES

Music: Harry Warren
Lyrics: Mack Gordon
Screenplay: Karl Tunberg & Darrel Ware
Produced by: William LeBaron for 20th Century-Fox
Directed by: Archie Mayo
Choreography: Nick Castle
Photography: Lucien Ballard
Cast: Glenn Miller & Orch. (incl. Ray Anthony, Billy May, Hal McIntyre, Tex Beneke, Marion Hutton, Ray Eberle, The Modernaires), George Montgomery, Ann Rutherford, Lynn Bari, Carole Landis, Cesar Romero, Jackie Gleason, Mary Beth Hughes, Virginia Gilmore, Harry Morgan, Tamara Geva, Nicholas Brothers
Songs: "People Like You and Me";"At Last"; "Serenade in Blue"; "I've Got a Gal in Kalamazoo"
Released: August 1942; 98 minutes

Though the plot about bitchy and jealous wives of band musicians was hardly one for the ages, *Orchestra Wives* retains interest chiefly because of the songs and the way they are performed by the Glenn Miller band. In addition, it is one of the rare movies to shed some light on the lives of the musicians and their experiences touring from city to city. Of course, the band is fictitious—Miller is called Gene Morrison—but the sidemen were all Miller's, including those who dubbed their instruments for the leading actors: trumpeter Johnny Best for George Montgomery, pianist Chummy MacGregor for Cesar Romero, and bassist Doc Goldberg for Jackie Gleason. (The vocalists were all Miller's too, except for Pat Friday who dubbed for Lynn Bari.)
Mercury ST.

SPRINGTIME IN THE ROCKIES

Music: Harry Warren
Lyrics: Mack Gordon
Screenplay: Walter Bullock & Ken Englund
Produced by: William LeBaron for 20th Century-Fox
Directed by: Irving Cummings
Choreography: Hermes Pan
Photography: Ernest Palmer, Henri Jaffa (Technicolor)
Cast: Betty Grable, John Payne, Carmen Miranda, Cesar Romero,
Charlotte Greenwood, Edward Everett Horton, Harry James Orch.,
Helen Forrest, Jackie Gleason, Chick Chandler
Songs: "Run Little Raindrop"; "I Had the Craziest Dream"; "Chattanooga
Choo-Choo"; "Pan-American Jubilee"
Released: September 1942; 91 minutes

When Alice Faye was unable to appear in *Springtime in the Rockies,* there was no problem in substituting Fox's other reigning musical queen, Betty Grable. Another of the studio's brightly colored musicals set in far-off locales, the movie is about two bickering musical-comedy performers, Miss Grable and John Payne, who break up when Betty goes off to Chateau Lake Louise in the Canadian Rockies with former dancing partner Cesar Romero. After Payne follows Betty, they discover—as expected—that they are in love. Apart from Miss Grable's dancing, the movie benefits from the comic performances of such stalwarts as Carmen Miranda (singing "Chattanooga Choo-Choo" in Portuguese to a samba beat), Charlotte Greenwood, and Edward Everett Horton. Harry James' Orchestra introduces the movie's hit song, "I Had the Craziest Dream," sung, not by Miss Grable, but by the band's vocalist Helen Forrest.
H'wood Soundstage ST. Key VC.

Springtime in the Rockies. Betty Grable and Cesar
Romero in the "Pan-American Jubilee" finale.

YOU WERE NEVER LOVELIER

Music: Jerome Kern
Lyrics: Johnny Mercer
Screenplay: Michael Fessier, Ernest Pagano, Delmer Daves
Produced by: Louis F. Edelman for Columbia
Directed by: William A. Seiter
Choreography: Val Raset (Fred Astaire uncredited)
Photography: Ted Tetzlaff
Cast: Fred Astaire, Rita Hayworth, Adolphe Menjou, Xavier Cugat & Orch., Leslie Brooks, Adele Mara, Isabel Elsom, Gus Schilling, Larry Parks, Lina Romay, Fidel Castro
Songs: "Dearly Beloved"; "I'm Old Fashioned"; "Shorty George"; "Wedding in the Spring"; "You Were Never Lovelier"
Released: October 1942; 98 minutes

Though its "You-Never" title might indicate a kinship with the previous Fred Astaire-Rita Hayworth *You'll Never Get Rich, You Were Never Lovelier* has a far more romantic theme and score. Based on an Argentinean movie, the film was originally relocated to Rio de Janeiro and titled *Carnival in Rio,* but the setting was switched back to Buenos Aires before shooting began. Actually, with its new innocuous title, lack of local color, and songs by Jerome Kern and Johnny Mercer that avoided Latin American rhythms, the movie could have been set just about anywhere that stylish, affluent people live. The story concerns Fred Astaire as a New York dancer who has gone to Buenos Aires to relax and play the horses. But he quickly loses his money, and is forced to seek employment at a plush hotel owned by Adolphe Menjou. Anxious to have daughter Rita Hayworth show some interest in matrimony, Menjou pens anonymous love letters, accompanied by orchids, and Rita thinks they are from Fred. After the ruse is revealed, Fred wins the lady on his own by appearing under her window as Lochinvar.

Oddly, Astaire had to wait some 35 minutes before the script gave him the chance to show his dancing skills as he auditions for Menjou. "I'm Old Fashioned" (Rita's singing was dubbed by Nan Wynn), and "You Were Never Lovelier," provide accompaniment for two loving, elegant dances by Fred and Rita. Casting note: Among the extras who appeared in the movie was the 15-year-old Fidel Castro.
Curtain Calls ST.   RCA/Columbia VC.

You Were Never Lovelier. Much to the chagrin of Adolphe Menjou, Rita Hayworth insists Fred Astaire is the one who's in love with her.

ROAD TO MOROCCO

Music: James Van Heusen
Lyrics: Johnny Burke
Screenplay: Frank Butler & Don Hartman
Produced by: Paul Jones for Paramount
Directed by: David Butler
Photography: William Mellor
Cast: Bing Crosby, Bob Hope, Dorothy Lamour, Anthony Quinn, Dona
Drake, Vladimir Sokoloff, George Givot, Andrew Tombes, Yvonne
DeCarlo, Dan Seymour, Leon Belasco
Songs: "Road to Morocco"; "Ain't Got a Dime to My Name"; "Constantly";
"Moonlight Becomes You"
Released: October 1942; 83 minutes

(See page 95.)

FOR ME AND MY GAL

Screenplay: Richard Sherman, Fred Finklehoffe, Sid Silvers
Produced by: Arthur Freed for MGM
Directed by: Busby Berkeley
Choreography: Bobby Connolly (Gene Kelly uncredited)
Photography: William Daniels
Cast: Judy Garland, George Murphy, Gene Kelly, Marta Eggerth,
Ben Blue, Richard Quine, Keenan Wynn, Stephen McNally
Songs: "Oh, You Beautiful Doll" (Nat Ayer-Seymour Brown); "For Me and
My Gal" (George Meyer-Edgar Leslie, E. Ray Goetz); "When You
Wore a Tulip" (Percy Wenrich-Jack Mahoney); "After You've Gone"
(Henry Creamoer-Turner Layton); "Till We Meet Again" (Richard
Whiting-Raymond Egan); "Ballin' the Jack" (Chris Smith-Jim Burris)
Released: November 1942; 104 minutes

After Gene Kelly had scored a success as the self-centered, ambitious song-and-dance man in the 1940 Broadway musical *Pal Joey*, it was logical that his first screen assignment would also find him playing a self-centered, ambitious song-and-dance man. This, however, was not the original idea since initially his role of a cocky hoofer in *For Me and My Gal* had been given to George Murphy, with Kelly slated for the lesser role that Murphy—much to his distress—was then forced to accept. The movie was the first in which Judy Garland had a partner other than Mickey Rooney, and her numbers with Kelly—such as their joyous performance of the film's title song—showed great advancement in her dancing ability. As a singer, especially with her rendition of "After You've Gone," she again proved that no one could surpass her in putting across a heart-tugging ballad.

Initially called *The Big Time,* the movie is a sentimental, nostalgic and patriotic show-business saga of vaudevillians Jo Hayden and Harry Palmer who meet and team up in Clifton Junction, Iowa, in 1916, work their way up through tank-town bookings, and two years later get an offer to appear at New York's prestigious Palace theatre. But Harry's dreams of glory are dashed when he gets his draft notice, and, to avoid service, he smashes his hand with the lid of a trunk. Shocked at his cowardice, Jo breaks up the team. ("I'm sorry for you. Terribly, desperately sorry. You'll never make the big time. Because you're small time in your heart.") A remorseful Harry goes overseas to entertain the troops as does Jo; Harry becomes a hero when he stops a convoy of ambulances from going through an ambush, and Jo is hailed as the Sweetheart of the AEF. After the war is over, they have a tearful reunion at—where else?—the Palace.
Sountrak ST.   MGM/UA VC.

Road to Morocco. Bing Crosby, Dorothy Lamour, and Bob Hope.

STAR SPANGLED RHYTHM

Music: Harold Arlen
Lyrics: Johnny Mercer
Screenplay: Harry Tugend
Produced by: Joseph Sistrom for Paramount
Directed by: George Marshall
Choreography: Danny Dare, George Balanchine
Photography: Leo Tover
Cast: Bing Crosby, Bob Hope, Fred MacMurray, Franchot Tone, Ray Milland, Victor Moore, Dorothy Lamour, Paulette Goddard, Vera Zorina, Mary Martin, Dick Powell, Betty Hutton, Eddie Bracken, Veronica Lake, Alan Ladd, Eddie "Rochester" Anderson, William Bendix, Jerry Colonna, Macdonald Carey, Walter Abel, Susan Hayward, Marjorie Reynolds, Dona Drake, Lynne Overman, Johnnie Johnston, Gil Lamb, Cass Daley, Sterling Holloway, Ernest Truex, Katherine Dunham, Arthur Treacher, Walter Catlett, Golden Gate Quartet, Cecil B. DeMille, Preston Sturges,
Songs: "Hit the Road to Dreamland"; "On the Swing Shift"; "I'm Doing It for Defense"; "A Sweater, a Sarong and a Peek-a-boo Bang" "That Old Black Magic"; "Old Glory"
Released: December 1942; 99 minutes

A phenomenon of the World War II years was the star-studded movies that used a slender plot as an excuse to offer a variety of songs and comic sketches. Beginning with *Star Spangled Rhythm*, these films included *Stage Door Canteen*, *Thank Your Lucky Stars*, *Hollywood Canteen*, *Thousands Cheer*, *Two Girls and a Sailor*, and *Follow the Boys*. Another of their ilk, Warners' *Starlift*, came along during the Korean War.

Star Spangled Rhythm benefited from two songs on the Harold Arlen-Johnny Mercer score: "Hit the Road to Dreamland" (introduced on a train by Mary Martin and Dick Powell with the Golden Gate Quartet) and "That Old Black Magic" (sung by soldier Johnnie Johnston and danced to by vision Vera Zorina). As for the plot, it has to do with the efforts of sailor Eddie Bracken and switchboard operator Betty Hutton to pass off studio guard Victor Moore, Bracken's father, as a Paramount executive to impress Bracken's shipmates. *Curtain Calls ST.*

HELLO, FRISCO, HELLO

Screenplay: Robert Ellis, Helen Logan, Richard Macauley
Produced by: Milton Sperling for 20th Century-Fox
Directed by: H. Bruce Humberstone
Choreography: Val Raset
Photography: Charles Clarke, Allen Davey (Technicolor)
Cast: Alice Faye, John Payne, Jack Oakie, Lynn Bari, Laird Cregar, June
Havoc, Ward Bond, George Barbier
Songs: "Hello, Frisco" (Louis Hirsch-Gene Buck); "You'll Never Know"
(Harry Warren-Mack Gordon); "They Always Pick on Me" (Harry
Von Tilzer-Stanley Murphy); "Has Anybody Here Seen Kelly?"
(Charles Moore, C.W. Murphy-William McKenna); "By the Light of
the Silvery Moon" (Gus Edwards-Edward Madden)
Released: March 1943; 98 minutes

After a year and a half absence from the screen, Alice Faye returned to her Lillian Russell
period in *Hello, Frisco, Hello,* a show-business saga costarring her for the fourth and last
time with John Payne (their previous movies together: *Tin Pan Alley, The Great American
Broadcast,* and *Week-End in Havana).* Taking place in the years just prior to MGM's *San
Francisco* (but playing its title song during the credits), the movie tells the story of four
Barbary Coast entertainers, Faye, Payne, Jack Oakie, and June Havoc. Go-getter Payne
manages to acquire enough money to open a successful nightspot, The Grizzly Bear, but
he unwisely marries socialite Lynn Bari, who is the cause of his losing his money, his
nightclub and his singing star. Meanwhile, Miss Faye becomes a favorite in London, then
returns to San Francisco and secretly provides the funds for Payne (now divorced) to
reopen The Grizzly Bear, where the two hold a grand and hopefully permanent reunion.
(The plot is actually a variation on Fox's 1935 musical, *King of Burlesque,* with Miss Faye
and Mr. Oakie in virtually the same roles in both.) Almost all of the songs were period
pieces—though of a slightly later period—with one new ballad, "You'll Never Know," written
specially for the film.
H'wood Soundstage ST.

Hello, Frisco, Hello. Alice Faye and John Payne.

Cabin in the Sky. Ethel Waters (singing "Li'l Black Sheep"), Butterfly McQueen and Eddie "Rochester" Anderson in church.

CABIN IN THE SKY

Music: Vernon Duke*; Harold Arlen**
Lyrics: John Latouche*; E.Y. Harburg**
Screenplay: Joseph Schrank
Produced by: Arthur Freed for MGM
Directed by: Vincente Minnelli
Choreography: (Busby Berkeley uncredited)
Photography: Sidney Wagner
Cast: Ethel Waters, Eddie "Rochester" Anderson, Lena Horne, Louis Armstrong, Duke Ellington Orch., Rex Ingram, Kenneth Spencer, John Bubbles, Ford Buck, Mantan Moreland, Oscar Polk, Willie Best, Butterfly McQueen, Hall Johnson Choir
Songs: "Li'l Black Sheep"***; "Happiness Is a Thing Called Joe"***; "Cabin in the Sky" *; "Taking a Chance on Love" * (lyric with Ted Fetter); "Life's Full of Consequence"***; "Shine"* (Ford Dabney-Cecil Mack); "Honey in the Honeycomb"*
Released: April 1943; 99 minutes

Cabin in the Sky was the first all-black Hollywood musical since Hallelujah in 1929. It also marked the first Hollywood assignment for director Vincente Minnelli, whose career included 16 musicals, all but four for MGM producer Arthur Freed. Adapted from a 1940 Broadway musical with book by Lynn Root, the movie retained two members of the original cast, Ethel Waters (in her only starring role in films) and Rex Ingram. Also retained were three of the 14 songs (including "Taking a Chance on Love"), to which were added three new songs by Harold Arlen and E. Y. Harburg (including "Happiness Is a Thing Called Joe").

In this folkish parable, Little Joe Jackson (Eddie "Rochester" Anderson), a compulsive gambler, is—apparently—killed during a crap game, but his wife Petunia (Waters) prays so hard that the Lord gives Joe six months on earth to redeem himself (similar to the later Carousel). This sets off a struggle for Joe's soul between the Lord's General (Kenneth Spencer) and Lucifer Junior (Ingram), which looks like no contest when the Devil sends seductive Georgia Brown (Lena Horne) to vamp Joe (similar to the later Damn Yankees). However, when Petunia is shot at the Paradise Dancehall, the Lord again shows mercy and lets Joe squeeze through the Pearly Gates. Then—contrary to the play's ending—the whole thing turns out to be a dream.

H'wood Soundstage ST. MGM/UA VC.

Coney Island. George Montgomery registers displeasure at Betty Grable's outfit.

CONEY ISLAND

Music: Ralph Rainger, etc.
Lyrics: Leo Robin, etc.
Screenplay: George Seaton
Produced by: William Perlberg for 20th Century-Fox
Directed by: Walter Lang
Choreography: Hermes Pan
Photography: Ernest Palmer (Technicolor)
Cast: Betty Grable, George Montgomery, Cesar Romero, Charles Winninger, Phil Silvers, Andrew Tombes, Hermes Pan
Songs: "Beautiful Coney Island"; "Put Your Arms Around Me, Honey" (Albert Von Tilzer-Junie McCree); "When Irish Eyes Are Smiling" (Ernest Ball-Chauncey Olcott, George Graff); "Cuddle Up a Little Closer" (Karl Hoschna-Otto Harbach); "Pretty Baby" (Egbert Van Alstyne, Tony Jackson-Gus Kahn); "Miss Lulu from Louisville"; "Take It from There"; "The Darktown Strutters' Ball" (Shelton Brooks); "There's Danger in a Dance"
Released: May 1943; 96 minutes

According to the annual poll of exhibitors, from 1942 to 1951 Betty Grable's name appeared on the list of ten most popular screen performers more often than any other female musical star. In 1943, with *Coney Island* and *Sweet Rosie O'Grady* among the year's biggest boxoffice attractions, the armed forces' favorite pin-up girl ranked No. 1 on the list. The first of the two movies is a turn-of-the-century tale in which the Brooklyn amusement park is depicted as an elaborate midway with sideshows, cabarets and theatres. George Montgomery and Cesar Romero, as battling partners, turn Betty into a major draw at their Ocean Gardens nightspot, but Betty's ambition is to appear at William Hammerstein's Victoria Theatre on Broadway. This, understandably, provokes all sorts of conflicts and misunderstandings until the anticipated happy ending. Only seven years later, Fox remade *Coney Island* as *Wabash Avenue* and simply shifted the story to Chicago in 1892. Miss Grable was on hand to repeat her role, but Victor Mature took over from Montgomery, Phil Harris from Romero, James Barton from Winninger, and Reginald Gardiner from Phil Silvers.

Stormy Weather. Babe Wallace, Lena Horne, and Bill Robinson.

STORMY WEATHER

Screenplay: Frederick Jackson & Ted Koehler
Produced by: William LeBaron for 20th Century-Fox
Directed by: Andrew Stone
Choreography: Clarence Robinson, Nick Castle
Photography: Leon Shamroy, Fred Sersen
Cast: Bill Robinson, Lena Horne, Cab Calloway & Orch., Fats Waller,
       Katherine Dunham Dancers, Nicholas Brothers, Dooley Wilson,
       Flournoy Miller, Ada Brown, Zutty Singleton, Benny Carter, Babe
       Wallace
Songs: "There's No Two Ways About Love" (J.P. Johnson-Ted Koehler);
       "That Ain't Right" (Nat King Cole-Irving Mills); "Ain't Misbehavin'"
       (Fats Waller, Harry Brooks-Andy Razaf); "Diga Diga Doo" (Jimmy
       McHugh-Dorothy Fields); "I Can't Give You Anything but Love"
       (McHugh-Fields); "Geechee Joe" (Cab Calloway); "Stormy
       Weather" (Harold Arlen-Koehler); "My, My, Ain't That Somethin'?"
       (Pinky Tomlin-Harry Tobias)
Released: May 1943; 77 minutes

Forget the story. This show-business saga—something about the pursuit of singer Lena
Horne by tap-dancer Bill Robinson from the end of World War I until they are reunited in
the early forties—is nothing more than a wobbly peg on which to hang a succession of song-
and-dance numbers featuring a stellar array of black talent. Besides Miss Horne (who sang
"Stormy Weather" for the first time in this film) and Robinson (who was given his only
starring role), the picture offers Cab Calloway's exuberant singing, the Nicholas Brothers'
spirited dancing, Fats Waller's zesfful piano playing, and the exciting Katherine Dunham
Dancers in their only screen appearance.
Sountrak ST.   Key VC.

THIS IS THE ARMY

Music & lyrics: Irving Berlin
Screenplay: Casey Robinson & Claude Binyon
Produced by: Jack L. Warner & Hal B. Wallis for Warner Bros.
Directed by: Michael Curtiz
Choreography: LeRoy Prinz, Robert Sidney
Photography: Bert Glennon, Sol Polito (Technicolor)
Cast: George Murphy, Joan Leslie, Ronald Reagan, George Tobias, Alan Hale, Charles Butterworth, Rosemary DeCamp, Dolores Costello, Una Merkel, Ruth Donnelly, Ezra Stone, Julie Oshins, Alan Manson, Earl Oxford, Philip Truex, Irving Berlin, Kate Smith, Joe Louis, Frances Langford, Gertrude Niesen, Victor Moore, Ernest Truex
Songs: "We're on Our Way to France"; "God Bless America"; "This Is the Army, Mr. Jones"; "I'm Getting Tired So I Can Sleep"; "The Army's Made a Man Out of Me"; "How About a Cheer for the Navy?"; "I Left My Heart at the Stage Door Canteen"; "With My Head in the Clouds"; "American Eagles"; "Oh, How I Hate to Get Up in the Morning"; "This Time"
Released: July 1943; 121 minutes

For the screen version of Irving Berlin's celebrated all-soldier revue, *This Is The Army,* Warners retained most of the principals in the original cast and 12 of the 16 songs. For some reason, it was also deemed essential to add a story line. The one devised begins in 1918 when song-and-dance man George Murphy is drafted and puts on an Army show called *Yip, Yip Yaphank* (actually the name of the show Berlin wrote during World War I). In one sequence, replicating a scene from *Alexander's Ragtime Band,* the soldiers grimly sing "We're on Our Way to France" as they march off the stage through the theatre aisles and onto a waiting convoy of transport trucks. Comes World War II and George Murphy's son, Ronald Reagan (are you still with me?), stages another all-soldier show, *This Is The Army,* which makes a special stop in Washington. (Reagan to cast: "You know who's out in front? Our boss, the President of the United States.")

Among the highlights are Kate Smith's stirring "God Bless America" (not part of the original score); the scene at the Stage Door Canteen where theatre luminaries are impersonated by soldiers and where a young GI leaves his heart; and Irving Berlin, in his World War I uniform, singing "Oh, How I Hate to Get Up In The Morning" (though no one troubles to explain who he is or why he is in the show). All the profits of *This Is The Army,* the sixth highest theatre rental musical of the Forties, were assigned to the Army Emergency Relief Fund.
H'wood Soundstage ST. Video Yesteryear VC.

This Is the Army. Irving Berlin singing "Oh, How I Hate to Get Up in the Morning."

THANK YOUR LUCKY STARS

Music: Arthur Schwartz
Lyrics: Frank Loesser
Screenplay: Norman Panama, Melvin Frank, James Kern
Produced by: Mark Hellinger for Warner Bros.
Directed by: David Butler
Choreography: LeRoy Prinz
Photography: Arthur Edeson
Cast: Humphrey Bogart, Eddie Cantor, Bette Davis, Olivia DeHavilland, Errol Flynn, John Garfield, Joan Leslie, Ida Lupino, Dennis Morgan, Ann Sheridan, Dinah Shore, Alexis Smith, Jack Carson, Alan Hale, George Tobias, Edward Everett Horton, S.Z. Sakall, Hattie McDaniel, Ruth Donnelly, Don Wilson, Spike Jones City Slickers, Henry Armetta, Mark Hellinger, David Butler
Songs: "Thank Your Lucky Stars"; "Ridin' for a Fall"; "We're Staying Home Tonight"; "Goin' North"; "Love Isn't Born, It's Made"; "The Dreamer"; "Ice Cold Katie"; "How Sweet You Are"; "That's What You Jolly Well Get"; "They're Either Too Young or Too Old"; "Good Night, Good Neighbor"
Released: August 1943; 131 minutes

Surmounting an inane plot involving three Hollywood hopefuls who get to appear in a star-studded benefit show, *Thank Your Lucky Stars* offered such a rich array of Arthur Schwartz-Frank Loesser songs that it is the most entertaining of all the all-star wartime movies. Of special appeal are the numbers performed by actors not normally associated with song-and-dance routines—Bette Davis lamenting "They're Either Too Young or Too Old," Ann Sheridan offering pragmatic advice that "Love Isn't Born, It's Made," and Errol Flynn mocking his own heroic image in "That's What You Jolly Well Get." One curious aspect of *Thank Your Lucky Stars* is that Eddie Cantor, in a dual role, was willing to portray himself as a talentless, egotistical bully.
Curtain Calls ST. MGM/UA VC.

SWEET ROSIE O'GRADY

Music: Harry Warren
Lyrics: Mack Gordon
Screenplay: Ken Englund
Produced by: William Perlberg for 20th Century-Fox
Directed by: Irving Cummings
Choreography: Hermes Pan
Photography: Ernest Palmer (Technicolor)
Cast: Betty Grable, Robert Young, Adolphe Menjou, Reginald Gardiner, Virginia Grey, Phil Regan, Sig Rumann, Alan Dinehart, Hermes Pan
Songs: "My Heart Tells Me"; "Sweet Rosie O'Grady" (Maude Nugent); "The Wishing Waltz"; "Going to the County Fair"
Released: September 1943; 74 minutes

Following *Coney Island,* Betty Grable again donned bonnet and bustle for her second and equally popular period musical of 1943. The setting is once more New York and Betty is again a song-and-dance performer aspiring to success on Broadway. This time she is Madeline Marlowe who, after stardom in London, returns to her hometown where she had once been a burlesque dancer under her real name of Rosie O'Grady. When nosey *Police Gazette* reporter Sam McGee (Robert Young) tries to get the lowdown, Madeline takes advantage of the situation by appearing in a show called *Sweet Rosie O'Grady.* Oh, yes, star and reporter eventually fall in love. The movie is probably best remembered for the scene in which Betty, covered with soap bubbles, sings "My Heart Tells Me" in a bathtub. In 1950, Warners made *The Daughter of Rosie O'Grady* with June Harver playing both daughter and, in flashback, her mother. It was neither sequel nor successor to the Fox film.

Best Foot Forward. "The Three B's" sung by June Allyson, Gloria DeHaven, and Nancy Walker.

BEST FOOT FORWARD

Music & lyrics: Hugh Martin & Ralph Blane
Screenplay: Irving Brecher & Fred Finklehoffe
Produced by: Arthur Freed for MGM
Directed by: Edward Buzzell
Choreography: Charles Walters
Photography: Leonard Smith (Technicolor)
Cast: Lucille Ball, William Gaxton, Virginia Weidler, Tommy Dix, Nancy Walker, June Allyson, Kenny Bowers, Gloria DeHaven, Beverly Tyler, Chill Wills, Henry O'Neill, Donald MacBride, Harry James Orch.
Songs: "Wish I May Wish I Might"; "Three Men on a Date"; "Ev'ry Time"; "The Three B's"; "Shady Lady Bird"; "My First Promise"; "Alive and Kicking"; "You're Lucky"; "Buckle Down, Winsocki"
Released: October 1943; 95 minutes

When he was a student as a prep school near Philadelphia, playwright John Cecil Holm invited movie star Betty Compson to be his prom date. Though she declined, Holm developed the situation into a 1941 Broadway musical that showed the comic complications that might have ensued had Miss Compson showed up. *Best Foot Forward* was energetically transferred to the screen, with June Allyson and Nancy Walker (in their film debuts) repeating their stage roles, and Tommy Dix elevated from a minor role to the juvenile male lead (but still belting out "Buckle Down, Winsocki"). The movie also retained seven of the original 14 songs (e.g. "Ev'ry Time" and "Shady Lane Bird," though the latter was performed without lyrics), to which were added three new Martin and Blane songs, plus two Harry James specialties. Another change: because of the war, Winsocki Prep was now Winsocki Military Academy.

Columbia's chief Harry Cohn had been the first to bid for the screen rights to of *Best Foot Forward,* in which he planned to star Shirley Temple as the unhappy date whose beau has also invited movie queen Rita Hayworth to the prom where Glenn Miller's orchestra is to supply the music. Part of the deal to ease Arthur Freed's acquisition was MGM's agreement to lend Gene Kelly to Columbia for *Cover Girl.* Though Freed originally wanted Lana Turner, he eventually turned to Lucille Ball (with Martha Mears' singing voice) who gamely played the part of a publicity hungry, slightly faded Hollywood star named Lucille Ball.
MGM/UA VC.

GIRL CRAZY

Music: George Gershwin
Lyrics: Ira Gershwin
Screenplay: Fred Finklehoffe
Produced by: Arthur Freed for MGM
Directed by: Norman Taurog (Busby Berkeley uncredited)
Choreography: Charles Walters, Busby Berkeley
Photography: William Daniels, Robert Planck
Cast: Mickey Rooney, Judy Garland, Tommy Dorsey Orch., Gil Stratton, Robert Strickland, Rags Ragland, June Allyson, Nancy Walker, Guy Kibbee, Henry O'Neill, Charles Walters, Don Taylor, Peter Lawford, Georgia Carroll, Roger Moore
Songs: "Treat Me Rough"; "Bidin' My Time"; "Could You Use Me?"; "Embraceable You"; "Fascinating Rhythm"; "But Not for Me"; "I Got Rhythm "
Released: November 1943; 99 minutes

The Mickey Rooney-Judy Garland *Strike Up The Band* had used nothing more than the title and the title song from George and Ira Gershwin's 1930 Broadway musical. However, in *Girl Crazy,* based on another Gershwin musical of the same year, the youthful team got to perform six of the original 14 numbers plus an additional Gershwin piece, "Fascinating Rhythm," with Rooney at the piano backed by Tommy Dorsey's orchestra. Even more unusual, the screenplay actually bears a passing resemblance to the Guy Bolton-John McGowan original story. In something of a genetic reversal of *Too Many Girls,* the tale concerns playboy Danny Churchill (Rooney) who, to avoid predatory females, is sent West by his father to the all-male Cody College of Mines and Agriculture, where he meets and falls in love with the local postmistress, Ginger Gray (Garland). As a finale, of course, the kids get to put on their own show—really a humongous Busby Berkeley creation—though this time it's not to advance their careers but to save the debt ridden college from closing its doors. Musical highlights: Judy's sly rendition of "Bidin' My Time" and the roughhouse duet, "Could You Use Me?"

There were two other screen versions of *Girl Crazy.* In 1934 RKO filmed the first one with Bert Wheeler and Robert Woolsey; in 1965, MGM filmed it again under the title *When the Boys Meet the Girls.* It featured Connie Francis, Harve Presnell, Louis Armstrong, Liberace, and Herman's Hermits.
DRG (Garland, Rooney LP); H'wood Soundstage ST. MGM/UA VC.

Girl Crazy. Busby Berkeley's "I Got Rhythm" finale with Mickey Rooney, Judy Garland, and Tommy Dorsey's Orchestra.

THE GANG'S ALL HERE

Music: Harry Warren
Lyrics: Leo Robin
Screenplay: Walter Bullock
Produced by: William LeBaron for 20th Century-Fox
Director-choreographer: Busby Berkeley
Photography: Edward Cronjager (Technicolor)
Cast: Alice Faye, Carmen Miranda, Phil Baker, Benny Goodman Orch.,
Eugene Pallette, Charlotte Greenwood, Edward Everett Horton,
Tony DeMarco, James Ellison, Sheila Ryan, June Haver, Jeanne
Crain, Leon Belasco, Frank Faylen
Songs: "Minnie's in the Money"; "The Lady in the Tutti-Frutti Hat"; "A
Journey to a Star"; "No Love, No Nothin'"; "Paducah"; "The Polka
Dot Polka"
Released: November 1943; 103 minutes

Busby Berkeley's first Technicolor musical offered him the chance to let his imagination run
riot with two surrealistic fantasies masquerading as nightclub production numbers—"The
Lady in the Tutti-Frutti Hat" (Carmen Miranda, hundreds of waving bananas, and kaleidoscopic patterns) and "The Polka Dot Polka" (Alice Faye and psychedelic color designs).
The Gang's All Here (a meaningless title that was changed in the United Kingdom to the
equally meaningless *The Girls He Left Behind)* focuses on the romance between a showgirl
at the Club New Yorker (Faye) who is elevated to featured attraction (singing "No Love, No
Nothin' "), and her romance with a well-heeled handsome soldier (James Ellison). The film
marked Miss Faye's last musical in a starring role until she returned 19 years later in Fox's
remake of *State Fair.*
Classic Intl. ST.

The Gang's All Here. Carmen Miranda performing "The Lady in the Tutti-Frutti Hat" at the
Club New Yorker.

UP IN ARMS

Music: Harold Arlen, etc.
Lyrics: Ted Koehler, etc.
Screenplay: Don Hartman, Allen Boretz, Robert Pirosh
Produced by: Samuel Goldwyn (released by RKO Radio)
Directed by: Elliott Nugent
Choreography: Danny Dare
Photography: Ray Rennahan (Technicolor)
Cast: Danny Kaye, Dinah Shore, Dana Andrews, Constance Dowling, Louis Calhern, George Mathews, Benny Baker, Lyle Talbot, Walter Catlett, Elisha Cook Jr., Margaret Dumont, Virginia Mayo
Songs: "Theatre Lobby Number" (Sylvia Fine-Max Liebman); "Now I Know"; "All Out for Freedom"; "Tess's Torch Song"; "Melody in 4-F" (Fine-Liebman)
Released: February 1944; 106 minutes

With some 80 releases, 1944 was Hollywood's peak year for movie musicals. *Up In Arms,* the year's first major production, was Danny Kaye's feature-film debut and the first of six musicals the comedian made for producer Samuel Goldwyn. In a role supposedly based on the character Eddie Cantor had played in Goldwyn's *Whoopee* (but actually closer to the Jerry Lewis misfits of a decade later), Kaye is seen as a hypochondriacal sad sack who gets drafted and eventually becomes a hero by capturing 20 Japanese soldiers on a Pacific island. The film gave Kaye ample leeway to indulge in some spastic mugging, disguise his voice with a Scottish burr, go through a mad jitterbug routine, speak in gibberish Japanese, and perform two of his favorite specialty numbers, a tongue-twisting patter description of a typical movie and a scat-sung saga of a draftee.
Sountrak ST. Nelson VC.

GOING MY WAY

Music: James Van Heusen, etc.
Lyrics: Johnny Burke, etc.
Screenplay: Frank Butler & Frank Cavett
Produced by: Leo McCarey for Paramount
Directed by: Leo McCarey
Photography: Lionel Lindon
Cast: Bing Crosby, Risë Stevens, Barry Fitzgerald, Frank McHugh, Jean Heather, Gene Lockhart, William Frawley, Stanley Clements, Carl Switzer, Adeline DeWalt Reynolds
Songs: "The Day After Forever"; "Silent Night" (Franz Gruber); "Too-Ra-Loo-Ra-Loo-Ral" (J.B. Shannon); "Habanera" (Bizet); "Going My Way"; "Ave Maria" (Schubert); "Swinging on a Star"
Released: February 1944; 130 minutes

According to the nation's exhibitors' annual poll, beginning in 1934 Bing Crosby was one of the ten most popular screen actors for 15 years, the longest period of any musical star. Moreover, Crosby held the No. 1 position from 1944 through 1948. The film that assured him that place of honor in 1944 was *Going My Way,* an unconventional musical that was one of the most successful attractions of the year. Its origin began with director Leo McCarey, who persuaded Crosby to take the part of a regular-guy parish priest despite the actor's qualms that he would not be accepted in such a role. In the story, Crosby's Father Chuck O'Malley finds himself frequently at odds with Barry Fitzgerald's crusty, authoritarian Father Fitzgibbon, his superior at St. Dominick's Church, whom he has been sent to supervise without the older man's knowledge. In the sentimental ending, Fitsgibbon is reunited at Christmas with his 90-year-old mother (Adeline DeWalt Reynolds), whom O'Malley and an opera-star friend (Risë Stevens) had arranged to fly over from Ireland.

The Bells of St. Mary's, made at RKO the following year, offered a similar tale in which Crosby again played Chuck O'Malley under McCarey's direction, and with Ingrid Bergman as the initially antagonistic Sister Superior of a parochial school. Crosby and Fitgerald were also teamed in Paramount's 1947 release, *Welcome Stranger,* though this time they were battling doctors.
MCA (Crosby CD). MCA VC.

Cover Girl. Gene Kelly and Rita Hayworth.

COVER GIRL

Music: Jerome Kern
Lyrics: Ira Gershwin
Screenplay: Virginia Van Upp (Sidney Buchman uncredited)
Produced by: Arthur Schwartz for Columbia
Directed by: Charles Vidor
Choreography: Val Raset, Seymour Felix (Gene Kelly, Stanley Donen uncredited)
Photography: Rudolph Maté, Allen Davey (Technicolor)
Cast: Rita Hayworth, Gene Kelly, Lee Bowman, Phil Silvers, Jinx Falkenburg, Leslie Brooks, Eve Arden, Otto Kruger, Jess Barker, Anita Colby, Edward Brophy, Thurston Hall, Shelley Winters, Curt Bois
Songs: "Sure Thing"; "Make Way for Tomorrow" (lyric with E.Y. Harburg); "Put Me to the Test"; "Long Ago and Far Away"; "Cover Girl"
Released: March 1944; 107 minutes

Though Gene Kelly is primarily associated with a series of landmark musicals at MGM, it was at Columbia that he first got the chance to show his range both as dancer and choreographer. Actually, Kelly was last-minute choice to costar with Rita Hayworth in *Cover Girl* since Columbia's boss, Harry Cohn, initially tried to find a suitable actor already under contract (among them Larry Parks). When that failed, Cohn reluctantly agreed to borrow Kelly from MGM, despite his misgivings that the actor was too short for Hayworth. The movie tells the tale of Rusty Parker (Hayworth, with her singing dubbed by Martha Mears), an ambitious dancer in a Brooklyn nightclub owned by her beau, Danny McGuire (Kelly). Rusty gets the chance to be a cover girl because *Vanity* magazine publisher (Otto Kruger) finds that she is not only the granddaughter of the girl he had loved and lost but also— since she is played, in flashback, by Miss Hayworth—her spit and image. After a taste of the glamorous life, Rusty happily and predictably returns to Brooklyn and to Danny.

Cover Girl was the first of Kelly's three films (the others were *Singing' in the Rain* and *It's Always Fair Weather*) to feature a solo street dance. Here it was the "alter-ego" number, a purely cinematic creation in which Kelly moodily dances with his own image to reveal two sides of his personality. Another street dance, the joyous "Make Way for Tomorrow" performed with Miss Hayworth and Phil Silvers, has the trio cavort down a Brooklyn street that obligingly furnishes them with such props as garbage-can lids, a mailbox, and a brownstone stoop.
Curtain Calls ST. RCA/Columbia VC.

TWO GIRLS AND A SAILOR

Screenplay: Richard Connell & Gladys Lehman
Produced by: Joe Pasternak for MGM
Directed by: Richard Thorpe
Choreography: Sammy Lee
Photography: Robert Surtees
Cast: June Allyson, Gloria DeHaven, Van Johnson, Tom Drake, Jimmy Durante, Lena Horne, Carlos Ramirez, Harry James Orch., Helen Forrest, Xavier Cugat Orch., Lina Romay, Jose Iturbi, Amparo Iturbi, Virginia O'Brien, Gracie Allen, Albert Coates, Ben Blue, Frank Jenks, Henry Stephenson, Henry O'Neill, Ava Gardner
Songs & instrumentals: "Sweet and Lovely" (Gus Arnheim-Jules Lemare, Harry Tobias); "A-Tisket A-Tasket" (Ella Fitzgerald-Van Alexander); "A Love Like Ours" (Mann Holiner-Alberta Nichols); "Granada" (Agustin Lara); "My Mother Told Me" (Jimmy McHugh-Ralph Freed); "Take It Easy" (Albert DeBru, Vic Mizzy-Irving Taylor); "Concerto for Index Finger"; "In a Moment of Madness" (McHugh-Freed); "Young Man With a Horn" (George Stoll-Freed); "Inka Dinka Doo" (Jimmy Durante-Ben Ryan); "Ritual Fire Dance" (Falla); "Paper Doll" (John Black)
Released: April 1944; 124 minutes

Another star-filled wartime entertainment, *Two Girls and a Sailor* was about two sisters, June Allyson and Gloria DeHaven, who succeed as a double act in both vaudeville and nightclubs. With the anonymous help of sailor Van Johnson, they become owners of a huge warehouse which they turn into a servicemen's canteen (run by ex-vaudevillian Jimmy Durante). Among those who show up to entertain: Xavier Cugat, Lina Romay, and Virginia O'Brien ("Take It Easy"), Gracie Allen ("Concerto for Index Finger"), Harry James ("Young Man With A Horn"), José and Amparo Iturbi (Falla's "Ritual Fire Dance"), and Lena Horne ("Paper Doll").
MGM/UA VC.

CAN'T HELP SINGING

Music: Jerome Kern
Lyrics: E.Y. Harburg
Screenplay: Lewis Foster & Frank Ryan
Produced by: Felix Jackson for Universal
Directed by: Frank Ryan
Photography: Woody Bredell, W. Howard Greene (Technicolor)
Cast: Deanna Durbin, Robert Paige, Akim Tamiroff, Leonid Kinskey, David Bruce, Thomas Gomez
Songs: "Can't Help Singing"; "Elbow Room"; "Any Moment Now"; "More and More"; "Californ-i-ay"
Released: December 1944; 89 minutes

Attempting to capitalize on the fame of Broadway's *Oklahoma!* (which would also influence *The Harvey Girls* two years later), *Can't Help Singing* was a musical celebration of the American pioneer spirit. It brought together Universal's reigning diva, Deanna Durbin, with composer Jerome Kern and lyricist E. Y. Harburg (in their only collaboration), and it even gave Miss Durbin a male singer, Robert Paige, to share the duets. Though the story, set in 1847, about a senator's daughter who finds love on a wagon train heading for Sonora, California, was as lumbering as the wagons, the score offered Miss Durbin the best original songs of any in her career. They include the lilting title song (sung by both leads in outdoor wooden bathtubs separated by a wall); the wistful "Any Moment Now," sung near the Grand Canyon; the romantically revelatory "More and More"; and the rollicking, waltzing ode to "Californ-i-ay", where "The hills have more splendor, the girls have more gender."

MEET ME IN ST. LOUIS

Music & lyrics: Hugh Martin & Ralph Blane, etc.
Screenplay: Irving Brecher & Fred Finklehoffe
Produced by: Arthur Freed for MGM
Directed by: Vincente Minnelli
Choreography: Charles Walters
Photography: George Folsey (Technicolor)
Cast: Judy Garland, Margaret O'Brien, Mary Astor, Lucille Bremer, Leon Ames, Tom Drake, Marjorie Main, Harry Davenport, June Lockhart, Hugh Marlowe, Chill Wills, Darryl Hickman, Joan Carroll, Henry Daniels Jr.
Songs: "Meet Me in St. Louis, Louis" (Kerry Mills-Andrew Sterling); "The Boy Next Door"; " Under the Bamboo Tree" (J. Rosamond Johnson-Bob Cole); "The Trolley Song"; "You and I" (Nacio Herb Brown-Arthur Freed); "Have Yourself a Merry Little Christmas"
Released: December 1944; 113 minutes

A leisurely, affectionate view of a turn-of-the-century upper middle-class family, with little action or conflict, *Meet Me In St. Louis* was made into one of Metro's most acclaimed and successful musicals, second only to *Gone With the Wind* as the studio's highest grossing film up to that time. The movie originated as a series of short stories that Sally Benson had written for *The New Yorker* magazine based on her recollections of growing up in a large St. Louis family. On screen, the Smith family consists of father Alonzo (Leon Ames) and mother Anna (Mary Astor), two teenage daughters, Rose (Lucille Bremer) and Esther (Judy Garland), two younger daughters, Agnes (Joan Carroll) and Tootie (Margaret O'Brien), one teenage son, Lon Jr. (Henry Daniels Jr.), one grandfather (Harry Davenport), and one maid (Marjorie Main).

The movie is divided into four sections, each covering a season during a yearlong period from 1903 to 1904, and each preceded by a sepia-tinted picture-card view (with appropriate filigree border) of the Smith family's American Gothic house at 5135 Kensington Avenue. Summer finds the family prematurely singing of meeting at the St. Louis Fair (which would not open until the following spring), and reveals Esther's feelings about the boy next door (played by Tom Drake in a part intended for Van Johnson). Autumn covers Tootie's frightening experience on Halloween, a sequence that was almost cut from the film. Winter takes up the vexing problem of who will escort whom to a Christmas dance and the crushing news that father has been offered another position in his firm's New York office (which, to the relief of his family, he eventually declines). Spring shows the happy Smith clan on the opening day of the Fair. And that, more or less, was that.

Though the movie had been written with Judy Garland in mind as Esther, the actress had to be talked into doing it because, at 21, she felt she was ready for more adult roles. The songs by Hugh Martin and Ralph Blane yielded three standards—"The Boy Next Door" (with a lyric that manages to include two cumbersome addresses, 5133 and 5135 Kensington Avenue), "The Trolley Song," and "Have Yourself a Merry Little Christmas" (whose lyric was changed, at Miss Garland's urging, to make it a song of hope rather than despair). Authentic period pieces were also used, with "Under the Bamboo Tree" serving for a memorable Garland-O'Brien cakewalk. In 1989 the movie was adapted as a Broadway musical.

Following *Meet Me In St. Louis,* other screen musicals sought to capture the home-and-hearth spirit of American family life. Fox came up with both *State Fair,* about the Frake family of Brunswick, Iowa, and *Centennial Summer,* about the Rogers family of Philadelphia during the Centennial Exposition of 1876. Paramount's *Isn't It Romantic?* was concerned with the Camerons of Blakesville, Indiana. MGM followed up with *Summer Holiday,* about the Millers of Danville, Connecticut, which even offered a successor to "The Trolley Song" in "The Stanley Steamer" (again with a lyric by Ralph Blane). And Warner Bros. released *On Moonlight Bay* and its sequel *By the Light of the Silvery Moon,* with Leon Ames once more playing the paterfamilias, this time of the Winfields of Indiana.
AEI (Garland LP). MGM/UA VC.

Meet Me in St. Louis. Margaret O'Brien and Judy Garland strutting through the cakewalk number, "Under the Bamboo Tree."

RHAPSODY IN BLUE

Music: George Gershwin
Lyrics: Ira Gershwin, etc.
Screenplay: Howard Koch & Elliot Paul
Produced by: Jesse L. Lasky for Warner Bros.
Directed by: Irving Rapper
Choreography: LeRoy Prinz
Photography: Sol Polito
Cast: Robert Alda, Joan Leslie, Alexis Smith, Charles Coburn, Julie Bishop, Albert Basserman, Morris Carnovsky, Rosemary DeCamp, Herbert Rudley, Al Jolson, Paul Whiteman Orch., Oscar Levant, George White, Hazel Scott, Anne Brown, Tom Patricola, Johnny Downs, Andrew Tombes, Odette Myrtil, Mark Stevens
Songs & Instrumentals: "Swanee" (Irving Caesar); "Somebody Loves Me" (B.G.DeSylva, Ballard Macdonald); "Oh, Lady Be Good"; "Rhapsody in Blue"; "The Man I Love"; "Clap Yo' Hands"; "Fascinating Rhythm"; "Embraceable You"; "An American in Paris"; "Mine"; "Summertime" (DuBose Heyward); "Love Walked In"; "Piano Concerto in F"
Released: June 1945; 139 minutes

Having succeeded so well with the fictitious George M. Cohan biography, *Yankee Doodle Dandy,* Warners followed it up with a fictitious biography of a later and more accomplished Broadway composer, George Gershwin, with newcomer Robert Alda in the part. Retained from the Cohan movie were Rosemary DeCamp, who had played Cohan's Irish-American mother, to play Gershwin's Jewish mother, and Joan Leslie again to play the love interest. Lending a certain authenticity to the proceedings were appearances by people associated with the composer's career, such as Al Jolson (singing "Swanee"), Broadway producer George White, Paul Whiteman (conducting "Rhapsody in Blue"), song-and-dance man Tom Patricola (singing "Somebody Loves Me"), *Porgy and Bess* star Anne Brown (singing "Summertime"), and Oscar Levant (playing the "Piano Concerto in F"). Still, for whatever reason, most of the songs were entrusted to Miss Leslie (whose vocals were dubbed by Louanne Hogan) and Hazel Scott. While the story may have been plodding and banal, the movie did offer enough musical riches—some 24 pieces from "Swanee" to "Love Walked In"—to win *Rhapsody in Blue* a place among the most popular musicals of the year.

ANCHORS AWEIGH

Music: Jule Styne, etc.
Lyrics: Sammy Cahn, etc.
Screenplay: Isobel Lennart
Produced by: Joe Pasternak for MGM
Directed by: George Sidney
Choreography: Gene Kelly
Photography: Robert Planck, Charles Boyle (Technicolor)
Cast: Frank Sinatra, Kathryn Grayson, Gene Kelly, José Iturbi, Dean
Stockwell, Pamela Britton, Carlos Ramirez, Leon Ames, Rags
Ragland, Edgar Kennedy, Henry O'Neill, Henry Armetta, Billy
Gilbert, Grady Sutton, Harry Barris
Songs: "I Begged Her"; "Jealousy" (Jacob Gade-Vera Bloom); "What
Makes the Sunset?"; "All of a Sudden My Heart Sings" (Herpin-
Harold Rome); "The Charm of You"; "I Fall in Love Too Easily";
"Waltz Serenade" (Tschaikowsky-Earl Brent)
Released: July 1945;140 minutes

Frank Sinatra may have been the singing rage of the mid-Forties, but RKO's *Higher and Higher* and *Step Lively,* his first two starring films, caused no box office stampede. He did considerably better at MGM, particularly in the three musicals he made with Gene Kelly—*Anchors Aweigh, Take Me Out to the Ball Game,* and *On the Town*—with the first establishing the characters of the girl-shy Frank and the girl-chasing Gene that they would play in their subsequent films together. In *Anchors Aweigh,* following the pattern of *Follow the Fleet, Born to Dance,* and *The Fleet's In,* they are sailors on leave. This time the locale is Hollywood, where they meet singing hopeful Kathryn Grayson and try to get her an audition with Metro's reigning maestro, José Iturbi. Kelly is paired with Grayson and Sinatra finds the perfect girl for him (Pamela Britton) because she too is from Brooklyn.

Kelly's most ambitious dance specialty was "The King Who Couldn't Dance." For the second time on screen (the first was Disney's *The Three Caballeros*), live action was combined with animated cartoon characters—principally Jerry the Mouse—a feat achieved by synchronizing 10,000 painted frames to Kelly's dance movements. One of the year's leading moneymakers, *Anchors Aweigh* was the first musical to cost over $2 million. *Curtain Calls ST. MGM/UA VC.*

Anchors Aweigh. Frank Sinatra and Gene
Kelly's "I Begged Her" routine performed in
a Los Angeles servicemen's dorm.

STATE FAIR

Music: Richard Rodgers
Lyrics & screenplay: Oscar Hammerstein II
Produced by: William Perlberg for 20th Century-Fox
Directed by: Walter Lang
Photography: Leon Shamroy (Technicolor)
Cast: Jeanne Crain, Dana Andrews, Dick Haymes, Vivian Blaine, Charles Winninger, Fay Bainter, Donald Meek, Frank McHugh, Percy Kilbride, Harry Morgan, William Marshall
Songs: "Our State Fair"; "It Might as Well Be Spring"; "It's a Grand Night for Singing"; "That's for Me"; "Isn't It Kinda Fun?"; "All I Owe Ioway"
Released: August 1945; 100 minutes

State Fair was the first "family" musical to come along after Meet Me In St. Louis. As in the previous film, the title song was used to introduce some of the principal characters by having them express anticipation about going to the forthcoming fair. But State Fair was less of a rustic St Louis than a modern, midwestern Oklahoma!, since the second collaboration of Rodgers and Hammerstein—and their only original screen musical—contained the same sort of bucolic flavor and homespun good humor as did their initial trailblazing musical.

The movie is about the Frake family of Brunswick, Iowa, consisting of farmer Abel (Charles Winninger), his wife Melissa (Fay Bainter), and their children, the restless, spring feverish Margy (Jeanne Crain, with her singing dubbed by Louanne Hogan) and the serious, clean-cut Wayne (Dick Haymes). At the fair, Margy finds true love with newspaper reporter Pat Gilbert (Dana Andrews), Wayne is temporarily smitten by band singer Emily Edwards (Viviane Blaine), Melissa wins first prize for her mince pie, and Abel's pet boar, Blue Bell, wins the blue ribbon. And then they go home.

Fox had previously made a nonmusical adaptation of Phil Stong's novel in 1933. Will Rogers, Louise Dresser, Janet Gaynor, and Norman Foster were the Frakes, and Sally Eilers and Lew Ayres showed up at the fair. The musical State Fair was remade in 1962, with José Ferrer directing. This time, taking advantage of CinemaScope, the Frakes were moved to Texas and to the Dallas State Fair. The family was made up of Tom Ewell, Alice Faye, Pamela Tiffin (Anita Gordon supplied the singing), and Pat Boone. Bobby Darin and Ann-Margret provided romantic distractions. Five of the six original songs were retained, with five new ones—both words and music—by Richard Rodgers.

Classic Intl. ST (1945); Dot ST (1962). CBS/Fox VC (1945); CBS/Fox VC (1962).

State Fair. Jeanne Crain and Dana Andrews.

THE DOLLY SISTERS

Screenplay: John Larkin & Marian Spitzer
Produced by: George Jessel for 20th Century-Fox
Directed by: Irving Cummings
Choreography: Seymour Felix
Photography: Ernest Palmer (Technicolor)
Cast: Betty Grable, John Payne, June Haver, S. Z. Sakall, Reginald Gardiner, Frank Latimore, Gene Sheldon, Sig Rumann, Lester Allen, Andre Charlot, Mae Marsh
Songs: "I Can't Begin to Tell You" (James Monaco-Mack Gordon); "Give Me the Moonlight, Give Me the Girl" (Albert Von Tilzer-Lew Brown); "Carolina in the Morning" (Walter Donaldson-Gus Kahn); "Powder, Lipstick and Rouge" (Harry Revel-Gordon); "I'm Always Chasing Rainbows" (Harry Carroll-Joseph McCarthy); "Darktown Strutters' Ball" (Shelton Brooks); "The Sidewalks of New York" (James Blake-Charles Lawlor)
Released: September 1945; 114 minutes

Hungarian-born Jennie and Rosie Dolly (née Janszieka and Roszika Deutsch) were dark-haired, dark-complexioned identical twins who danced their way from headliners in vaudeville to the *Ziegfeld Follies of 1911* and other entertainments on Broadway and throughout Europe. On screen, they were portrayed by blonde, all-American Betty Grable and June Haver (who inherited her part when Alice Faye refused to come out of retirement). Their song-and-dance routines compensated for the bland, fictitious tale that held the musical numbers together, and were the main reason why the movie showed up among the most popular musicals of the year. The film marked the fourth and final appearance together of Miss Grable and leading man John Payne (their previous three movies: *Tin Pan Alley, Footlight Serenade,* and *Springtime in the Rockies*).
Classic Intl. ST.

ROAD TO UTOPIA

Music: James Van Heusen
Lyrics: Johnny Burke
Screenplay: Norman Panama & Melvin Frank
Produced by: Paul Jones for Paramount
Directed by: Hal Walker
Choreography: Danny Dare
Photography: Lionel Linden
Cast: Bing Crosby, Bob Hope, Dorothy Lamour, Robert Benchley, Hillary Brooke, Douglass Dumbrille, Jack LaRue, Robert Barrat, Ferdinand Munier, Nestor Paiva
Songs: "Sunday, Monday or Always"; "Goodtime Charlie"; "It's Anybody's Spring"; "Personality"; "Welcome to My Dream"; "Put It There, Pal"; "Would You?"
Released: December 1945; 90 minutes

(See page 95.)

ZIEGFELD FOLLIES

Sketches: Harry Tugend, George White, Billy K. Wells, David Freedman
Produced by: Arthur Freed for MGM
Directed by: Vincente Minnelli, also George Sidney, Robert Lewis, Lemuel
       Ayers, Roy Del Ruth
Choreography: Robert Alton, also Eugene Loring, Charles Walters (Fred
       Astaire, Gene Kelly uncredited)
Photography: George Folsey, Charles Rosher (Technicolor)
Cast: Fred Astaire, Lucille Ball, Lucille Bremer, Fanny Brice, Judy Garland,
       Kathryn Grayson, Lena Horne, Gene Kelly, James Melton, Victor
       Moore, Red Skelton, Esther Williams, William Powell, Edward Arnold,
       Marion Bell, Bunin's Puppets, Cyd Charisse, Hume Cronyn, William
       Frawley, Robert Lewis, Virginia O'Brien, Keenan Wynn, Grady Sutton,
       Eugene Loring
Songs: "Here's to the Girls" (Roger Edens-Ralph Freed); "Libiamo ne' lieti
       calici" (Verde-Piave); "This Heart of Mine" (Harry Warren-Arthur
       Freed); "Love" (Hugh Martin-Ralph Blane); "Limehouse Blues"
       (Philip Braham-Douglas Furber); "Madame Crematon" (Edens-Kay
       Thompson); "The Babbitt and the Bromide" (George Gershwin-
       Ira Gershwin)
Released: January 1946; 110 minutes

Not since the early days of the talkies had a studio attempted a movie that would adhere to the traditionally plotless format of the Broadway revue, and not since *Ziegfeld Follies* has one been attempted. Arthur Freed's dream of producing a purely cinematic revue inspired by the legendary Ziegfeld productions had been germinating for a number of years, during which time some 17 songs or sketches were eliminated (enough material for *a Ziegfeld Follies II!*). Of the stellar cast, only Fanny Brice had ever been in a *Follies* on Broadway, and her sketch, "The Sweepstakes Ticket," had originated in a *Follies* that came along four years after the impresario's death. As prologue, Ziegfeld (played by William Powell, who had starred in *The Great Ziegfeld)* is shown in Heaven planning a new revue. Among the musical highlights were three involving Fred Astaire—the elegant "This Heart of Mine" with Lucille Bremer, the melodramatic "Limehouse Blues" again with Miss Bremer, and the high-spirited "Babbitt and the Bromide" with Gene Kelly.
Curtain Calls ST. MGM/UA VC.

Ziegfeld Follies. Fred Astaire and Lucille Bremer in the "Limehouse Blues" sequence.

The Harvey Girls. Judy Garland shows her bravery though Stephen McNally and Angela Lansbury seem sceptical.

THE HARVEY GIRLS

Music: Harry Warren
Lyrics: Johnny Mercer
Screenplay: Edmund Beloin, Nathaniel Curtis, Samson Raphaelson
Produced by: Arthur Freed for MGM
Directed by: George Sidney
Choreography: Robert Alton
Photography: George Folsey (Technicolor)
Cast: Judy Garland, John Hodiak, Ray Bolger, Angela Lansbury, Preston Foster, Virginia O'Brien, Kenny Baker, Cyd Charisse, Marjorie Main, Chill Wills, Selena Royle, Stephen McNally
Songs: "In the Valley Where the Evening Sun Goes Down"; "Wait and See"; "On the Atchison, Topeka and the Santa Fe"; "It's a Great Big World", "The Wild Wild West"
Released: January 1946; 104 minutes

According to *The Harvey Girls,* the Harvey girls brought civilization—i.e., spotless silverware, crumbless napery, and chastity—to America's lawless frontier in the 1880s. The movie also brought Susan Bradley (Judy Garland), to Sandrock, New Mexico, where she joins the waitresses of Fred Harvey's restaurant chain, which Harvey established to provide reputable eating places for train passengers traveling through the disreputable West. Susan and her co-workers quickly come in conflict with the girls of the Alhambra saloon, led by Em (Angela Lansbury with the singing voice of Virginia Reese), and its co-owners, the villainous Sam Purvis (Preston Foster) and the more straightforward Ned Trent (John Hodiak). Fearful of the competition, Purvis has the Harvey building set on fire. He is given a sound thrashing by Trent who, not unexpectedly, is the only man for whom Susan will soon be preparing breakfast.

Though MGM had originally planned to film the Samuel Hopkins Adams story as a nonmusical with Lana Turner, producer Arthur Freed turned it into a musical for two reasons: the success of Rodgers and Hammerstein's *Oklahoma!,* and the chance it gave to star Judy Garland in a different kind of American saga after *Meet Me In St. Louis.* In the flavorsome score was the rousing "On the Atchison, Topeka and the Santa Fe," used for the scene welcoming the Harvey girls as they arrive on Engine Number 49 on its way from Philadel-phi-ay to Californ-i-ay.
AEI (Garland LP); H'wood Soundstage ST. MGM/UA VC.

CENTENNIAL SUMMER

Music: Jerome Kern
Lyrics: Leo Robin, etc.
Screenplay: Michael Kanin
Producer-director: Otto Preminger for 20th Century-Fox
Choreography: Dorothy Fox
Photography: Ernest Palmer (Technicolor)
Cast: Jeanne Crain, Cornel Wilde, Linda Darnell, William Eythe, Walter
Brennan, Constance Bennett, Dorothy Gish, Kathleen Howard,
Barbara Whiting, Larry Stevens, Avon Long, Charles Dingle
Songs: "The Right Romance"; "Up With the Lark"; "In Love in Vain"; "All
Through the Day" (lyric: Oscar Hammerstein II); "Cinderella Sue"
(lyric: E. Y. Harburg)
Released: May 1946; 102 minutes

Jerome Kern's last score, either for stage or screen, was composed for *Centennial Summer,* a rather blatant attempt to cash in on the success of both *Meet Me In St. Louis* and *State Fair* (Jeanne Crain was again playing the lovesick daughter, with Louanne Hogan again dubbing her singing). Once more we have a closely knit family—the Rogerses of Philadelphia—and once more the story has to do with a fair, this time the Centennial Exposition honoring the 100th anniversary of the Declaration of Independence. But the crises of the plot were even more trying on audiences than they were on the family, and the film's pleasures were largely reserved for the songs, among them the daydreaming ballad, "All Through the Day," performed as a demonstration of magic lantern slides.
Classic Intl. ST.

NIGHT AND DAY

Music & lyrics: Cole Porter
Screenplay: Charles Hoffman, Leo Townsend, William Bowers
Produced by: Arthur Schwartz for Warner Bros.
Directed by: Michael Curtiz
Choreography: LeRoy Prinz
Photography: J. Peverell Marley, William Skall (Technicolor)
Cast: Cary Grant, Alexis Smith, Monty Woolley, Ginny Simms, Mary Martin,
Jane Wyman, Eve Arden, Victor Francen, Alan Hale, Dorothy Malone,
Selena Royle, Donald Woods, Henry Stephenson, Paul Cavanaugh,
Sig Rumann, Carlos Ramirez, Milada Mladova, Herman Bing, Mel Tormé
Songs: "In the Still of the Night"; "Old Fashioned Garden"; "Let's Do It";
"You Do Something to Me"; "Miss Otis Regrets"; "What Is This Thing
Called Love?"; "I've Got You Under My Skin"; "Night and Day"; "It
Was Just One of Those Things"; "You're the Top"; "I Get a Kick Out
of You"; "My Heart Belongs to Daddy"; "Begin the Beguine"
Released: July 1946; 128 minutes

Warners' treatment of the life of Broadway composer-lyricist Cole Porter (with Cary Grant in the part) was similar to its treatment of the life of George Gershwin in *Rhapsody in Blue* the previous year. (Alexis Smith, who had played one of Gershwin's passing fancies, even showed up as Porter's wife.) The aim was simply to offer a procession of well-known songs—21 in all—ranging from throbbing, minor-key ballads ("Night and Day," Begin the Beguine") to witty comic numbers ("Let's Do It," "You're the Top") held together by a totally fabricated account of the songwriter's life. Monty Woolley and Mary Martin (she introduced "My Heart Belongs to Daddy") were the only Porter associates to appear in the film. Most of the numbers were sung by Jane Wyman and Ginny Sims, the latter playing a singer who apparently starred in just about every one of the composer's shows. Like *Rhapsody in Blue,* *Night and Day* turned out to be a box office—if not critical—success.
Motion Pic. Tracks ST. MGM/UA VC.

THREE LITTLE GIRLS IN BLUE

Music: Josef Myrow
Lyrics: Mack Gordon
Screenplay: Valentine Davies
Produced by: Mack Gordon for 20th Century-Fox
Directed by: H. Bruce Humberstone
Choreography: Seymour Felix
Photography: Ernest Palmer (Technicolor)
Cast: June Haver, George Montgomery, Vivian Blaine, Celeste Holm, Vera-Ellen, Frank Latimore, Charles Smith, Thurston Hall
Songs: "Three Little Girls in Blue"; "On the Boardwalk at Atlantic City"; "Somewhere in the Night"; "If You Can't Get a Girl in the Summertime"; "This Is Always" (music: Harry Warren); "You Make Me Feel So Young"
Released: September 1946; 90 minutes

The same 1938 London play, *Three Blind Mice,* that had been filmed first as a nonmusical, then turned into a 1941 screen musical, *Moon Over Miami* (see page 103), served once again as the basis for *Three Little Girls in Blue.* This time the period is 1902. Three farming sisters from Red Bank, New Jersey, decide to spend their small inheritance on a trip to Atlantic City, "The Millionaire's Playground," with hopes of entrapping at least one millionaire while posing as a wealthy heiress (June Haver), the heiress's secretary (Vivian Blaine), and the heiress's maid (Vera-Ellen). Complications ensue when supposedly rich George Montgomery turns out to be a fortune hunter too, but matters do get straightened out—just as they always did in the past. One particular advantage this version has is the period-flavored score by Josef Myrow and Mack Gordon that even, on occasion, is integrated into the story.
H'wood Soundstage ST.

The Jolson Story. Larry Parks (with Al Jolson's voice) singing "The Spaniard That Blighted My Life."

THE JOLSON STORY

Screenplay: Stephen Longstreet (Sidney Buchman uncredited)
Produced by: Sidney Skolsky for Columbia
Directed by: Alfred E. Green
Choreography: Jack Cole
Photography: Joseph Walker (Technicolor)
Cast: Larry Parks, Evelyn Keyes, William Demarest, Ludwig Donath, Tamara Shayne, Bill Goodwin, Ernest Cossart, Scotty Beckett
Songs: "Let Me Sing and I'm Happy" (Irving Berlin); "My Mammy" (Walter Donaldson-Sam Lewis, Joe Young); "I'm Sittin' on Top of the World" (Ray Henderson-Lewis, Young); "You Made Me Love You" (James Monaco-Joseph McCarthy); "Swanee" (George Gershwin-Irving Caesar); "Toot, Toot, Tootsie" (Ted Fiorito, Robert King-Gus Kahn); "April Showers" (Louis Silvers-B. G. DeSylva); "California, Here I Come" (Joseph Meyer-DeSylva); "Liza" (Gershwin-Ira Gershwin, Kahn); "Avalon" (Vincent Rose-Al Jolson); "Anniversary Song" (Ion Ivanovici-Saul Chaplin); "Waiting for the Robert E. Lee" (Lewis Muir-L. Wolfe Gilbert); "Rockabye Your Baby With a Dixie Melody" (Jean Schwartz-Lewis, Young)
Released: September 1946; 128 minutes

A sentimentalized, cliché-filled movie about the life of a has-been entertainer was turned into the most popular show-business saga since *Yankee Doodle Dandy*. Though Al Jolson was a ruthless egomaniac, *The Jolson Story* presents him as an easy-going extrovert whose only possible flaw is his total dedication to entertaining his adoring public. In the movie—which has a plot unavoidably similar to that of *The Jazz Singer,* Jolson's pioneering effort in 1927—young Asa Yoelson, a cantor's son, runs away from home to go into vaudeville. He changes his name, adopts his blackface, down-on-one-knee, eye-rolling trademarks, wins acclaim on Broadway and in Hollywood, and marries a dancer who yearns only for home and hearth. At his wife's urging, Al retires from show business, but the couple break up when it becomes evident that Jolson can never be happy staying away from the spotlight.

For years, Hollywood columnist Sidney Skolsky had sought to interest the major studios in a movie about Jolson but only Columbia's Harry Cohn saw the possibilities. To play the leading role (which Jolson, then over 60, wanted to do himself), Cohn auditioned Richard Conte, Danny Thomas, and José Ferrer, then settled on studio contract player Larry Parks, who lip-synched the songs as Jolson sang them on the soundtrack (even though Parks's speaking voice and Jolson's singing voice didn't seem to be coming from the same throat). Though the movie is concerned with the romance between the singer and Ruby Keeler, his third wife, she was portrayed by Evelyn Keyes as his first wife and given the name of Julie Benson.

Because of the huge success of *The Jolson Story* (the seventh highest theatre rental musical of the forties), Cohn made a sequel, *Jolson Sings Again*—which became the tenth highest theatre rental musical of the forties (see page 155). Released in 1949, the movie begins with Al back on Broadway in something called *You Ain't Heard Nothin' Yet* (a show dreamed up in Hollywood), but he leaves to entertain the troops in World War II. After collapsing from exhaustion, Jolson is cared for by nurse Ellen Clark (Barbara Hale), whom he marries. (Actually, his fourth wife's name was Erle Galbraith and she was not a nurse). Following another retirement, he scores a hit in a Hollywood benefit show, which sparks the idea for the movie biography. Scenes of preparation for *The Jolson Story* even include the sight of Larry Parks as Al Jolson shaking hands with Larry Parks as Larry Parks. William Demarest, Ludwig Donath, Tamara Shayne, and Bill Goodwin all played the same supporting roles in both films.
Decca (Jolson LP). RCA/Columbia VC.

BLUE SKIES

Music & lyrics: Irving Berlin
Screenplay: Arthur Sheekman
Produced by: Sol C. Siegel for Paramount
Directed by: Stuart Heisler
Choreography: Hermes Pan, David Robel (Fred Astaire uncredited)
Photography: Charles Lang Jr., William Snyder (Technicolor)
Cast: Bing Crosby, Fred Astaire, Joan Caulfield, Billy DeWolfe, Olga San
Juan, Cliff Nazarro
Songs: "I've Got My Captain Working for Me Now"; "You'd Be Surprised";
"All By Myself"; "Puttin' on the Ritz"; "(I'll See You in) C-U-B-A";
"A Couple of Song and Dance Men"; "You Keep Coming Back Like
a Song"; "Blue Skies"; "Russian Lullaby"; "Everybody Step"; "How
Deep Is the Ocean?"; "(Running Around in Circles) Getting
Nowhere"; "Heat Wave"; "White Christmas"
Released: September 1946; 104 minutes

Originally, *Blue Skies* was to have reunited three of the principals who had been associated
with *Holiday Inn*—Bing Crosby, Irving Berlin, and producer-director Mark Sandrich. Instead
of Fred Astaire, however, the new movie would costar Crosby with dancer Paul Draper. But
the plans fell apart when Sandrich died soon after shooting had begun, and his replacements, producer Sol C. Siegel and director Stuart Heisler, dropped Draper for Astaire.

Blue Skies was a variation of *Holiday Inn*. Crosby and Astaire again play former song-
and-dance partners who compete for the same girl (Joan Caulfield) and again the girl
prefers Bing (they even get married twice). This time, however, instead of fitting appropriate Berlin songs to American holidays in one nightclub over a one-year period, the movie
fitted appropriate Berlin songs to a variety of nightclubs over a 27-year period. The standout
routine was "Puttin' on the Ritz," in which Astaire dances with a row of miniature Astaires
behind him. Proving there was still magic in the Crosby-Astaire-Berlin combination, *Blue
Skies* was the eighth highest domestic theatre rental musical of the forties.
MCA (Crosby, Astaire CD); Sountrak ST. MCA VC.

Blue Skies. Fred Astaire leading eight miniature Fred Astaires in "Puttin' on the Ritz."

Till the Clouds Roll By. June Allyson and Ray McDonald dancing to the title song.

TILL THE CLOUDS ROLL BY

Music: Jerome Kern
Lyrics: Oscar Hammerstein II, etc.
Screenplay: Myles Connolly & Jean Holloway
Produced by: Arthur Freed for MGM
Directed by: Richard Whorf, Vincente Minnelli (George Sidney uncredited)
Choreography: Robert Alton
Photography: Harry Stradling, George Folsey (Technicolor)
Cast: June Allyson, Lucille Bremer, Judy Garland, Kathryn Grayson, Van Heflin, Lena Horne, Van Johnson, Tony Martin, Dinah Shore, Frank Sinatra, Robert Walker, Gower Champion, Cyd Charisse, Angela Lansbury, Ray McDonald, Virginia O'Brien, Dorothy Patrick, Caleb Peterson, Wilde Twins, Sally Forrest
Songs: "Make Believe"; "Can't Help Lovin' dat Man"; "Ol' Man River"; "How'd You Like to Spoon With Me?" (Edward Laska); "They Didn't Believe Me" (M.E. Rourke); "Till the Clouds Roll By" (P. G. Wodehouse); "Look for the Silver Lining" (B. G. DeSylva); "Who?"; "I Won't Dance" (Dorothy Fields); "Smoke Gets in Your Eyes" (Otto Harbach); "The Last Time I Saw Paris"; "Long Ago and Far Away" (Ira Gershwin); "All the Things You Are"; "Why Was I Born?"
Released: November 1946; 137 minutes

Though it was released after Warners' pseudo-biographies of George Gershwin and Cole Porter, MGM's treatment of the life of Jerome Kern, the most influential of all Broadway composers, had been delayed two years because of legal problems involving copyrights. As in *Rhapsody in Blue* and *Night and Day, Till the Clouds Roll By* tells a success story (Robert Walker played Kern) with little conflict and not much adherence to biographical accuracy. MGM, however, made amends by including appearances by most of the major singing and dancing talents then on the payroll. Highlights are a 15-minute condensation of *Show Boat*, three numbers from Kern's Princess Theatre shows performed by June Allyson and Ray McDonald, and two Judy Garland sequences (both directed by Vincente Minnelli) with Judy, as Marilyn Miller. But then there is the ludicrous finale (staged by George Sidney) culminating in Frank Sinatra, in a white tuxedo standing on a white pedestal, singing "Ol' Man River." *Till the Clouds Roll By* spurred similar star-studded MGM epics spotlighting the catalogues of Rodgers and Hart *(Words and Music)* and Sigmund Romberg *(Deep in My Heart).*
MCA ST; Sountrak ST. MGM/UA VC.

THE SHOCKING MISS PILGRIM

Music: George Gershwin
Lyrics: Ira Gershwin
Screenplay: George Seaton
Produced by: William Perlberg for 20th Century-Fox
Directed by: George Seaton
Photography: Leon Shamroy (Technicolor)
Cast: Betty Grable, Dick Haymes, Anne Revere, Allyn Joslyn, Gene Lockhart, Elizabeth Patterson, Arthur Shields
Songs: "Changing My Tune"; "Aren't You Kind of Glad We Did?"; "Back Bay Polka"; "One, Two, Three"; "For You, For Me, For Evermore"
Released: January 1947; 85 minutes

Miss Cynthia Pilgrim (Betty Grable) shocks proper Boston in 1874 by not only invading male territory by getting a job as typewriter at the Prichard Shipping Company (at $8 per week with hours from 8 to 6), but also by joining the suffragette movement. Though she and her boss, John Prichard (Dick Haymes), fall in love, they break up—temporarily of course—over John's inability to cope with her feminist views. A surprisingly timely film, *The Shocking Miss Pilgrim,* however, disappointed 1947 audiences by not giving star Betty Grable the opportunity to show her celebrated legs. It was also unusual in that it contained a score assembled from unpublished music by George Gershwin, who had died eight years before the movie was made, with lyrics rewritten by George's brother Ira. Apart from the romantic expressions, "Changing My Tune" and "For You, For Me, For Evermore," it includes the double-entendre duet, "Aren't You Kind of Glad We Did?" (what they did was dine together in a restaurant without a chaperone) and the put-down of Boston's then stern moral code, "Back Bay Polka."
Classic Intl. ST.

The Shocking Miss Pilgrim. Gene Lockhart keeps an eye on Betty Grable.

Mother Wore Tights. "On a Little Two-Seat Tandem" sung by Betty Grable and Dan Dailey.

MOTHER WORE TIGHTS

Music: Josef Myrow, etc.
Lyrics: Mack Gordon, etc.
Screenplay: Lamar Trotti
Produced by: Lamar Trotti for 20th Century-Fox
Directed by: Walter Lang
Choreography: Seymour Felix, Kenny Williams
Photography: Harry Jackson (Technicolor)
Cast: Betty Grable, Dan Dailey, Mona Freeman, Vanessa Brown, Connie Marshall, Robert Arthur, Sara Allgood, William Frawley, Sig Rumann, Lee Patrick, Chick Chandler, Señor Wences, Kathleen Lockhart
Songs: "You Do"; "Burlington Bertie from Bow" (William Hargreaves); "This Is My Favorite City"; "Kokomo, Indiana"; "Tra-la-la" (music: Harry Warren); "There's Nothing Like a Song"; "On a Little Two-Seat Tandem"
Release date: August 1947; 107 minutes

In none of her previous 12 movies for Fox had Betty Grable been costarred with a male dancing partner. That was finally remedied in *Mother Wore Tights* when the studio chose Dan Dailey (Miss Grable had been expecting either Fred Astaire or James Cagney) and the two clicked so well together that they would be reunited in three subsequent Fox musicals, *When My Baby Smiles at Me, My Blue Heaven,* and *Call Me Mister.* Beginning in 1900, *Mother Wore Tights* (based on a book by Miriam Young) tells the nostalgic, sentimental tale (narrated by Anne Baxter) of a barnstorming vaudeville couple and their problems raising two daughters, especially the one who turns snooty. Grossing $4.15 million in theater rental fees, the picture was Miss Grable's most successful box office vehicle. *Classic Intl. ST.*

ROAD TO RIO

Music: James Van Heusen
Lyrics: Johnny Burke
Screenplay: Edmund Beloin & Jack Rose
Produced by: Daniel Dare for Paramount
Directed by: Norman Z. McLeod
Choreography: Bernard Pearce, Billy Daniels
Photography: Ernest Laszlo
Cast: Bing Crosby, Bob Hope, Dorothy Lamour, Andrews Sisters, Gale Sondergaard, Robert Barrat, Jerry Colonna, Wiere Brothers, Raul Roulien
Songs: "Apalachicola, Fla."; "You Don't Have to Know the Language"; "Experience"; "But Beautiful"
Released: November 1947; 100 minutes

(See page 95.)

GOOD NEWS

Music: Ray Henderson, etc.
Lyrics: B. G. DeSylva & Lew Brown, etc.
Screenplay: Betty Comden & Adolph Green
Produced by: Arthur Freed for MGM
Directed by: Charles Walters
Choreographers: (Robert Alton, Charles Walters uncredited)
Photography: Charles Schoenbaum (Technicolor)
Cast: June Allyson, Peter Lawford, Patricia Marshall, Joan McCracken, Mel Tormé, Ray McDonald, Robert Strickland, Donald MacBride, Clinton Sundberg
Songs: "Good News"; "Be a Ladies Man" (added lyric: Roger Edens & Kay Thompson); "Lucky in Love"; "The French Lesson" (Edens-Betty Comden, Adoph Green); "The Best Things in Life Are Free"; "Pass That Peace Pipe" (Edens-Hugh Martin, Ralph Blane); "Just Imagine"; "The Varsity Drag"
Released: December 1947; 83 minutes

Good News ushered in a period in which, with six films in a row, Arthur Freed established himself as Hollywood's most consistent producer of quality musicals. It was also the first movie with a screenplay by Broadway librettists Betty Comden and Adolph Green as well as the first directed by choreographer Charles Walters. The film was based on the 1927 Broadway musical comedy that was the prototype of all the jazzy collegiate shows populated by flat-chested flappers and slick-haired sheiks. Half of the 12 original songs were retained for the picture with two new numbers added.

It is 1927 and we are at Tait College where everyone does the "Varsity Drag" and where poor Connie Lane (June Allyson) is smitten by ladies' man and football hero Tommy Marlowe (Peter Lawford), who has a crush on campus flirt Pat McClellan (Patricia Marshall). Because Tommy has failed his French course (on the stage it had been astronomy), he is barred from playing in The Big Game, a decision that is reversed after Connie tutors him. Tait, of course, wins the game and Connie, of course, wins Tommy. After being planned for Mickey and Judy, *Good News* was then to have costarred Van Johnson opposite Miss Allyson, but Johnson was replaced by the incongruously cast London-born Peter Lawford. Another change was the substitution of Patricia Marshall for Gloria De Haven. Metro's first version of the story, in 1930, featured Mary Lawlor (of the Broadway cast), Stanley Smith, Bessie Love, and Lola Lane.
MCA ST; Sountrak ST.   MGM/UA VC.

Good News. The "Pass That Peace Pipe" number led by Joan McCracken and Ray McDonald at the college ice-cream parlor.

THE PIRATE

Music & lyrics: Cole Porter
Screenplay: Frances Goodrich & Albert Hackett
Produced by: Arthur Freed for MGM
Directed by: Vincente Minnelli
Choreography: Robert Alton, Gene Kelly
Photography: Harry Stradling (Technicolor)
Cast: Judy Garland, Gene Kelly, Walter Slezak, Gladys Cooper, Reginald
    Owen, Nicholas Brothers, George Zucco, Lester Allen, Cully
    Richards, Lola Albright, Jerry Bergen, Ben Lessy, Lola Deem, Ellen
    Ross, Mary Jo Ellis
Songs: "Niña"; "Mack the Black"; "You Can Do No Wrong"; "Be a
    Clown"; "Love of My Life"
Released: March 1948; 102 minutes

The Pirate stemmed from a 1942 Broadway production that had starred the theatre's most distinguished acting couple, Alfred Lunt and Lynn Fontanne. Adapted by S.N. Behrman from a German play, *Der Seeräuber* by Ludwig Fulda, the stylish play, set on a Caribbean island in the early 1800's, was concerned with daydreaming Manuela, the wife of Don Pedro, the stuffy village mayor, who is secretly enamored of a legendary swashbuckling pirate named Escamundo. Aware of this, Serafin, the leader of a band of itinerant actors, convinces Manuela that he is the notorious pirate, but the lady soon discovers the ruse and is furious at the deception. At one of Serafin's performances, Don Pedro is mesmerized into revealing that he is the real Escamundo—an admission that ends Manuela's infatuation with the outlaw and begins her free-spirited days with Serafin.

Somehow, the play seemed to producer Arthur Freed to be just right for Judy Garland, especially if it could have songs by Cole Porter and direction by her then husband, Vincente Minnelli. With that taken care of, Gene Kelly was added to play the flamboyant male lead, thus reuniting the Garland-Kelly team for the first time since *For Me and My Gal* six years earlier. A few changes, however, were in order: Manuela would be Don Pedro's fiancée, not his wife, and the pirate's name—since it would be easier for Porter to fit into a song lyric—would be changed from Escamundo to Macoco, better known as Mack the Black. There were, however, two songs, "Manuela" and "Voodoo," that could not be fitted into the movie.

Though problems plagued the filming because of Miss Garland's illness and frequent absences, the result was a brightly colored, purposely artificial romantic satire with a sophistication somewhat ahead of its time. It offered Miss Garland the opportunity to show the full range of her comic gifts, particularly in her unbridled assault on Kelly after discovering his fabrication, and it gave Kelly the chance to do takeoffs on both Douglas Fairbanks's gymnastics and John Barrymore's histrionics. In the actor's major dance routine (an expansion of his "La Cumparsita" number in *Anchors Aweigh),* he leaps fleetingly and bounds flirtingly from one senorita to another—all of whom he calls Niña—as he climbs balconies, scales rooftops, slides down poles, and stomps out a Flamenco. At Kelly's request, Porter also contributed the boisterous "Be a Clown," a celebration of the joys that come only to those who play the fool. Kelly performs it first with the Nicholas Brothers, then repeats it at the end of the film with Judy Garland when both appear sporting putty noses and baggy clown costumes, sing directly to the audience, and have a whale of a time.

MCA ST.   MGM/UA VC.

The Pirate. Judy Garland getting even with Gene Kelly for his deception.

Easter Parade. Fred Astaire, Judy Garland as a "A Couple of Swells."

EASTER PARADE

Music & lyrics: Irving Berlin
Screenplay: Sidney Sheldon, Frances Goodrich & Albert Hackett
Produced by: Arthur Freed for MGM
Directed by: Charles Walters
Choreography: Robert Alton (Charles Walters, Fred Astaire uncredited)
Photography: Harry Stradling (Technicolor)
Cast: Judy Garland, Fred Astaire, Peter Lawford, Ann Miller, Jules Munshin, Clinton Sundberg, Richard Beavers, Benay Venuta, Lola Albright, Dee Turnell
Songs: "Happy Easter"; "Drum Crazy"; "It Only Happens When I Dance With You"; "Everybody's Doin' It"; "I Want to Go Back to Michigan"; "Beautiful Faces Need Beautiful Clothes"; "A Fella With an Umbrella"; "I Love a Piano"; "Snookey Ookums"; "Ragtime Violin"; "When the Midnight Choo-Choo Leaves for Alabam'"; "Shaking the Blues Away"; "Steppin' Out With My Baby"; "A Couple of Swells"; "The Girl on the Magazine Cover"; "Better Luck Next Time"; "Easter Parade"
Released: June 1948; 103 minutes

Following *The Pirate,* Arthur Freed signed Judy Garland, Gene Kelly, director Vincente Minnelli, choreographer Robert Alton, writers Frances Goodrich and Albert Hackett, and cameraman Harry Stradling to work on his next production, *Easter Parade.* The special attraction was that the picture would feature a cornucopia of Irving Berlin songs—ten old, seven new—performed within the context of a show-business saga covering the period from the day before Easter in 1912 to Easter Sunday the following year. Since the story would be about a vaudeville headliner who recruits and trains a new partner with whom he eventually falls in love, their relationship would have something of the flavor of Garland and Kelly's first film together, *For Me and My Gal.*

But work did not proceed smoothly. Minnelli was taken off the film for personal reasons concerning Miss Garland, his wife at the time, and was replaced by Charles Walters. Then Kelly had to bow out because of a broken ankle. His recommended replacement: Fred Astaire. Astaire had retired after making *Blue Skies* two years earlier but *Easter Parade* offered the irresistible lure of working with Judy Garland and singing and dancing Irving Berlin songs. Thus, Fred Astaire was back on the screen, still playing the singing and dancing romantic lead at the age of 48 (Judy was then 25). (Another cast replacement was Ann Miller, as Fred's former partner, who took over when Cyd Charisse also met with an accident.)

The tale of how Don Hewes, a nimble-footed Pygmalion, and Hannah Brown, his quick-witted Galatea, make it from vaudeville to Broadway within a year provides a serviceable background for some unforgettable song-and-dance routines —Fred and Judy's ragtime medley as they hit their stride in vaudeville . . . Ann Miller's electrifying tapping to "Shaking the Blues Away" . . . Fred's dazzling slow-motion leaps to "Steppin' Out With My Baby" while the chorus in the background dances at regular speed . . . the mocking, mischievous "A Couple of Swells" (a worthy successor to Cole Porter's "Be a Clown" in *The Pirate),* performed by Fred and Judy as two seedy tramps putting on airs . . . Judy's anguished "Better Luck Next Time."

Notwithstanding the film's replacements and delays, *Easter Parade,* a perennial springtime attraction on television, placed high on the list of the most popular box-office attractions of the year.
CBS ST. MGM/UA VC.

WORDS AND MUSIC

Music: Richard Rodgers
Lyrics: Lorenz Hart
Screenplay: Fred Finklehoffe
Produced by: Arthur Freed for MGM
Directed by: Norman Taurog
Choreography: Robert Alton, Gene Kelly
Photography: Charles Rosher, Harry Stradling (Technicolor)
Cast: June Allyson, Perry Como, Judy Garland, Lena Horne, Gene Kelly,
Mickey Rooney, Ann Sothern, Tom Drake, Cyd Charisse, Betty
Garrett, Janet Leigh, Marshall Thompson, Mel Tormé, Vera-Ellen,
Richard Quine, Dee Turnell, Allyn Ann McLerie, Blackburn Twins,
Clinton Sundberg
Songs: "Manhattan"; "There's a Small Hotel"; "Mountain Greenery";
"Where's That Rainbow?"; "On Your Toes"; "Thou Swell"; "Where
or When"; "The Lady Is a Tramp"; "I Wish I Were in Love Again";
"Johnny One Note"; "Blue Moon"; "Spring Is Here"; "Slaughter on
Tenth Avenue" (instrumental); "With a Song in My Heart"
Released: December 1948; 121 minutes

After Hollywood's biographical treatments of Broadway composers Gershwin, Porter, and
Kern, it was time to distort the lives of Richard Rodgers and Lorenz Hart (portrayed by Tom
Drake and Mickey Rooney). But MGM came to the rescue by spotlighting guest stars to
perform 17 of the team's most memorable songs. Some of the notable musical scenes are
Lena Horne's stylized way with "Where and When" and "The Lady Is a Tramp," Gene Kelly
and Vera-Ellen's smoldering dance to "Slaughter on Tenth Avenue," and Judy Garland and
Mickey Rooney's explosive "I Wish I Were In Love Again"—their last screen appearance
together—and Judy's solo of "Johnny One Note." (The last two songs, from the original
score of *Babes in Arms,* had been omitted from the Mickey-Judy screen version.) One of
the box-office leaders of 1949, *Words and Music* takes the songwriters from their first
meeting, covers some of their Broadway and London successes, and ends with Hart's
tragic death at the age of 48 (caused, according to the movie, by the lyricist's unrequited
love for a fictitious nightclub singer, played by Betty Garrett).
MCA ST. MGM/UA VC.

Words and Music. Mickey Rooney and
Judy Garland performing "I Wish I Were
in Love Again."

Take Me Out to the Ball Game. Frank Sinatra, Gene Kelly, and Jules Munshin.

TAKE ME OUT TO THE BALL GAME

Music: Roger Edens, etc.
Lyrics: Betty Comden & Adolph Green, etc.
Screenplay: Harry Tugend & George Wells
Produced by: Arthur Freed for MGM
Directed by: Busby Berkeley
Choreography: Gene Kelly & Stanley Donen
Photography: George Folsey (Technicolor)
Cast: Frank Sinatra, Esther Williams, Gene Kelly, Betty Garrett, Edward Arnold, Jules Munshin, Blackburn Twins, Sally Forrest
Songs: "Take Me Out to the Ball Game" (Albert Von Tilzer-Jack Norworth); "Yes, Indeedy"; "O'Brien to Ryan to Goldberg"; "The Right Girl for Me"; "It's Fate Baby, It's Fate" (lyric: Roger Edens); "The Hat My Father Wore Upon St. Patrick's Day" (Jean Schwartz-William Jerome)
Released: April 1949; 93 minutes

Gene Kelly and Frank Sinatra may have doffed their *Anchors Aweigh* sailor suits in favor of baseball uniforms in *Take Me Out to the Ball Game,* but they still portrayed the same basic characters of brashy Gene and bashful Frank. In the turn-of-the-century tale (from a story dreamed up by Kelly and Stanley Donen), they play shortstop and second baseman for a professional ball team known as the Wolves, have a separate career as vaudevillians during the off-season, and spend much of their time clowning with first baseman Jules Munshin (in a part originally intended for baseball manager Leo Durocher). At their Sarasota training camp, the Wolves find themselves with a new owner in the unlikely person of Esther Williams (who replaced first Kathryn Grayson then Judy Garland), a bit of casting that required both a new screenplay and even a new songwriting team. Romantic complications—which really weren't too complicated—involve man-hungry Betty Garrett chasing Sinatra who loves Williams who loves Kelly. The movie was retitled *Everybody's Cheering* in Great Britain.
Curtain Calls ST. MGM/UA VC.

THE BARKLEYS OF BROADWAY

Music: Harry Warren, etc.
Lyrics: Ira Gershwin
Screenplay: Betty Comden & Adolph Green
Produced by: Arthur Freed for MGM
Directed by: Charles Walters
Choreography: Robert Alton, Hermes Pan (Fred Astaire uncredited)
Photography: Harry Stradling (Technicolor)
Cast: Fred Astaire, Ginger Rogers, Oscar Levant, Billie Burke, Jacques
Francois, Gale Robbins, George Zucco, Hans Conried, Joyce
Matthews, Lennie Hayton, Dee Turnell
Songs & instrumentals: "Swing Trot" (instrumental); "Sabre Dance"
(Khatchaturian); "You'd Be Hard to Replace"; "Bouncin' the Blues"
(instrumental); "My One and Only Highland Fling"; "A Weekend in the
Country"; "Shoes With Wings On"; Piano Concerto in B-flat Minor
(excerpt) (Tschaikowsky); "They Can't Take That Away from Me"
(music: George Gershwin); "Manhattan Downbeat"
Released: May 1949;109 minutes

With *Easter Parade* one of the biggest moneymakers of 1948, producer Arthur Freed was quick to make plans for another show-business tale that would again costar Judy Garland and Fred Astaire. Since the previous movie had ended with a bickering vaudeville couple winning acclaim in their first Broadway show, it occurred to screenwriters Betty Comden and Adolph Green that a modern story could be woven around bickering married couple, Josh and Dinah Barkley, who have apparently been enjoying nothing but success as the musical theatre's answer to Alfred Lunt and Lynn Fontanne. The conflict in the film would center on the way they cope with the crisis—fortunately only temporary—of Dinah's deserting musicals in favor of heavy drama. (The writers even had Dinah appear in a play as Sarah Bernhardt and recite the "Marseillaise" in French!)

For the project, Freed brought together many of the same people who had worked with him on *Easter Parade:* director Charles Walters, choreographer Robert Alton, associate producer Roger Edens, director of photography Harry Stradling, art director Cedric Gibbons, and editor Albert Akst. For the songs, however, he turned to composer Harry Warren and lyricist Ira Gershwin for what would be the only project on which they ever worked together.

After rehearsals for *The Barkleys of Broadway* had already begun, Miss Garland's illness caused the actress to be absent so often that Freed was forced to replace her—which led him to Astaire's most celebrated dancing partner, Ginger Rogers. (It was their first film together in nine years and their tenth and final costarring appearance.) The cast change required alterations to both the script and the songs (no less than nine numbers were discarded), plus the addition of the interpolated George and Ira Gershwin ballad, "They Can't Take That Away from Me," which had been first sung by Fred to Ginger in *Shall We Dance,* and is here performed as a formal song-and-dance routine during a benefit show.

Among the film's memorable musical scenes are the seemingly spontaneous Astaire-Rogers rehearsal dance to the instrumental "Bouncin' the Blues"; Fred's solo "Shoes With Wings On," performed in a shoe-repair store with dozens of disembodied tapping shoes; and the Scottish duet, "My One and Only Highland Fling," burred by Fred and Ginger wearing tam-o'-shanters, kilts, and dour expressions. In Great Britain the movie was known as *The Gay Barkleys.*
Sountrak St. MGM/UA VC.

The Barkleys of Broadway. Ginger Rogers and Fred Astaire doing the "Bouncin' the Blues" number during a rehearsal.

NEPTUNE'S DAUGHTER

Music & lyrics: Frank Loesser
Screenplay: Dorothy Kingsley
Produced by: Jack Cummings for MGM
Directed by: Edward Buzzell
Choreography: Jack Donohue
Photography: Charles Rosher (Technicolor)
Cast: Esther Williams, Red Skelton, Ricardo Montalban, Betty Garrett, Keenan Wynn, Xavier Cugat Orch., Mel Blanc
Songs: "I Love Those Men"; "My Heart Beats Faster"; "Baby, It's Cold Outside"
Released: June 1949; 93 minutes

With theatre rental earnings of $3.45 million, *Neptune's Daughter* was not only among the biggest draws of 1949, it was also the most popular of the 18 splashy musicals in which Esther Williams appeared. In the movie, Hollywood's only female natant star plays an amateur swimming champion who becomes a successful swimsuit designer and manufacturer. When a South American polo team, led by Ricardo Montalban, comes to New York, Esther stages a fashion show in and around the polo club's pool. Her man-hungry sister, Betty Garrett, mistakes the club's masseur, Red Skelton, for Montalban and Esther is angry at Montalban for breaking her sister's heart. Take it from there. The musical highlight of the film is the duet, "Baby, It's Cold Outside," which had originally been written by composer-lyricist Frank Loesser as a song that he and his wife could sing at parties. Curiously, just before it is sung in the picture, Montalban urges Miss Williams to stay with him on "this warm summer evening."
MGM/UA VC.

IN THE GOOD OLD SUMMERTIME

Screenplay: Albert Hackett, Frances Goodrich, Van Tors
Produced by: Joe Pasternak for MGM
Directed by: Robert Z. Leonard
Choreography: Robert Alton
Photography: Harry Stradling (Technicolor)
Cast: Judy Garland, Van Johnson, S. Z. Sakall, Spring Byington, Clinton
Sundberg, Buster Keaton, Marcia Van Dyke, Liza Minnelli
Songs: "In the Good Old Summertime" (George Evans-Ren Shields);
"Meet Me Tonight in Dreamland" (Leo Friedman-Beth Whitson);
"Put Your Arms Around Me, Honey" (Albert VonTilzer-Junie
McCree); "Play That Barbershop Chord" (Lewis Muir-William
Tracey); "I Don't Care" (Harry Sutton-Jean Lenox); "Merry
Christmas" (Fred Spielman-Janice Torre)
Released: June 1949; 102 minutes

In the Good Old Summertime began life as a Hungarian play, *Parfumerie* by Miklos Laszlo, which was first filmed in 1939 by Ernst Lubitsch as *The Shop Around the Corner* with Margaret Sullavan and James Stewart. (In 1963, the original version would be adapted as a Broadway musical, *She Loves Me*). For *In the Good Old Summertime* (actually, the film covers the period from summer to Christmas), the locale was changed from modern Budapest to Chicago after the turn of the century, and Maraczek's leather goods and novelty shop became Oberkugen's Music Store. The main story of two antagonistic shop clerks who anonymously carry on a romantic postal correspondence was retained, but the conflict caused by the store owner's unfaithful wife was changed to one caused when the owner's beloved Stradivarius is lent to a music student without his permission.

After pregnant June Allyson had to bow out of the film, Judy Garland was signed to star opposite Van Johnson. To give the movie an authentic period flavor, six of the songs dated from the century's first decade, though there was a new song, "Merry Christmas," inserted as something of a successor to "Have Youself a Merry Little Christmas." In the final scene showing the once battling shop clerks now happily married, their progeny was played by Miss Garland's own three-year-old daughter, Liza Minnelli.
MCA ST. MGM/UA VC.

In the Good Old Summertime. S.Z.Sakall, Van Johnson, and Judy
Garland in Oberkugen's Music Store.

JOLSON SINGS AGAIN

Screenplay: Sidney Buchman
Produced by: Sidney Buchman for Columbia
Directed by: Henry Levin
Photography: William Snyder (Technicolor)
Cast: Larry Parks, Barbara Hale, William Demarest, Ludwig Donath, Tamara Shayne, Bill Goodwin, Myron McCormick
Songs: "Is It True What They Say About Dixie?" (Gerald Marks-Irving Caesar, Sammy Lerner); "For Me and My Gal" (George Meyer - Edgar Leslie, E. Ray Goetz); "Back in Your Own Back Yard" (Dave Dreyer-Billy Rose); "I'm Looking Over a Four Leaf Clover" (Harry Woods-Mort Dixon); "When the Red Red Robin Comes Bob Bob Bobbin' Along" (Woods); "Give My Regards to Broadway" (George M. Cohan); "Chinatown My Chinatown" (Jean Schwartz-William Jerome); "I'm Just Wild About Harry" (Eubie Blake-Noble Sissle); "Sonny Boy" (Ray Henderson-B. G. DeSylva, Lew Brown); "Carolina in the Morning" (Walter Donaldson-Gus Kahn); "Rockabye Your Baby With a Dixie Melody" (Schwartz-Sam Lewis, Joe Young)
Released: August 1949; 96 minutes

(See page 139.)

CINDERELLA

Music & lyrics: Al Hoffman, Jerry Livingston, Mack David
Screenplay: Kenneth Anderson, Ted Sears, Homer Brightman, Joe Rinaldi, William Peet, Harry Reeves, Winston Hibler, Erdman Penner
Produced by: Walt Disney (released by RKO Radio)
Directed by: Wilfred Jackson, Hamilton Luske, Clyde Geronimi (Technicolor)
Voices: Ilene Woods, William Phipps, Eleanor Audley, Rhoda Williams, Lucille Bliss, Verna Felton, Luis Van Rooten
Songs: "Bibbidi Bobbidi Boo"; "So This Is Love"; "A Dream Is a Wish Your Heart Makes"; "Cinderella"; "Sing, Sweet Nightingale"; "The Work Song"
Released: December 1949; 74 minutes

According to the most recent Guinness Book on the movies, *Cinderella* has had more screen versions than any other story. Five of these productions have been musicals—*First Love* (1939) with Deanna Durbin; the Walt Disney cartoon feature *Cinderella* (1949); *The Glass Slipper* (1955) with Leslie Caron; *Cinderfella* (1960) with Jerry Lewis; and *The Slipper and the Rose* (1976) with Gemma Craven. Disney's version, whose latest reissue was in 1987, has been by far the most successful (at latest count, it has taken in $41 million in domestic theatre rental fees). The cartoon follows the general fairy-tale formula established by *Snow White and the Seven Dwarfs,* while adding new characters such as Cinderella's resourceful rodent chums, Jacques and Gus, who get the other mice to make a ball gown for our heroine. Though its exact origins are obscure, *Cinderella* as we know it today was first written by Charles Perrault, a 17th Century French writer who called it *Cendrillon ou la Petite Pantoufle de Vair,* though through the years the slipper of squirrel fur *(vair)* was changed to one of glass *(verre).*
Disney VC.

ON THE TOWN

Music: Leonard Bernstein*; Roger Edens**
Lyrics & screenplay: Betty Comden & Adolph Green
Produced by: Arthur Freed for MGM
Directors-choreographers: Gene Kelly & Stanley Donen
Photography: Harold Rosson (Technicolor)
Cast: Gene Kelly, Frank Sinatra, Betty Garrett, Ann Miller, Jules Munshin,
Vera-Ellen, Florence Bates, Alice Pearce, Hans Conried, Carol
Haney, George Meader, Bea Benaderet
Songs: "I Feel Like I'm Not Out of Bed Yet"*; "New York, New York"*; "Miss
Turnstiles"* ballet (instrumental); "Prehistoric Man"**; "Come Up to
My Place"*; " Main Street"**; "You're Awful"**; "On the Town"**;
"Count on Me"**; A Day in New York"* ballet (instrumental)
Released: December 1949; 98 minutes

A ballet titled *Fancy Free* was the genesis of *On the Town,* the successful 1944 stage
musical that served to introduce Broadway to the talents of composer Leonard Bernstein,
lyricists-librettists Betty Comden and Adolph Green, and choreographer Jerome Robbins.
Its tale focuses on three sailors on 24-hour shore leave in New York, the sights they see,
and the three girls they meet and fall for before it is time to return to their ship. The story
may have been slight—and slightly familiar—but the treatment was so inventive, both
musically and choreographically, that the show played an influential role in the development of the American musical theatre.

For the screen, producer Arthur Freed put Gene Kelly and Frank Sinatra back in the
sailor uniforms they had worn in *Anchors Aweigh* (which had also been about gobs on leave
trying to pick up girls) and added Jules Munshin and Betty Garrett from *Take Me Out to the
Ball Game* (with Miss Garrett again playing a boy-crazy girl chasing a girl-shy Sinatra).
Vera-Ellen and Ann Miller rounded out the sextet as the girls fancied by Kelly and Munshin.
The first film co-directed and choreograhed by Gene Kelly and Stanley Donen, *On the Town*
utilized dance as a major component of the action in ways that had never before been
attempted on the screen. It marked the first movie to have a musical sequence shot on
location on New York. (the exuberant "New York, New York" number) and there was an
imaginative ballet for Vera-Ellen as the winner of the subway's "Miss Turnstiles" competition. (Kelly would create a similar dance for Leslie Caron in *An American in Paris* two years
later.) There was also a joyous routine atop the Empire State Building (actually filmed in
Culver City), though the extended "Day in New York" ballet unnecessarily repeated the
movie's plot.

Comden and Green were assigned to write the screenplay, but because Freed did not
like it, Bernstein's score was limited to three songs and two ballets, with the rest of it
replaced by five numbers written by Roger Edens and Comden and Green. Of the original
Broadway cast, only Alice Pearce was engaged to recreate her role as Miss Garrett's
sniffling roommate. The last of the three Kelly-Sinatra movies, *On the Town* placed among
the box office winners of 1950.

Five years later, as something of a sequel, *It's Always Fair Weather* , also written by
Comden and Green, took up the subject of a New York reunion of three army buddies
played by Kelly, Dan Dailey and Michael Kidd, with Cyd Charisse and Dolores Gray in the
leading female roles (see page 197).
DRG (studio cast LP). MGM/UA VC.

On the Town. The "Count on Me" number performed by Betty Garrett, Ann Miller, Gene Kelly, Jules Munshin, Frank Sinatra, and Alice Pearce.

YOUNG MAN WITH A HORN

Screenplay: Carl Foreman & Edmund North
Produced by: Jerry Wald for Warner Bros.
Directed by: Michael Curtiz
Photography: Ted McCord
Cast: Kirk Douglas, Lauren Bacall, Doris Day, Hoagy Carmichael, Juano Hernandez, Jerome Cowan, Mary Beth Hughes
Songs: "The Very Thought of You" (Ray Noble); "Too Marvelous for Words" (Richard Whiting-Johnny Mercer); "I May Be Wrong" (Henry Sullivan-Harry Ruskin); "With a Song in My Heart" (Richard Rodgers-Lorenz Hart); "Can't We Be Friends?" (Kay Swift-Paul James); "I Only Have Eyes for You" (Harry Warren-Al Dubin); "Get Happy" (Harold Arlen-Ted Koehler)
Released: January 1950; 112 minutes

Like most films dealing with jazz and pop musicians (e.g. *Blues in the Night, The Glenn Miller Story*), *Young Man With a Horn* was yet another tale of a dedicated jazzman striving to play his kind of music his way. In this case, the story was based on a fictionalized biography by Dorothy Baker of legendary trumpeter Bix Beiderbecke, with the leading role played by Kirk Douglas (whose trumpet was dubbed by Harry James). The plot traces the career of Rick Martin, who has professional problems conforming to the requirements of a commercial dance orchestra (Beiderbecke had been a sideman for Paul Whiteman), and personal problems with a neurotic wife (Lauren Bacall). After hitting the bottle and losing his job, Rick is eventually saved by the love of a devoted band singer (Doris Day). Because "horn" is British slang for erection, the movie was retitled *Young Man of Music* when it was released in Great Britian.
Warner VC.

Annie Get Your Gun. Betty Hutton singing "Doin" What Comes Natur'lly."

ANNIE GET YOUR GUN

Music & lyrics: Irving Berlin
Screenplay: Sidney Sheldon
Produced by: Arthur Freed for MGM
Directed by: George Sidney
Choreography: Robert Alton
Photography: Charles Rosher (Technicolor)
Cast: Betty Hutton, Howard Keel, Louis Calhern, J. Carrol Naish, Edward Arnold, Keenan Wynn, Benay Venuta, Clinton Sundberg, Andre Charlot, Mae Clarke, Chief Yowlachie, Bradley Mora, Diana Dick, Susan Odin, Eleanor Brown
Songs: "Colonel Buffalo Bill"; "Doin' What Comes Natur'lly"; "The Girl That I Marry"; "You Can't Get a Man With a Gun"; "There's No Business Like Show Business"; "They Say It's Wonderful"; "My Defenses Are Down"; "I'm an Indian, Too"; "I Got the Sun in the Morning"; "Anything You Can Do"
Released: April 1950; 107 minutes

Ethel Merman may have been the Queen of Broadway Musicals and *Annie Get Your Gun* may have given her her longest reign, but when MGM bought the screen rights to the 1946 smash (at a record price of $700,000), the studio had no other star in mind but Judy Garland. After recording all her songs and performing before the camera for almost two months under Busby Berkeley's direction, Miss Garland, as she had during the preparation of *The Barkleys of Broadway*, became too sick to continue. Metro put her on suspension, considered Betty Garrett as her replacement, but ultimately gave the plum role of sharp-shooter Annie Oakley to Betty Hutton, thus becoming her only musical assignment away from Paramount. (The MGM brass had most likely seen her in *Incendiary Blonde,* in which, as Texas Guinan, Miss Hutton first wins acclaim in a Wild West show.) Following a five-month delay, shooting resumed with two other major changes —George Sidney replaced Berkeley as director and Louis Calhern replaced Frank Morgan as Buffalo Bill following Morgan's death. *Annie Get Your Gun* also marked the screen debut of Howard Keel, who won the leading male role over John Raitt.

The biggest box office musical success of 1950, the movie version retained ten of the 15 songs in Irving Berlin's original hit-filled score, though "Moonshine Lullaby" and "Let's Go West Again," which were supposed to be in the film were casualties, and "Doin' What Comes Natur'lly" was both laundered and shortened. Adapted from the libretto by Dorothy and Herbert Fields, Sidney Sheldon's screen treatment was a faithful transference that also took full advantage of the medium, as in the spectacular "There's No Business Like Show Business" finale.

In the tale, which made no attempt at historical accuracy, tomboyish hillbilly marksman Annie Oakley, smitten by Frank Butler, the star attraction of Buffalo Bill's Wild West Show, joins the show and not only becomes Frank's rival but even boasts that anything he can do she can do better. Annie, however, stifles her competitiveness and bows to male chauvinism by purposely losing a marksmanship contest with Frank—and thereby winning her man.

The success of *Annie Get Your Gun* was the catalyst for Warners' 1953 musical, *Calamity Jane,* a pale variation starring Doris Day and, again, Howard Keel (as Wild Bill Hickock). In 1935, RKO Radio had released a nonmusical film, *Annie Oakley,* with Barbara Stanwyck and Preston Foster as the shooting stars.
MGM ST.

THREE LITTLE WORDS

Music: Harry Ruby, etc.
Lyrics: Bert Kalmar, etc.
Screenplay: George Wells
Produced by: Jack Cummings for MGM
Directed by: Richard Thorpe
Choreography: Hermes Pan (Fred Astaire uncredited)
Photography: Harry Jackson (Technicolor)
Cast: Fred Astaire, Red Skelton, Vera-Ellen, Arlene Dahl, Keenan Wynn, Gale Robbins, Gloria DeHaven, Phil Regan, Debbie Reynolds, Carleton Carpenter, Harry Barris, Harry Ruby
Songs: "Where Did You Get That Girl?" (music: Harry Puck); "My Sunny Tennessee" (with Herman Ruby); "So Long, Oo-Long"; "Who's Sorry Now?" (with Ted Snyder); "Nevertheless"; "All Alone Monday"; "I Wanna Be Loved by You" (music with Herbert Stothart); "Thinking of You"; "I Love You So Much"; "Three Little Words"
Released: July 1950; 103 minutes

Hollywood had just about run out of major Broadway songwriters to provide catalogues upon which some semblance of biographical fact and fiction could be strung, when MGM decided to film the life story of Bert Kalmar and Harry Ruby. In dealing with these prolific though relatively obscure writers, producer Jack Cummings avoided the all-star, elaborate approach in favor of concentrating on the skills, both musical and comedic, of its two stars, Fred Astaire and Red Skelton, as well as on the pleasures of the 15 numbers paraded throughout the film. Among them was "I Wanna Be Loved By You," for which Debbie Reynolds (as Helen Kane) did the mouthing to Miss Kane's own boop-boop-a-doop dubbing. The movie also gave Astaire a new dancing partner, Vera-Ellen, though it limited his terpsichorean efforts by having Kalmar, depicted as a vaudeville hoofer, break his leg about a quarter of the way through the film, thus forcing him to become a full-time lyricist. (Actually, the real Kalmer had a magic and comedy act.) The plot is primarily concerned with Kalmar's efforts to keep Ruby away from gold-digging females by shipping him off to a Florida baseball training camp to be with his beloved Washington Senators. The men squabble, break up, and come back together to accidentally write one of their biggest hits, "Three Little Words."
MGM ST. MGM/UA VC.

SUMMER STOCK

Music: Harry Warren, etc.
Lyrics: Mack Gordon, etc.
Screenplay: George Wells, Sy Gomberg
Produced by: Joe Pasternak for MGM
Directed by: Charles Walters
Choreography: Nick Castle (Gene Kelly, Charles Walters uncredited)
Photography: Robert Planck (Technicolor)
Cast: Judy Garland, Gene Kelly, Eddie Bracken, Gloria DeHaven, Marjorie Main, Phil Silvers, Ray Collins, Carleton Carpenter, Hans Conried, Carol Haney
Songs: "Happy Harvest"; "If You Feel Like Singing, Sing"; "You Wonderful You" (lyric: Jack Brooks, Saul Chaplin); "Friendly Star"; "Heavenly Music" (Chaplin); "Get Happy" (Harold Arlen-Ted Koehler)
Released: August 1950; 108 minutes

The story is all about a theatrical troupe of young Broadway hopefuls having all kinds of problems trying out a new show in a Connecticut barn—so let's page Mickey and Judy! That, at least, was the original plan of producer Joe Pasternak, but he had second thoughts because the Judy Garland-Gene Kelly combination seemed like a stronger box office bet. And so the couple appeared together for the third and last time in a film that also happened to be Miss Garland's 27th and final picture at MGM. In this unpretentious, predictable tale, Judy played the farmer on whose land the barn is located and Gene the leader of the acting company that Judy, against her will, has allowed to stay on her property.

The stars' duet "You Wonderful You" was a highlight as was Kelly's dance on a newspaper covering the barn's squeaky floor. Judy's health problems caused so many delays that the shooting schedule was forced to run over eight months. They were also responsible for her being noticeably overweight. Two months after filming had stopped, however, when she returned to do the classic "Get Happy" number, Judy had shed 20 pounds and was back to her normal figure. The film's title—something of a misnomer since it was not really about a summer stock company—was changed in Great Britain to *If You Feel Like Singing*.
CBS ST. MGM/UA VC.

Summer Stock. Gene Kelly and Judy Garland dancing to "You Wonderful You."

ROYAL WEDDING

Music: Burton Lane
Lyrics & screenplay: Alan Jay Lerner
Produced by: Arthur Freed for MGM
Directed by: Stanley Donen
Choreography: Nick Castle (Fred Astaire uncredited)
Photography: Robert Planck (Technicolor)
Cast: Fred Astaire, Jane Powell, Peter Lawford, Sarah Churchill, Keenan Wynn, Albert Sharpe, Viola Roache, Mae Clarke
Songs: "Open Your Eyes"; "The Happiest Day of My Life"; "How Could You Believe Me When I Said I Love You When You Know I've Been a Liar All My Life"; "Too Late Now"; "You're All the World to Me"; "I Left My Hat in Haiti"
Released: March 1951; 93 minutes

Royal Wedding grew out of Arthur Freed's desire to produce a musical that would take advantage of the 1947 marriage of Princess Elizabeth and Philip Mountbatten. For his first Hollywood assignment, Alan Jay Lerner contributed a story loosely paralleling the relationship between Fred Astaire and his sister and first partner, Adele. In 1928, the Astaires took their Broadway hit *Funny Face* to London. While there, Adele met Lord Charles Cavendish, whom she subsequently married, thereby ending her professional career. In *Royal Wedding,* Tom Bowen (Astaire) and his sister Ellen (Jane Powell) take their Broadway hit *Every Night at Seven* to London. On the ship going over, Ellen meets Lord John Brindale (Peter Lawford), whom she weds soon after the show's West End opening, thereby ending her professional career. To flesh out Fred's part, the dancer finds romance with a publican's daughter (Sir Winston's daughter, Sarah Churchill). To tie it all in with the royal nuptials, both couples get married on the same day as the Princess and the Duke.

The film had originally been intended for Astaire and June Allyson. Miss Allyson, however, became pregnant and was succeeded by Judy Garland. Then Miss Garland began missing rehearsals and had to be replaced by Miss Powell. Astaire's standout dance solo takes place in his London hotel room, where he seemingly defies gravity by dancing all over the walls and ceiling. Lest Britons mistake the picture for a documentary, the movie was retitled *Wedding Bells* in Great Britain.

MCA ST. MGM/UA VC.

Royal Wedding. Fred Astaire and Jane Powell doing the comic "Liar Song."

The Great Caruso. Jarmila Novotna, Mario Lanza, and Ian Wolfe meeting at the Metropolitan Opera House.

THE GREAT CARUSO

Screenplay: Sonia Levien & William Ludwig
Produced by: Joe Pasternak for MGM
Directed by: Richard Thorpe, Peter Herman Adler
Photography: Joseph Ruttenberg (Technicolor)
Cast: Mario Lanza, Ann Blyth, Dorothy Kirsten, Jarmila Novotna, Richard Hageman, Carl Benton Reid, Eduard Franz, Ludwig Donath, Mae Clarke, Ian Wolfe
Songs & arias: "La donna e mobile" (Verdi); 'Celeste Aida" (Verdi); "Torna a Surriento" (DeCurtis); "O Paradiso" (Verdi); "Che gelida manina" (Puccini); "Vesti la Giubba" (Leoncavallo); "Ave Maria" (Bach-Gounod); "The Loveliest Night of the Year" (Juventino Rosas, Irving Aaronson-Paul Francis Webster); "Sextet" (Donizetti); "M'Appari" (Flotow); "'Tis the Last Rose of Summer" (Thomas Moore)
Released: April 1951; 109 minutes

Mario Lanza appeared in only seven films and dubbed the soundtrack of an eighth *(The Student Prince)*, but so great was his appeal that the robust, temperamental tenor did more to popularize opera than any other movie star. Lanza's biggest hit, the sugar-coated biography of the legendary opera singer, traces Enrico Caruso's story from his humble beginnings in Naples, through his idyllic marriage to a New York socialite (there is no mention of a previous common-law wife and their two sons, nor of Caruso's notorious womanizing), to his death of pleurisy at the age of 48 (Lanza himself died of a heart attack at 38). The ancient Mexican waltz known as "Over the Waves," usually associated with performing seals, was revised for the film and called "The Loveliest Night of the Year." Though sung by Ann Blyth as Mrs. Caruso, the song became a hit only after Lanza recorded it.

An Italian screen biography, *Enrico Caruso, Legend of a Voice,* with Ermanno Randi, was released the same year as *The Great Caruso.* The American film was followed by three other Hollywood biographies of opera stars: *So This Is Love* (1953), with Kathryn Grayson as Grace Moore (Miss Moore had played Jenny Lind in her 1930 biography, *A Lady's Morals); Melba* (1953), with Patrice Munsel as Nellie Melba; and *Interrupted Melody* (1955), with Eleanor Parker (with the voice of Eileen Farrell) as Marjorie Lawrence. *RCA ST. MGM/UA VC.*

ON THE RIVIERA

Music & lyrics: Sylvia Fine
Screenplay: Phoebe & Henry Ephron
Produced by: Sol C. Siegel for 20th Century-Fox
Directed by: Walter Lang
Choreography: Jack Cole
Photography: Leon Shamroy (Technicolor)
Cast: Danny Kaye, Gene Tierney, Corinne Calvert, Marcel Dalio, Clinton Sundberg, Sig Rumann, Gwen Verdon
Songs: "On the Riviera"; "Rhythm of a New Romance"; "Ballin' the Jack" (Chris Smith); "Popo the Puppet"; "Happy Ending"
Released: April 1951; 89 minutes

In 1935 it had been used for *Folies Bergere de Paris,* in 1941 it had served for *That Night in Rio,* and in 1951 the well-tested tale of the impersonator who doubles for a celebrated playboy showed up once more in *On the Riviera.* With Danny Kaye in a variation on the dual role previously played by Maurice Chevalier and Don Ameche, the story was again moved to a different locale and filmed in dazzling color (cameraman Leon Shamroy had the distinction of working on all three movies). The funniest version of all, *On the Riviera* gave Danny Kaye more comic opportunities than his predecessors, as well as four new numbers written to his specifications by his wife, Sylvia Fine. (There was even an "in" joke in which Kaye does an imitation of Chevalier while singing the title song.)

SHOW BOAT

Music: Jerome Kern
Lyrics: Oscar Hammerstein II
Screenplay: John Lee Mahin
Produced by: Arthur Freed for MGM
Directed by: George Sidney
Choreography: Robert Alton
Photography: Charles Rosher (Technicolor)
Cast: Kathryn Grayson, Ava Gardner, Howard Keel, Joe E. Brown, Marge & Gower Champion, Robert Sterling, Agnes Moorehead, Leif Erickson, William Warfield, Regis Toomey, Fuzzy Knight, Chick Chandler
Songs: "Make Believe"; "Can't Help Lovin' Dat Man"; "I Might Fall Back on You"; "Ol' Man River"; "You Are Love"; "Why Do I Love You?"; "Bill" (lyric with P.G. Wodehouse); "Life Upon the Wicked Stage"; "After the Ball" (Charles K. Harris)
Released: June 1951; 108 minutes

Not counting the abridgement in *Till the Clouds Roll By* (which also featured Kathryn Grayson), there have been three movie versions of the 1927 landmark Broadway production (see page 57 for the 1936 film). During the first part of the 1951 adaptation, the script keeps close to the original Oscar Hammerstein libretto, including the love-at-first-sight meeting between Magnolia Hawks and riverboat gambler Gaylord Ravenal, the revelation that the showboat's star attraction, Julie La Verne, is part Negro and must leave the company, and Magnolia and Gay's marriage and their move to Chicago. Then the dramatic structure is considerably tightened by having Ravenal, now penniless, walk out on Magnolia while she is pregnant, and by having Magnolia, after singing in a Chicago nightclub on New Year's Eve, return with her father to the showboat to bring up her daughter (in the original, both she and daughter become musical-comedy stars on Broadway). Instead of waiting some 20 years until their accidental reunion, Magnolia and Gay are separated only about four years, and it is the tragic Julie who plays a crucial role in bringing them together. Initially, either Judy Garland or Dinah Shore seemed set for the role of Julie, but the part went to Ava Gardner (with her songs dubbed by Annette Warren, though the "soundtrack" album used Miss Gardner's voice).
CBS ST. MGM/UA VC.

Show Boat. The *Cotton Blossom* comes to town.

AN AMERICAN IN PARIS

Music: George Gershwin
Lyrics: Ira Gershwin
Screenplay: Alan Jay Lerner
Produced by: Arthur Freed for MGM
Directed by: Vincente Minnelli
Choreography: Gene Kelly
Photography: Alfred Gilks, John Alton (Technicolor)
Cast: Gene Kelly, Leslie Caron, Oscar Levant, Georges Guetary, Nina Foch, Benny Carter Orch., Andre Charisse, Eugene Borden, Martha Bamattre, Ann Codee, Dudley Field Malone
Songs & instrumentals: "Embraceable You"; "By Strauss"; "I Got Rhythm"; "Tra-La-La"; "Love Is Here to Stay"; "I'll Build a Stairway to Paradise" (lyric with B.G. DeSylva); "Piano Concerto in F" (third movement); " 'S Wonderful"; "An American in Paris" (ballet)
Released: August 1951; 113 minutes

He had no story or score, but producer Arthur Freed was certain of three things: the movie would be about an American in Paris, it would be called *An American in Paris,* and it would somehow use the Gershwin orchestral suite as part of the story. The next logical step was to have an all-Gershwin score and Freed, joined by director Vincente Minnelli and his staff, came up with about a dozen songs plus the third movement of the Piano Concerto in F. Once it was decided to create a ballet as the movie's climax, Gene Kelly became the logical choice for the title role.

Screenwriter Alan Jay Lerner devised an accommodating tale about a carefree, impecunious painter, former GI Jerry Mulligan (Kelly), who needs no more than one look to fall hopelessly in love with pert young Parisian Lise Bourvier (French ballet dancer Leslie Caron, then 19, in her film debut). Lise somehow finds herself succumbing to the aggressively gauche American—particularly when they dance to "Love Is Here to Stay" on a Seine River embankment—but there is a complication: she is engaged to an older man, popular music hall singer Henri Baurel (Georges Guetary, who was actually two-and-a-half years younger than Kelly). Another complication arises when wealthy American Milo Richards (Nina Foch), who has taken a fancy to Jerry, offers to set him up in an elegant studio and introduce him to all the right people. (This situation was doubtlessly prompted by the Broadway musical *Pal Joey,* in which Kelly had first won recognition.) Through a mutual friend, composer Adam Cook (Oscar Levant), Jerry and Henri become acquainted without being aware that each loves the same girl. At the film's end, of course, Jerry wins Lise with Henri's blessing.

When Miss Foch was forced to miss work for a few days because of illness, the delay gave Kelly time to concentrate on the *American in Paris* ballet. He came up with the idea of having Jerry, brooding about his lost love, think about Paris and Lise and what they both mean to him, with the dance evolving as Jerry's way of expressing his varied emotions as he pursues Lise throughout the city. Because Jerry is an artist, each section of Paris is shown in the style of a famous painter— Dufy for the Place de la Concorde, Renoir for the Pont Neuf, Utrillo for Montmartre, Rousseau for the zoo, Van Gogh for the Place de l'Opera, and Toulouse-Lautrec for the Moulin Rouge. Lasting 17 minutes, the ballet took one month to shoot and cost $542,000.

Initially, Kelly wanted to film the musical sequences in Paris, but economic considerations forced Freed to shoot everything in Culver City. Despite forebodings that audiences wouldn't sit still for the ballet finale, *An American in Paris* placed high among the top money-makers of 1951.

CBS ST. MGM/UA VC.

An American in Paris. Gene Kelly and Leslie Caron in the ballet.

WITH A SONG IN MY HEART

Screenplay: Lamar Trotti
Produced by: Lamar Trotti for 20th Century-Fox
Directed by: Walter Lang
Choreography: Billy Daniels
Photography: Leon Shamroy (Technicolor)
Cast: Susan Hayward, David Wayne, Thelma Ritter, Rory Calhoun, Una
         Merkel, Richard Allan, Max Showalter, Leif Erickson, Robert Wagner,
         Lyle Talbot
Songs: "Blue Moon" (Richard Rodgers-Lorenz Hart); "With a Song in My
         Heart" (Rodgers-Hart); "Embraceable You" (George Gershwin-Ira
         Gershwin); "Tea for Two" (Vincent Youmans-Irving Caesar); "It's
         a Good Day" (Dave Barbour-Peggy Lee); "They're Either Too
         Young or Too Old" (Arthur Schwartz-Frank Loesser); "I'll Walk
         Alone" (Jule Styne-Sammy Cahn); "Indiana" (James Hanley-
         Ballard MacDonald); "Deep in the Heart of Texas" (Don Swander-
         June Hershey)
Released: February 1952; 117 minutes

A leading radio, nightclub, and recording attraction during the 1930s and 1940s, Jane
Froman suffered a crippling accident early in 1943 when she was injured in a plane crash
off Lisbon as she was flying to entertain the troops. The story of the singer's battle to recover
her health and her gallant professional comeback was the subject of a highly popular if
sudsy biography, in which Susan Hayward gave a strong performance and Miss Froman
supplied the vocal dubbing on the soundtrack for over 20 songs (including "I'll Walk Alone,"
which became one of the singer's best-selling records).
Capitol ST.

With a Song in My Heart. Jane Froman (Susan Hayward) entertaining the troops.

THE BELLE OF NEW YORK

Music: Harry Warren
Lyrics: Johnny Mercer
Screenplay: Robert O'Brien & Irving Elinson
Produced by: Arthur Freed for MGM
Directed by: Charles Walters
Choreography: Robert Alton (Fred Astaire uncredited)
Photography: Robert Planck (Technicolor)
Cast: Fred Astaire, Vera-Ellen, Marjorie Main, Keenan Wynn, Alice Pearce, Clinton Sundberg, Gale Robbins, Lisa Ferraday, Benny Rubin
Songs: "When I'm Out With the Belle of New York"; "Seeing's Believing"; "Baby Doll"; "Oops!"; "Naughty but Nice"; "I Wanna Be a Dancin' Man"
Released: February 1952; 82 minutes

Raiding the Broadway stage for material on which to base screen musicals has been going on ever since the earliest days of talkies. No one, however, had ever gone back as far as Arthur Freed when he put into production a variation on the 1897 musical, *The Belle of New York.* In the film version, with a new score by Harry Warren and Johnny Mercer, the period is roughly the same as that of *Easter Parade,* and the story has to do with a playboy who gives up his prodigal ways when he falls in love with an officer in the Salvation Army (here called the Daughters of the Right). Following *Royal Wedding* on Fred Astaire's agenda, the movie gave an even more amazing demonstration of gravitational defiance. In the previous film Fred has danced on the walls and ceiling of his hotel room; in the current one he walks and dances on air (though it's an ability one always suspected he possessed). An extended dance sequence performed before a series of seasonal backdrops inspired by Currier and Ives lithographs was another high spot, as was the song-and-dance number "I Wanna Be a Dancin' Man," which became a joyously personal expression for Astaire. *The Belle of New York* was the second and last time Astaire was teamed with Vera-Ellen (whose singing voice belonged to Anita Ellis).
MCA ST. MGM/UA VC.

SINGIN' IN THE RAIN

Music: Nacio Herb Brown
Lyrics: Arthur Freed
Screenplay: Betty Comden & Adolph Green
Produced by: Arthur Freed for MGM
Directors-choreographers: Gene Kelly & Stanley Donen
Photography: Harold Rosson (Technicolor)
Cast: Gene Kelly, Donald O'Connor, Debbie Reynolds, Jean Hagen,
   Millard Mitchell, Cyd Charisse, Rita Moreno, Jimmy Thompson
Songs: "Singin' in the Rain"; "Fit as a Fiddle" (music: Al Hoffman, Al
   Goodhart); "All I Do Is Dream of You"; "Make 'Em Laugh"; "I've
   Got a Feelin' You're Foolin'"; "Should I?"; "Beautiful Girl"; "You
   Were Meant for Me"; "Good Morning"; "Would You?"
Released: March 1952;103 minutes

Since Arthur Freed had recently produced a movie built around the Gershwin catalogue *(An American in Paris),* and since he himself had begun his career as the lyricist partner of composer Nacio Herb Brown, why not, he reasoned, build a movie around the Freed catalogue? For the project Betty Comden and Adolph Green were chosen to concoct an appropriate tale with no more inspirational guide than the songs Freed and Brown had written for MGM movies during the late 1920s and early 1930s. Because these songs evoked the flavor of the period, the writers came up with a spoofing but affectionate story about the traumatic days when Hollywood abandoned the silent screen in favor of the sound screen. And since the leading male role would be that of a former song-and-dance man who becomes a Hollywood star, the part was eminently suited to Gene Kelly, who was also signed as co-director-choreographer with Stanley Donen. In addition to Comden, Green, Kelly, and Donen, *Singin' in the Rain* also reunited others in the Freed Unit who had worked together on *On the Town*—associate producer Roger Edens, art director Cedric Gibbons, music director Lennie Hayton, and cameraman Harold Rosson. As in the case of *An American in Paris,* the studio hierarchs wanted a fresh face for the female lead, and they chose the one belonging to Debbie Reynolds.

The story tells of silent screen idol Don Lockwood who accidentally meets Kathy Selden following the premiere of Don's latest swashbuckler, *The Royal Rascal.* Kathy is a struggling young actress who, with the advent of the talkies, gets a job dubbing the speaking voice of a temperamental star, Lina Lamont (Jean Hagen), whose barely understandable squeak would have ended her career. Eventually, the ruse is revealed and Kathy wins both stardom and Don. One curious aspect of *Singin' in the Rain* is that it actually perpetuates the kind of auditory deception that it ridicules. The cultured speaking tones emanating from Miss Hagen's mouth were really her own since Miss Reynolds' Texas twang would have been unsuitable, and even Debbie's singing of "Would You?" had to be dubbed by Betty Noyes.

The picture has a number of standout musical sequences, especially Kelly's splash dance to "Singin' in the Rain," which became his trademark. Donald O'Connor (as Don's sidekick Cosmo Brown) had a funny slapstick number in "Make 'Em Laugh" (though the music and general idea had been snitched from Cole Porter's "Be a Clown"), and there was an exuberant "Good Morning" for Kelly, Reynolds, and O'Connor to perform all over Lockwood's house. The lengthy, self-contained "Broadway Ballet" (which seems to have come out of another film called *Left Field*), finds Kelly playing a young hoofer who wins success on the Great White Way but loses the seductive moll (Cyd Charisse) whom he adores.

Singin' in the Rain is usually on anyone's list of the screen's most favored musicals. Two stage productions were based on the movie. In 1983, a London version with Tommy Steele had a run of two years; in 1985, a Broadway version with Don Correia hung on for ten months.
CBS ST. MGM/UA VC.

Singin' in the Rain. Gene Kelly's dance to the title song.

Lovely to Look At. Marge Champion, Kathryn Grayson, and Ann Miller.

LOVELY TO LOOK AT

Music: Jerome Kern
Lyrics: Otto Harbach*; Dorothy Fields**
Screenplay: George Wells & Harry Ruby
Produced by: Jack Cummings for MGM
Directed by: Mervyn LeRoy, Vincente Minnelli
Choreography: Hermes Pan
Photography: George Folsey (Technicolor)
Cast: Kathryn Grayson, Red Skelton, Howard Keel, Marge & Gower Champion, Zsa Zsa Gabor, Kurt Kasznar, Marcel Dalio
Songs: "Lovely to Look At"***; "I'll Be Hard to Handle" (lyric: Bernard Dougall); "Yesterdays" *; "The Most Exciting Night" **; "You're Devastating"*; "I Won't Dance"***; "Smoke Gets in Your Eyes"*; "The Touch of Your Hand"*
Released: May 1952; 112 minutes

Alice Duer Miller's novel *Gowns by Roberta* was the genesis of the 1933 Broadway musical *Roberta*, RKO's 1935 screen version (see page 40), and MGM's 1952 version, retitled *Lovely to Look At*. Three of the original Jerome Kern songs—"I'll Be Hard to Handle," "Yesterdays," and "Smoke Gets in Your Eyes"—were in both movies; two—"I Won't Dance" and "Lovely to Look At"—were written for the first film and retained for the second; and two—"Lafayette" and "The Most Exciting Night"—were introduced in the 1952 treatment. All clear? This time out the story is about three would-be Broadway producers, Howard Keel, Red Skelton, and Gower Champion, who, accompanied by nightclub dancer and investor Ann Miller, go to Paris to sell Skelton's half interest in a fashionable dress salon known as Madame Roberta's. In Paris they meet sisters Kathryn Grayson and Marge Champion, owners of the other half interest in the salon, which is in dire financial trouble. To stave off creditors, they all take part in a mammoth fashion show (staged by Vincente Minnelli) featuring a display of some 42 costumes designed by Adrian. Hermes Pan, who devised the film's dance routines (Ann Miller's flashy "I'll Be Hard to Handle" was a standout), had also choreographed the earlier film version of the story.
MCA ST.

Where's Charley? In a dream sequence, Ray Bolger and Allyn McLerie dance to the music of "Pernambuco."

WHERE'S CHARLEY?

Music & lyrics: Frank Loesser
Screenplay: John Monks Jr.
Produced by: Gerry Blattner for Warner Bros.
Directed by: David Butler
Choreography: Michael Kidd
Photography: Erwin Hillier (Technicolor)
Cast: Ray Bolger, Allyn McLerie, Robert Shackleton, Mary Germaine,
    Horace Cooper, Margaretta Scott
Songs: "Once in Love With Amy"; "My Darling, My Darling"; "Make a
    Miracle"; "Pernambuco"; "Where's Charley?"; "The New
    Ashmoleon Marching Society and Student Conservatory Band"
Released: July 1952; 97 minutes

For his first Broadway assignment, Hollywood composer-lyricist Frank Loesser was engaged to write the score for the 1948 musical *Where's Charley?,* adapted from Brandon Thomas's durable farce, *Charley's Aunt.* The Thomas play, which premiered in London in 1892, concerns two Oxford undergraduates, Charley Wykeham and Jack Chesney who, in order to entertain two proper young ladies in their rooms, cajole a third student, Lord Fancourt Babberly, to act as chaperon by posing as Charley's aunt from Brazil, "where the nuts come from." (Jack Benny starred in the movie version of *Charley's Aunt* in 1941.) In the musical adaptation, the third character was eliminated and the aunt in drag was played by Charley himself, with the humor resulting from the quick costume changes as Charley runs around trying to play both the aunt and the ardent suitor. Ray Bolger as Charley, Allyn McLerie as his inamorata, and Horace Cooper as Miss McLerie's guardian repeated their stage roles in the screen adaptation, which also retained most of the songs in Loesser's score (including Bolger's showstopping "Once in Love With Amy" and his proposal duet with Miss McLerie, "Make a Miracle"). Part of the film was shot at Oxford.

ROAD TO BALI

Music: James Van Heusen
Lyrics: Johnny Burke
Screenplay: Frank Butler, Hal Kanter, William Morrow
Produced by: Harry Tugend for Paramount
Directed by: Hal Walker
Choreography: Charles O'Curran
Photography: George Barnes (Technicolor)
Cast: Bing Crosby, Bob Hope, Dorothy Lamour, Murvyn Vye, Peter Coe,
        Bob Crosby, Jane Russell, Dean Martin, Jerry Lewis, Carolyn Jones
Songs: "Chicago Style"; "Moonflowers"; "Hoot Mon"; "To See You"; "Merry
        Go Runaround"
Released: November 1952; 91 minutes

(See page 95.)

Road to Bali. The "Hoot Mon" number performed by Bing Crosby, Dorothy Lamour, and Bob Hope at an island feast.

HANS CHRISTIAN ANDERSEN

Music & lyrics: Frank Loesser
Screenplay: Moss Hart
Produced by: Samuel Goldwyn (released by RKO Radio)
Directed by: Charles Vidor
Choreography: Roland Petit
Photography: Harry Stradling (Technicolor)
Cast: Danny Kaye, Farley Granger, Jeanmaire, Joey Walsh, Erik Bruhn, Roland Petit
Songs: "The King's New Clothes"; "I'm Hans Christian Andersen"; "Wonderful Copenhagen"; "Thumbelina"; "The Ugly Duckling"; "Anywhere I Wander"; "The Inch Worm"; "No Two People"
Released: November 1952; 120 minutes

It took five years and 21 scripts before producer Samuel Goldwyn gave his approval to go ahead with the musical about Hans Christian Andersen—and then he ran into trouble with the Danish government for distorting the writer's life. Actually, the Moss Hart screenplay made no attempt at biographical accuracy, and the Danes were mollified when the movie was preceded by the explanation that it was "a fairy tale about a great spinner of fairy tales." With a subdued Danny Kaye in the title role, the plot, set in 1830, tells of a cobbler who entertains children in his native Odense by spinning stories, much to the displeasure of town officials. Andersen takes off for Copenhagen where he makes shoes for a ballerina (Jeanmaire), with whom he falls hopelessly in love and for whom he writes a 17-minute ballet, "The Little Mermaid." Back home in Odense the heartsick storyteller at last wins the appreciation of all his neighbors. More important to the success of the film than its somewhat downbeat script were the four ballets (comprising some 25% of the footage) and the imaginative Frank Loesser score, half of which was based on Andersen's fairy tales. Goldwyn's most lavish production to date, *Hans Christian Andersen* was one of the leading box office attractions of 1953.

A stage variation—which used the songs but not the script—opened in London in 1974 under the title *Hans Andersen*. Tommy Steele had the starring role.
Decca (Kaye LP). Nelson VC.

Hans Christian Andersen. Danny Kaye singing the tale of "The King's New Clothes" to the children of Odense.

Call Me Madam. Ethel Merman belting "Something to Dance About" as she entertains at an embassy party.

CALL ME MADAM

Music & lyrics: Irving Berlin
Screenplay: Arthur Sheekman
Produced by: Sol C. Siegel for 20th Century-Fox
Directed by: Walter Lang
Choreography: Robert Alton
Photography: Leon Shamroy (Technicolor)
Cast: Ethel Merman, George Sanders, Donald O'Connor, Vera-Ellen, Billy DeWolfe, Helmut Dantine, Walter Slezak, Ludwig Stossel, Charles Dingle, Walter Woolf King, Johnny Downs
Songs: "The Hostess With the Mostes' "; "Can You Use Any Money Today?"; "Marrying for Love"; "It's a Lovely Day Today"; "That International Rag"; "The Ocarina"; "What Chance Have I With Love?"; "The Best Thing for You"; "Something to Dance About"; "You're Just in Love"
Released: March 1953; 117 minutes

Of Ethel Merman's nine Broadway musicals that were turned into movies, only two retained her services—*Anything Goes* in 1936 and *Call Me Madam* 17 years later. A Broadway hit of 1950, *Call Me Madam* had a book by Howard Lindsay and Russel Crouse based on President Harry Truman's surprise choice of wellheeled Washington party-giver Perle Mesta as Ambassador to Luxembourg, and the musical was replete with satirical thrusts at politics, foreign affairs, and the behavior of the comically gauche Americans abroad. The film version—which gave Miss Merman her best screen role—was a close approximation of the show, with virtually all the Irving Berlin songs intact. In the story, when Sally Adams, the hostess with the mostes' on the ball, becomes Ambassador to the mythical Duchy of Lichtenburg, she charms the local gentry with her brash, no-nonsense style. She also finds herself in a romantic foreign entanglement with diplomat Cosmo Constantine (George Sanders in his only screen musical), and helps her young aide, Kenneth Gibson (Donald O'Connor), recognize romantic symptoms in the contrapuntal duet, "You're Just in Love." *DRG ST.*

Gentlemen Prefer Blondes. Jane Russell and Marilyn Monroe take over a Paris street to sing and dance "When Love Goes Wrong."

GENTLEMEN PREFER BLONDES

Music: Jule Styne*; Hoagy Carmichael**
Lyrics: Leo Robin*; Harold Adamson**
Screenplay: Charles Lederer
Produced by: Sol C. Siegel for 20th Century-Fox
Directed by: Howard Hawks
Choreography: Jack Cole
Photography: Harry Wild (Technicolor)
Cast: Jane Russell, Marilyn Monroe, Charles Coburn, Elliott Reid, Tommy Noonan, Taylor Holmes, Steven Geray, Norma Varden, Larry Kert, George Chakiris
Songs: "A Little Girl from Little Rock" *; "Bye, Bye Baby" *; "Ain't There Anyone Here for Love?" **; "When Love Goes Wrong" * *; "Diamonds Are a Girl's Best Friend"*
Released: June 1953; 91 minutes

On Broadway, where it opened in 1949, *Gentlemen Prefer Blondes* was a spoof of the madcap Twenties which gave Carol Channing her first starring role; on the screen, it was an up-to-date spoof of sex which gave Marilyn Monroe her first starring role in a musical. Freely adapted from Anita's Loos's novel, the movie tells of the adventures of two little girls from Little Rock, money-hungry Lorelei (Monroe) and man-hungry Dorothy Shaw (Jane Russell), who take an ocean liner to France. They meet some accommodating gentlemen, are accused of filching a diamond tiara, do a saucy turn on a Paris street ("When Love Goes Wrong"), become entertainers in a cabaret (where Miss Monroe wiggles through "Diamonds Are a Girl's Best Friend"), and end up with suitable mates for a joint wedding ceremony aboard a ship returning to New York. Only three songs from the original Jule Styne-Leo Robin score were retained, with two others by Hoagy Carmichael and Harold Adamson added. The film was followed two years later by United Artists' *Gentlemen Marry Brunettes,* also from a book by Miss Loos and also starring Jane Russell.
DRG ST. CBS/Fox VC.

The Band Wagon. Fred Astaire, Nanette Fabray, and Jack Buchanan as "Triplets."

THE BAND WAGON

Music: Arthur Schwartz
Lyrics: Howard Dietz
Screenplay: Betty Comden & Adolph Green
Produced by: Arthur Freed for MGM
Directed by: Vincente Minnelli
Choreography: Michael Kidd
Photography: Harry Jackson (Technicolor)
Cast: Fred Astaire, Cyd Charisse, Oscar Levant, Nanette Fabray, Jack Buchanan, James Mitchell, Thurston Hall, Ava Gardner, Julie Newmar, Matt Mattox, LeRoy Daniels
Songs: "By Myself"; "A Shine on Your Shoes"; "That's Entertainment"; "Dancing in the Dark"; "Something to Remember You By"; "High and Low"; "I Love Louisa"; "New Sun in the Sky"; "I Guess I'll Have to Change My Plan"; "Louisiana Hayride"; "Triplets"; "The Girl Hunt" ballet (narration: Alan Jay Lerner)
Released: July 1953; 112 minutes

With the male lead of *Easter Parade*, the director of *An American in Paris,* and the writers of *Singin' in the Rain, The Band Wagon* became the fourth Arthur Freed production to spotlight the catalogue of a major songwriter or team. This time out it was composer Arthur Schwartz and lyricist Howard Dietz (he also doubled as head of MGM's promotion and publicity department), whose songs graced some of Broadway's most sophisticated revues. One of them even supplied the movie with a title. Since the original *Band Wagon* had also starred Fred Astaire (along with his sister Adele), and since Fred would be playing the leading role in the picture, this somehow sparked the idea of a backstage story in which four of the leading characters would be based on actual people. Fred's own career suggested the role of an aging Hollywood song-and-dance man. Comden and Green used themselves as models for two Broadway writers (played by Nanette Fabray and Oscar Levant), and the part of a flamboyant director (played by Jack Buchanan after it had been turned down by Clifton Webb) was a combination of Orson Welles, José Ferrer, and director Minnelli himself.

In the story, Tony Hunter, washed up in Hollywood, comes to New York to make a comeback in a musical comedy created by his friends Lily and Lester Marton. The show is to be directed by Broadway's latest genius, Jeffrey Cordova, and the leading lady is to be ballerina Gabrielle Gerard (Cyd Charisse, with India Adams' singing voice). The biggest problem along the show's bumpy road to New York is that Cordova has turned the Martons' lighthearted script into an arty modern version of *Faust.* Disaster! So in true Mickey and Judy style ("Gosh, with all this raw talent around, why can't us kids get together and put on ourselves a show!," was Levant's line), the actors take over the production from Cordova (though he appears in it) and transform it into a Broadway smash. Simple as that.

Among the unforgettable musical numbers are Astaire's rueful "By Myself" in Grand Central Terminal . . . his exuberant "Shine on Your Shoes" with LeRoy Daniels as they scamper around a 42nd Street penny arcade . . . the witty "That's Entertainment" (the only song written for the film) . . . the languid Astaire-Charisse dance to "Dancing in the Dark" performed in Central Park . . . Astaire and Buchanan's debonair song-and-dance to "I Guess I'll Have to Change My Plan" . . .the comic "Triplets" with Astaire, Fabray, and Buchanan on their knees in baby clothes . . . and "The Girl Hunt" ballet (with narration written anonymously by Alan Jay Lerner), a takeoff on Mickey Spillane detective novels featuring Astaire and Charisse.

Four years before *The Band Wagon* reached the screen, Fox had used three songs from the original stage revue in *Dancing in the Dark,* in which William Powell played a washed-up Hollywood actor. Earlier in the same year as *The Band Wagon,* Warners' *She's Back on Broadway* also told of a has-been movie star (Virginia Mayo) who attempts a comeback in a stage musical. (She's a hit but the show isn't.)
CBS ST. MGM/UA VC.

THE BEGGAR'S OPERA

Music: Sir Arthur Bliss
Lyrics: John Gay, Christopher Fry
Screenplay: Denis Cannan & Christopher Fry
Produced by: Laurence Olivier & Herbert Wilcox for British Lion
Directed by: Peter Brook
Photography: Guy Green (Technicolor)
Cast: Laurence Olivier, Stanley Holloway, Dorothy Tutin, George Devine, Mary Clare, Hugh Griffith, Daphne Anderson, Athene Seyler, Margot Grahame, Kenneth Williams, George Rose, Laurence Naismith
Songs: "In the Days of My Youth"; "Pretty Polly Say"; "Were I Laid on When I Was Down Greenland Coast"; "If the Heart of a Man"; "Youth's the Season Made for Joy"; "At the Gallows I'll Serve Her With Pleasure"; "How Happy Would I Be With Either"; "Come, Sweet Lass"; "Would I Might Be Hang'd"
Released: August 1953; 94 minutes

John Gay's London hit of 1728, the first ballad opera (or musical comedy), was a satire on both corrupt politicians and bombastic Italian operas. It was also the first movie directed by Peter Brook and the first musical starring Laurence Olivier, who did his own singing, horseback riding, and dueling. The British-made film opens in Newgate Prison where the notorious highwayman, Capt. Macheath (Olivier), meets a beggar (Hugh Griffith) who has written an opera glamorizing the outlaw. In the opera, redcoated Macheath is married to Polly (Dorothy Tutin), whose parents (George Devine and Mary Clare) betray him to the police and he is imprisoned at Newgate. He escapes with the help of Lucy Lockit (Daphne Anderson), the daughter of the gaoler (Stanley Holloway), but he is recaptured and sentenced to be hanged. The beggar, however, decides to give the outlaw a last minute reprieve, a verdict that is greeted by general rejoicing. Though the film was not a commercial success, its air of sophisticated merriment and its stylish sardonic viewpoint make it one of the everlasting delights of the musical screen.

The original *Beggar's Opera* was the progenitor of Kurt Weill's *Threepenny Opera*, which was brought to the screen in 1930, 1965, and 1990.

Kiss Me Kate. Howard Keel taming his shrew Kathryn Grayson. Looking on are Bob Fosse, Bobby Van, Ann Miller, and Tommy Rall.

KISS ME KATE

Music & lyrics: Cole Porter
Screenplay: Dorothy Kingsley
Produced by: Jack Cummings for MGM
Directed by: George Sidney
Choreography: Hermes Pan (Bob Fosse uncredited)
Photography: Charles Rosher (Ansco Color)
Cast: Kathryn Grayson, Howard Keel, Ann Miller, Tommy Rall, Keenan Wynn, James Whitmore, Bobby Van, Bob Fosse, Kurt Kasznar, Ron Randell, Willard Parker, Carol Haney, Jeanne Coyne, Claud Allister, Dave O'Brien
Songs: "So in Love" "Too Darn Hot"; "Why Can't You Behave?"; "Wunderbar"; ' We Open in Venice"; "Tom, Dick or Harry"; "I've Come to Wive It Wealthily in Padua"; "I Hate Men"; "Were Thine That Special Face"; "Where Is the Life That Late I Led?"; "Always True to You (in My Fashion)"; "Brush Up Your Shakespeare"; "From This Moment On"
Released: October 1953; 109 minutes

Kiss Me Kate had its genesis in 1935 when Saint Subber, then a stagehand for a Theatre Guild production of Shakespeare's *Taming of the Shrew*, couldn't help but observe that its stars, Alfred Lunt and Lynn Fontanne, battled almost as fiercely offstage as they did in the play. Convinced that this had the makings of a Broadway musical, Subber, who by 1948 had become a producer, took his idea to Cole Porter and playwrights Bella and Samuel Spewack. The result was Porter's most acclaimed work which, in turn, became the most satisfying of all the composer's eight stage musicals adapted to the screen, with virtually the entire score both intact and effectively staged. (Because of censorship, however, "stuck a pig" was changed to "met a bore" in "I've Come to Wive It Wealthily in Padua," and "virgin" became "maiden" in "I Hate Men.")

The movie reunited Kathryn Grayson and Howard Keel for their third and final appearance together (their other films were *Show Boat* and *Lovely to Look At*), though initially producer Jack Cummings had tried to get Laurence Oliver for the male lead. Miss Grayson was seen as Lilli Vanessi, a temperamental actress, and Keel played her ex-husband, Fred Graham, an egotistical actor and director, who is anxious to have Lilli costar with him in a musical version of *The Taming of the Shrew* (even Cole Porter, in the person of Ron Randell, shows up to persuade her). Despite misgivings, Lilli agrees, and the story focuses on the show's final rehearsal and out-of-town opening, with the action moving from backstage to onstage. (As in the 1929 film, *On With the Show*, the progress of the play, though seen only in segments, can be easily followed by the movie audience.) Hermes Pan's choreography for Ann Miller's sizzling "Too Darn Hot," and especially for the numbers involving Miss Miller, Tommy Rall, Bobby Van, Bob Fosse, Carol Haney, and Jeanne Coyne, turned the screen version into even more of a dancing show than the original. Fosse, in fact, made his choreographic debut with a segment in the sequence featuring "From This Moment On," a song that had been dropped from another Porter musical, *Out of This World*.

Kiss Me Kate was the only musical filmed in the three-dimensional—or 3D— process, an innovation that accounts for the distraction of seeing various items thrown directly at the camera, as well as for the staging of Keel's solo, "Where Is the Life That Late I Led?," on a runway jutting into the on-screen audience. Other movie musicals derived from Shakespearean sources were *The Boys from Syracuse* (1940) from *The Comedy of Errors*; *West Side Story* (1961) from *Romeo and Juliet*; and both *All Night Long* (1961) and *Catch My Soul* (1974) from *Othello*.
CBS ST. MGM/UA VC.

GIVE A GIRL A BREAK

Music: Burton Lane
Lyrics: Ira Gershwin
Screenplay: Frances Goodrich & Albert Hackett
Produced by: Jack Cummings for MGM
Directed by: Stanley Donen
Choreography: Gower Champion, Stanley Donen
Photography: William Mellor (Technicolor)
Cast: Debbie Reynolds, Marge & Gower Champion, Bob Fosse, Helen
Wood, Kurt Kasznar, Larry Keating, William Ching, Robert Anderson
Songs: "Give a Girl a Break"; "Nothing Is Impossible"; "In Our United
State"; "It Happens Every Time"; "Applause, Applause"
Released: December 1953; 82 minutes

When the star of a Broadway-bound musical walks out after a fight with director Gower Champion, he decides to follow the advice of the show's title, *Give a Girl a Break,* and hold auditions for an unknown to replace her. The three finalists are Debbie Reynolds (whom assistant director Bob Fosse fancies), Marge Champion (Gower's former dancing partner), and Helen Wood (the favorite of composer Kurt Kasznar). Through elimination, the starring role goes to Debbie, since Helen is pregnant and Marge is more interested in Gower than in her career. The unpretentious film was filled with attractive people, some engaging dance routines by the Champions and Bob Fosse, and a bright score by Burton Lane and Ira Gershwin, here collaborating for the only time.

The Glenn Miller Story. James Stewart as Glenn Miller.

THE GLENN MILLER STORY
Screenplay: Valentine Davies & Oscar Brodney
Produced by: Aaron Rosenberg for Universal
Directed by: Anthony Mann
Photography: William Daniels (Technicolor)
Cast: James Stewart, June Allyson, Harry Morgan, Charles Drake, George Tobias, Frances Langford, Louis Armstrong, Gene Krupa, Ben Pollack, Barton MacLane, Sig Rumann, Kathleen Lockhart
Songs: "Basin Street Blues" (Spencer Williams); "Over the Rainbow" (Harold Arlen-E. Y. Harburg); "I Know Why" (Harry Warren-Mack Gordon); "String of Pearls" (Jerry Gray-Eddie DeLange); "Pennsylvania 6-5000" (Gray-Carl Sigman); "Tuxedo Junction" (Erskine Hawkins, William Johnson, Julian Dash-Buddy Feyne); "Chattanooga Choo-Choo" (Warren-Gordon)
Released: January 1954; 116 minutes

A highly sentimentalized biography of one of the major figures of the big-band era, *The Glenn Miller Story* was Hollywood's most popular movie about the life of an orchestra leader (it had the eighth highest theatre rental fees of any musical released during the 1950s). James Stewart gave a sensitive performance in the title role (Joe Yukl dubbed his trombone playing), which helped overcome some of the excesses in the cliché-filled script dealing with Miller's domestic life (June Allyson played the understanding little woman) and his messianic search for "my own sound." Miller himself appeared in *Sun Valley Serenade* (1941) and *Orchestra Wives* (1942). Other screen biographies of bandleaders of the period were *The Fabulous Dorseys* (Jimmy and Tommy played themselves), *The Benny Goodman Story* (Steve Allen), *The Eddy Duchin Story* (Tyrone Power), and *The Gene Krupa Story* (Sal Mineo).
MCA ST. MCA VC.

ROSE MARIE
Music: Rudolf Friml, etc.
Lyrics: Otto Harbach & Oscar Hammerstein II*; Paul Francis Webster**
Screenplay: Ronald Millar & George Froeschel
Producer-director: Mervyn LeRoy for MGM
Choreography: Busby Berkeley
Photography: Paul Vogel (Eastman Color; CinemaScope)
Cast: Ann Blyth, Howard Keel, Fernando Lamas, Bert Lahr, Marjorie Main, Joan Taylor, Ray Collins
Songs: "The Right Place for a Girl" **; "Free to Be Free" **; "Indian Love Call"*; "Rose Marie"*; "Totem Tom-Tom"* (music with Herbert Stothart); "I'm a Mountie Who Never Got His Man" (George Stoll-Herbert Baker); "I Have the Love"***; "The Mounties" * (music with Stothart)
Released: March 1954; 115 minutes

In plot, at least, the 1954 *Rose Marie* was closer to the original Broadway hit of 1924 than it was to the Jeanette MacDonald-Nelson Eddy screen version (see page 51). The heroine (Ann Blyth) is now a French-Canadian trapper's daughter, not an opera star, and she loses her heart not to a Mountie (Howard Keel), but to a prospector (Fernando Lamas) falsely accused of murder. As in the 1936 Hollywood treatment, however, only four songs were retained from the original score, though composer Rudolf Friml was on hand to write four new pieces with lyricist Paul Francis Webster. Unfortunately, this widescreen remake did not enjoy the box office success of its predecessor.
MCA ST.

Seven Brides for Seven Brothers. The barn-raising sequence.

SEVEN BRIDES FOR SEVEN BROTHERS

Music: Gene de Paul
Lyrics: Johnny Mercer
Screenplay: Frances Goodrich, Albert Hackett, Dorothy Kingsley
Produced by: Jack Cummings for MGM
Directed by: Stanley Donen
Choreography: Michael Kidd
Photography: George Folsey (Ansco Color; CinemaScope)
Cast: Jane Powell, Howard Keel, Jeff Richards, Russ Tamblyn, Tommy Rall, Marc Platt, Matt Mattox, Jacques d'Amboise, Julie Newmar, Virginia Gibson, Kelly Brown
Songs: "Bless Your Beautiful Hide"; "Wonderful, Wonderful Day"; "When You're in Love"; "Goin' Co'tin'"; "Lonesome Polecat"; "Sobbin' Women"; "Spring, Spring, Spring"
Released: June 1954; 103 minutes

Based on Stephen Vincent Benet's story, "The Sobbin' Women"—which had been based on Plutarch's "Rape of the Sabine Women"—*Seven Brides for Seven Brothers* switched the locale from the Tennessee Valley to the Oregon backwoods in 1850 and turned the tale into a thick slice of robust Americana. Farmer Adam Pontipee (Howard Keel) goes to town looking for a wife and quickly finds a cook named Milly (Jane Powell) to marry him. Milly soon discovers, much to her horror, that Adam shares his isolated farmhouse with six surly, unwashed younger brothers. She tries teaching them social graces ("Goin' Co'tin"), but the young men are so romantically frustrated that they take direct action by kidnapping six young women from town. Because an avalanche blocks the mountain pass to the farm, the brothers cannot be apprehended until spring. By then, however, the captives have grown to love their honorably intentioned captors (the girls sleep in the farmhouse, the boys in the barn), and—as the title indicates—the film ends in matrimony for all.

What makes the movie memorable is its ambitious use of dance and the fact that all six younger Pontipees are played by expert dancers. Choreographer Michael Kidd gave them two outstanding sequences: the vaulting, somersaulting barn-raising number which builds to a free-for-all when the brothers square off against the young men from town, and the "Lonesome Polecat" scene in the snow in which the Pontipee boys reveal their misery at being without female companionship. In 1982, a stage version starring Debbie Boone had a brief run on Broadway.
MCA ST.   MGM/UA VC.

THE STUDENT PRINCE

Music: Sigmund Romberg*; Nicholas Brodszky**
Lyrics: Dorothy Donnelly*; Paul Francis Webster**
Screenplay: Sonia Levien & William Ludwig
Produced by: Joe Pasternak for MGM
Directed by: Richard Thorpe
Photography: Paul Vogel (Ansco Color; CinemaScope)
Cast: Edmund Purdom, Ann Blyth, Louis Calhern, Edmund Gwenn, S. Z.
Sakall, Evelyn Varden, John Williams, John Hoyt, John Ericson
Songs: "Come Boys, Let's All Be Gay Boys" *; "Summertime in
Heidelberg"**; "Drinking Song"*; "Serenade"*; "Deep in My Heart,
Dear"*; "Beloved"***; "I Walk With God"**; "Golden Days" *
Released: June 1954; 107 minutes

It seemed like a box office natural: Mario Lanza in *The Student Prince*. Lanza was then at the peak of his popularity, and the 1924 Sigmund Romberg-Dorothy Donnelly operetta about a prince's brief romance with a waitress in the university city of Heidelberg, had been a Broadway smash. And, oddly enough, it had been filmed only once before, in 1927, when Ernst Lubitsch directed a silent version with Norma Shearer and Ramon Novarro. But the unpredictable Lanza, in a fit of temperament, walked off the picture and out of his MGM contract—though not before he had recorded all of his songs. Thus, producer Joe Pasternak was able to salvage the project by casting Edmund Purdom as the student prince and dubbing Lanza's distinctive singing voice. The result may have been a vocal hybrid, but the movie did have all that emotion-stirring music (augmented by songs by Nicholas Brodszky and Paul Francis Webster), as well as atmospheric locales and some of Hollywood's nimblest scene-stealing character actors. Previous screen musicals concerned with the prince-commoner theme were MGM's *The Night Is Young* with Ramon Novarro, Evelyn Laye, and Romberg music (1935), and Fox's *Thin Ice* with Tyrone Power and Sonja Henie (1937).
RCA (Lanza LP)

WHITE CHRISTMAS

Music & lyrics: Irving Berlin
Screenplay: Norman Krasna, Norman Panama, Melvin Frank
Produced by: Robert Dolan for Paramount
Directed by: Michael Curtiz
Choreography: Robert Alton
Photography: Loyal Griggs (Technicolor; VistaVision)
Cast: Bing Crosby, Danny Kaye, Rosemary Clooney, Vera-Ellen, Dean
Jagger, Grady Sutton, Sig Rumann, Barrie Chase, George Chakiris
Songs: "White Christmas"; "The Old Man"; "Blue Skies"; "Sisters"; "The Best
Things Happen While You're Dancing"; "Snow"; "Mandy"; "Count
Your Blessings Instead of Sheep"; "Love, You Didn't Do Right by Me"
Released: August 1954; 120 minutes

Planned as the third Bing Crosby-Fred Astaire-Irving Berlin musical, *White Christmas* suffered the loss of Astaire when Fred took sick and had to be replaced by Donald O'Connor. Then O'Connor took sick and had to be replaced by Danny Kaye. None of the changes affected the box office: grossing $12 million in theatre rentals, the movie held the No. 1 position as the top money-making picture of 1954, and it also ranks fifth among the highest rental musicals of the decade. The story easily shows its *Holiday Inn-Blue Skies* roots, with Crosby and Kaye as successful Broadway partners who become romantically involved with sisters Rosemary Clooney and Vera-Ellen. On vacation in Vermont, they stay at a ski resort owned by Bing and Danny's former Army General (Dean Jagger) where they are the only guests because there's no snow. The boys help out the General by staging their Broadway-bound revue at the resort and Crosby makes a television appeal to his army buddies to show up on Christmas Eve. They do, it snows, and everyone sings "White Christmas."
MCA ST. Paramount VC.

Brigadoon. Cyd Charisse and Gene Kelly.

BRIGADOON

Music: Frederick Loewe
Lyrics & screenplay: Alan Jay Lerner
Produced by: Arthur Freed for MGM
Directed by: Vincente Minnelli
Choreography: Gene Kelly
Photography: Joseph Ruttenberg (Ansco Color; CinemaScope)
Cast: Gene Kelly, Cyd Charisse, Van Johnson, Elaine Stewart, Barry Jones, Hugh Laing, Albert Sharpe, Virginia Bosler
Songs: "Once in the Highlands"; "Brigadoon"; "Waitin' for My Dearie"; "I'll Go Home with Bonnie Jean"; "Heather on the Hill"; "Almost Like Being in Love"
Released: September 1954; 108 minutes

Lerner and Loewe's 1947 Broadway fantasy about a slumbering Scottish village that miraculously comes to life for one day every hundred years unfortunately seldom came to life on the screen. The initial plan was to shoot the outdoors sequences in the Scottish Highlands but economic considerations forced producer Arthur Freed and director Vincente Minnelli to film everything on the MGM backlot. Freed and Minnelli also wanted to make it more of a dancing musical than it had been on the stage which led them to sign Gene Kelly for both the leading role and the choreography. They also hoped to get British ballerina Moira Shearer, with the Sadler's Wells Ballet Company used for the ensemble, but that didn't work out either and Cyd Charisse was picked as Kelly's costar (with Carol Richards doing her singing). While no one was entirely satisfied with the results, the movie was partially redeemed by the atmospheric songs (half the original 14 were retained), and the lyrical Kelly-Charisse pas de deux to "The Heather on the Hill."
CBS ST. MGM/UA VC.

A STAR IS BORN

Music: Harold Arlen, etc.
Lyrics: Ira Gershwin, etc.
Screenplay: Moss Hart
Produced by: Sidney Luft for Warner Bros.
Directed by: George Cukor
Choreography: Richard Barstow
Photography: Sam Leavitt (Technicolor; CinemaScope)
Cast: Judy Garland, James Mason, Jack Carson, Charles Bickford, Tommy Noonan, Lucy Marlow, Grady Sutton, Laurindo Almeida, Amanda Blake, Irving Bacon, Louis Jean Heydt, Chick Chandler, Rex Evans, Mae Marsh
Songs: "Gotta Have Me Go With You"; "The Man That Got Away"; "Born in a Trunk" (Roger Edens-Leonard Gershe); "Swanee" (George Gershwin-Irving Caesar); "It's a New World"; "Here's What I'm Here For"; "Someone at Last"; "Lose That Long Face"
Released: September 1954; 154 minutes

Ever since appearing in a radio adaptation of *A Star Is Born* in 1942, Judy Garland had tried to interest MGM in the property. It was not, however, until the studio cancelled her contract nine years later that she again thought of the venerable Hollywood saga. Judy's then husband, Sidney Luft, made a deal with Warner Bros, and lined up director George Cukor (for his first musical), writer Moss Hart, and songwriters Harold Arlen and Ira Gershwin. Cary Grant, Ray Milland, Humphrey Bogart, Marlon Brando, and Laurence Olivier were sought for the male lead which eventually went to James Mason. The picture cost over $6 million and took ten months to make. Delays were caused by the decision, after eight days' shooting, to film it in CinemaScope, plus Judy's frequent absences from the set, and assorted firings and hirings. After the filming had been completed, the rousing but superfluous 15 minute mini-musical, "Born in a Trunk," was added. This made the running time more than three hours, which—over Cukor's objections—forced the removal of some crucial scenes and the elimination of two songs, "Here's What I'm Here For" and "Lose That Long Face." In 1983, however, most of the deleted sequences were restored and the film was rereleased in a version running 170 minutes.

The basic story first showed up in 1932 in David O. Selznick's *What Price Hollywood,* also directed by Cukor, with Constance Bennett as a waitress who becomes a star and Lowell Sherman as her mentor, a heavy-drinking director who hits the skids and shoots himself to death. The second version, in 1937—now called *A Star Is Born*—was again produced by Selznick. This time the movie played up the romantic relationship by having the rising star (Janet Gaynor) fall in love with and marry a boozy falling star (Fredric March) who ends his life by drowning in the Pacific. (The character was partly based on silent film actor John Bowers, an alcoholic who committed suicide in the same way.)

The emotion-draining musical version of 1954 concerns Esther Blodgett (Garland), a band singer in Hollywood, who, while appearing in a benefit show, encounters a soused movie star, Norman Maine (Mason), when he staggers onstage to join her act. Once he hears Esther sing "The Man That Got Away" in a deserted nightclub, Maine becomes convinced that she could become a great movie actress. With his help, Esther (now known as Vicki Lester) wins a starring role, becomes a sensation, and the couple marries. But Norman's career goes steadily downhill until, to keep from being a burden, the actor walks out of his Malibu beach house and drowns himself. Months later, Esther bravely appears at a benefit show at the Shrine Auditorium. Greeted by an ovation, she steps to the microphone, fights back the tears, and utters the imperishable line, "Hello, everybody. This is . . . Mrs. Norman Maine." (One curious aspect of the film is that the character of the alcoholic, self-destructive actor was more closely identified with Judy Garland's own life than the part she herself played.)

For a second musical version of *A Star Is Born,* see page 263.
CSP ST. Warner VC.

A Star Is Born. "Gotta Have Me Go With You" sing Jack Harman, Judy Garland, and Don McCabe during a benefit show at the Shrine Auditorium, Los Angeles.

CARMEN JONES

Music: Georges Bizet
Lyrics: Oscar Hammerstein II
Screenplay: Harry Kleiner
Producer-director: Otto Preminger for 20th Century-Fox
Choreography: Herbert Ross
Photography: Sam Leavitt (Deluxe Color; CinemaScope)
Cast: Dorothy Dandridge, Harry Belafonte, Olga James, Pearl Bailey, Diahann Carroll, Joe Adams, Brock Peters, Carmen DeLavallade
Songs: "Dat's Love"; "You Talk Just Like My Maw"; "Dere's a Cafe on de Corner"; "Beat Out Dat Rhythm on a Drum"; "Stan' Up an' Fight"; "Dis Flower"; "My Joe"
Released: October 1954; 105 minutes

French novelist Prosper Mérimée's *Carmen* was brought to the screen ten times as a silent, but it was not until 1948 that the story was filmed in Hollywood with sound (Columbia's *The Loves of Carmen* with Rita Hayworth). The first time, however, that an American studio filmed it with the music of Bizet's 1875 opera was when Fox released *Carmen Jones,* based on Oscar Hammerstein's all-black Broadway version of 1943. The action is now set during World War II mostly in the South and the leading characters are Carmen (Dorothy Dandridge dubbed by Marilyn Horne), a worker in a parachute factory; Joe (Harry Belafonte dubbed by LeVern Hutcherson), an Army corporal who falls in love with the temptress; Cindy Lou (Olga James) the country girl who loves Joe; and Husky Miller (Joe Adams dubbed by Marvin Hayes), a prizefighter who is the cause of Joe's strangling Carmen in a jealous rage. The most recent screen adaptation of Bizet's original opera was in 1984 with Julia Migenes-Johnson.
RCA ST.

THE COUNTRY GIRL

Music: Harold Arlen
Lyrics: Ira Gershwin
Screenplay: George Seaton
Produced by: William Perlberg for Paramount
Directed by: George Seaton
Choreography: Robert Alton
Photography: John F. Warren
Cast: Bing Crosby, Grace Kelly, William Holden, Anthony Ross, Gene
        Reynolds, Jacqueline Fontaine
Songs: "The Search Is Through"; "Dissertation on the State of Bliss" ("Love
        and Learn"); "It's Mine, It's Yours"; "The Land Around Us"
Released: November 1954; 104 minutes

Based on Clifford Odets' 1950 Broadway play, *The Country Girl* (a rather misleading title) was more of a drama with songs than a musical drama. It also gave Bing Crosby (who had originally turned it down) the most challenging role of his career, and the four Harold Arlen-Ira Gershwin songs seem to have been included to give Crosby confidence rather than to fulfill an essential need in the story. The plot of the film (one of 1955's box office winners) concerns an alcoholic, washed-up singer attempting to make a comeback on the stage in an *Oklahoma!* type musical called *The Land Around Us,* and his relationships with his long-suffering wife (Grace Kelly replaced Jennifer Jones before shooting began), and the show's director (William Holden) who, at first, fails to understand the actor's dependence on his spouse. *The Country Girl* marked Bing Crosby's 45th and penultimate appearance in a Paramount picture.
Decca (Crosby LP). Paramount VC.

The Country Girl. Bing Crosby recording "The Search Is Through."

Deep in My Heart. José Ferrer, as Sigmund Romberg, cavorting through *Jazzadoo.*

DEEP IN MY HEART

Music: Sigmund Romberg
Lyrics: Oscar Hammerstein II, etc.
Screenplay: Leonard Spigelgass
Produced by: Roger Edens for MGM
Directed by: Stanley Donen
Choreography: Eugene Loring
Photography: George Folsey (Eastman Color)
Cast: José Ferrer, Merle Oberon, Helen Traubel, Walter Pidgeon, Paul Heinreid, Rosemary Clooney, Gene Kelly, Fred Kelly, Jane Powell, Vic Damone, Ann Miller, Cyd Charisse, Howard Keel, Tony Martin, Doe Avedon, Tamara Toumanova, Paul Stewart, Isobel Elsom, William Olvis, James Mitchell, Joan Weldon, David Burns, Jim Backus
Songs: "Leg of Mutton" (Roger Edens); "You Will Remember Vienna"; "Softly, as in a Morning Sunrise"; "Mr. and Mrs." (Cyrus Wood'); "I Love to Go Swimmin' with Women" (Ballard MacDonald); "The Road to Paradise" (Rida Johnson Young); "Will You Remember" (Young); "It"; "Serenade" (Dorothy Donnelly); "One Alone" (lyric with Otto Harbach); "Your Land and My Land" (Donnelly); "Lover, Come Back to Me"; "Stouthearted Men"; "When I Grow Too Old to Dream"
Released: December 1954; 132 minutes

The fourth and final MGM salute to Broadway songwriters did homage to the contributions of Sigmund Romberg, whose 56 shows over a 40-year period made him the most prodigious composer of all. The film was the first to be produced solely by Roger Edens, who had been Arthur Freed's associate for nine years, and it continued the tradition of playing hobs with the facts of a composer's life and career. Originally announced with Kurt Kasznar as Romberg, the part went to the more versatile José Ferrer, whose manic performance outlining the plot of an imaginary musical comedy called *Jazzadoo* was a memorable turn. The composer's fame may have rested on his lush operetta scores, but his livelier, lesser-known numbers provide the movie's high spots: the Ferrer-Helen Traubel duet "Leg of Mutton"; the Ferrer-Rosemary Clooney (then Mrs. Ferrer) duet "Mr. and Mrs."; Gene and Fred Kelly's dance to "I Love to Go Swimmin' With Women"; and Ann Miller's dance to "It".
MCA ST. MGM/UA VC.

THERE'S NO BUSINESS LIKE SHOW BUSINESS

Music & lyrics: Irving Berlin
Screenplay: Henry & Phoebe Ephron
Produced by: Sol C. Siegel for 20th Century-Fox
Directed by: Walter Lang
Choreography: Robert Alton, Jack Cole
Photography: Leon Shamroy (DeLuxe Color; CinemaScope)
Cast: Ethel Merman, Donald O'Connor, Marilyn Monroe, Dan Dailey, Johnnie Ray, Mitzi Gaynor, Hugh O'Brian, Frank McHugh, Lee Patrick, Chick Chandler, Lyle Talbot
Songs: "When the Midnight Choo-Choo Leaves for Alabam'"; "Play a Simple Melody"; "After You Get What You Want You Don't Want It"; "A Man Chases a Girl (Until She Catches Him)"; You'd Be Surprised"; "Heat Wave"; "Alexander's Ragtime Band"
Released: December 1954; 117 minutes

Because of Ethel Merman's success in *Call Me Madam,* Fox's Darryl Zanuck signed her to appear in a second film with songs by Irving Berlin (including the title number, which Miss Merman had introduced in *Annie Get Your Gun*). The new picture also had the same producer, director, choreographer (Robert Alton), art directors (Lyle Wheeler, John DeCuir), music director (Alfred Newman), choral director (Ken Darby), and editor (Robert Simpson), and the stellar cast included Dan Dailey (as Miss Merman's husband and vaudeville partner), Donald O'Connor, Mitzi Gaynor, and Johnnie Ray (as their dancing and singing children), and, as O'Connor's love interest, Marilyn Monroe (who does a sexy "Heat Wave"). Berlin's score, the last one he worked on for the movies, consisted of 12 songs from the trunk and two new ones.
Decca ST. CBS/Fox VC.

There's No Business Like Show Business. Ethel Merman, Dan Dailey in their vaudeville number, "When the Midnight Choo-Choo Leaves for Alabam'."

HIT THE DECK

Music: Vincent Youmans
Lyrics: Leo Robin*, Clifford Grey #, etc.
Screenplay: Sonya Levien & William Ludwig
Produced by: Joe Pasternak for MGM
Directed by: Roy Rowland
Choreography: Hermes Pan
Photography: George Folsey (Eastman Color; CinemaScope)
Cast: Jane Powell, Tony Martin, Debbie Reynolds, Walter Pidgeon, Vic
          Damone, Gene Raymond, Ann Miller, Russ Tamblyn, Kay Armen,
          J. Carrol Naish, Jane Darwell, Allan King
Songs: "Join the Navy"* #; "Sometimes I'm Happy" (lyric: Irving Caesar);
          "Keeping Myself for You" (lyric: Sidney Clare); "Ciribiribin"
          (Albert Pestalozza); "Why, Oh Why?"* #; "I Know That You Know"
          (lyric: Anne Caldwell); "More Than You Know" (lyric: Edward Eliscu,
          Billy Rose); "Lady from the Bayou" *; "Hallelujah!" * #
Released: March 1955; 112 minutes

Ostensibly adapted from the 1927 Broadway musical, which had been based on Hubert Osborne's 1922 play *Shore Leave*, *Hit the Deck* kept seven of the 10 songs in the Vincent Youmans-Leo Robin-Clifford Grey score and discarded the Herbert Fields book. To replace it, producer Joe Pasternak used a plot that he felt would better display the talents of MGM's younger singers and dancers. In a San Francisco setting, sailor Russ Tamblyn discovers actress Debbie Reynolds, Petty Officer Tony Martin resumes his romance with nightclub dancer Ann Miller, and sailor Vic Damone takes up with Jane Powell, the admiral's daughter and Tamblyn's sister. Augmented by four Youmans songs from other sources, his 11 numbers represent the largest collection of the composer's works to be heard in one movie. The first screen version of *Hit the Deck* was released by RKO in 1930 and featured Jack Oakie and Polly Walker; the second variation, retitled *Follow the Fleet*, was released six years later with Fred Astaire and Ginger Rogers and a new score by Irving Berlin.
MCA ST. MGM/UA VC.

LADY AND THE TRAMP

Music & lyrics: Sonny Burke & Peggy Lee
Screenplay: Erdman Penner, Joe Rinaldi, Ralph Wright, Donald Da Gradi
Produced by: Walt Disney (released by Buena Vista)
Directed by: Hamilton Luske, Clyde Geronimi, Wildred Jackson (Technicolor;
          Cinema-Scope)
Voices: Peggy Lee, Barbara Luddy, Larry Roberts, Bill Thompson, Bill
          Baucon, Stan Freberg, Verna Felton, Alan Reed, George Givot
Songs: "He's a Tramp"; "La La Lu"; "Siamese Cat Song"; "Peace on Earth";
          "Bella Notte"
Released: April 1955; 75 minutes

Based on an original story by Ward Greene, *Lady and the Tramp* was put together by a creative staff including over 150 animators and artists. It was also the first Walt Disney cartoon feature in two years and the first in CinemaScope. The film's locale is a New England town in 1910, and the story concerns Lady, a pampered cocker spaniel owned by the improbably named Darling and Jim Dear, who becomes friendly with Tramp, a raffish street mutt from the wrong side of town. When the Dears have a child, Lady not only feels rejected but must also cope with the antagonism of her owners' Aunt Sarah. Lady and Tramp save the life of the newborn baby from a ferocious rat, an act of heroism that is misunderstood by Sarah, who has the dog catcher take Tramp away. The mutt is rescued with the help of Jock, a Scottish terrier, and Trusty, a basset hound, and when last seen Lady and Tramp are the proud parents of a litter of four.
Decca (Lee LP). Disney VC.

Daddy Long Legs. Fred Astaire and Leslie Caron dancing to "Something's Gotta Give" on a Manhattan terrace.

DADDY LONG LEGS

Music & lyrics: Johnny Mercer
Screenplay: Phoebe & Henry Ephron
Produced by: Samuel G. Engel for 20th Century-Fox
Directed by: Jean Negulesco
Choreography: David Robel, Roland Petit (Fred Astaire uncredited)
Photography: Leon Shamroy (DeLuxe Color; CinemaScope)
Cast: Fred Astaire, Leslie Caron, Terry Moore, Thelma Ritter, Fred Clark, Ralph Dumke, Larry Keating, Ray Anthony Orch.
Songs: "History of the Beat"; "Dream"; "Sluefoot"; "Something's Gotta Give"
Released: May 1955; 126 minutes

First filmed in 1919 (with Mary Pickford and Mahlon Hamilton), then in 1931 (with Janet Gaynor and Warner Baxter), the Jean Webster novel gave Fred Astaire, in his mid-fifties, the chance to play an unconventional character of his own age who, though not a performer, likes nothing better than singing, dancing, and playing the drums. In the tale, a wealthy businessman, to forestall gossip about his motive, becomes the anonymous sponsor of an orphan girl's education. They meet without the girl knowing who he is, they fall in love, and eventually the truth comes out. The musical version alters the basic story slightly by making the girl a French orphan (because Darryl Zanuck cast Leslie Caron in the part) who is sent to school in the United States. (The title refers to the fact that initially the only sight the girl has of her benefactor is his distorted, spidery shadow which prompts her to dub him her "Daddy Long Legs"—or in this case, "Papa Faucheux.") Johnny Mercer's score yielded "Something's Gotta Give" (an amatory application of the physical law about irresistible forces and immovable objects), and there were two extended dance sequences—both performed to the song "Dream" in which Miss Caron fantasizes about her middle-aged guardian angel.

Love Me or Leave Me. James Cagney and Doris Day in a tense situation.

LOVE ME OR LEAVE ME

Screenplay: Daniel Fuchs & Isobel Lennart
Produced by: Joe Pasternak for MGM
Directed by: Charles Vidor
Choreography: Alex Romero
Photography: Arthur Arling (Eastman Color; CinemaScope)
Cast: Doris Day, James Cagney, Cameron Mitchell, Robert Keith, Tom Tully, Claude Stroud, Harry Bellaver, Richard Gaines, Joe Pasternak
Songs: "It All Depends on You" (Ray Henderson-B. G. DeSylva, Lew Brown); "You Made Me Love You" (James Monaco-Joe McCarthy); "Everybody Loves My Baby" (Spencer Williams-Jack Palmer); "Sam the Old Accordion Man" (Walter Donaldson); "Shaking the Blues Away" (Irving Berlin); "Ten Cents a Dance" (Richard Rodgers-Lorenz Hart); "I'll Never Stop Loving You" (Nicholas Brodszky-Sammy Cahn); "At Sundown" (Donaldson); "Love Me or Leave Me" (Donaldson-Gus Kahn)
Released: May 1955; 122 minutes

Temporarily freed from her accustomed ginger-peachy girl-next-door roles, Doris Day starred in the first Hollywood biography offering a view of a singer's life that was not excessively sentimentalized or glamorized. *Love Me or Leave Me* tells the story of torch singer Ruth Etting who, beginning as a dime-a-dance hostess, goes on to win fame in nightclubs, the *Ziegfeld Follies,* and movies (though in real life the singer appeared in only three films). What gives a special edge to the story is the character of Gimp Snyder (memorably played by James Cagney), a brutish, but somehow sympathetic mobster who worships Ruth, uses strongarm methods to clear her path to success ("Whoever I am, kiddo, I'm what makes you tick"), and is ultimately cuckolded by his beloved. But producer Joe Pasternak, long associated with family-style musicals, made sure to tack on a happy ending. After Gimp has served time for shooting (but not killing) Ruth's accompanist and lover (Cameron Mitchell), all three are reunited at the opening of Snyder's new nightclub. *Love Me or Leave Me* helped pave the way for such other attempts at a more realistic approach to show-business biographies as *I'll Cry Tomorrow* (Susan Hayworth as Lillian Roth), *The Joker Is Wild* (Frank Sinatra as Joe E. Lewis) and *The Helen Morgan Story* (Ann Blyth with Gogi Grant's singing voice).
CSP ST. MGM/UA VC.

PETE KELLY'S BLUES

Screenplay: Richard L. Breen
Producer-director: Jack Webb for Warner Bros.
Photography: Hal Rosson (WarnerColor; CinemaScope)
Cast: Jack Webb, Janet Leigh, Edmond O'Brien, Peggy Lee, Andy Devine, Lee Marvin, Ella Fitzgerald, Martin Milner, Jayne Mansfield, Mort Marshall, Matty Matlock, George Van Epps, Nick Fatool, Snub Pollard
Songs: "Sugar" (Maceo Pinkard-Sidney Mitchell, Edna Alexander); "Somebody Loves Me" (George Gershwin-B. G. DeSylva, Ballard Macdonald); "Bye Bye Blackbird" (Ray Henderson-Mort Dixon); "What Can I Say After I Say I'm Sorry?" (Walter Donaldson, Abe Lyman); "He Needs Me" (Arthur Hamilton); "Sing a Rainbow" (Hamilton); "Pete Kelly's Blues" (Ray Heindorf-Sammy Cahn)
Released: July 1955; 95 minutes

Best known as the frozen-faced detective in the television series *Dragnet,* Jack Webb (with his cornet playing dubbed by Dick Cathcart) appears in this musical melodrama as a frozen-faced jazz bandleader fronting Pete Kelly's Big Seven (actually Matty Matlock's Dixie-landers) in a 1927 Kansas City speakeasy. The club's owner, a sadistic bootlegger (Edmond O'Brien) trying to strong-arm his way into the talent agency business, is also instrumental in the band hiring has-been vocalist Peggy Lee (giving an unusually dramatic performance), who sings nine of the 12 songs (the other three are sung by Ella Fitzgerald). The movie was inspired by a 1951 radio show of the same name, in which Cathcart had led the Matlock group.
Decca (Lee, Fitzgerald LP). Warner VC.

It's Always Fair Weather. Michael Kidd, Gene Kelly, and Dan Dailey dancing in the street.

IT'S ALWAYS FAIR WEATHER

Music: André Previn
Lyrics & screenplay: Betty Comden & Adolph Green
Produced by: Arthur Freed for MGM
Directors-choreographers: Gene Kelly & Stanley Donen
Photography: Robert Bronner (Eastman Color; CinemaScope)
Cast: Gene Kelly, Dan Dailey, Cyd Charisse, Dolores Gray, Michael Kidd,
David Burns, Jay C. Flippen, Hal March
Songs: "March, March"; "The Time for Parting"; "Blue Danube" ("Why
Are We Here?") (music: Johann Strauss); "Stillman's Gym"; "Baby,
You Knock Me Out"; "Situation-Wise"; "Once Upon a Time"; "Music
Is Better Than Words" (lyric with Roger Edens); "I Like Myself"; "Thanks a
Lot but No Thanks"
Released: August 1955; 101 minutes

After having written the screenplays for *On the Town* and *Singin' in the Rain*, both with Gene Kelly and both produced by Arthur Freed and directed and choreographed by Kelly and Stanley Donen, Betty Comden and Adolph Green came up with a new project for the five to work on—a sequel to *On the Town*, again with Kelly, Frank Sinatra and Jules Munshin, in which they would show what happens when the three sailors get together again ten years after their day-long spree in New York. Because Sinatra wasn't interested, his part went to dancer-choreographer Michael Kidd (in his first acting role) and Munshin's part went to Dan Dailey. Along the way, the three sailors became three soldiers, music director André Previn was given the assignment to compose the score (though three of his songs and a ballet sequence were dropped), and by the time everyone was finished with it, *It's Always Fair Weather* had taken on a far more cynical and satirical tone than the lighthearted *On the Town.*

A decade following the end of World War II, Kelly is a brash fly-by-night fight manager, Dailey is a stuffy, pill-popping advertising executive, and Kidd (whose singing was dubbed by Jud Conlin) is an unpolished rube who owns a greasy spoon in Schenectady named the Cordon Bleu. At their reunion, the men discover that they can't stand each other and are not particularly happy with the way their lives have turned out either. A television program coordinator and boxing fan (Cyd Charisse) gets the bright notion of having the three veterans show up as surprise guests on "The Throb of Manhattan," a human-interest segment of a program presided over by an excessively gushy mistress of ceremonies (Dolores Gray in her screen debut). The show becomes the occasion for a battle royal caused by a crooked fight promoter (Jay C. Flippen) who has been chasing Kelly, and by the time it's all over the ex-Army buddies have a better understanding of each other and themselves.

Taking advantage of CinemaScope and the special talents of its stars, *It's Always Fair Weather* includes a number of striking sequences including a drunken dance down Third Avenue with garbage-can lids attached to the three men's feet (recalling the spirit and locale of the "Make Way for Tomorrow" routine in *Cover Girl*); Miss Charisse flashing her legs as she leads a group of pugs at Stillman's Gym in "Baby, You Knock Me Out"; the trio's split-screen dance to "Once Upon a Time"; Kelly's jaunty solo street dance roller skating down Broadway after proclaiming "I Like Myself"; and Miss Gray's slinky way with the comic rejection of material wealth, "Thanks a Lot but No Thanks."
MCA ST. MGM/UA VC.

Oklahoma! Shirley Jones and Gordon MacRae.

OKLAHOMA!

Music: Richard Rodgers
Lyrics: Oscar Hammerstein II
Screenplay: Sonya Levien & William Ludwig
Produced by: Arthur Hornblow Jr. for Magna
Directed by: Fred Zinnemann
Choreography: Agnes de Mille
Photography: Robert Surtees (Eastman Color; Todd-AO)
Cast: Gordon MacRae, Gloria Grahame, Shirley Jones, Charlotte Greenwood, Eddie Albert, Gene Nelson, James Whitmore, Rod Steiger, Jay C. Flippen, Marc Platt, James Mitchell, Bambi Linn, Kelly Brown, Barbara Lawrence
Songs: "Oh, What a Beautiful Mornin' "; "The Surrey With the Fringe on Top"; "Kansas City"; "I Cain't Say No"; "Many a New Day"; "People Will Say We're in Love"; "Pore Jud"; "Out of My Dreams"; "The Farmer and the Cowman"; "All er Nothin'"; "Oklahoma"
Released: October 1955; 145 minutes

An acknowledged Broadway landmark, *Oklahoma!,* which opened in 1943, was a major step in the evolution of a more closely integrated form of musical theatre. It also launched the partnership of Richard Rodgers and Oscar Hammerstein II, who based their work on a 1931 play by Lynn Riggs, *Green Grow the Lilacs.* Set in Oklahoma Territory shortly after the turn of the century, the simple tale tells of ranchhand Curly McLain who loves Laurey Williams and hopes to escort her—in his imaginary surrey with the fringe on top—to a box social. Matters are complicated, however, when in a fit of spite Laurey accepts the invitation of the menacing farmhand, Jud Fry. Eventually, Laurey and Curly are married and celebrate the event by leading everyone in singing the praises of their brand new state. The merry-making is interrupted when Jud picks a fight with Curly and accidentally stabs himself to death. Curly is exonerated on the spot and he and Laurey drive off for their honeymoon in a real surrey with the fringe on top. A contrasting comic plot involves Ado Annie Carnes, the girl who cain't say no, and her two admirers, rancher Will Parker and itinerant Persian peddler Ali Hakim. The stage *Oklahoma!* prompted at least two Western movie musicals, *Can't Help Singing* and *The Harvey Girls,* which were released before the show was brought to the screen.

Unwilling to jeopardize *Oklahoma!'s* success on the stage, Rodgers and Hammerstein waited until after the record-breaking Broadway run and the national tour had ended before entering into an agreement with a new company, Magna Theatre Corporation, to produce *Oklahoma!* as the first film released in a new wide-screen process known as Todd-AO (though a year after its initial showing, the film was rereleased by 20th Century-Fox in CinemaScope).

Of the original Broadway cast, only dancers Bambi Linn and Marc Platt were in the film version, though the movie did retain the services of choreographer Agnes de Mille, music director Jay Blackton, and orchestrator Robert Russell Bennett. Two songs, "It's a Scandal! It's a Outrage!" and "Lonely Room" were dropped from the original score.

Fred Zinnemann, who had never before worked on a musical, was chosen to direct. Before the major roles were assigned to Gordon MacRae, Shirley Jones (in her first film), and Rod Steiger, Paul Newman and James Dean had been tested for Curly, Joanne Woodward for Laurey, and Eli Wallach for Jud. Charlotte Greenwood, who had been sought for the role of Laurey's aunt in the original production, played the part in the screen version. Though the interiors were filmed in Culver City, most of the exterior locations were shot near Nogales, Arizona, because its terrain was considered closer to turn-of-the-century Oklahoma than the state being celebrated.
Capitol ST. CBS/Fox VC.

GUYS AND DOLLS

Music & lyrics: Frank Loesser
Screenplay: Joseph L. Mankiewicz
Produced by: Samuel Goldwyn (released by MGM)
Directed by: Joseph L. Mankiewicz
Choreography: Michael Kidd
Photography: Harry Stradling (Eastman Color; CinemaScope)
Cast: Marlon Brando, Jean Simmons, Frank Sinatra, Vivian Blaine, Robert Keith, Stubby Kaye, B. S. Pully, Johnny Silver, Sheldon Leonard, Danny Dayton, George E. Stone, Regis Toomey, Kathryn Givney, Veda Ann Borg
Songs: "Fugue for Tinhorns"; "The Oldest Established"; "I'll Know"; "Pet Me, Poppa"; "Adelaide's Lament"; "Guys and Dolls"; "Adelaide"; "A Woman in Love"; "If I Were a Bell"; "Take Back Your Mink"; "Luck Be a Lady"; "Sue Me"; "Sit Down, You're Rockin' the Boat"
Released: November 1955; 150 minutes

Samuel Goldwyn paid a record $1 million (plus 10% of the world gross) to secure the screen rights to the classic 1950 stage musical about Broadway's gambling tinhorns (based on Damon Runyon's "The Idyll of Miss Sarah Brown"), then spent $5.5 million of his own money to produce the film. To protect his investment, Goldwyn signed Vivian Blaine to recreate her role of Miss Adelaide, the leading attraction at the Hot Box nightclub, rounded up three of the show's flashiest performers, Stubby Kaye (to repeat his memorable "Sit Down, You're Rockin' the Boat"), B. S. Pully and Johnny Silver, and chose the original stage choreographer, Michael Kidd, for the dances. He also retained 11 of Frank Loesser's 16 songs, to which the composer added "Pet Me, Poppa" (replacing "A Bushel and a Peck"), the Latin-flavored "A Woman in Love" (replacing "I've Never Been in Love Before"), and "Adelaide."

The producer, however, was not above doing some gambling of his own by casting the principal roles with actors who had never before sung in front of a camera—Marlon Brando as the highrolling Sky Masterson (after the more logical first choice, Gene Kelly, had been unable to secure a loanout from MGM) and Jean Simmons as the straitlaced Miss Sarah Brown, the Save-a-Soul Mission doll who falls in love with the smooth-talking guy. Frank Sinatra was tapped for the uncharacteristic role of Nathan Detroit, the harried proprietor of "the oldest established permanent floating crap game in New York," though he was convinced he would have been more suited to the part of Sky Masterson. Goldwyn took another gamble by entrusting both the film's direction and adaptation (of Abe Burrows' libretto) to Joseph Mankiewicz, who had had no previous experience working on a musical. But the most daring decision of all was to try to avoid the realism inherent in movies by having Broadway designer Oliver Smith create purposely stylized, two-dimensional sets that emphasized the artificiality of the hard-shelled but soft-centered characters who populate the very special world of Damon Runyon. Risky or not, it all paid off commercially—if not artistically—when *Guys and Dolls* topped the list as the biggest money-maker of 1956.

The first movie with songs that was derived from a Damon Runyon story was *Little Miss Marker*, a Shirley Temple vehicle of 1934, which was remade three times. After *Guys and Dolls* opened on Broadway, its success spawned three other Runyon-derived releases with songs—*The Lemon Drop Kid* in 1951 (Bob Hope), *Bloodhounds of Broadway* in 1952 (Mitzi Gaynor), and *Money from Home* in 1953 (Dean Martin and Jerry Lewis). In 1989, *Bloodhounds of Broadway* was remade with Madonna in a leading role.
Motion Pic. Tracks ST. CBS/Fox VC.

Guys and Dolls. Led by Frank Sinatra, Johnny Silver, and Stubby Kaye, the barbershop customers sing the gamblers' anthem, "The Oldest Established."

Guys and Dolls. "Luck Be a Lady" sings Marlon Brando as he throws the dice. Among the onlookers: B.S. Pully, Sheldon Leonard, Johnny Silver, Frank Sinatra, and Stubby Kaye.

KISMET

Music: Robert Wright & George Forrest, based on Alexander Borodin
Lyrics: Robert Wright & George Forrest
Screenplay: Charles Lederer & Luther Davis
Produced by: Arthur Freed for MGM
Directed by: Vincente Minnelli (Stanley Donen uncredited)
Choreography: Jack Cole
Photography: Joseph Ruttenberg (Eastman Color; CinemaScope)
Cast: Howard Keel, Ann Blyth, Vic Damone, Dolores Gray, Monty
Woolley, Sebastian Cabot, Jay C. Flippen, Aaron Spelling
Songs: "Fate"; "Not Since Nineveh"; "Baubles, Bangles, and Beads";
"Stranger in Paradise"; "Bored"; "Night of My Nights"; "The Olive
Tree"; "And This Is My Beloved"; "Sands of Time"
Released: December 1955; 113 minutes

Set in and around ancient Baghdad, *Kismet* relates the adventures of a public poet (Howard Keel) who in a 24-hour period from dawn to dawn assumes the identity of a beggar named Hajj, then manages to win a fortune, escape from the police, drown the wicked Wazir of Police (Sebastian Cabot), gain appointment to a high government post, and make off with the Wazir's voluptuous wife (Dolores Gray). Oh, yes, he also sees his daughter (Ann Blyth) marry the handsome Caliph (Vic Damone). The movie was an opulent adaptation (written by the show's librettists, Charles Lederer and Luther Davis) of the successful 1953 stage production starring Alfred Drake, for which Robert Wright and George Forrest had created songs based on themes by Alexander Borodin, e.g., "Stranger in Paradise" from the Polovtsian Dances, and both "And This Is My Beloved" and "Baubles, Bangles and Beads" from the D-major String Quartet. *Kismet* dates back to a 1911 play by Edward Knoblock, written as a vehicle for Otis Skinner, who appeared in the 1920 and 1930 screen versions (the latter with Loretta Young). A third nonmusical treatment in 1944 costarred Ronald Colman and Marlene Dietrich.
CBS ST. MGM/UA VC.

I'LL CRY TOMORROW

Screenplay: Helen Deutsch & Jay Richard Kennedy
Produced by: Lawrence Weingarten for MGM
Directed by: Daniel Mann
Photography: Arthur Arling
Cast: Susan Hayward, Richard Conte, Eddie Albert, Jo Van Fleet, Don
Taylor, Ray Danton, Margo
Songs: "Sing You Sinners" (W. Franke Harling-Sam Coslow); "When the
Red Red Robin Comes Bob Bob Bobbin' Along" (Harry Woods);
"Happiness Is a Thing Called Joe" (Harold Arlen-E. Y. Harburg)
Released: December 1955; 117 minutes

I'll Cry Tomorrow followed in the path of two previous screen biographies of popular female singers. Like *With a Song in My Heart*, the story of Jane Froman, it again starred Susan Hayward in the central dramatic role and it was again concerned with the rehabilitation of a life and a career (this time wrecked by alcoholism). Like *Love Me or Leave Me*, the story of Ruth Etting, it was another look at the seamy side of show business as well as an unflinching picture of marital discord (including wife beating). Based on the best-selling autobiography of Lillian Roth, a vivacious, dark-haired singer who had appeared in Broadway revues and early Hollywood musicals (including *The Love Parade),* the box office success featured an emotion-charged performance by Miss Hayward (who did her own singing) and strong support from Jo Van Fleet as Miss Roth's pushy mother, and Don Taylor, Richard Conte, and Eddie Albert as the men she married.
MGM/UA VC.

THE COURT JESTER

Music & lyrics: Sylvia Fine & Sammy Cahn
Screenplay: Norman Panama & Melvin Frank
Producers & directors: Norman Panama & Melvin Frank for Paramount
Choreography: James Starbuck
Photography: Ray June (Technicolor; VistaVision)
Cast: Danny Kaye, Glynis Johns, Basil Rathbone, Angela Lansbury, Cecil
  Parker, Mildred Natwick, John Carradine
Songs: "They'll Never Outfox the Fox"; "Baby, Let Me Take You Dreaming"; "My
  Heart Knows a Lovely Song"; "The Maladjusted Jester" (Fine alone)
Released: January 1956; 101 minutes

In this broad spoof of the Robin Hood legend, Danny Kaye is a carnival clown who joins the
Black Fox's outlaw group to do battle against the forces of King Rupert the Tyrant. The tale
lets Kaye indulge in much comic horseplay involving mistaken identity, hypnosis that
changes him from an awkward buffoon to an accomplished swordsman and back again,
and a madcap induction into knighthood. And there is the famous exchange in which Lady
in Waiting Mildred Natwick warns Kaye of the plot to poison him.
  Natwick: I've put a pellet of poison in one of the vessels.
  Kaye: Which one?
  Natwick: The one with a figure of a pestle.
  Kaye: The vessel with a pestle?
  Natwick: Yes. But you don't want the vessel with the pestle. You want the little crystal
  chalice with the figure of a palace.
  Kaye: Does the chalice with the palace have the pellet with the poison?
  Natwick: No, the pellet with the poison is in the vessel with the pestle.
  And on and on.
MCA ST. Paramount VC.

CAROUSEL

Music: Richard Rodgers
Lyrics: Oscar Hammerstein II
Screenplay: Henry & Phoebe Ephron
Produced by: Henry Ephron for 20th Century-Fox
Directed by: Henry King
Choreography: Rod Alexander, Agnes de Mille
Photography: Charles Clarke (DeLuxe Color; CinemaScope)
Cast: Gordon MacRae, Shirley Jones, Cameron Mitchell, Barbara Ruick,
  Claramae Turner, Robert Rounseville, Gene Lockhart, Audrey Christie,
  Jacques d'Amboise, Susan Luckey
Songs: "Carousel Waltz" (instrumental); "You're a Queer One, Julie Jordan"; "Mr.
  Snow"; "If I Loved You"; "June Is Bustin' Out All Over"; "When the Children
  Are Asleep", "Soliloquy"; "A Real Nice Clambake"; "What's the Use of
  Wond'rin'?"; "You'll Never Walk Alone"
Released: February 1956; 128 minutes

The second of Rodgers and Hammerstein's six musicals brought to the screen, *Carousel*
(based on Ferenc Molnar's play *Liliom*) was originally to have costarred Frank Sinatra and
Shirley Jones, but Sinatra walked off the set when it was decided to shoot the film in both
35 mm. and 55 mm. CinemaScope. Gordon MacRae then got the part—thus reuniting the
movie leads of R & H's *Oklahoma!* Filmed mostly in Boothbay Harbor, Maine, *Carousel* is
set in and around a fishing village in the late 1890s. Factory girl Julie Jordan meets carousel
barker Billy Bigelow and they immediately fall in love. Billy loses his job and marries Julie,
but the couple find little happiness together, a situation complicated by Billy's impending
fatherhood. In desperation, he attempts a robbery but kills himself rather than face a jail
term. He is, however, granted a day back on earth in which to help his lonely, unhappy
daughter gain greater self-confidence.
Capitol ST. CBS/Fox VC.

The King and I. Deborah Kerr showing the Siamese king's wives what she wears under her skirt.

The King and I. Martin Benson, Deborah Kerr, Yul Brynner, Alan Mowbray, and Geoffrey Toone.

THE KING AND I

Music: Richard Rodgers
Lyrics: Oscar Hammerstein II
Screenplay: Ernest Lehman
Produced by: Charles Brackett for 20th Century-Fox
Directed by: Walter Lang
Choreography: Jerome Robbins
Photography: Leon Shamroy (DeLuxe Color; CinemaScope)
Cast: Deborah Kerr, Yul Brynner, Rita Moreno, Martin Benson, Terry Saunders, Rex Thompson, Carlos Rivas, Patrick Adiarte, Alan Mowbray, Yuriko, Michiko, Gemze de Lappe, Geoffrey Toone, Charles Irwin
Songs: "I Whistle a Happy Tune";"March of the Siamese Children" (instrumental); "Hello, Young Lovers"; "A Puzzlement"; "Getting to Know You"; "We Kiss in a Shadow"; "Something Wonderful"; "The Small House of Uncle Thomas" (ballet); "Song of the King"; "Shall We Dance?"
Released: March 1956;133 minutes

Ever since its first Broadway engagement in 1951, *The King and I* has been one of the five most frequently revived Rodgers and Hammerstein musicals. On screen, along with *The Sound of Music* (also produced at Fox), it was one of the two best realized adaptations of the partners' works, placing seventh in domestic theatre rental fees of all musical films released in the fifties. Keeping faithful to its source, while embellishing it with appropriately exotic backgrounds, the movie retained the services of Yul Brynner as King Mongkut of Siam, as well as that of choreographer Jerome Robbins, costume designer Irene Sharaff, plus four of the featured dancers. It also kept 10 of the original 13 songs ("My Lord and Master" was the only major musical omission), the instrumental "March of the Siamese Children," and the ballet variations on *Uncle Tom's Cabin* called "The Small House of Uncle Thomas."

Taking place in Bangkok in the 1860s, the story is about English school teacher-governess Anna Leonowens (Deborah Kerr with Marni Nixon's singing voice) who has been employed to care for the Siamese monarch's numerous offspring. The strong-willed Anna and the semi-barbaric autocratic ruler come into immediate conflict, though eventually Anna realizes how hard Mongkut is struggling to reform his backward kingdom. Without being fully aware of their own feelings, teacher and king even find themselves falling in love as they twirl merrily to the music of "Shall We Dance?" After Mongkut dies, Anna remains at court as an advisor to Crown Prince Chowfa Chulalongkorn, who assumes the throne pledging to carry out his father's plans to modernize the country. A secondary plot concerns the ill-starred romance between Tuptim (Rita Moreno with a vocal assist from Leona Gordon), one of the king's wives, and Lun Tha (Carlos Rivas with singing by Reuben Fuentes), one of the soldiers at court. The film also capped the career of veteran director Walter Lang, who had previously been responsible for a number of Betty Grable musicals as well as Rodgers and Hammerstein's *State Fair.*

The origin of *The King and I* was Mrs. Leonowens' diary, *The English Governess at the Siamese Court,* the basis for Margaret Landon's best-selling novel, *Anna and the King of Siam.* In 1946, Fox turned the story into a movie with Irene Dunne, Rex Harrison, and Linda Darnell. It was principally because of Gertrude Lawrence's desire to play the part of Anna in a musical stage version that Rodgers and Hammerstein were won over to the idea of creating the songs and libretto.
Capitol ST. CBS/Fox VC.

INVITATION TO THE DANCE

Produced by: Arthur Freed for MGM
Directeor-choreographer: Gene Kelly
Photography: F. A. Young, Joseph Ruttenberg (Technicolor)
Cast: Igor Youskevitch, Gene Kelly, Claire Sombert, Claude Bessy,
Tommy Rall, Tamara Toumanova, Belita, Irving Davies,
Diana Adams, Carol Haney
Music: "The Circus" (Ibert); "Ring Around the Rosy" (André Previn);
"Sinbad the Sailor" (Rimsky-Korsakov)
Released: May 1956; 92 minutes

Though neither an artistic nor a commercial success, *Invitation to the Dance* occupies a special niche in movie annals as the only feature to consist solely of newly choreographed ballets without a single word of dialogue. It had been Gene Kelly's dream for some time to create a film that would appeal to people who had never before been exposed to ballet and initially he did not plan to appear in it (but the MGM brass insisted). The production contains three separate sequences, most of them shot in Boreham Wood, England, in 1952. (A fourth, a choreographed interpretation of a dozen popular songs, was cut by the studio.) "The Circus" is about a white-faced clown in Pierrot costume (modeled on the main character in Marcel Carné's French classic *Les Enfants du Paradis)* and his tragic love for a ballerina. "Ring Around the Rosy" (modeled on Arthur Schnitzler's *La Ronde)* is about a bracelet that is passed from husband to wife to artist to model to hoofer to vamp to nightclub singer to nightclub hatcheck girl to Marine to streetwalker and back to husband and wife. "Sinbad the Sailor," like the movie *Anchors Aweigh,* gives Kelly a chance to be seen dancing with animated cartoon characters. Because of Metro's lack of confidence in *Invitation to the Dance,* it was delayed some four years before being released to the general public.
MCA ST. MGM/UA VC.

High Society. Frank Sinatra and Bing Crosby clowning through "Well, Did You Evah?"

HIGH SOCIETY

Music & lyrics: Cole Porter
Screenplay: John Patrick
Produced by: Sol C. Siegel for MGM
Director-choreographer: Charles Walters
Photography: Paul Vogel (Technicolor; VistaVision)
Cast: Bing Crosby, Grace Kelly, Frank Sinatra, Celeste Holm, John Lund, Louis Calhern, Sidney Blackmer, Louis Armstrong & Band (Edmond Hall, Trummy Young, Billy Kyle, Arvell Shaw, Barrett Deems), Margalo Gilmore, Lydia Reed
Songs: "High Society Calypso"; "Little One"; "Who Wants to Be a Million-aire?", "True Love"; "You're Sensational"; "I Love You, Samantha"; "Now You Has Jazz"; "Well, Did You Evah?"; "Mind If I Make Love to You?"
Released: July 1956; 107 minutes

The locale was changed from Philadelphia to Newport (where the movie was shot mostly in and around Clarendon Court, then owned by Claus von Bülow), and one of the leading male characters was changed from an idle socialite to a song-writing socialite who also runs the local jazz festival (an event never shown in the film to which he devotes the least possible time and serves only as an excuse for the appearance of Louis Armstrong). Nonetheless, *High Society* is still basically *The Philadelphia Story,* Philip Barry's 1939 play in which Katharine Hepburn, Joseph Cotten, Van Heflin, and Shirley Booth had appeared on Broadway, and which had been filmed the following year with Miss Hepburn, Cary Grant, James Stewart, and Ruth Hussey. In the musical version, it was outfitted with songs by Cole Porter (his first screen assignment in eight years), and its cast was headed by two authentic singing legends, Bing Crosby and Frank Sinatra (they would also appear together in the 1962 film, *The Road to Hong Kong,* and the 1964 film, *Robin and the 7 Hoods),* plus Grace Kelly (who happened to have been a member of one of Philadelphia's most socially prominent families).

The frothy plot of *High Society* deals with the complications that arise when Tracy Lord (Miss Kelly), about to wed self-made businessman George Ketteridge (John Lund), finds herself falling in love with two other men who are also at the nuptuals—ex-husband C.K.Dexter Haven (Crosby), to whom she eventually returns, and magazine writer Mike Connor (Sinatra) who, with photographer Liz Imbrie (Celeste Holm), has come to Newport to cover the event for *Spy,* a *Life-*type magazine (in the original stage production it had been called *Destiny).*

Inspired by writing for such talents as Crosby, Sinatra, and Armstrong, Porter turned out an appropriately romantic and rhythmic score, including "True Love" (sung in a flashback by Crosby on a sailboat of the same name, and harmonized briefly by Miss Kelly), which became one of the most popular songs the composer ever wrote. Crosby and Sinatra got together for a roistering commentary on the behavior of the upper crust called "Well, Did You Evah?," a number that director Charles Walter had introduced with Betty Grable in the 1939 Broadway musical, *DuBarry Was a Lady.* One of the year's biggest box office attractions, *High Society* marked the final screen appearance of the future Princess Grace of Monaco.

In 1987, a stage adaptation of *High Society* was produced in London with Natasha Richardson, Trevor Eve, and Stephen Rea.
Capitol ST. MGM/UA VC.

FUNNY FACE

Music: George Gershwin*; Roger Edens**
Lyrics: Ira Gershwin*; Leonard Gershe**
Screenplay: Leonard Gershe
Produced by: Roger Edens for Paramount
Directed by: Stanley Donen
Choreography: Eugene Loring (Fred Astaire uncredited)
Photography: Ray June (Technicolor; VistaVision)
Cast: Audrey Hepburn, Fred Astaire, Kay Thompson, Michel Auclair, Robert Flemyng, Dovima, Virginia Gibson, Suzy Parker, Ruta Lee, Sue England
Songs: "Think Pink"**; "How Long Has This Been Going On?"*; "Funny Face"*; "Bonjour, Paris!"**; "Let's Kiss and Make Up" *; "He Loves and She Loves"*; "On How to Be Lovely"**; "Clap Yo' Hands"*; "'S Wonderful"*
Released: March 1957; 103 minutes

Funny Face was put together by combining the title and songs of one stage musical with the story intended for another—and was put on the screen by combining one Hollywood studio with key production personnel of another. Screenwriter Leonard Gershe had written the book for an unproduced musical called *Wedding Day,* which was bought by MGM producer Roger Edens. Edens' idea was to add songs to it that George and Ira Gershwin had contributed to the 1927 Broadway show *Funny Face,* and he lined up director Stanley Donen and costars Audrey Hepburn and Fred Astaire (who had appeared in the Gershwin production with his sister Adele). But Miss Hepburn was under contract to Paramount and Astaire had just signed with the same studio. Moreover, Warner Bros. owned the rights to the Gershwin songs. After much negotiating, Warners agreed to permit the *Funny Face* score to be licensed to MGM, which then made a deal with Paramount lending the services of Edens, Gershe, and Donen.

In the stunningly photographed movie, Astaire plays a fashion photographer who is charmed by a black-stockinged Greenwich Village intellectual (Miss Hepburn) and even persuades her to accompany him to Paris to pose for a layout in *Quality* magazine. Under the romantic influence of the city of lights (where, despite frequently inclement weather, most of the exterior filming was shot), the young lady eventually sheds her cerebral pretentions and is won over to the photographer's glittering superficial world. Like Astaire's earlier film *The Band Wagon, Funny Face* is something of a *roman à clef.* Fashion photographer Richard Avery suggests fashion photographer Richard Avedon (who served as the movie's "visual consultant"), Kay Thompson's magazine editor is modeled on Carmel Snow of *Harper's Bazaar,* and Michel Auclair's Professor Flostre, the leader of a philosophical movement called Empathicalism, is given a name combining both Jean-Paul Sartre, the founder of the Existentialist movement, and the Cafe de Flore, Sartre's well-publicized hangout.

The film's hybrid score utilized five Gershwin numbers written for the original *Funny Face* (though "How Long Has This Been Going On?" had been cut before the show's New York opening), one Gershwin number, "Clap Yo' Hands," written for another musical, and three new songs contributed by producer Edens and screenwriter Gershe. Two of the movie's most distinguished dance sequences were Astaire's courtyard solo to "Let's Kiss and Make Up" with the dancer's umbrella and raincoat used as props for a lightning matador-style sword-and-cape routine, and Astaire and Hepburn's misty morning dance on the grass around a pond. Miss Hepburn even had a vocal solo, to "How Long Has This Been Going On?," which she plaintively sang all by herself. In 1928, Fred and Adele Astaire had been tested for a possible screen version of the Broadway *Funny Face,* but the project never materialized. Eight years later, however, a British screen version was released under the title *She Knew What She Wanted.*
DRG ST. Paramount VC.

Funny Face. Fred Astaire and Audrey Hepburn performing their gossamer dance to "He Loves and She Loves."

Silk Stockings. Cyd Charisse and Fred Astaire dancing to "All of You."

SILK STOCKINGS

Music & lyrics: Cole Porter
Screenplay: Leonard Gershe & Leonard Spigelgass (Harry Kurnitz
   uncredited)
Produced by: Arthur Freed for MGM
Directed by: Rouben Mamoulian
Choreography: Eugene Loring, Hermes Pan (Fred Astaire uncredited)
Photography: Robert Bronner (Metrocolor; CinemaScope)
Cast: Fred Astaire, Cyd Charisse, Janis Page, Peter Lorre, Jules Munshin,
   George Tobias, Joseph Buloff, Wim Sonneveld, Barrie Chase, Belita,
   Tybee Afra, Betty Uitti, Kaaren Verne, Rolfe Sedan, Eugene Borden
Songs: "Too Bad"; "Paris Loves Lovers"; "Stereophonic Sound"; "It's
   a Chemical Reaction, That's All"; "All of You"; "Satin and Silk";
   "Without Love"; "Fated to Be Mated"; "Josephine"; "Siberia";
   "The Red Blues"; "The Ritz Roll and Rock"
Released: July 1957; 118 minutes

It was only a coincidence, but in *Funny Face* and *Silk Stockings,* his two movies of 1957, Fred Astaire was cast as an enterprising American whose work takes him to Paris. In both he meets a plainly dressed, serious-minded young woman who belittles his work and the world in which he lives. Eventually, under the influence of both Paris and Fred's singing and dancing, the young woman develops a taste for materialistic pleasures, particularly feminine finery, and the two fall in love. They surmount a breakup, of course, because nothing can keep this oddly matched couple from ending up in each other's arms. (A further coincidence was that Leonard Gershe was involved in writing the screenplays of both pictures.)

The basic plot of *Silk Stockings* dates back to 1939 when, as *Ninotchka,* it emerged under Ernst Lubitsch's direction as a sophisticated tale (based on a story by Melchior Lengyel), in which Greta Garbo had played a dedicated Soviet official on a mission to Paris, and Melvyn Douglas the suave Parisian count who breaks down her resistance and wins her heart. Sixteen years later, outfitted with a Cole Porter score (his last for a stage musical), the story was adapted by George S. Kaufman, Leueen McGrath, and Abe Burrows into a fairly blunt satire with Hildegarde Neff as the Communist official and Don Ameche as a Hollywood agent who has come to Paris to represent his clients working on a movie based on Tolstoy's *War and Peace.*

When Arthur Freed decided to make a screen version of the stage version, he and director Rouben Mamoulian retained the basic story line but, since the leads were being played by Fred Astaire (whose role was changed to that of a Hollywood producer) and Cyd Charisse (with Carol Richards' singing voice), they put more of the emphasis on dancing. As a result, two minor songs were dropped in favor of two new ones expressly created for dancing sequences—"Fated to Be Mated," a joyous marriage proposal, and "The Ritz Roll and Rock," a bouncing, top-hatted Astaire specialty that was more Ritz than rock. Choreographer Eugene Loring also added Miss Charisse's dance in which—to the background accompaniment of the title song—the once ascetic commissar symbolically removes her drab garments and dons newly purchased satins and silks that she had hidden in various parts of her hotel room.

Because *Funny Face* had pretty well exhausted all the authentic Paris scenes, *Silk Stockings* was filmed in Hollywood and allowed the French capitol's hypnotic appeal to be conveyed exclusively through dialogue and song (especially "Paris Loves Lovers"). The only actor to repeat his stage role in the film, playing the Soviet Commissar of Arts, was George Tobias, who had also been seen as a Soviet official in *Ninotchka.*
CBS ST. MGM/UA VC.

THE PAJAMA GAME

Music & lyrics: Richard Adler & Jerry Ross
Screenplay: George Abbott & Richard Bissell
Producers-directors: George Abbott & Stanley Donen for Warner Bros.
Choreography: Bob Fosse
Photography: Harry Stradling (WarnerColor)
Cast: Doris Day, John Raitt, Carol Haney, Eddie Foy Jr., Reta Shaw, Barbara Nichols, Thelma Pelish, Peter Gennaro, Kenneth LeRoy, Buzz Miller, Ralph Dunn
Songs: "The Pajama Game"; "Racing With the Clock"; "I'm Not at All in Love"; "I'll Never Be Jealous Again"; "Hey, There"; "Once-a-Year Day"; "Small Talk"; "There Once Was a Man"; "Steam Heat"; "Hernando's Hideaway"; "7-1/2 Cents"
Released: August 1957; 101 minutes

Except for the substitution of Doris Day for Janis Paige in the female lead, the chief players in the 1954 Broadway musical *The Pajama Game* were transferred virtually en masse to repeat their roles in the movie. As he had been in the original, George Abbott was again in charge, serving as co-author with Richard Bissell (on whose novel, *7-1/2 Cents,* the musical had been based), and co-producer and co-director with Stanley Donen. And to further assure authenticity, 11 of the original 15 songs were retained. The movie is concerned with the romance between the new plant superintendent (John Raitt) at the Sleep Tite Pajama Factory in Cedar Rapids, Iowa, and one of tha union leaders (Miss Day) who leads the strike for a seven-and-a-half cent hourly pay increase.
CSP ST. Warner VC.

THE JOKER IS WILD

Screenplay: Oscar Saul
Produced by: Samuel Briskin for Paramount
Directed by: Charles Vidor
Choreography: Josephine Earl
Photography: Daniel Fapp (VistaVision)
Cast: Frank Sinatra, Jeanne Crain, Mitzi Gaynor, Eddie Albert, Beverly Garland, Jackie Coogan, Hank Henry, Walter Woolf King
Songs: "At Sundown" (Walter Donaldson); "I Cried for You" (Gus Arnheim, Abe Lyman-Arthur Freed); "If I Could Be With You One Hour Tonight" (Jimmy Johnson-Henry Creamer); "All the Way" (James Van Heusen-Sammy Cahn)
Released: August 1957; 126 minutes

Following those two other deglamorizing show business biographies, *Love Me or Leave Me* and *I'll Cry Tomorrow, The Joker Is Wild* (adapted from Art Cohn's book) gives us the supposed unvarnished lowdown on the life of Joe E. Lewis, a raspy voiced nightclub comic specializing in self-deprecating humor revolving around his drinking and gambling. As portrayed by his friend, Frank Sinatra, Lewis began as a Sinatra soundalike in Chicago speakeasies whose singing career came to an end when his face and vocal chords were slashed by hoodlums after he had left one mobster's club to sing in another's. The almost unremittingly downbeat film (it was directed by Charles Vidor who had also directed *Love Me or Leave Me)* involves the comedian with two women whom he marries and divorces, socialite Jeanne Crain and nightclub cutie Mitzi Gaynor. Because the song "All the Way" became such a big hit, the film was later reissued as *All the Way* (even though the point of the film was that Lewis could not go "all the way" in his devotion to one woman).

The Pajama Game. Doris Day leading the factory strikers in the "7-1/2 Cents" number.

PAL JOEY

Music: Richard Rodgers
Lyrics: Lorenz Hart
Screenplay: Dorothy Kingsley
Produced by: Fred Kohlmar for Columbia
Directed by: George Sidney
Choreography: Hermes Pan
Photography: Harold Lipstein (Technicolor)
Cast: Rita Hayworth, Frank Sinatra, Kim Novak, Barbara Nichols, Bobby
Sherwood, Hank Henry, Elizabeth Patterson, Hermes Pan
Songs: "That Terrific Rainbow"; "I Didn't Know What Time It Was"; "Great
Big Town"; "There's a Small Hotel"; "Zip"; "I Could Write a Book";
"The Lady Is a Tramp"; "Bewitched"; "My Funny Valentine"
Released: September 1957; 111 minutes

Soon after Vivienne Segal and Gene Kelly had opened on Broadway in *Pal Joey* late in
1940, Columbia's chief Harry Cohn secured the screen rights—but the picture had to wait
16 years before being filmed. Initially, as a result of their success in *Cover Girl,* Kelly was
sought to play opposite Rita Hayworth again, but MGM, the actor's studio, refused the
loanout. After years of announcing various stars for the leads, Cohn eventually settled on
Frank Sinatra and his original choice, Rita Hayworth, though now playing the older woman
rather than the ingenue. The character of Joey Evans (which had originated in short stories
by John O'Hara) was changed from a nightclub dancer to a nightclub singer and the locale
was moved from Chicago to San Francisco. Other alterations involved Miss Hayworth's
Vera Simpson (now not only a wealthy Nob Hill widow but also a former burlesque stripper)
and Kim Novak's Linda English (now a naive chorus girl instead of a naive stenographer).
The film even allows a mushy ending with Joey and Linda going off together arm in arm with
a misplaced Golden Gate Bridge in the background. Of the 14 original Rodgers and Hart
songs, eight were retained (two as instrumental pieces) and four numbers were added from
other shows involving the songwriting team. The singing voices of Misses Hayworth and
Novak were, respectively, those of Jo Ann Greer and Trudy Erwin.
Capitol ST. RCA/Columbia VC.

Pal Joey. Frank Sinatra and Rita Hayworth.

Les Girls. Mitzi Gaynor, Kay Kendall, Gene Kelly, and Taina Elg.

LES GIRLS

Music & lyrics: Cole Porter
Screenplay: John Patrick
Produced by: Sol C. Siegel for MGM
Directed by: George Cukor
Choreography: Jack Cole (Gene Kelly uncredited)
Photography: Robert Surtees (Metrocolor; CinemaScope)
Cast: Gene Kelly, Mitzi Gaynor, Kay Kendall, Taina Elg, Jacques Bergerac,
Henry Daniell, Patrick Macnee, Leslie Phillips
Songs: "Les Girls"; "Ça, C'est L'Amour"; "Ladies in Waiting"; "You're Just
Too, Too"; "Why Am I So Gone About That Gal?"
Released: October 1957; 114 minutes

Producer Sol C. Siegel, screenwriter John Patrick and composer-lyricist Cole Porter, who
had worked together on *High Society*, were reunited for another sophisticated romp, *Les
Girls,* which turned out to be Porter's last screen assignment as well as Gene Kelly's 18th
and final MGM musical. As in the Japanese film classic, *Rashomon,* the movie (based on
a story by Vera Caspery) is concerned with various people's perception of the truth,
specifically what really did happen in Paris in 1949 between song-and-dance man Gene
Kelly and his shapely trio known as Les Girls (Mitzi Gaynor, Kay Kendall, and Taina Elg).
Most memorable is the performance of the stately madcap Miss Kendall, particularly her
rendition of the "Habañera" while slightly sozzled, and her seemingly spontaneous routine
with Kelly to "You're Just Too, Too." When first announced in 1955, the film was to have
had four girls, three of whom were to be played by Cyd Charisse, Leslie Caron, and Carol
Haney.
MCA ST. MGM/UA VC.

SOUTH PACIFIC

Music: Richard Rodgers
Lyrics: Oscar Hammerstein II
Screenplay: Paul Osborn
Produced by: Buddy Adler for Magna (released by 20th Century-Fox)
Directed by: Joshua Logan
Choreography: LeRoy Prinz
Photography: Leon Shamroy (Technicolor; Todd-AO)
Cast: Rossano Brazzi, Mitzi Gaynor, John Kerr, Ray Walston, Juanita Hall, France Nuyen, Russ Brown, Ken Clark, Floyd Simmons, Candace Lee, Warren Hsieh, Archie Savage, Jack Mullaney, Beverly Aadland, Tom Laughlin
Songs: "Bloody Mary"; "There Is Nothin' Like a Dame"; "Bali Ha'i"; "A Cock-Eyed Optimist", "Twin Soliloquies"; "Some Enchanted Evening"; "Dites-moi" ("Tell Me Why"); "I'm Gonna Wash That Man Right Outa My Hair"; "A Wonderful Guy"; "Younger Than Springtime"; "Happy Talk"; "Honey Bun"; "My Girl Back Home"; "You've Got to Be Carefully Taught"; "This Nearly Was Mine"
Released: March 1958; 171 minutes

The movie version of *South Pacific* continued Rodgers and Hammerstein's association with 20th Century-Fox, employing the same music directors (Alfred Newman and Ken Darby), orchestrators (Edward Powell and Bernard Mayers), art directors (Lyle Wheeler and John DeCuir), cinematographer (Leon Shamroy), and editor (Robert Simpson) as *The King and I*. It also retained the services of two veterans of the original 1949 stage production, director Joshua Logan (who had also collaborated with Hammerstein on the book) and actress Juanita Hall (though her singing was dubbed by Muriel Smith who had been in the London company), plus two veterans of the touring company, Ray Walston and Russ Brown. To replace Mary Martin and Ezio Pinza, the stars of the original Broadway production, the movie offered Mitzi Gaynor (also under consideration had been Elizabeth Taylor and Doris Day) and Rossano Brazzi (whose singing was through the courtesy of Giorgio Tozzi).

All the songs in the stage score were kept in the film (though not in exactly the same sequence), plus "My Girl Back Home," which had been cut before the New York opening. Apart from being cinematically overblown, the film (shot mostly on the Hawaiian island of Kauai) made its most serious miscalculation by using various color filters for the musical sequences in a misguided effort to establish different moods and to help audiences adjust to the artificiality of people expressing their emotions through song rather than through speech. (Still, the picture did manage to become the fourth highest domestic theatre rental musical of the 1950s.)

The genesis of *South Pacific* was two stories in James Michener's wartime collection, *Tales of the South Pacific.* The catalyst was Logan, who felt strongly that the stories could be adapted into a successful musical and he urged Rodgers and Hammerstein to read the book. One story, "Our Heroine," was about young Nellie Forbush (Gaynor), a naive Navy nurse from Little Rock, and mature Emile de Becque (Brazzi), a worldly French planter, who meet on an unnamed island in the Pacific and fall in love on an enchanted evening. The other story, "Fo' Dolla'," was about a romance between Lt. Joe Cable (John Kerr, with the soundtrack voice of Bill Lee singing his impassioned "Younger Than Springtime") and Liat (France Nuyen), the daughter of the Polynesian native Bloody Mary (Hall), which is tragically ended when Joe is killed while on a mission with deBecque behind Japanese lines. *RCA ST. CBS/Fox VC .*

South Pacific. Juanita Hall (with Muriel Smith's voice) singing "Happy Talk" to France Nuyen and John Kerr.

South Pacific. Rossano Brazzi reunited with Mitzi Gaynor and his children, Candace Lee and Warren Hsieh.

Gigi. Maurice Chevalier reprises "Thank Heaven for Little Girls" in the Bois de Boulogne as Leslie Caron and Louis Jourdan stroll by.

GIGI

Music: Frederick Loewe
Lyrics & screenplay: Alan Jay Lerner
Produced by: Arthur Freed for MGM
Directed by: Vincente Minnelli (Charles Walters uncredited)
Photography: Joseph Ruttenberg (Metrocolor; CinemaScope)
Cast: Leslie Caron, Maurice Chevalier, Louis Jourdan, Hermione Gingold, Eva Gabor, Jacques Bergerac, Isabel Jeans, John Abbott, Monique Van Vooren
Songs: "Thank Heaven for Little Girls"; "The Parisians"; "It's a Bore"; "Gossip"; "She Is Not Thinking of Me"; "The Night They Invented Champagne"; "I Remember It Well"; "Gigi"; "I'm Glad I'm Not Young Anymore"; "Say a Prayer for Me Tonight"
Released: May 1958; 116 minutes

Because it was about a tomboyish young girl who is transformed into an elegant lady and wins the heart of a wealthy confirmed bachelor, and because it followed *My Fair Lady* by two years, *Gigi* is regarded as something of a Gallic variation of Lerner and Loewe's previous work. The story, however, had originated in 1942 as a novella by the French writer Colette and had already been turned into a French film in 1950 starring Danielle Delormé and a Broadway play (by Anita Loos) in 1954 starring Audrey Hepburn. After Miss Hepburn showed no interest in appearing in the new film, Leslie Caron, who had played Gigi in London, was signed (though her singing was dubbed by Betty Wand). The male romantic lead went to Louis Jourdan after Lerner's original choice, Dirke Bogard, proved unavailable. The part of the hero's philandering uncle, a minor character in the book who did not even appear in the play, was significantly expanded to fit the talents of Maurice Chevalier, and the role of Gigi's regal aunt went to Isabel Jeans after being turned down by such distinguished actresses as Gladys Cooper, Ina Claire, and Yvonne Printemps.

Gigi reunited four of the principal people who had been associated with *An American in Paris*—producer Arthur Freed, director Vincente Minnelli, screenwriter Lerner, and Miss Caron. It was Lerner and Loewe's first screen collaboration (their only other original movie was *The Little Prince* in 1974) and it was the first American musical shot almost entirely in Paris. Locales included not just the familiar attractions such as Maxim's, the Bois de Boulogne, the Palais de Glaces, and the Tuilleries, but also interior scenes that customarily would have been filmed in Hollywood (such as the Musée Jacquemort-André which served as an elegant town house). Because the shooting schedule ran overtime, however, two musical sequences did have to be shot at MGM—the nostalgic Maurice Chevalier-Hermione Gingold duet "I Remember It Well" and the exuberant "The Night They Invented Champagne" (both directed by Charles Walters). *Gigi* placed ninth in domestic theatre rental fees of all the musicals released in the fifties.

In the story, set during *La Belle Epoque*, Gaston Lachailles, the bored nephew of boulevardier Honoré Lachailles, is a close chum of former courtesan Inez Alvarez, whose granddaughter Gigi is something of a madcap. Gigi's family has a proud tradition of courtesanship and she is coached in such vital matters of the trade as charm, femininity, deportment ("Bad table manners have broken up more households than infidelity"), and the importance of avoiding marriage. Gaston, suddenly aware that little Gigi has been growing up before his very eyes, would like to do the honorable thing and make her his mistress, but Gigi demurs. She then shocks her grandmother and aunt by being the first woman in her family to accept a marriage proposal.

In 1973, with virtually its entire score intact, and with the addition of five new songs, *Gigi* became the first Hollywood musical to be made into a Broadway musical. Lerner himself wrote the libretto, and the cast was headed by Alfred Drake (Honoré), Daniel Massey (Gaston), Maria Karnilova (Inez), Agnes Moorehead (Alicia), and Karin Wolfe (Gigi). *CBS ST. MGM/UA VC.*

DAMN YANKEES

Music & lyrics: Richard Adler & Jerry Ross
Screenplay: George Abbott
Producers-directors: George Abbott & Stanley Donen for Warner Bros.
Choreography: Bob Fosse
Photography: Harold Lipstein (Technicolor)
Cast: Gwen Verdon, Tab Hunter, Ray Walston, Russ Brown, Shannon Bolin, Robert Shafer, Nathaniel Frey, James Komack, Albert Linville, Bob Fosse
Songs: "Goodbye, Old Girl"; "Heart"; "Shoeless Joe from Hannibal, Mo.";
"A Little Brains, a Little Talent"; "Who's Got the Pain?"; "Two Lost Souls"
Released: September 1958; 110 minutes

Just as the 1956 stage musical *Damn Yankees* had been put together by virtually the same team that had created *The Pajama Game,* so its movie version—like its predecessor's—retained the services of the same key men, director-writer George Abbott and choreographer Bob Fosse, who had brought it to Broadway. (Abbott, however, was again joined by co-producer and co-director Stanley Donen.) Also following the lead of its *Pajama Game,* Warners' *Damn Yankees* kept all the major actors from the stage (except for the substitution of Tab Hunter for Stephen Douglass), and nine of the 12 songs were retained. Based on Douglass Wallopp's novel *The Year the Yankees Lost the Pennant,* the fantasy tells of a middle-aged baseball fan who temporarily sells his soul to the Devil (Ray Walston) in order to play with his beloved Washington Senators. Transformed into a young man (Hunter), he becomes a star player and even manages to withstand the temptations of Lola, the Devil's accomplice (Gwen Verdon). Because of the titular expletive, the movie was retitled *What Lola Wants* when shown in Britain.
RCA ST. Warner VC.

PORGY AND BESS

Music: George Gershwin
Lyrics: DuBose Heyward*; Ira Gershwin#
Screenplay: N. Richard Nash
Produced by: Samuel Goldwyn (released by Columbia)
Directed by: Otto Preminger
Choreography: Hermes Pan
Photography: Leon Shamroy (Technicolor; Todd-AO)
Cast: Sidney Poitier, Dorothy Dandridge, Sammy Davis Jr., Pearl Bailey, Brock Peters, Diahann Carroll, Ruth Attaway, Leslie Scott
Songs: "Summertime"*; "A Woman Is a Sometime Thing"*; "My Man's Gone Now"*; "I Got Plenty o' Nuttin'"* #; "Bess, You Is My Woman Now"* #; "It Ain't Necessarily So"* #; "I Loves You, Porgy"* #; "There's a Boat Dat's Leavin' Soon for New York"#; "Oh, Bess, Where's My Bess?"#
Released: June 1959; 138 minutes

It had taken Samuel Goldwyn 10 years of negotiations before he secured the screen rights to *Porgy and Bess*—and then he had to contend with such problems as a devastating soundstage fire, disagreements with Rouben Mamoulian, the original director who was replaced by Otto Preminger, and opposition from civil-rights groups protesting what they felt was an unfavorable view of Negro life. Because of the score's vocal demands, Sidney Poitier's Porgy was dubbed by Robert McFerrin, Dorothy Dandridge's Bess by Adele Addision, Diahann Carroll's Clara by Loulie Jean Norman, and Ruth Attaway's Serena by Inez Matthews. *Porgy and Bess* began life in 1925 as a novel by DuBose Heyward called *Porgy,* all about a crippled beggar who lives in Catfish Row, Charleston, S.C., and his love for the temptress known as Bess. Two years later it was turned into a play by Heyward and his wife, Dorothy, and eight years after that Gershwin turned it into an opera.
CBS ST.

Can-Can. Frank Sinatra, Shirley MacLaine, and Maurice Chevalier.

CAN-CAN

Music & lyrics: Cole Porter
Screenplay: Dorothy Kingsley & Charles Lederer
Produced by: Jack Cummings for 20th Century-Fox
Directed by: Walter Lang
Choreography: Hermes Pan
Photography: William Daniels (DeLuxe Color; Todd-AO)
Cast: Frank Sinatra, Shirley MacLaine, Maurice Chevalier, Louis Jourdan,
        Juliet Prowse, Marcel Dalio, Leon Belasco
Songs: "C'est Magnifique"; "You Do Something to Me"; "Let's Do It"; "It's All
        Right With Me"; "Live and Let Live"; "Come Along With Me"; "Just
        One of Those Things"
Released: March 1960; 131 minutes

Abe Burrows' libretto for the 1953 Broadway musical about efforts to suppress the
scandalous dance known as the can-can in *fin de siècle* Paris was distorted considerably
in its screen version—which nevertheless ended up as one of the two most popular
musicals of 1960. A role was added for Frank Sinatra as a lawyer who defends—and falls
in love with—Shirley MacLaine, the proprietor of the Montmartre cabaret in which the dance
takes place, and the minor role of an easy-going judge was enlarged to give Maurice
Chevalier a part similar to the one he had played in *Gigi* (with Louis Jourdan, cast as
Sinatra's romantic rival, again playing Chevalier's confidant.) Of the 14 Cole Porter songs
in the original (which had featured Lilo, Peter Cookson, and Gwen Verdon), eight were in
the movie ("I Love Paris," the most popular in the show, was sung only over the credits),
augmented by three Porter standards from other sources. Before shooting began, Juliet
Prowse took over the second female lead from Barrie Chase.
Capitol ST. CBS/Fox VC.

BELLS ARE RINGING

Music: Jule Styne
Lyrics & screenplay: Betty Comden & Adolph Green
Produced by: Arthur Freed for MGM
Directed by: Vincente Minnelli
Choreography: Charles O'Curran
Photography: Milton Krasner (Metrocolor; CinemaScope)
Cast: Judy Holliday, Dean Martin, Fred Clark, Eddie Foy Jr., Jean Stapleton, Dort Clark, Frank Gorshin, Bernie West, Gerry Mulligan, Hal Linden
Songs: "It's a Perfect Relationship"; "Do It Yourself"; "It's a Simple Little System"; "Better Than a Dream"; "I Met a Girl"; "Just in Time"; "Drop That Name"; "The Party's Over"; "I'm Going Back"
Released: June 1960; 126 minutes

A 1956 Broadway vehicle for Judy Holliday, *Bells Are Ringing* was brought to the screen with its original star plus three original cast members, Jean Stapleton, Dort Clark and Bernie West. Librettists Betty Comden and Adolph Green wrote the adaptation themselves, and 12 of the musical's 16 songs were retained ("On My Own" was replaced by "Do It Yourself" and "Long Before I Knew You" by "Better Than a Dream"). With some of its exterior locales photographed in New York (including a Sutton Place mansion), the film concerns a meddlesome telephone service message taker who comes to the aid of an insecure playwright (Dean Martin) with whom she inevitably falls in love. The film marked the 13th and final association between producer Arthur Freed and director Vincente Minnelli, and the 11th and final screen appearance of Judy Holliday.
Capitol ST. MGM/UA VC.

West Side Story. Led by Russ Tamblyn, the Jets taunt the Sharks' leader, George Chakiris.

WEST SIDE STORY

Music: Leonard Bernstein
Lyrics: Stephen Sondheim
Screenplay: Ernest Lehman
Produced by: Robert Wise for The Mirisch Company (released by
United Artists)
Directed by: Robert Wise & Jerome Robbins
Choreography: Jerome Robbins
Photography: Daniel Fapp (Technicolor; Panavision)
Cast: Natalie Wood, Richard Beymer, Russ Tamblyn, Rita Moreno,
George Chakiris, Simon Oakland, John Astin, Eliot Feld, David
Winters, Anthony Teague
Songs: "Jet Song"; "Something's Coming"; "Maria"; "America"; "Tonight";
"Gee, Officer Krupke!"; "I Feel Pretty"; "One Hand, One Heart";
"Cool"; "A Boy Like That"; "I Have a Love"; "Somewhere"
Released: September 1961; 151 minutes

Based on a "conception" by director-choreographer Jerome Robbins, *West Side Story* is a modern retelling of Shakespeare's *Romeo and Juliet* with New York street gangs, known as the Jets and Sharks, substituted for Montagues and Capulets. The dynamic fusion of Arthur Laurents' libretto, Leonard Bernstein and Stephen Sondheim's score, and Robbins' dances was acclaimed when the musical was first presented on Broadway in 1957 (with Carol Lawrence and Larry Kert in the leads), and the screen version won further encomia. The entire score was retained (though with a slight rearrangement in the order of songs), and Robbins was credited as co-director (with Robert Wise) as well as choreographer. George Chakiris, who had been in the London company, was the only film principal to have appeared in *West Side Story* on the stage. Romantic leads Natalie Wood and Richard Beymer had their singing voices dubbed by Marni Nixon and Jim Bryant, and Rita Moreno, as Natalie's best friend, received vocal assistance from Betty Wand. Location shooting for the movie took place in New York on West 64th Street, now the site of the Lincoln Center Performing Arts complex.

Foreshadowing director Wise's opening for *The Sound of Music* four years later, the movie starts with aerial views of Manhattan, shot straight down, then zooms in on the finger-snapping Jets as they dance menacingly through the streets. Instead of Romeo and Juliet, the star-crossed lovers are now Tony, a native-born American of Polish background and former Jets' leader, and Maria, a recent arrival from Puerto Rico and sister of the Sharks' leader, Bernardo; instead of a balcony they now make do with a fire escape (where they sing "Tonight"); and instead of well-meaning Friar Lawrence, they now have well-meaning Doc, a local druggist. When Tony, who has left the life of a street gang leader, tries to break up a rumble between the warring ethnic gangs, he kills Bernardo (George Chakiris) after Bernardo has killed Riff (Russ Tamblyn), the leader of the Jets. Unlike Shakespeare, however, the authors of *West Side Story* did not end their drama with a double suicide; Tony is killed by an avenging Puerto Rican gang member and the grief-stricken Maria lives on.

Despite its grim subject matter, the movie turned out to be the biggest moneymaking musical of 1962 with the fifth highest rental of any musical of the sixties. Possibly part of its acceptability was due to the fact that its somewhat overage delinquents were all so well-scrubbed and neatly garbed. In 1989, Robert Wise directed an updated variation on *West Side Story* called *Rooftops*.

For other movie musicals based on Shakespeare's plays, see *Kiss Me Kate* (page 181). *Columbia ST. MGM/UA VC.*

FLOWER DRUM SONG

Music: Richard Rodgers
Lyrics: Oscar Hammerstein II
Screenplay: Joseph Fields
Produced by: Ross Hunter & Joseph Fields for Universal-International
Directed by: Henry Koster
Choreography: Hermes Pan
Photography: Russell Metty (Eastman Color; Panavision)
Cast: Nancy Kwan, James Shigeta, Miyoshi Umeki, Juanita Hall, Benson Fong, Jack Soo, Reiko Sato
Songs: "You Are Beautiful"; "A Hundred Million Miracles"; "I Enjoy Being a Girl"; "I Am Going to Like It Here"; "Chop Suey"; "Don't Marry Me"; "Grant Avenue"; "Love, Look Away"; "The Other Generation"; "Sunday"
Released: November 1961; 133 minutes

With a cast headed by actors who were Eurasian (Nancy Kwan), Hawaiian (James Shigeta), Japanese (Miyoshi Umeki, Japanese-American (Jack Soo), and African-American (Juanita Hall), *Flower Drum Song* was Hollywood's only musical about the Chinese-Americans. Chin Y. Lee's delicate novel of a picture bride (Umeki) who has come from China, and her adjustment to San Francisco's more uninhibited ways was first turned into an elaborate Broadway musical in 1958 by Rodgers and Hammerstein. Joseph Fields, who served as co-librettist with Hammerstein, adapted the story for the screen, and Misses Umeki and Hall repeated their original roles. Except for "Like a God," the score was kept intact, as were the basic story and the mixed-culture witticisms ("You got egg foo yong all over your face"). Among the dubbed singing voices were those of B. J. Baker for Miss Kwan and Marilyn Horne for Reiko Sato.
MCA ST. MCA VC.

Flower Drum Song. Miyoshi Umeki entertaining a San Francisco crowd singing "A Hundred Million Miracles."

The Music Man. Shirley Jones and Robert Preston leading the finale.

THE MUSIC MAN

Music & lyrics: Meredith Willson
Screenplay: Marion Hargrove
Producer-director: Morton DaCosta for Warner Bros.
Choreography: Onna White
Photography: Robert Burks (Technicolor; Technirama)
Cast: Robert Preston, Shirley Jones, Buddy Hackett, Hermione Gingold, Paul Ford, Pert Kelton, Ronny Howard, The Buffalo Bills, Timmy Everett, Susan Luckey, Mary Wickes
Songs: "Trouble"; "Goodnight, My Someone"; "Seventy-Six Trombones"; "Sincere"; "The Sadder-but-Wiser Girl"; "Pick-a-Little, Talk-a-Little"; "Marian the Librarian"; "Being in Love"; "Gary, Indiana"; "Wells Fargo Wagon"; "Lida Rose"; "Shipoopi"; "Till There Was You"
Released: April 1962; 151 minutes

Although Robert Preston's dynamic performance in the 1957 Broadway musical *The Music Man* became closely identified with title role, the actor won the starring part in the screen version only after Cary Grant had turned it down. Also on hand from the original production were Pert Kelton and the Buffalo Bills singing quartet, director Morton DaCosta, and choreographer Onna White. The only change in the Meredith Willson score was the substitution of "Being in Love" for "My White Knight." Based on Willson's recollections of growing up in a small Iowa town, the story deals with con man "Professor" Harold Hill who invades River City on the Fourth of July, and rouses its citizenry into believing that the town's youngsters are heading for trouble if they don't learn how to play musical instruments. He then hoodwinks the rustics into buying the instruments from him on the condition that he will do the teaching, which he has neither the talent nor the inclination to do. Reformed through the love of Marian the Librarian (Shirley Jones), Hill remains to accomplish the impossible task. The picture ends with the youngsters joined by thousands of colorfully uniformed musicians marching down the street blaring out their thumping ode to the "Seventy-Six Trombones" that once led the town's biggest parade.
Warner ST. Warner VC.

THE ROAD TO HONG KONG

Music: James Van Heusen
Lyrics: Sammy Cahn
Screenplay: Norman Panama & Melvin Frank
Produced by: Norman Panama & Melvin Frank (released by United Artists)
Directed by: Norman Panama
Choreography: Jack Baker & Sheila Meyers
Photography: Jack Hildyard
Cast: Bing Crosby, Bob Hope, Joan Collins, Dorothy Lamour, Robert Morley, Peter Sellers, Walter Gotell, Felix Aylmer, David Niven, Jerry Colonna, Frank Sinatra, Dean Martin, Dave King
Songs: "Teamwork"; "The Road to Hong Kong"; "Let's Not Be Sensible"; "Warmer Than a Whisper"
Released: May 1962; 91 minutes

(See page 95.)

GYPSY

Music: Jule Styne
Lyrics: Stephen Sondheim
Screenplay: Leonard Spigelgass
Producer-director: Mervyn LeRoy for Warner Bros.
Choreography: Robert Tucker
Photography: Harry Stradling (Technicolor; Technirama)
Cast: Rosalind Russell, Natalie Wood, Karl Malden, Paul Wallace, Betty Bruce, Ann Jillian, Faith Dane, Roxanne Arlen, Harry Shannon, Harvey Korman, Danny Lockin, Jack Benny
Songs: "Small World"; "Some People"; "Mr. Goldstone"; "Little Lamb"; "You'll Never Get Away from Me"; "If Mama Was Married"; "All I Need Is the Girl"; "Everything's Coming Up Roses"; "Together Wherever We Go"; "You Gotta Have a Gimmick"; "Let Me Entertain You"; "Rose's Turn"
Released: September 1962; 149 minutes

There should have been a law prohibiting anyone other than Ethel Merman, who had starred in *Gypsy* on Broadway in 1959, from playing her role in the film version. Rosalind Russell tried gamely, but only Merman could have turned the basically tawdry story into the artistic triumph that it had been on stage. Still, the picaresque saga based on Arthur Laurents' adaptation of Gypsy Rose Lee's memoirs was a faithful treatment— with all its great songs intact—about a monstrously ambitious stage mother who stops at nothing to help her daughters, first June (Ann Jillian) then Louise (Natalie Wood, with her singing dubbed by Marni Nixon), become headliners. Louise makes it as a burlesque stripper. Though Miss Russell claimed to have done all her own singing, Lisa Kirk has been credited with a vocal assist on some numbers. Only two actors, Paul Wallace (singing and dancing "All I Need Is the Girl") and Faith Dane (in the "You Gotta Have a Gimmick" number), were holdovers from the original New York production.
Warner ST. Warner VC.

Jumbo. Jimmy Durante serenading his bride, Martha Raye, with "The Most Beautiful Girl in the World."

JUMBO

Music: Richard Rodgers
Lyrics: Lorenz Hart
Screenplay: Sidney Sheldon
Produced by: Joe Pasternak & Martin Melcher for MGM
Directed by: Charles Walters
Choreography: Busby Berkeley
Photography: William Daniels (Metrocolor; Panavision)
Cast: Doris Day, Stephen Boyd, Jimmy Durante, Martha Raye, Dean Jagger, Grady Sutton
Songs: "Over and Over Again"; "The Circus Is on Parade"; "Why Can't I?"; "This Can't Be Love"; "The Most Beautiful Girl in the World"; "My Romance"; "Little Girl Blue"; "Sawdust, Spangles and Dreams" (Roger Edens)
Released: December 1962; 125 minutes

By the time *Jumbo* reached the screen, the 1935 stage extravaganza underwent a number of changes. On Broadway, Jimmy Durante had played a circus press agent in the Ben Hecht-Charles MacArthur story and the tanbark Romeo and Juliet tale ended with the merger of two rival circuses. On film, Durante plays a debt-ridden circus owner and the story relates how the son of a more prosperous owner underhandedly gains control of Durante's circus for his father. But since the young man (Stephen Boyd, with James Joyce's singing voice) is in love with Durante's daughter, Doris Day, he is eventually forgiven. The picture ends with Boyd, Day, Durante, and Martha Raye (as Mrs. Durante) singing "Sawdust, Spangles and Dreams" as they dream of rebuilding the Durante circus. Augmented by two Rodgers and Hart songs from other sources, only half the team's original score was included in the movie which, at the insistence of the self-effacing producer of the stage musical, was officially known as *Billy Rose's Jumbo.* The production also marked the 42nd and final film with choreography by Busby Berkeley.
CSP ST. MGM/UA VC.

BYE BYE BIRDIE

Music: Charles Strouse
Lyrics: Lee Adams
Screenplay: Irving Brecher
Produced by: Fred Kohlmar for Columbia
Directed by: George Sidney
Choreography: Onna White
Photography: Joseph Biroc (Eastman Color, Panavision)
Cast: Janet Leigh, Dick Van Dyke, Ann-Margret, Maureen Stapleton, Bobby
        Rydell, Jesse Pearson, Ed Sullivan, Paul Lynde, Frank Albertson, Gil
        Lamb, Robert Paige
Songs: "Bye Bye Birdie"; "The Telephone Hour"; "How Lovely to Be a
        Woman"; "Honestly Sincere"; "One Boy"; "Put on a Happy Face";
        "Kids"; "One Last Kiss", "A Lot of Livin' to Do"; "Rosie"
Released: April 1963; 112 minutes

Broadway's first rock-and-roll musical swiveled its way onto the stage in 1960 and onto the screen three years later. Dick Van Dyke (in his movie debut) repeated his role of Albert Peterson, the manager of an Elvis Presley-type singer named Conrad Birdie (Jesse Pearson), who is about to be drafted into the Army. To give Conrad the perfect sendoff, Albert and his secretary, Rose Grant (Janet Leigh), put the singer on Ed Sullivan's television show to sing Albert's song "One Last Kiss" and bestow that kiss on teenager Kim McAfee (Ann-Margret) of Sweet Apple, Ohio. Hollywood changed Albert from a would-be English teacher in Michael Stewart's original libretto to a former biochemist so that the picture ends with him going into the fertilizer business with Kim's father (Paul Lynde, who had originated the part on Broadway). Five songs were cut from the Strouse-Adams score and a title song was added for the movie. Cinematic highlights were the split-screen "Telephone Hour" and the imaginative staging of "Put on a Happy Face."
RCA ST.   RCA/Columbia VC.

Bye Bye Birdie. Ann-Margret singing "How Lovely
to Be a Woman."

VIVA LAS VEGAS

Screenplay: Sally Benson
Produced by: Jack Cummings & George Sidney for MGM
Directed by: George Sidney
Choreography: David Winters
Photography: Joseph Biroc (Metrocolor; Panavision)
Cast: Elvis Presley, Ann-Margret, Cesare Danova, William Demarest, Nicky Blair, Jack Carter, Eddie Quillan
Songs: "Viva Las Vegas" (Doc Pomus-Mort Shuman); "The Lady Loves Me" (Sid Tepper-Roy Bennett); "Appreciation" (Marvin Moore-Bernie Wayne); "I Need Somebody to Lean On" (Pomus); "My Rival" (Moore-Wayne); "If You Think I Don't Need You" (Red West)
Released: May 1964; 86 minutes

Elvis Presley was one of the few modern singers also to have a successful movie career. Acting in 31 films from 1956 to 1970 (and voted by distributors among the ten most popular screen stars for seven years between 1957 and 1966), he was in a succession of undistinguished—and frequently indistinguishable—musicals that generally found the pouting, pompadoured rock star as an outdoorsy, misunderstood free spirit who can't help but become involved with nubile young ladies who readily succumb to the swivel-hipped singer's appeal. Grossing $5,152,000 in domestic rentals, *Viva Las Vegas* was the most popular of all the Presley films. Despite its title, however, the movie takes place mostly on the city's outskirts where Presley, a racecar driver, finds temporary employment in a resort hotel and permanent distraction in the arms of swimming instructor Ann-Margret. *MGM/UA VC.*

THE UNSINKABLE MOLLY BROWN

Music & lyrics: Meredith Willson
Screenplay: Helen Deutsch
Produced by: Lawrence Weingarten for MGM
Directed by: Charles Walters
Choreography: Peter Gennaro
Photography: Daniel Fapp (Metrocolor; Panavision)
Cast: Debbie Reynolds, Harve Presnell, Ed Begley, Jack Kruschen, Hermione Baddeley, Vassili Lambrinos, Harvey Lembeck, Martita Hunt, Audrey Christie, Grover Dale, Maria Karnilova, Anna Lee
Songs: "I Ain't Down Yet"; "Colorado My Home"; "Belly Up to the Bar, Boys"; "I'll Never Say No to You"; "He's My Friend"; "Leadville Johnny Brown"
Released: July 1964; 128 minutes

The movie version of the 1960 Broadway musical (starring Tammy Grimes) was the last of the traditional bigtime MGM musicals. With only five of the original 17 Meredith Willson songs retained (plus one addition, "He's My Friend"), the film is embellished with dances by the original choreographer, Peter Gennaro, and enhanced by location shooting at Black Canyon in the Gunnison National Monument, Colorado. Loosely based on the exploits of a legendary figure of the Colorado mining days, librettist Richard Morris's tale concerns hillbilly Molly Tobin (Debbie Reynolds), who marries gold prospector "Leadville Johnny" Brown (Harve Presnell in the role he had created on the stage) and suddenly finds herself in the chips. But spunky, social climbing Molly is snubbed by Denver society and the Browns take off for Europe for a little polishing. Though Johnny returns to Leadville, Molly stays on to become the toast of the titled set. Lonesome for her husband, she books passage on the maiden voyage of the *S.S. Titanic* which, on April 15,1912, hits an iceberg and goes down. Molly, being unsinkable, survives, is acclaimed a hero, and is reunited with her Johnny high in the Colorado Rockies. *MCA ST. MGM/UA VC.*

Robin and the 7 Hoods. Dean Martin, Sammy Davis Jr., Frank Sinatra, Bing Crosby, and Barbara Rush.

ROBIN AND THE 7 HOODS

Music: James Van Heusen
Lyrics: Sammy Cahn
Screenplay: David Schwartz
Produced by: Frank Sinatra for Warner Bros.
Directed by: Gordon Douglas
Photography: William Daniels (Technicolor; Panavision)
Cast: Frank Sinatra, Dean Martin, Sammy Davis Jr., Bing Crosby, Peter Falk, Edward G. Robinson, Barbara Rush, Victor Buono, Hank Henry, Allen Jenkins, Jack LaRue, Hans Conried, Sig Rumann, Philip Crosby
Songs: "Bang! Bang!"; "Style"; "Mister Booze"; "Don't Be a Do-Badder"; "My Kind of Town"
Released   August 1964; 103 minutes

Spoofing the Robin Hood legend, *Robin and the 7 Hoods* offers Frank Sinatra as Robbo, a Prohibition gangster leading his merry band of altruistic Chicago outlaws, including Little John (Dean Martin), Will (Sammy Davis Jr.), and Allen A. Dale (Bing Crosby), as they do battle against a rival gang led by Guy Gisborn (Peter Falk). Romance is supplied by Barbara Rush as Marian, the daughter of an old-time mobster (Edward G. Robinson doing a guest bit in his "Little Caesar" role), and musical highlights are supplied by the vaudeville-type "Style" for strawhatted Sinatra, Martin, and Crosby, and Sinatra's ode to Chicago "My Kind of Town." The movie was originally to have been produced by Gene Kelly for Sinatra's production firm but the two men had a disagreement and Sinatra took personal charge. It marked the third and last time Sinatra and Crosby appeared together (*High Society* and *The Road to Hong Kong* had been the first two), and it was the last musical film for both men: Sinatra had been in 20, Crosby in 61.
Reprise LP. Warner VC.

A Hard Day's Night. The Beatles and their adoring fans.

A HARD DAY'S NIGHT

Music & lyrics: John Lennon & Paul McCartney
Screenplay: Alun Owen
Produced by: Walter Shenson (released by United Artists)
Directed by: Richard Lester
Photography: Gilbert Taylor
Cast: John Lennon, Paul McCartney, George Harrison, Ringo Starr, Wilfred Brambell, Norman Rossington, Victor Spinetti, Kenneth Haigh, Anna Quayle
Songs: "A Hard Day's Night"; "I Should Have Known Better"; "All My Loving"; "If I Fell"; "Can't Buy Me Love"; "And I Love Her"; "I'm Happy Just to Dance With You"; "Tell Me Why"; "She Loves You"
Released: August 1964; 85 minutes

The four mop-haired Liverpudlians who soared to international acclaim with their winning performances and the infectious beat of their music were starred in a fast-paced movie that greatly influenced other comic films that followed. Motivation for the low-budget film was simply to capitalize on the hysteria the foursome then engendered in order for United Artists to reap the financial rewards by issuing the soundtrack album. But the charm of the Beatles' laid-back personalities, plus director Richard Lester's frenetic *cinema vérité* approach, the non sequitur dialogue, and the bright songs by John Lennon and Paul McCartney all combined to win critical acclaim as well as box-office success. The fictionalized documentary purports to be a typical day's activity as it shows the boys—along with Paul's foxy grandpa (Wilfred Brambell)—cutting up on a train, fleeing from their adoring fans, rehearsing their numbers, dodging the police, and ending with a television performance before a wildly screaming audience of pubescent young ladies.

The quartet acted together in one other film (*Help!*), sang on the soundtrack of *Yellow Submarine,* and were seen in rock documentaries. Though they did not appear in the 1978 release, *I Wanna Hold Your Hand,* the movie was all about the wave of Beatlemania that attended their first engagement on the Ed Sullivan television Show. After the group's breakup in 1970, Lennon (who was murdered in 1980) and Starr continued their separate careers acting in movies, and McCartney has written a number of film songs. In 1984, Starr and McCartney were reunited in McCartney's movie, *Give My Regards to Broad Street.* UA ST. MPI VC.

Mary Poppins. One-man band Dick Van Dyke entertaining Londoners with "Chim-Chim-Cheree."

Mary Poppins. Julie Andrews leading the chimney sweeps in the "Step in Time" number.

MARY POPPINS

Music & lyrics: Richard M. Sherman & Robert B. Sherman
Screenplay: Bill Walsh & Donald Da Gradi
Produced by: Walt Disney (released by Buena Vista)
Directed by: Robert Stevenson
Choreography: Marc Breaux & DeeDee Wood
Photography: Edward Colman (Technicolor)
Cast: Julie Andrews, Dick Van Dyke, David Tomlinson, Glynis Johns, Ed Wynn, Hermione Baddeley, Karen Dotrice, Matthew Garber, Elsa Lanchester, Arthur Treacher, Reginald Owen, Reta Shaw, Jane Darwell
Songs: "Chim Chim Cheree"; "Sister Suffragette"; "The Life I Lead"; "A Spoonful of Sugar"; "Jolly Holiday"; "I Love to Laugh"; "Supercalifragilisticexpialidocious"; "Stay Awake"; "Feed the Birds"; "Step in Time"; "Let's Go Fly a Kite"
Released: September 1964; 140 minutes

After scoring a success in the Broadway musical *My Fair Lady,* Julie Andrews was passed over for the leading female role in the film version in favor of Audrey Hepburn. Miss Andrews, however, was amply compensated when Walt Disney persuaded her to make her screen debut in the title role of the adaptation of Pamela Travers' children's classic, *Mary Poppins.*

A fantasy combining live action with animated cartoon characters, the film turned out to be one of the most popular and highly acclaimed productions ever to come out of the Disney Studio, and second only to *The Sound of Music* (also starring Miss Andrews) as the highest domestic theatre rental musical of the 1960s. Set in London in 1910, the tale concerns stuffy banker George Banks (David Tomlinson), his suffragette wife Winifred (Glynis Johns) and their two young children, Jane and Michael (Karen Dotrice and Matthew Garber), who live at 17 Cherry Tree Lane. Because Jane and Michael are in need of a new nanny, they write a "help-wanted" newspaper ad which their father throws into the fireplace. Miraculously, the paper flies through the chimney and into the hands of Mary Poppins sitting on her favorite cloud. She is hired for the position ("I'm practically perfect in every way"), then quickly sets about tidying up the children's room which she accomplishes with a snap of her fingers while singing "A Spoonful of Sugar." In the park, the nanny and her charges meet Bert (Dick Van Dyke), a one-man band and a street chalk artist, and the foursome proceed to have a "Jolly Holiday" in the country by simply walking through one of Bert's pictures. In the movie's most imaginative sequence, they meet up with a variety of cartoon characters—farm animals, turtles that carry them over a pond, dancing penguin waiters at an outdoor restaurant, and merry-go-round horses that leap off the carousel and turn into race horses. After riding one of them to victory, Mary Poppins describes her feelings to a group of reporters ("Supercalifragilisticexpialidocious!") and joins Bert and some banjo-plucking buskers in a song and dance. A sudden downpour washes the chalk drawing away and the four are back in London.

Displeased that Mary Poppins wastes his children's time, Papa Banks takes Jane and Michael to his bank to learn something useful. There they meet Mr. Dawes (also played by Van Dyke), the doddering bank president, and inadvertently cause a run on the bank. Though Banks is dismissed, he turns into a more understanding parent and even manages to get his job back. And Mary Poppins, her mission accomplished, happily soars off into the sky.

The huge success of *Mary Poppins* prompted two other big-budget musical fantasies adapted from British children's books —*Doctor Dolittle* in 1967 and *Chitty Chitty Bang Bang* the following year. Even more reminiscent was the Disney studio's own 1971 release, *Bedknobs and Broomsticks,* another London-based tale about a flying heroine (played by Angela Lansbury), which shared the same screenwriters, producer, director, songwriters, music director (Irwin Kostal), and featured actor (David Tomlinson).
Buena Vista ST. Disney VC.

MY FAIR LADY

Music: Frederick Loewe
Lyrics & screenplay: Alan Jay Lerner
Produced by: Jack L. Warner for Warner Bros.
Directed by: George Cukor
Choreography: Hermes Pan
Photography: Harry Stradling (Technicolor; Super Panavision 70)
Cast: Audrey Hepburn, Rex Harrison, Stanley Holloway, Wilfred Hyde-White, Gladys Cooper, Jeremy Brett, Theodore Bikel, Mona Washbourne, Isobel Elsom, Henry Daniell, Grady Sutton, Charles Fredericks, John Holland, Owen McGiveney, Lily Kemble Cooper, Moyna MacGill, Olive Reeves-Smith, Barbara Pepper, Baroness Bina Rothschild
Songs: "Why Can't the English?"; "Wouldn't It Be Lovely?"; "I'm an Ordinary Man"; "With a Little Bit of Luck"; "Just You Wait"; "The Rain in Spain"; "I Could Have Danced All Night"; "Ascot Gavotte"; "On the Street Where You Live"; "Embassy Waltz" (instrumental); "You Did It"; "Show Me"; "Get Me to the Church on Time"; "A Hymn to Him"; "Without You"; "I've Grown Accustomed to Her Face"
Released: October 1964; 170 minutes

According to Greek mythology, Pygmalion, King of Cyprus carved an ivory statue of a woman and fell in love with it. The statue came to life, she was named Galatea, and Pygmalion married her. The myth so intrigued playwright George Bernard Shaw that he wrote a variation on the legend about a phonetics professor who, aided by her cooperation and skill, manages to transform a Cockney flower seller into a lady so refined she is accepted as a duchess. The unsentimental playwright, however, carefully avoided any sign of love between the two and left their relationship ambivalent at the end. The play, written for Mrs. Patrick Campbell, gave its first performance in London in 1914, then opened in New York later the same year.

In 1956, Alan Jay Lerner and Frederick Loewe turned Shaw's work into a musical, starring Rex Harrison and Julie Andrews, and not only retained most of the original dialogue but also borrowed from Anthony Asquith's 1938 film version of *Pygmalion,* with Leslie Howard and Wendy Hiller. The story was expanded to include scenes at Tottenham Court Road, the Ascot race meeting, and the Embassy Ball, and it also indicated a more permanent relationship between the sharp-tongued bachelor, Professor Henry Higgins, and his star pupil, Eliza Doolittle.

In one more transformation—stage to screen—the musical was faithfully adapted by Lerner himself, who not only kept all the musical numbers but even restored two lines, eliminated before the New York opening, at the end of "You Did It"—"'I know each language on the map,' said he, 'And she's Hungarian as the first Hungarian Rhapsody.' " Also on hand from the original were costume designer Cecil Beaton (now in charge of designing the entire production) and Harrison (after Cary Grant had refused the part), plus Stanley Holloway as Eliza's carousing father, Alfred P. Doolittle. Miss Andrews, however, was replaced by Audrey Hepburn (with her singing dubbed by Marni Nixon) because producer Jack L. Warner wanted to protect his investment with a proven box office draw since Miss Andrews had never before appeared in a movie. (This left her free to take the leading role in *Mary Poppins.)*

The cost of securing the screen rights to *My Fair Lady,* a record at the time, was $5.5 million (plus other emoluments). Though the action was opened up more than in the stage production, director George Cukor carefully avoided a too realistic approach by recreating Covent Garden (the film's first scene) and Ascot on the studio backlot rather than on location.

Columbia ST. CBS/Fox VC.

My Fair Lady. Jeremy Brett, Audrey Hepburn, Rex Harrison, and Wilfred Hyde-White at Ascot.

My Fair Lady. Stanley Holloway and his fellow pub-crawlers performing "Get Me to the Church on Time."

The Sound of Music. Late as usual, Julie Andrews runs into a cold reception from Peggy Wood, Portia Nelson, Anna Lee, Marni Nixon, and Evadne Baker.

The Sound of Music. Julie Andrews and the Von Trapp children sing about "The Lonely Goatherd."

THE SOUND OF MUSIC

Music: Richard Rodgers
Lyrics: Oscar Hammerstein II
Screenplay: Ernest Lehman
Producer-director: Robert Wise for 20th Century-Fox
Choreography: Marc Breaux & DeeDee Wood
Photography: Ted McCord (DeLuxe Color; Todd-AO)
Cast: Julie Andrews, Christopher Plummer, Eleanor Parker, Richard
Haydn, Peggy Wood, Charmian Carr, Bil Baird Marionettes, Anna
Lee, Portia Nelson, Marni Nixon, Daniel Truhitte, Norma Varden,
Evadne Baker
Songs: "The Sound of Music"; "How Do You Solve a Problem Like Maria";
"I Have Confidence in Me" (lyric: Richard Rodgers); "Sixteen Going
on Seventeen"; "My Favorite Things"; "Do Re Mi"; "Lonely Goatherd";
"Edelweiss"; "So Long, Farewell"; "How Can Love Survive?"; "Climb
Ev'ry Mountain"; "Something Good" (lyric: Rodgers)
Released: March 1965; 174 minutes

A young woman is employed as governess to a large brood of children of a gruff-speaking autocrat, and soon wins their affection. She also succeeds in making the autocrat a more understanding and humane person, and the two fall in love while dancing. So far that plot outline could apply equally to Rodgers and Hammerstein's *The King and I* (set in Siam in the 1860s) and to their *Sound of Music* (set in Austria in 1938), both of which were based on true stories. But unlike the first, in *The Sound of Music* governess Maria Rainer and employer Captain Georg Von Trapp get married—only to have their happiness dashed by the invasion of the German army. At the end of the musical as the Nonnberg Abbey nuns sing "Climb Ev'ry Mountain," the Von Trapps and their seven children begin the perilous journey climbing over the Alps to freedom in Switzerland.

The Sound of Music, which opened on Broadway in 1959, had a book by Howard Lindsay and Russel Crouse partly based on a German film, *Die Trapp Familie,* starring Ruth Leuwerik, about the celebrated family of folk singers who began concertizing in Austria, then continued for 17 years after coming to the United States. It was Rodgers and Hammerstein's last collaboration and the sixth of their nine stage works to be filmed. Not only was it their most financially successful movie, it held the record as the biggest domestic box office attraction of any motion picture between 1966 and 1969 (by the end of 1989, its total domestic theatre rentals still placed it 20th among the top moneymakers of all time). Mary Martin had starred as the postulant-turned-governess on the stage, but for the film (after Doris Day, Audrey Hepburn, and Romy Schneider had been considered), the part went to Julie Andrews even before the release of her first movie, *Mary Poppins.* William Wyler was signed to direct but he withdrew early in the preparations and was replaced by Robert Wise. Shot mostly on location in and around Salzburg, *The Sound of Music* took full advantage of the camera, offering many atmospheric views of the picture-postcard city and the Tyrolean Alps. Particularly striking were the opening scenes of the mountains which introduced the story in a manner similar to the technique Wise had used at the beginning of *West Side Story.* (More than 20 years before, director Joe May had opened *Music in the Air,* which also had songs with Hammerstein lyrics, with panoramic views of the Bavarian Alps.)

Three of the original songs in the score were not sung in the movie though two new ones were added that had lyrics as well as music by Richard Rodgers: "I Have Confidence in Me" and "Something Good" (which replaced "An Ordinary Couple"). In the matter of voice dubbing, it was Bill Lee who sang for Christopher Plummer (as Capt. Georg Von Trapp) and Margery McKay who did the singing for Peggy Wood (as the Mother Abbess).
RCA ST. CBS/Fox VC.

HELP!

Music & lyrics: John Lennon & Paul McCartney
Screenplay: Marc Behm & Charles Wood
Produced by: Walter Shenson (released by United Artists)
Directed by: Richard Lester
Photography: David Watkin (Eastman Color)
Cast: John Lennon, Paul McCartney, George Harrison, Ringo Starr, Leo McKern, Eleanor Bron, Victor Spinetti, Roy Kinnear, Patrick Cargill, Alfie Bass, Warren Mitchell, Dandy Nichols
Songs: "Help!"; "You're Gonna Lose That Girl"; "You've Got to Hide Your Love Away"; "Ticket to Ride"; "I Need You" (George Harrison); "The Night Before"; "Another Girl"
Released: August 1965; 90 minutes

Combining Marx Brothers gags with a James Bond spoof in a manner predating television's *Monty Python,* the Beatles' follow-up to their memorable *A Hard Day's Night* finds the quartet pursued by members of an Eastern religious sect that is hell-bent on retrieving a sacrificial ring belonging to High Priest Leo McKern, that a fan has given to Ringo Starr. The picture also has something to do with a mad scientist who wants to rule the world if he can get a government grant. As he had in their first film, director Richard Lester put the boys through a frenzied pace which found John, Paul, George, and Ringo—each one seemingly a variation on the three others—performing their numbers on a television screen, at a recording session, in their London flat, on Salisbury Plain (where they are protected from their adversaries by army tanks), in the snow, and on a Bahamian beach.
UA ST. Criterion VC.

Help! John Lennon, George Harrison, Ringo Starr, and Paul McCartney.

HOW TO SUCCEED IN BUSINESS WITHOUT REALLY TRYING

Music & lyrics: Frank Loesser
Screenplay: David Swift
Producer-director: David Swift for The Mirisch Corp. (released by United Artists)
Choreography: Dale Moreda (based on Bob Fosse)
Photography: Burnett Guffey (DeLuxe Color, Panavision)
Cast: Robert Morse, Michele Lee, Rudy Vallee, Anthony Teague, Maureen Arthur, Murray Matheson, Sammy Smith, Ruth Kobart, Robert Q. Lewis, Paul Hartman, Joey Faye, Don Koll
Songs: "The Company Way"; "A Secretary Is Not a Toy"; "Been a Long Day"; "Grand Old Ivy"; "Rosemary"; "I Believe in You"; "Brotherhood of Man"
Released: March 1966; 121 minutes

Transferred virtually in toto to the screen, *How to Succeed in Business Without Really Trying* was based on the 1961 Abe Burrows-Frank Loesser Pulitzer Prize-winning satiric farce about the most efficient—and devious—methods of getting ahead in the business world. In the leading roles were the two stars of the Broadway show—Robert Morse as the innocent-looking window washer-turned-executive, J. Pierpont Finch, and Rudy Vallee (in his first screen musical in 11 years) as the stuffy president of the World Wide Wicket Company, J. B. Biggley. Also retained from the New York company were Michele Lee (who had succeeded the original female lead), Sammy Smith, and Ruth Kobart, with Maureen Arthur (as Biggley's mistress, Hedy LaRue) recruited from the touring company. All but five songs from the score were sung in the film, and the dances were reproductions of Bob Fosse's original choreography.
UA ST.   MGM/UA VC.

How to Succeed in Business Without Really Trying.
Rudy Vallee and Robert Morse pledging allegiance to "Grand Old Ivy."

THOROUGHLY MODERN MILLIE

Screenplay: Richard Morris
Produced by: Ross Hunter for Universal
Directed by: George Roy Hill
Choreography: Joe Layton
Photography: Russell Metty (Technicolor; Panavision)
Cast: Julie Andrews, Mary Tyler Moore, Carol Channing, James Fox,
        Beatrice Lillie, John Gavin, Jack Soo, Buddy Schwab, Benny Rubin
Songs: "Thoroughly Modern Millie" (James Van Heusen-Sammy Cahn);
        "Jimmy" (Kay Thompson); "The Tapioca" (Van Heusen-Cahn);
        "Jazz Baby" (Blanche Merrill-M. K. Jerome); "Poor Butterfly"
        (Raymond Hubbell-John Golden); "Baby Face" (Harry Akst-Benny
        Davis); "Do It Again" (George Gershwin-B. G. DeSylva)
Released: March 1967; 138 minutes

In 1954, upon seeing Julie Andrews on Broadway in *The Boy Friend,* a British sendup of musical comedies of the Twenties, producer Ross Hunter first tried unsuccessfully to win the screen rights, then got the notion of a different kind of period spoof for Miss Andrews. Camping out in New York in 1922, *Thoroughly Modern Millie* involves cloche-hatted flapper Millie Dilmount (Miss Andrews) and her new friend, Miss Dorothy Brown (Mary Tyler Moore), who is surprised when a taxi driver refuses her check for 35 cents. Both are residents of the Priscilla Hotel for Single Young Ladies, run by the sinister Mrs. Meers (Beatrice Lillie in a rare movie appearance), who turns out to be a dealer in white slavery. In its affectionate spoofing of the jazz age, the picture takes advantage of silent-screen techniques such as wipes, iris-ins, and title cards. It also kids females fashions (Millie must appear flatchested so that her beads hang straight); pipe-smoking, Arrow Collar ad-type heroes (John Gavin); and the Harold Lloyd-type juvenile (James Fox), who gets the chance to teeter on the ledge of an office building. One of the most popular musicals of the decade (it placed seventh in theatre rental fees), the film included four new numbers along with eight period songs.
MCA ST. MCA VC.

Thoroughly Modern Millie. Mary Tyler Moore,
Julie Andrews, and Carol Channing.

Camelot. Franco Nero, Richard Harris, and Vanessa Redgrave.

CAMELOT

Music: Frederick Loewe
Lyrics & screenplay: Alan Jay Lerner
Produced by: Jack L. Warner for Warner Bros.
Directed by: Joshua Logan
Photography: Richard H. Kline (Technicolor; Panavision)
Cast: Richard Harris, Vanessa Redgrave, Franco Nero, David Hemmings, Lionel Jeffries, Laurence Naismith, Estelle Winwood, Pierre Olaf
Songs: "I Wonder What the King Is Doing Tonight"; "The Simple Joys of Maidenhood"; "Camelot"; "C'est Moi"; "The Lusty Month of May"; "Follow Me"; "How to Handle a Woman"; "Then You May Take Me to the Fair"; "If Ever I Would Leave You"; "What Do the Simple Folk Do?"; "I Loved You Once in Silence"; "Guenevere"
Released: October 1967; 179 minutes

The people who had brought *My Fair Lady* to the stage—Frederick Loewe, Alan Jay Lerner, and director Moss Hart—were reunited in 1960 for a musical about the Arthurian legend adapted from T. H. White's book, *The Once and Future King*. Not nearly as well received as the previous work, *Camelot* was a stately, opulent production in which the idealistic monarch (played by Richard Burton) sees his dream of peace and justice—as personified by his Knights of the Round Table— totally destroyed when his wife, Queen Guenevere (Julie Andrews), and his closest friend, Sir Lancelot (Robert Goulet), violate the spirit of Camelot by their adulterous fall from grace. Jack L. Warner, who had produced the movie version of *My Fair Lady,* put *Camelot* on the screen with most of the original songs (chief loss: "Before I Gaze at You Again"), a script by Lerner, and the tragic triangle now acted by Richard Harris (he would tour as Arthur during the 1980s), Vanessa Redgrave, and Franco Nero (whose singing was dubbed by Gene Merlina). With exterior shooting in Spain (because of the castles), the somber extravaganza lost one character (Arthur's sister Morgan Le Fay) and used the song "If Ever I Would Leave You" for a two-year flashback of Lancelot and Guenevere's illicit affair. Though it was the tenth highest ranking musical of the sixties in domestic theatre rental fees, the $15 million production was a financial failure.
Warner ST. Warner VC.

Doctor Dolittle. Rex Harrison singing "When I Look in Your Eyes" to Sophie the Seal.

DOCTOR DOLITTLE

Music & lyrics: Leslie Bricusse
Screenplay: Leslie Bricusse
Produced by: Arthur P. Jacobs for 20th Century-Fox
Directed by: Richard Fleischer
Choreography: Herbert Ross
Photography: Robert Surtees (DeLuxe Color; Todd-AO)
Cast: Rex Harrison, Samantha Eggar, Anthony Newley, Richard Attenborough, William Dix, Peter Bull, Geoffrey Holder, Portia Nelson, Norma Varden
Songs: "My Friend the Doctor"; "Talk to the Animals"; "I've Never Seen Anything Like It"; "Beautiful Things"; "When I Look in Your Eyes"; "After Today"; "Fabulous Places"; "Where Are the Words?"; "I Think I Like You"; "Doctor Dolittle"; "Something in Your Smile"
Released: December 1967; 144 minutes

Doctor Dolittle was created in an attempt to cash in on the popularity of two recent hits— like *Mary Poppins* it was another turn-of-the-century fantasy based on a popular children's book by an English author, and like *My Fair Lady* it again starred Rex Harrison as an authority on language. Here, however, the former Henry Higgins who had once taught Eliza Doolittle how to speak proper English is now John Dolittle who has been taught by his pet parrot how to talk to the animals. Hugh Lofting's good doctor, in fact, can converse in almost 500 animal languages— from Alligatorese to Zebran—and the rambling, whimsical tale finds Dolittle and his chums (Samantha Eggar, Anthony Newley, and William Dix) in a series of adventures involving such zoological oddities as the Pushmi-Pullyu (a two-headed llama), the Great Pink Sea Snail, and the Giant Lunar Moth. The seaside village of Puddleby-on-the-Marsh was recreated in the inland village of Castle Combe, England, and scenes involving the floating Sea Star Island were filmed on the Caribbean island of St. Lucia.
20th Century-Fox ST. CBS/Fox VC.

FINIAN'S RAINBOW

Music: Burton Lane
Lyrics: E. Y. Harburg
Screenplay: E. Y. Harburg & Fred Saidy
Produced by: Joseph Landon for Warner Bros.-Seven Arts
Directed by: Francis Coppola
Choreography: Hermes Pan (Fred Astaire uncredited)
Photography: Philip Lathrop (Technicolor; Panavision)
Cast: Fred Astaire, Petula Clark, Tommy Steele, Don Francks, Keenan Wynn, Al Freeman Jr., Barbara Hancock, Avon Long
Songs: "How Are Things in Glocca Morra?"; "Look to the Rainbow"; "If This Isn't Love"; "Something Sort of Grandish"; "That Great Come-and-Get-It Day"; "Old Devil Moon"; "When the Idle Poor Become the Idle Rich"; "When I'm Not Near the Girl I Love"; "The Begat"
Released: August 1968; 145 minutes

There were at least seven unsuccessful attempts to transfer the 1947 Broadway musical to the screen, including an animated cartoon feature with the voices of Frank Sinatra, Judy Garland, Ella Fitzgerald, and Louis Armstrong heard on the soundtrack. The version that did make it to the screen, with a script E. Y. Harburg and Fred Saidy adapted from their stage libretto, starred 68-year-old Fred Astaire in his 35th and final musical film. Astaire plays the role of Finian McLonergan who, with his daughter Sharon (Petula Clark), has come from Ireland to mingle with the good folks of Rainbow Valley, Missitucky. Finian has a crock of gold which he has stolen from Og the leprechaun (Tommy Steele), and his aim is to bury it in the ground near Fort Knox since it is sure to grow and make him rich. The whimsical satire, which had featured Albert Sharpe, Ella Logan, and David Wayne on the stage, retained all but one of the songs ("Necessity" was filmed but cut before the picture's release), changed the romantic lead's occupation from that of a union organizer to the manager of a co-op, and enlarged the role of Finian so that Astaire would have plenty to sing and dance about.
Warner ST. Warner VC.

HOW ARE THINGS IN GLOCCA MORRA?

Lyrics by E. Y. HARBURG
Music by BURTON LANE

FRED ASTAIRE · PETULA CLARK in "FINIAN'S RAINBOW"
—TOMMY STEELE—
CHAPPELL & CO., INC./609 FIFTH AVE., NEW YORK

FUNNY GIRL

Music: Jule Styne, etc.
Lyrics: Bob Merrill, etc.
Screenplay: Isobel Lennart
Produced by: Ray Stark for Columbia & Rastar
Directed by: William Wyler (Herbert Ross uncredited)
Choreography: Herbert Ross
Photography: Harry Stradling (Technicolor; Panavision)
Cast: Barbra Streisand, Omar Sharif, Kay Medford, Anne Francis, Walter Pidgeon, Lee Allen, Mae Questel, Tommy Rall
Songs: "I'm the Greatest Star"; "If a Girl Isn't Pretty"; "Roller Skate Rag"; "His Love Makes Me Beautiful"; "I'd Rather Be Blue Over You" (Fred Fisher-Billy Rose); "Second Hand Rose" (James Hanley-Grant Clarke); "People"; "You Are Woman, I Am Man"; "Don't Rain on My Parade"; "Sadie, Sadie"; "The Swan"; "Funny Girl"; "My Man" (Maurice Yvain-Channing Pollock)
Released: September 1968; 145 minutes

Producer Ray Stark had originally planned a biography of his mother-in-law, comedienne Fanny Brice, as a film and assigned Isobel Lennart to write the screenplay. But when Stark failed to get studio backing, he decided to offer it first as a stage musical with Miss Lennart now writing the libretto. The show opened on Broadway in 1964 and had a successful run, chiefly because of the impact of the relatively unknown Barbra Streisand. The story contrasts Fanny Brice's acclaim in the *Ziegfeld Follies* with her stormy marital relationship with smooth-talking gambler and embezzler Nick Arnstein which ends in divorce after Nick serves time in prison. (The 1939 Fox film, *Rose of Washington Square*, found Alice Faye and Tyrone Power in a tale so similar to her own life that Miss Brice took legal action and won an out-of-court settlement.) In addition to Miss Streisand, stage performers who repeated their roles in the film were Kay Medford as Fanny's pushy mother and Lee Allen (a Broadway cast replacement) as her best friend, but with Omar Sharif replacing Sydney Chaplin as Nick.

Of the 16 songs in the original Jule Styne-Bob Merrill score, seven—including the pop standard "People"—were retained in the screen treatment. The team also wrote three new numbers, "Roller Skate Rag," the ballet spoof "The Swan," and a new title song. In addition, three songs associated with Fanny Brice were included: "I'd Rather Be Blue Over You," "Second Hand Rose," and Miss Brice's trademark, "My Man" (replacing "The Music That Makes Me Dance"). The most cinematic presentation involved "Don't Rain on My Parade," which Miss Streisand, in frantic pursuit of her man, sings while rushing through a train station, riding on a train, driving a car, dashing across a pier, and standing on the bridge of a tugboat as it passes the Statue of Liberty. Before shooting began, director Sidney Lumet was replaced by William Wyler, though choreographer Herbert Ross was responsible for over half the direction.

The movie's success (it placed fourth in domestic theatre rental fees of all the decade's musicals) prompted a sequel in 1975 called *Funny Lady*, which was another box office winner (see page 262). Barbra Streisand again starred in the Ray Stark production, with Omar Sharif returning as Nick for some brief scenes. Herbert Ross was credited as director as well as choreographer, and the film, like its predecessor, again combined old songs with new (written by John Kander and Fred Ebb). Taking over where *Funny Girl* left off, *Funny Lady* (with little concern for biographical accuracy) shows Fanny as an established Broadway star still carrying the torch for Nick, who has remarried. Fanny's unhappiness is somewhat alleviated by her marriage to the brash songwriter-producer Billy Rose (James Caan), but that comes to an end when she catches Billy in bed with aquatic star Eleanor Holm. ("Don't just lay there," says Fanny. "Swim something.")
Columbia ST (Funny Girl); Bay Cities ST (Funny Lady). RCA/Columbia VC.

Funny Girl. Barbra Streisand defiantly warning "Don't Rain on My Parade" from the bridge of a tugboat.

STAR!

Screenplay: William Fairchild
Produced by: Saul Chaplin for 20th Century-Fox
Directed by: Robert Wise
Choreography: Michael Kidd
Photography: Ernest Laszlo (DeLuxe Color; Todd-AO)
Cast: Julie Andrews, Richard Crenna, Michael Craig, Daniel Massey, Robert Reed, Bruce Forsyth, Beryl Reid, Garrett Lewis, Don Koll
Songs: "Star!" (James Van Heusen-Sammy Cahn); " 'N Everything" (B. G. DeSylva-Gus Kahn); "Burlington Bertie from Bow" (William Hargreaves); "Parisian Pierrot" (Noel Coward); "Limehouse Blues" (Philip Braham-Douglas Furber); "Someone to Watch Over Me" (George Gershwin-Ira Gershwin); "Do, Do, Do" (Gershwin-Gershwin); "Has Anybody Seen Our Ship?" (Coward); "Someday I'll Find You" (Coward); "The Physician" (Cole Porter); "My Ship" (Kurt Weill-Gershwin); "Jenny" (Weill-Gershwin)
Released: October 1968; 175 minutes

The men who brought us *The Sound of Music,* producer-director Robert Wise and associate producer Saul Chaplin, teamed again (with Chaplin replacing Wise as producer) to put together Julie Andrews' fourth screen musical, a biography of the flamboyant London and New York stage star, Gertrude Lawrence. The big budget film turned out to be a lengthy, rather ponderous affair, though redeemed occasionally by the authenticity of the locales and the period flavor, as well as the effectiveness of some of the early musical staging. Noel Coward, who was closely associated with Miss Lawrence's career, was portrayed by Daniel Massey, but Beatrice Lillie, another close associate, was neither portrayed nor mentioned. The film was subsequently rereleased under the title *Those Were the Happy Times,* with its running time pared by almost an hour.
20th Century Fox ST.

YELLOW SUBMARINE

Music & lyrics: John Lennon & Paul McCartney
Screenplay: Lee Minoff, Al Brodax, Jack Mendelsohn, Erich Segal
Produced by: Al Brodax for Apple Films (released by United Artists)
Directed by: George Dunning (DeLuxe Color)
Voices: John Lennon, Paul McCartney, George Harrison, Ringo Starr, Paul Angelus, John Chie, Dick Emery, Geoff Hughes, Lance Percival
Songs: "Yellow Submarine"; "Eleanor Rigby"; "All Together Now"; "When I'm Sixty-Four"; "Nowhere Man"; "Lucy in the Sky With Diamonds"; "All You Need Is Love"; "Sgt. Pepper's Lonely Hearts Club Band"
Released: November 1968; 85 minutes

Following *A Hard Day's Night* and *Help!,* the third Beatles movie, *Yellow Submarine,* was a pop-art, psychedelic animated cartoon feature in which the foursome are caricatured with their speaking voices dubbed and their singing voices heard on the soundtrack—though they do show up live at the end. In the surrealistic film, created by a staff of artists under Heinz Edelmann, idyllic Pepperland is overrun by the sourfaced, music-hating Blue Meanies, and John, Paul, George, and Ringo get on board a yellow submarine (skippered by the leader of Sergeant Pepper's Lonely Hearts Club Band) that is able to fly through the air as well as travel underwater. It takes them to fantastic places for fantastic encounters with the Snapping Turks, the Ferocious Flying Glove, the Count Down Clock, and Jeremy the Nowhere Man, before they return to rout the Blue Meanies. Somehow, all this goes to prove that love conquers all. Of the 10 songs in *Yellow Submarine,* seven had been hits prior to being sung in the film.
UA ST. MGM/UA VC.

Chitty Chitty Bang Bang. The "Toot Sweet" number with Sally Ann Howes and Dick Van Dyke leading the candy factory workers.

CHITTY CHITTY BANG BANG

Music & lyrics: Richard M. Sherman & Robert B. Sherman
Screenplay: Roald Dahl & Ken Hughes
Produced by: Albert R. Broccoli (released by United Artists)
Directed by: Ken Hughes
Choreography: Marc Breaux & DeeDee Wood
Photography: Christopher Challis (Technicolor; Super-Panavision)
Cast: Dick Van Dyke, Sally Ann Howes, Lionel Jeffries, Gert Frobe, Anna Quayle, Benny Hill, James Robertson Justice, Robert Helpmann, Max Wall, Bernard Spear, Heather Ripley, Adrian Hill, Barbara Windsor
Songs: "Toot Sweet"; "Hushabye Mountain"; "Me Ol' Bamboo"; "Chitty Chitty Bang Bang"; "Truly Scrumptious"; "Lovely Lonely Man"; "Posh!"; "Chu-Chi Face"
Released: November 1968;156 minutes

Attempting to repeat the huge success of Walt Disney's *Mary Poppins*, producer Albert Broccoli not only chose another children's fantasy set in Edwardian England, he chose some of his key personnel from among those who had been associated with the Disney film—costar Dick Van Dyke (paired with Sally Ann Howes, the nearest thing to Julie Andrews), Richard and Robert Sherman for the songs, Marc Breaux and DeeDee Wood for the dances, and Irwin Kostal as music director. Based on a book by Ian Fleming, the excessively jolly tale involves an eccentric widowed inventor named Caractacus Potts (Van Dyke) who dreams up spindly Ronald Searle-type inventions (created by Ronald Searle). His greatest achievement is a flying motorcar, which comes in mighty handy in getting Potts, his two children, and his lady friend Truly Scrumptious (Howes) into and out of an extremely inhospitable Teutonic barony called Vulgaria.
UA ST. MGM/UA VC.

Oliver! Ron Moody explaining "You've Got to Pick a Pocket or Two" to Jack Wild and Mark Lester.

OLIVER!

Music & lyrics: Lionel Bart
Screenplay: Vernon Harris
Produced by: John Woolf for Columbia
Directed by: Carol Reed
Choreography: Onna White
Photography: Oswald Morris (Technicolor; Panavision)
Cast: Ron Moody, Oliver Reed, Harry Secombe, Shani Wallis, Mark Lester, Jack Wild, Hugh Griffith, Leonard Rossiter, James Hayter, Fred Emney
Songs: "Food, Glorious Food"; "Boy for Sale"; "Where Is Love?"; "You've Got to Pick a Pocket or Two"; "Consider Yourself"; "It's a Fine Life"; "As Long As He Needs Me"; "I'd Do Anything"; "Who Will Buy?"; "Reviewing the Situation"; "Oom-Pah-Pah"
Released: December 1968; 153 minutes

With only two songs cut from the original stage score, Lionel Bart's *Oliver!* was transformed into an impressive screen achievement. Based on Charles Dickens' novel *Oliver Twist*, the musical originated in London in 1960, then was successfully moved to Broadway three years later. Set in 1830, the tale concerns poorhouse foundling Oliver Twist (Mark Lester), who unwittingly falls in with a den of young thieves presided over by the avuncular villain Fagin (Ron Moody in a role he created on the stage). In time, Oliver is rescued by his long-lost great uncle. Throughout the film, director Carol Reed contrasts the grimy alleys and bustling street markets of London with the elegant residential areas of the city, utilizing choreography (by Onna White) to a far greater extent than it had been in the theatre.

The choreographic highlight, set in Bloomsbury Square, opens on an early-morning flower seller repeating the street cry, "Who will buy my sweet red roses?" As other vendors join in, their cries develop into the song "Who Will Buy?," through which Oliver expresses his joy at being alive on such a wonderful morning. Presently, the screen is filled with schoolchildren, bobbies, tweenies, nannies, and marching bandsmen who turn the number into a glorious affirmation of life. *Oliver!* had the sixth highest domestic theatre rental of all the musicals of the sixties. Among the seven previous film versions of the Dickens novel, all titled *Oliver Twist*, were those featuring Lon Chaney and Jackie Coogan (1922), Irving Pichel and Dickie Moore (1933), and Alec Guinness and John Howard Davies (1948). In 1988, the Disney studio released an animated musical version, *Oliver & Company*, with the characters depicted as cats and dogs.
RCA ST. RCA/Columbia VC.

SWEET CHARITY

Music: Cy Coleman
Lyrics: Dorothy Fields
Screenplay: Peter Stone
Produced by: Robert Arthur for Universal
Director-choreograper: Bob Fosse
Photography: Robert Surtees (Technicolor, Panavision)
Cast: Shirley MacLaine, John McMartin, Ricardo Montalban, Sammy
        Davis Jr., Chita Rivera, Paula Kelly, Stubby Kaye, Ben Vereen, Lee
        Roy Reams
Songs: "My Personal Property"; "Big Spender"; "If My Friends Could See
        Me Now"; "There's Gotta Be Something Better Than This"; "It's a
        Nice Face"; "Rhythm of Life"; "Sweet Charity"; "I'm a Brass Band";
        "I Love to Cry at Weddings"; "Where Am I Going?"
Released: January 1969; 157 minutes

On its way to the Broadway musical stage in 1966, Federico Fellini's film *Nights of Cabiria* was changed from the story of a gullible waiflike Roman prostitute to that of a gullible waiflike New York taxi dancer (Gwen Verdon). On the screen *Sweet Charity* was preserved more or less faithfully, except that Bob Fosse, the original director here making his movie debut, decked out the fragile story with all the cinematic tricks he could think of, including quick cutting, slow motion, dissolves, frame freezes, and monochromatic sequences. Miss Verdon (for whom librettist Neil Simon had written the part of Charity) was succeeded by Shirley MacLaine for the film, but John McMartin repeated his original role of Charity's Brooks Brothers suitor, and her chums at the Fan-Dango Ballroom were Chita Rivera (she had played Charity in the touring company) and Paula Kelly (she'd been in the London production). Three of the 11 songs in the film were new—"My Personal Property" (replacing "You Should See Yourself"), "It's a Nice Face" (for "I'm the Bravest Individual"), and a revised title song. Scenes were shot on location in New York including the "I'm a Brass Band" sequence filmed on Wall Street, the Brooklyn Bridge, and at Lincoln Center. Originally, *Sweet Charity* was to have been produced by Ross Hunter and written by I. A. L. Diamond.
MCA ST. MCA VC.

Sweet Charity. "There's Gotta Be Something Better Than This" danced by Paula Kelly, Shirley MacLaine, and Chita Rivera.

GOODBYE, MR. CHIPS

Music & lyrics: Leslie Bricusse
Screenplay: Terence Rattigan
Produced by: Arthur P. Jacobs for MGM
Directed by: Herbert Ross
Photography: Oswald Morris (Metrocolor; Panavision)
Cast: Peter O'Toole, Petula Clark, Michael Redgrave, George Baker,
Sean Phillips, Alison Leggatt, Jack Hedley
Songs: "Fill the World With Love"; "Where Did My Childhood Go?"; "London
Is London"; "And the Sky Smiled"; "When I Am Older"; "Walk
Through the World"; "What a Lot of Flowers"; "You and I"
Released: September 1969; 151 minutes

In transforming James Hilton's sentimental story about the dedicated schoolmaster known as Mr. Chips to the musical screen, writer Terence Rattigan updated the period from 1896-1933 to 1924-1969, made Chips' young wife, Katherine, a musical-comedy star when he meets her, and had her killed in a bombing raid during World War II instead of dying in childbirth. Helping to preserve the delicacy of the story, songs are sung on the soundtrack in counterpoint to the action rather than as interruptions, and muted, autumnal colors are used throughout. Peter O'Toole won high praise for his sensitive performance in the central role (Richard Burton had been the first choice), and authenticity was provided by the Sherborne School in Dorset, which served as stand-in for the fictitious Brookfield. *Goodbye, Mr. Chips* was first dramatized in 1938 when it was presented on the London stage with Leslie Banks in the lead, and the following year MGM filmed it with Robert Donat and Greer Garson. The 1969 movie version was adapted as a stage musical in 1982 and presented at England's Chichester Festival Theatre with John Mills.
MCA ST. MGM/UA VC.

Goodbye, Mr. Chips. Peter O'Toole and Petula Clark
at the ruins in Paestum, Italy.

Paint Your Wagon. Lee Marvin as Ben Rumson.

PAINT YOUR WAGON

Music: Frederick Loewe*; André Previn**
Lyrics & screenplay: Alan Jay Lerner
Produced by: Alan Jay Lerner for Paramount
Directed by: Joshua Logan
Choreography: Jack Baker
Photography: William Fraker (Technicolor, Panavision)
Cast: Lee Marvin, Clint Eastwood, Jean Seberg, Harve Presnell, Ray Walston, Alan Baxter, Tom Ligon
Songs: "I'm on My Way"*; "I Still See Elisa"*; "The First Thing You Know"**; "Hand Me Down That Can o' Beans"*; "They Call the Wind Maria"*; "A Million Miles Away Behind the Door"**; "There's a Coach Comin' In"*; "Gospel of No Name City"**; "I Talk to the Trees"*; "Best Things"**; "Wand'rin Star"*; "Gold Fever"**
Released: October 1969; 166 minutes

Abandoning the book he had fashioned for the 1951 Broadway musical, Alan Jay Lerner wrote the screen version based on an adaptation by Paddy Chayevsky. Over half the songs Lerner had written with composer Frederick Loewe were also discarded, with five new ones added with music by André Previn. The story, however, still takes place during the 1849 gold rush in California (though the movie was shot on location in Oregon), but now it is concerned with a polygamous affair in the mining town of No Name City where an indecisive young bride (Jean Seberg with Anita Gordon's singing voice) shares her affections with two gold-prospecting partners, the scruffy Lee Marvin and the more clean-cut Clint Eastwood. Eventually, as the gold peters out, the girl succumbs to respectability with Eastwood as Marvin goes off to follow his "wand'rin' star."
MCA ST. Paramount VC.

Hello, Dolly! Louis Armstrong and Barbra Streisand singing the title song at the Harmonia Gardens.

HELLO, DOLLY!

Music & lyrics: Jerry Herman
Screenplay: Ernest Lehman
Produced by: Ernest Lehman for 20th Century-Fox
Directed by: Gene Kelly
Choreography: Michael Kidd
Photography: Harry Stradling (DeLuxe Color; Todd-AO)
Cast: Barbra Streisand, Walter Matthau, Michael Crawford, Louis Armstrong, Marianne McAndrew, E. J. Peaker, Danny Lockin, Tommy Tune, Joyce Ames, Fritz Feld
Songs: "Just Leave Everything to Me"; "It Takes a Woman"; "Put On Your Sunday Clothes"; "Ribbons Down My Back"; "Dancing"; "Before the Parade Passes By"; "Elegance" (Bob Merrill); "Love Is Only Love"; "Hello, Dolly!"; "It Only Takes a Moment"; "So Long, Dearie"
Released: December 1969; 129 minutes

At 27 she was too young for the part, but Barbra Streisand beat out Carol Channing, Julie Andrews, and Elizabeth Taylor for the role of Dolly Levi in *Hello, Dolly!* simply because by 1969 she had become the screen's hottest box office attraction following her debut in *Funny Girl*. (In fact, 1969 was the first of six consecutive years that Miss Streisand would place among the ten most popular movie stars in the annual distributors' poll.) *Hello, Dolly!* had a lengthy gestation period. It originated in 1835 as a British play, *A Day Well Spent*, by John Oxenford, which, seven years later, turned up on the Vienna stage as *Einen Jux Will Er Sich Machen (He Wants to Have a Lark)* by Johann Nestroy. In 1938, American playwright Thornton Wilder transformed the Viennese play into a vehicle for Jane Cowl called *The Merchant of Yonkers,* and 16 years later wrote a new version for Ruth Gordon called *The Matchmaker.* Shirley Booth appeared in the 1958 film adaptation. The long-running 1964 Broadway musical, *Hello, Dolly!,* which librettist Michael Stewart based on the second Wilder play, gave Carol Channing the biggest hit of her career.

On screen, *Hello, Dolly!* retained nine of the 11 original songs, plus two additions: "Just Leave Everything to Me" (replacing "I Put My Hand In") and "Love Is Only Love" (which had been cut from *Mame).* Gene Kelly, directing his last screen musical, turned the movie into a colorful spectacle and choreographer Michael Kidd came up with some highly energetic (if endless) routines to "Put On Your Sunday Clothes," "Dancing," and the title number.

The picture opens on a motionless and soundless view of New York City's 14th Street in 1890, then comes to life as it focuses on the pushy, matchmaking widow, Dolly Levi, as she hops on a train to Yonkers to call upon the bilious hay and feed merchant Horace Vandergelder (Walter Matthau). Though she has arranged a date for him with milliner Irene Molloy (Marianne McAndrew), Dolly now decides to set her own chapeau for Horace. To help smooth her path to the altar, she sees to it that Vandergelder's chief clerk, Cornelius Hackl (Michael Crawford), and his assistant, Barnaby Tucker (Danny Lockin), escort Irene and her assistant, Minnie Fay (E. J. Peaker) to the elegant Harmonia Gardens on the Battery. There Dolly makes a triumphant entrance, welcomed by a host of excessively enthusiastic waiters and orchestra leader Louis Armstrong, and ends up trapping her matrimonial prize.

The extravagant film—it required over 3,700 extras alone for the mammoth 14th Street Parade—cost a record $24 million and lost money (even though it placed eighth among the musicals of the sixties with the highest domestic theatre rentals).
Casablanca ST. CBS/Fox VC.

Darling Lili. Julie Andrews entertaining the troops with "Whistling Away the Dark."

DARLING LILI

Music: Henry Mancini
Lyrics: Johnny Mercer
Screenplay: Blake Edwards & William Peter Blatty
Producer-director: Blake Edwards for Paramount
Choreography: Hermes Pan
Photography: Russell Harlan (Technicolor; Panavision)
Cast: Julie Andrews, Rock Hudson, Jeremy Kemp, Lance Percival,
      Michael Witney, Jacques Marin, Andre Maranne, Gloria Paul
Songs: "Whistling Away the Dark"; "The Girl in No Man's Land"; "I'll Give
      You Three Guesses"; "Smile Away Each Rainy Day"; "Darling Lili"
Released: December 1969; 136 minutes

The effort to alter the cool, crisp Julie Andrews image continued with the actress's fifth screen musical, *Darling Lili,* a World War I spy caper in which she was cast as a Mayfair version of Mata Hari. But Miss Andrews' first film with her husband, writer-director-producer Blake Edwards, found her as neither vamp nor villainess; she was again cool, crisp Julie Andrews, a.k.a .Lili Smith, whose father was German and who covers up her activities by entertaining Allied troops. Lili is ordered to France to collect information from American flying ace Major Bill Larrabee (Rock Hudson), but the two fall in love and the young woman is arrested for treason to the Fatherland. With Bill's help she escapes to Switzerland, and the lovers eventually hold a post-war reunion. Aided by appealing songs by Henry Mancini and Johnny Mercer (including the compelling "Whistling Away the Dark"), the big budget film, which was unsuccessful on its first release, has taken on something of a cult status. *RCA ST.*

ON A CLEAR DAY YOU CAN SEE FOREVER

Music: Burton Lane
Lyrics & screenplay: Alan Jay Lerner
Produced by: Howard W. Koch for Paramount
Directed by: Vincente Minnelli
Photography: Harry Stradling (Technicolor; Panavision)
Cast: Barbra Streisand, Yves Montand, Bob Newhart, Larry Blyden,
Simon Oakland, Jack Nicholson, John Richardson, Pamela Brown,
Irene Handl, Roy Kinnear, Don Koll
Songs: "Hurray, It's Lovely Up Here"; "Love With All the Trimmings"; "On a
Clear Day"; "Melinda"; "Go to Sleep"; "He Isn't You"; "What Did I
Have That I Don't Have?"; "Come Back to Me"
Released: June 1970; 129 minutes

Originating as a 1961 Broadway musical starring Barbara Harris and John Cullum, *On a Clear Day You Can See Forever* was inspired by librettist-lyricist Alan Jay Lerner's fascination with the phenomenon of extrasensory perception (ESP). In adapting his story to the screen, Lerner kept the basic plot though he dropped half the songs (while adding two new ones with composer Burton Lane, "Love With All the Trimmings" and "Go to Sleep"). Daisy Gamble (Barbra Streisand), a modern-day New Yorker, not only can make flowers grow by talking to them, she also has psychic powers that tell her when the telephone will ring, and—after being hypnotized by psychiatrist Marc Chabot (Yves Montand in a role first intended for Richard Harris)—even reveals that she had once had a previous life as social-climbing Melinda Tentrees in Regency England. Complications arise when Marc, much to Daisy's chagrin, finds himself falling in love with Melinda. For the flashback scenes, the movie was shot on location at the Royal Pavilion in Brighton. *CSP ST. Paramount VC.*

On a Clear Day You Can See Forever. Yves Montand hypnotizing Barbra Streisand.

SCROOGE

Music & lyrics: Leslie Bricusse
Screenplay: Leslie Bricusse
Produced by: Robert Solo for Cinema Center
Directed by: Ronald Neame
Choreography: Paddy Stone
Photography: Oswald Morris (Technicolor; Panavision)
Cast: Albert Finney, Edith Evans, Kenneth More, Alec Guinness, Laurence Naismith, Michael Medwin, David Collings, Anton Rodgers, Suzanne Neve, Richard Beaumont, Paddy Stone, Kay Walsh, Gordon Jackson, Roy Kinnear
Songs: "A Christmas Carol"; "Father Christmas"; "December the 25th"; "Happiness"; "I Like Life"; "The Beautiful Day"; "Thank You Very Much"; "I'll Begin Again"
Released: October 1970; 118 minutes

As those in charge must have reasoned, if Charles Dickens' *Oliver Twist* could be turned into a profitable singing and dancing movie, why not *A Christmas Carol?* Retitled *Scrooge,* the film, like its predecessor, is set in Victorian London with cantankerous Ebenezer Scrooge (played by Albert Finney) taking the place of cantankerous Fagin and innocent Tiny Tim Cratchit (Richard Beaumont) taking the place of innocent Oliver Twist. But before the reformed skinflint (in Santa Claus costume) can lead the Yuletide revelers in cavorting down the street, he must first be taught to mend his ways through the intervention of such apparitions as his long-dead partner Marley (Alec Guinness), and the Ghosts of Christmas Past (Edith Evans), Christmas Present (Kenneth More), and Christmas Future (Paddy Stone, also the film's choreographer). The earliest movie version of *A Christmas Carol* was released in 1901. Others were made in 1935 (with Seymour Hicks), 1938 (with Reginald Owen), and 1951 (with Alistair Sim, who was also Scrooge's voice in a 1972 cartoon feature).
Columbia ST. CBS/Fox VC.

Fiddler on the Roof. "If I Were a Rich Man" sung by Topol.

FIDDLER ON THE ROOF

Music: Jerry Bock
Lyrics: Sheldon Harnick
Screenplay: Joseph Stein
Producer-director: Norman Jewison for the Mirisch Company (released by
    United Artists)
Choreography: Tom Abbott (based on Jerome Robbins)
Photography: Oswald Morris (DeLuxe Color; Panavision)
Cast: Topol, Norma Crane, Leonard Frey, Molly Picon, Paul Mann,
    Rosalind Harris, Michele Marsh, Neva Small, Michael Glaser, Tutte
    Lemkow, Zvee Scooler, Elaine Edwards, Raymond Lovelock, Candy
    Bonstein
Songs: "Tradition"; "Matchmaker, Matchmaker"; "If I Were a Rich Man";
    "Sabbath Prayer"; "To Life"; "Miracle of Miracles"; "Tevye's
    Dream"; "Sunrise, Sunset"; "Wedding Celebration"; "Do You Love
    Me?"; "Far from the Home I Love"; "Chava Ballet" (instrumental);
    "Anatevka"
Released: October 1971; 180 minutes

To reproduce on the screen as closely as possible the international stage success which first opened on Broadway in 1964, Joseph Stein was signed to write the screenplay based on his original libretto, the dances were adapted from Jerome Robbins' original choreography by Tom Abbott, Robbins' assistant, and all but two of the musical numbers ("Now I Have Everything" and "I Just Heard") were retained from Jerry Bock and Sheldon Harnick's original score. In addition, the cast was headed by Israeli actor Topol, who had starred as Tevye in the London company (Zero Mostel had starred on Broadway), and included Leonard Frey, who had played Motel the tailor in the original Broadway production. To reproduce as closely as possible a Jewish settlement in Czarist Russia in 1905, director Norman Jewison took his cast and crew to Lakenik, near Zagreb, Yugoslavia, where they did most of the exterior shooting. To preserve the fantasy quality of the work—based on *Tevye's Daughters,* a collection of short stories by Yiddish writer Sholom Aleichem—the movie was filmed in the kind of colors associated with Russian artist Marc Chagall.

Fiddler on the Roof was the third highest ranking movie musical of the seventies on *Variety's* list of "All-Time Film Rental Champs." Released while the original New York production was still running, the picture was judged by critic Hollis Alpert in *Saturday Review* as "a stunning combination of frolicsome production numbers, touching rituals (a Sabbath supper, a wedding beneath the traditional canopy), ethnic comedy, and sure-fire poignance."

The story is primarily about Tevye, a dairyman who speaks to God ("It's no shame to be poor but it's no honor either") and his efforts to retain tradition in the face of change, particularly as revealed through his relationship with his three oldest daughters (Rosalind Harris, Michele Marsh, and Neva Small) and his feelings about the men they marry. At the end, when a Cossack pogrom has destroyed his village of Anatevka, Tevye still clings to his faith and his tradition as he sets off with what is left of his family to find a new life in America. The symbolic fiddler of the title was acted by Swedish mime Tutte Lemkow and his playing was by Isaac Stern.

In 1979, the movie was re-released in Dolby Stereo, with its running time shortened by some 32 minutes. The first screen version of the original stories was filmed in 1939 in Yiddish under the title *Tevye.*

Liberty ST. MGM/UA VC.

Cabaret. Liza Minnelli and Joel Grey singing "Money, Money" in the show at the Kit Kat Klub in Berlin.

CABARET

Music: John Kander
Lyrics: Fred Ebb
Screenplay: Jay Presson Allen
Produced by: Cy Feuer for Allied Artists & ABC
Director-choreographer: Bob Fosse
Photography: Geoffrey Unsworth (Technicolor; Panavision)
Cast: Liza Minnelli, Michael York, Helmut Griem, Joel Grey, Marisa
Berenson, Fritz Wepper, Elizabeth Neumann-Viertel, Oliver Collignon,
Angelika Koch, Louise Quick
Songs: "Willkommen"; "Mein Herr"; "Maybe This Time"; "Money,
Money"; "Two Ladies"; "Hieraten"; "Tomorrow Belongs to Me";
"If You Could See Her"; "Cabaret"
Released: January 1972; 124 minutes

Few Broadway musical productions have ever been recreated in such purely cinematic terms as *Cabaret*. In adapting the work, screenwriter Jay Presson Allen, assisted by the oddly credited "research consultant" Hugh Wheeler, not only based the script on Joe Masteroff's libretto for the 1966 stage musical, she also went back to the sources of that musical, Christopher Isherwood's *Berlin Stories* (a collection of short stories) and John van Druten's 1951 dramatic adaptation, *I Am a Camera,* which starred Julie Harris and William Prince on Broadway, and was itself transferred to the screen four years later with Miss Harris and Laurence Harvey.

Differences between the stage and screen *Cabaret* include the elimination of the Jewish fruit dealer, the lessening of the importance of the Berlin landlady, and the addition of two people who appeared only in the book and the play: a wealthy Jewish girl (Marisa Berenson) and her penniless suitor (Fritz Wepper). The film also added an entirely new character, the oleaginous bisexual aristocrat (Helmut Griem), and the nationalities of the two leading characters were changed. The hedonistic yet vulnerable Sally Bowles, who had been English, is now an American played by Liza Minnelli (scoring a triumph in her first screen musical since appearing as a tot in *In the Good Old Summertime),* and American writer Clifford Bradshaw is now English writer Brian Roberts (Michael York). Joel Grey, in a part created for the stage musical, reappeared in the movie as the epicene Master of Ceremonies at the Kit Kat Klub, a garish Berlin cabaret where Sally is the featured singer and whose floor shows become a metaphor for German decadence during the period just before Hitler's rise to power.

Of the 15 Kurt Weillish songs in the original John Kander-Fred Ebb score, six were retained for the screen version. Added were "Mein Herr" (which replaced "Don't Tell Mama" and which was staged in a manner recalling Marlene Dietrich in *The Blue Angel),* "Maybe This Time," (a song originally written for Liza Minnelli in 1963) and "Money, Money" (replacing "The Money Song" but using the same music as the eliminated "Telephone Song"). Even more than in the stage production, the musical numbers were limited to the environs of the nightclub, with only "Hieraten" ("Married") and "Tomorrow Belongs to Me" performed in different settings. Credit for the film's overall power belongs to the boldly imaginative direction of Bob Fosse whose use of cross-cutting was particularly effective (such as a slapping number in the nightclub floorshow contrasted with Nazis beating up a man in the street outside).

Cabaret placed sixth among the highest domestic theatre rentals of all musicals released in the seventies.
MCA ST. CBS/Fox VC.

LADY SINGS THE BLUES

Screenplay: Terence McCloy, Chris Clark, Suzanne de Passe
Produced by: Jay Weston & James White for Paramount
Directed by: Sidney J. Furie
Photography: John Alonzo (Eastman Color; Panavision)
Cast: Diana Ross, Billy Dee Williams, Richard Pryor, James Callahan,
Paul Hampton, Sid Melton, Virginia Capers, Scatman Crothers
Songs: "'Taint Nobody's Bizness if I Do" (Porter Grainger, Graham Prince,
Clarence Williams); "The Man I Love" (George Gershwin-Ira Gershwin);
"Them There Eyes" (Maceo Pinkard, William Tracey, Doris Tauber);
"Strange Fruit" (Lewis Allan); "What a Little Moonlight Can Do"
(Harry Woods); "Good Morning Heartache" (Dan Fisher, Ervin
Drake, Irene Higgenbotham); "Don't Explain" (Billie Holiday-Arthur
Herzog); "Lover Man" (Jimmy Sherman, Roger Ramirez, Jimmy
Davis); "Love Is Here to Stay" (Gershwin-Gershwin); "God Bless
the Child" (Holiday-Herzog)
Released: October 1972; 144 minutes

Something of a forerunner to *The Rose*, which was about Janis Joplin, *Lady Sings the Blues* tells the often harrowing story of the life of an earlier pop singer, Billie Holiday, who was also unable to deal with the pressures of her career and died of heroin addiction at the age of 44. Many of the events were fictionalized or rearranged (e.g. Artie Shaw, not the fictitious Reg Harney, hired Billie as the first black singer with a white band, and her first drug bust was in 1947 not 1936), but the picture did manage to capture the spirit of the singer's tragic life. Of particular help was the casting of Diana Ross who, in her first acting part, gave a convincing portrayal as well as a believable reinterpretation of Lady Day's singing style. *Motown ST. Paramount VC.*

1776

Music & lyrics: Sherman Edwards
Screenplay: Peter Stone
Produced by: Jack L. Warner for Columbia
Directed by: Peter Hunt
Choreography: Onna White
Photography: Harry Stradling (Technicolor; Panavision)
Cast: William Daniels, Howard Da Silva, Ken Howard, Donald Madden,
Blythe Danner, John Cullum, Roy Poole, David Ford, Virginia
Vestoff, Ronald Holgate, Ray Middleton, Rex Robbins, Patrick Hines
Songs: "Sit Down, John"; "Piddle, Twiddle and Resolve"; "Till Then";
"The Lees of Old Virginia"; "But, Mr. Adams"; "Yours, Yours,
Yours"; "He Plays the Violin"; "Momma Look Sharp"; "The Egg";
"Molasses to Rum"; "Is Anybody There?"
Released: November 1972; 141 minutes

A faithful—perhaps too faithful—adaptation of the 1969 Broadway musical, *1776* was brought to the screen by the original librettist, director, choreographer, and orchestrator (Eddie Sauter), and it used all but one song ("Cool, Cool Considerate Men") in the Sherman Edwards score. As for the cast, no less than 13 of the leading actors had already played their roles on the Broadway stage. The movie is a dramatized retelling of the debates and compromises that resulted in the signing of the Declaration of Independence by members of the Continental Congress meeting in Philadelphia during a sweltering summer. Led by John Adams (William Daniels), the pro-independence forces gradually wear down the opposition (the main issue is free states versus slave states), and the film ends with the stirring—if historically inaccurate—sight of the men affixing their signatures to the document on the Fourth of July. *Columbia ST. RCA/Columbia VC.*

Lady Sings the Blues. Diana Ross (as Billie Holiday) auditioning at a Harlem nightspot.

1776. Howard Da Silva, Ken Howard, and William Daniels singing "The Egg."

FUNNY LADY

Music: John Kander, etc.
Lyrics: Fred Ebb, etc.
Screenplay: Jay Presson Allen & Arnold Schulman
Produced by: Ray Stark for Columbia & Rastar
Director-choreographer: Herbert Ross
Photography: James Wong Howe (Technicolor; Panavision)
Cast: Barbra Streisand, James Caan, Omar Sharif, Roddy McDowall, Ben Vereen, Carole Wells
Songs: "Blind Date"; "More Than You Know" (Vincent Youmans-Edward Eliscu, Billy Rose); "I Found a Million Dollar Baby" (Harry Warren-Mort Dixon, Rose); "Great Day" (Youmans-Eliscu, Rose); "How Lucky Can You Get?"; "Isn't It Better?"; "If I Love Again" (Ben Oakland-J. P. Murray); "Let's Hear It for Me"
Released: March 1975; 137 minutes

(See page 244.)

NASHVILLE

Screenplay: Joan Tewkesbury
Producer-director: Robert Altman for ABC
Photography: Paul Lohmann (Metrocolor)
Cast: Barbara Baxley, Ned Beaty, Karen Black, Ronee Blakley, Timothy Brown, Keith Carradine, Geraldine Chaplin, Shelley Duvall, Allen Garfield, Henry Gibson, Jeff Goldblum, Barbara Harris, Michael Murphy, Lily Tomlin, Keenan Wynn, Julie Christie, Elliott Gould
Songs: "200 Years" (Richard Baskin-Henry Gibson); "It Don't Worry Me" (Keith Carradine); "For the Sake of the Children" (Baskin); "Keep a-Goin'" (Baskin-Gibson); "Memphis" (Karen Black); "Rolling Stone" (Black); "Tapedeck in His Tractor" (Ronee Blakley); "I'm Easy" (Carradine); "My Idaho Home" (Blakley)
Released: June 1975; 159 minutes

Just as *Cabaret* had used a gaudy Berlin nightclub as a metaphor for the decadence of pre-Hitler Germany, so Nashville used the home of country music as a metaphor for the entire country in the mid-seventies, illuminating such themes as fame, ambition, idolatry, vanity, rivalry, jealousy, political power, and just plain slippin' around. Using hand-held cameras and such cinematic techniques as quick cutting and overlapping dialogue, director Robert Altman created a complex, artful mosaic focusing on the interrelationship of 24 people directly or indirectly associated with the country-music scene.

The film gives the members of its large cast the opportunity to create vivid cameos, including Karen Black as an opportunistic country singer on her way up, Keith Carradine as a smarmy rock singer, Ronee Blakley as a sickly legendary star (suggesting Loretta Lynn), Henry Gibson as a self-conscious, self-important aging star (suggesting Hank Snow), Shelley Duvall as a vacuous groupie, Barbara Harris as a kookie would-be singer, Michael Murphy as a slick political operator, Lily Tomlin as an unhappy housewife, and Geraldine Chaplin as a flighty reporter filming a documentary for the BBC. Because of the presence of the reporter, the film at times takes on the quality of a documentary, and the scenes during performances at the Grand Ole Opry—both onstage and backstage—are strikingly realistic. An unusual feature of *Nashville* is that Gibson, Blakley, Black, and Carradine wrote some of the songs that they sing in the film.
ABC ST. Paramount VC.

Rocky Horror Picture Show. Tim Curry as Dr. Frank N. Furter.

ROCKY HORROR PICTURE SHOW

Music and Lyrics: Richard O'Brien
Screenplay: Tim Sharman and Richard O'Brien
Produced by: Michael White
Directed by: Tim Sharman
Photography: Peter Suschitzky (Eastmancolor)
Cast: Tim Curry, Susan Sarandon, Barry Bostwick, Richard O'Brien, Patricia Quinn, Little Nell, Jonathan Adams, Peter Hinwood, Meatloaf, Charles Gray
Songs: "Science Fiction/Double Feature"; "Damnit, Janet"; "Over at the Frankenstein Place"; "The Time Warp"; "Sweet Transvestite"; "I Can Make You a Man"; "Hot Patootie – Bless My Soul"; "Sword of Damoclies"; "Eddie's Teddy"; "Touch-A, Touch-A, Touch Me"; "Planet Schmanet"; "Rose Tint My World/Fan Fare/Don't Dream It Be It/Wild Untamed Thing"; "I'm Going Home"; "Super Heroes"
Released: September 1975; 100 minutes.

It was a dark and stormy night ... how else would you begin an over-the-top spoof of sci-fi/horror films? A painfully naïve couple finds themselves lost in the countryside with a broken-down car. Seeking help, they stumble out of the storm and into the lair of a mad scientist who is trying to construct the perfect man. Based on the hit stage musical, *The Rocky Horror Picture Show* was a failure when first released. A cult following soon developed, including midnight screenings enhanced by live, costumed casts in many cities. Zealous audience participation became an integral part of the film experience, with lighters, squirt guns and pieces of toast among the list of self-directed props. Tim Curry repeated his stage role, playing a "transvestite transsexual from Transylvania." Rocker Meat Loaf appears as Eddie. Sharman and O'Brien joined forces again for a 1981 sequel, Shock Treatment, which was neither an immediate nor a cult success.
Wea/Atlantic/Rhino ST. Fox VC.

A STAR IS BORN

Screenplay: John Gregory Dunne, Joan Didion, Frank Pierson
Produced by: Jon Peters for First Artists (released by Warner Bros.)
Directed by: Frank Pierson
Photography: Robert Surtees (Metrocolor; Panavision)
Cast: Barbra Streisand, Kris Kristofferson, Paul Mazursky, Gary Busey,
      Oliver Clark, M. G. Kelly, Sally Kirkland
Songs: "Queen Bee" (Robert Holmes); "Lost Inside of You" (Barbra
      Streisand-Leon Russell); "Evergreen" (Streisand-Paul Williams);
      "The Woman in the Moon" (Williams-Kenny Ascher); "I Believe
      in Love" (Kenny Loggins-Alan & Marilyn Bergman); "With One More
      Look at You" (Williams-Ascher); "Watch Closely Now"
      (Williams-Ascher)
Released: December 1976; 140 minutes

Though its source was credited to the same story (by William A. Wellman and Robert Carson) and it bore the same title as the 1937 nonmusical and the 1954 musical (see page 188), the 1976 *A Star Is Born* was reborn into an entirely different environment, with significant plot changes and a new score. Instead of being concerned with the romance between a rising movie star and a fading movie star, it is concerned with the romance between a rising rock star (Barbra Streisand) and a fading rock star (Kris Kristofferson in a part intended for Elvis Presley), and instead of having the has-been singer drown himself in the Pacific he kills himself by crashing his Ferrari. The picture is particularly effective in capturing the electricity of the rock concert milieu, and in showing how the young singer, in her very first concert (filmed before 11,000 in Tucson), could rouse a cheering crowd to its feet. *A Star Is Born,* for which Miss Streisand served as executive producer, was the fourth highest domestic theatre rental musical released during the seventies.
Columbia ST. Warner VC.

NEW YORK, NEW YORK

Screenplay: Earl MacRauch & Mardik Martin
Produced by: Irwin Winkler & Robert Chartoff for United Artists
Directed by: Martin Scorsese
Photography: Laszlo Kovacs (DeLuxe Color; Panavision)
Cast: Liza Minnelli, Robert DeNiro, Lionel Stander, Barry Primus, Mary
      Kay Place, Georgie Auld, Diahnne Abbott
Songs: "You Brought a New Kind of Love to Me" (Sammy Fain-Irving
      Kahal, Pierre Norman); "Once in a While" (Michael Edwards-Bud
      Green); "You Are My Lucky Star" (Nacio Herb Brown-Arthur Freed);
      "The Man I Love" (George Gershwin-Ira Gershwin); "Just You, Just
      Me" (Jesse Greer-Ray Klages); "Blue Moon" (Richard Rodgers-
      Lorenz Hart); "But the World Goes 'Round" (John Kander-Fred
      Ebb); "Theme from New York, New York" (Kander-Ebb);
      "Honeysuckle Rose" (Fats Waller-Andy Razaf)
Released: June 1977; 153 minutes

Using artificial backlot sets to evoke the atmosphere of the 1940s movies, *New York, New York* (whence came the metropolis' unofficial anthem) is a nostalgic view of the big-band era that shows off the singing talents of Liza Minnelli as a wide-eyed vocalist and the acting talents of Robert DeNiro as a highly strung saxophone player (with Georgie Auld doubling on the instrument). Minnelli and DeNiro play a couple who meet at the Rainbow Room on VJ Day, have a stormy marriage, and separate when DeNiro walks out after the birth of their child. One scene near the end puts the movie a bit out of sync by having Miss Minnelli sing "But the World Goes 'Round" in a manner suggesting her mother, Judy Garland, doing "The Man That Got Away" in *A Star Is Born*. In 1981, a deleted number, "Happy Endings," performed by Miss Minnelli and Larry Kert, was restored to the film print.
Liberty ST. MGM/UA VC.

Saturday Night Fever. Karen Lynn Gorney and John Travolta dancing to "More Than a Woman" at the 2001 Oddysey in Brooklyn.

SATURDAY NIGHT FEVER

Music & lyrics: Barry, Robin & Maurice Gibb
Screenplay: Norman Wexler
Produced by: Robert Stigwood for Paramount
Directed by: John Badham
Choreography: Lester Wilson
Photography: Ralf D. Bode (Movielab Color; Panavision)
Cast: John Travolta, Karen Lynn Gorney, Barry Miller, Joseph Cali, Paul Pape, Bruce Ornstein, Donna Pescow, Val Bisoglio, Julie Bovasso, Monte Rock III
Songs: "Staying Alive"; "Night Fever"; "More Than a Woman"; "How Deep Is Your Love?"
Released: December 1977; 119 minutes

In his first starring role, John Travolta played a 19-year-old dese-dems-and-dose dumbo who lives in Bay Ridge, Brooklyn, with his unemployed squabbling father and his lachrymose mother, and spends his days working in a paint store and his nights hanging out with his buddies. Skidding his car, copulating on the back seat, brawling with a rival gang, and horsing around on the steel cables of the Verrazano Bridge take care of Tony Manero's week nights, but Saturday night is reserved for the all-important ritual when he can put on a new silk shirt and adorn himself with gold chains and become like y'know the star attraction at the 2001 Oddysey, a local disco. Tony meets the upwardly mobile Stephanie Mangano (Karen Lynn Gorney), now living and working in Manhattan, who sizes him up ("You're nowhere on your way to noplace"), and with whom he teams to win $500 in the disco's dance contest. Eventually, after the suicide of one of his friends, he comes to realize the emptiness of his life. A grittier, more graphic *West Side Story*, *Saturday Night Fever* offers an alarming depiction of moral degeneracy, though tempered by the sound-track songs of the Bee Gees and the flashy dance routines devised by Lester Wilson. The movie, which was filmed in Brooklyn's Bay Ridge section, was the second highest domestic theatre rental musical of the seventies.

Six years later, *Saturday Night Fever* was followed by a sequel, *Staying Alive*, also starring Travolta, which shows what happens to Tony after he has moved to Manhattan in search of a career as a Broadway dancer. Sylvester Stallone directed.
RSO ST. Paramount VC.

Grease. Olivia Newton-John and John Travolta.

GREASE

Music & lyrics: Warren Casey & Jim Jacobs, etc.
Screenplay: Bronte Woodard
Produced by: Robert Stigwood & Allan Carr for Paramount
Directed by: Randal Kleiser
Choreography: Patricia Birch
Photography: Bill Butler (Metrocolor; Panavision)
Cast: John Travolta, Olivia Newton-John, Stockard Channing, Jeff Conaway, Didi Conn, Eve Arden, Frankie Avalon, Joan Blondell, Edd Byrnes, Sid Caesar, Alice Ghostley, Dody Goodman, Sha-Na-Na, Lorenzo Lamas, Fannie Flagg
Songs: "Grease" (Barry Gibb); "Summer Nights"; "Look at Me, I'm Sandra Dee"; "Hopelessly Devoted to You" (John Farrar); "Beauty School Dropout"; "Hound Dog" (Jerry Lieber-Mike Stoller); "Born to Hand Jive"; "There Are Worse Things I Could Do"; "You're the One That I Want" (Farrar); "We Go Together"
Released: June 1978; 110 minutes

To date the highest domestic theatre rental musical film of all time (it had grossed $96.3 million by the end of 1989), *Grease* celebrates youthful conformity by advocating that anyone is a loser whose values regarding dress, morality, and social behavior differ from that of the majority. The long-running stage musical, which opened Off-Broadway in 1972, was filmed with virtually all its original songs augmented by seven additional numbers, and with dances created by its choreographer, Patricia Birch. John Travolta, who had played a minor role in the show's touring company, and Jeff Conaway, who had replaced male lead Barry Bostwick on Broadway, were the only *Grease* veterans in the movie cast. The locale of Rydell High School was moved from an urban center to Southern California, and the story, set in the mid-Fifties, deals with the romance between students Danny Zuko (23-year-old Travolta), the leader of the black leatherjacketed T-Birds, and Australian Sandy Alston (29-year-old Olivia Newton-John), a member of the Pink Ladies. Sandy, however, is a social outcast since she chooses to dress tastefully and behave properly, but by the end of the last reel she has seen the errors of her ways and shows up looking just as tacky as all the others.

A sequel, *Grease 2*, was released by in 1982. Like its predecessor, it was produced by Robert Stigwood and Allan Carr with choreography by Patricia Birch (who also directed). Maxwell Caulfield and Michelle Pfeiffer had the leads.
RSO ST. Paramount VC.

THE BUDDY HOLLY STORY

Screenplay: Robert Gittler
Produced by: Freddy Bauer for Columbia
Directed by: Steve Rash
Photography: Stevan Larner (Metrocolor; Panavision)
Cast: Gary Busey, Don Stroud, Charles Martin Smith, Conrad Janis,
William Jordan, Maria Richwine, Amy Johnson, Dick O'Neil
Songs: "Rock Around the Ollie Vee" (Sonny Curtis); "That'll Be the Day"
(Jerry Allison, Buddy Holly, Norman Petty); "Oh, Boy" (Sonny West,
Bill Tilghman, Petty); "It's So Easy" (Holly, Petty); "Well All Right"
(Frances Faye, Don Raye, Dan Howell); "Chantilly Lace" (J. P.
Richardson); "Peggy Sue" (Allison, Holly, Petty)
Released: July 1978; 112 minutes

Buddy Holly was a gangly, scrawny, bespectacled early rock and roll singer who hailed from Lubbock, Texas, and whose life was tragically ended at the age of 22 in the same plane crash that also cost the life of another rock star, Ritchie Valens. (Valens was the hero of his own biographical film, *La Bamba,* released in 1987.) According to the movie, Holly was a clean-cut, dedicated artist who rose to fame with the success of "That'll Be the Day" and who became the first white performer ever booked at Harlem's Apollo Theatre where he scored a resounding success. In the title role, part-time musician Gary Busey gave a performance that captured both Holly's shyness and assurance, while also demonstrating what made the singer such a fireball on the stage. Holly was also played by Marshall Crenshaw in *La Bamba.*
Epic ST. RCA/Columbia VC.

HAIR

Music: Galt MacDermot
Lyrics: Gerome Ragni & James Rado
Screenplay: Michael Weller
Produced by: Lester Persky & Michael Butler (released by United Artists)
Directed by: Milos Forman
Choreography: Twyla Tharp
Photography: Miroslav Ondricek (Technicolor; Panavision)
Cast: John Savage, Treat Williams, Beverly D'Angelo, Annie Golden,
Dorsey Wright, Don Dacus, Cheryl Barnes, Melba Moore, Charlotte
Rae, Nicholas Ray, Twyla Tharp, Laurie Beechman, Nell Carter,
Ronnie Dyson, Charlaine Woodard
Songs: "Aquarius"; "Manchester"; "Ain't Got No"; "I Got Life"; "Hair";
"Where Do I Go?"; "Black Boys/White Boys"; "Easy to Be Hard";
"Good Morning, Starshine"; "The Flesh Failures"; "Let the Sunshine In"
Released: March 1979; 118 minutes

The long-running 1968 musical that shocked Broadway audiences was a bit dated by the time it reached the screen. The movie version, however, turned out to be a better structured work than the original, imaginatively recapturing the spirit of the Age of Aquarius in which hippies expressed their opposition to war, oppression, and conformity by advocating the truly good things of life—long hair, drugs, uncleanliness, rock music, boorish behavior, and promiscuous sex. In the story, an Oklahoma farmboy (John Savage) unaccountably travels all the way to New York for one last fling before being inducted into the army. In Central Park he comes across a tribe of social misfits who help him in his pursuit of a debutante (Beverly D'Angelo), and even manage to effect his escape—though with harrowing consequences—from his basic-training camp in Nevada. All but five songs from the original score were retained, as were two members of the Broadway cast, Melba Moore and Ronnie Dyson.
RCA ST. MGM/UA VC.

THE MUPPET MOVIE

Music & lyrics: Paul Williams & Kenny Ascher
Screenplay: Jerry Juhl & Jack Burns
Produced by: Jim Henson for ITC (Sir Lew Grade & Martin Starger)
Directed by: James Frawley
Photography: Isidore Mankofsky (Eastman Color)
Voices & cast: Jim Henson, Frank Oz, Jerry Nelson, Richard Hunt, Dave
         Goelz, Charles Durning, Austin Pendleton, Edgar Bergen, Milton
         Berle, Mel Brooks, James Coburn, Dom DeLuise, Elliott Gould,
         Bob Hope, Madeline Kahn, Carol Kane, Cloris Leachman, Steve
         Martin, Richard Pryor, Telly Savalas, Orson Welles, Paul Williams
Songs: "Rainbow Connection"; "Movin' Right Along"; "Can You Picture
         That?"; "Never Before, Never Again"; "I Hope That Something
         Better Comes Along"; "I'm Going to Go Back There Someday";
         "The Magic Store"
Released: May 1979; 94 minutes

Jim Henson and his entourage of television Muppeteers made such a successful adjustment to the large screen that *The Muppet Movie* placed sixth among the highest domestic
theatre rental musicals of the seventies. The familiar hand-operated characters—banjo-
playing Kermit the Frog, his inamorata Miss Piggy, Fozzie Bear, Rowlf, and the others—
were skillfully operated by remote control so that their hands and feet could move, while
real-live guest stars showed up in cameo roles throughout the story (something about
Kermit being pursued by a fiendish owner of a chain of fast food French fried frogs' legs
restaurants as he travels from a Georgia swamp to Hollywood). The movie was followed
by *The Great Muppet Caper* (1981) directed by Henson, and *The Muppets Take Manhattan*
(1984) directed by Franz Oz.
Atlantic ST. CBS/Fox VC.

The Muppet Movie. Miss Piggy and Kermit the Frog.

THE ROSE

Screenplay: Bill Kerby & Bo Goldman
Produced by: Marvin Worth & Aaron Russo for 20th Century-Fox
Directed by: Mark Rydell
Choreography: Toni Basil
Photography: Vilmos Zsigmond (DeLuxe Color; Panavision)
Cast: Bette Midler, Alan Bates, Frederic Forrest, Barry Primus, Sandra McCabe, David Keith, Harry Dean Stanton
Songs: "Whose Side Are You On?" (Kenny Hopkins-Charley Williams); "Midnight in Memphis" (Tony Johnson); "When a Man Loves a Woman" (Calvin Lewis-Andrew Wright); "Sold My Soul to Rock 'n' Roll" (Gene Pustilli); "Love Me With a Feeling" (Hudson Whittaker); "Stay With Me" (Jerry Ragavoy-George Weiss); "The Rose" (Amanda McBroom)
Released: November 1979; 134 minutes

Based largely on the life of self-destructive rock star Janis Joplin, who died in 1970 at the age of 27, *The Rose* gave Bette Midler the opportunity for a highly auspicious screen debut. Without bothering to explain how she got where she got, the movie begins after Rose's death, then flashes back to scenes of her wowing the corybantic crowds from concert to concert, all the while fighting with her manager (Alan Bates) about her need for time off from the pressures of her career. Unable to control her addiction to drugs and alcohol, the outrageous and pathetic singer suffers a breakdown during a concert in her home town and comes to the inevitable tragic end. Two other films based on the lives of rock stars (both of whom also died at young ages) were *The Buddy Holly Story* (1978), with Gary Busey as Holly, and *La Bamba* (1987), with Lou Diamond Phillips (using David Hidalgo's singing voice) as Ritchie Valens.
Atlantic ST. CBS/Fox VC.

ALL THAT JAZZ

Screenplay: Robert Alan Aurthur & Bob Fosse
Produced by: Robert Alan Aurthur for 20th Century-Fox & Columbia
Director-choreograper: Bob Fosse
Photography: Giuseppe Rotunno (Technicolor; Panavision)
Cast: Roy Scheider, Jessica Lange, Ann Reinking, Leland Palmer, Cliff Gorman, Ben Vereen, Erzsebet Foldi, Keith Gordon, John Lithgow
Songs: "On Broadway" (Barry Mann-Cynthia Weil-Jerry Leiber-Mike Stoller); "Everything Old Is New Again" (Peter Allen-Carole Sager); "After You've Gone" (Henry Creamer-Turner Layton); "There'll Be Some Changes Made" (W. B. Overstreet-Billy Higgins); "Some of These Days" (Shelton Brooks); "Bye Bye Love" (Boudleaux & Felice Bryant)
Released: December 1979; 123 minutes

With much the same atmosphere as the stage musical, *A Chorus Line* (and preceding its film version by six years), *All That Jazz* offers a seemingly authentic view of the creation of a high-powered musical show. Like Bob Fosse, the movie's director, choreographer, and co-author, the leading character, Joe Gideon (Roy Scheider), is an egocentric, hard-driving, death-obsessed, pill-popping, drug-taking, chain-smoking Broadway director-choreographer with a loyal ex-wife (Leland Palmer as Gwen Verdon), a patient mistress (Ann Reinking as Ann Reinking), and an adoring daughter (Erzsebet Foldi as Nicole Fosse). Also like Fosse, who had his first heart attack in 1974, Gideon is rushed to a hospital with a coronary. After the director literally bares his heart to the audience during open-heart surgery, Gideon's life and the film come to an end with a hallucinatory razzle-dazzle song-and-dance production number performed with Ben Vereen. Originally financed by Columbia Pictures, *All That Jazz* was rescued by 20th Century-Fox after the rival studio had threatened to halt production because of mounting costs. The infusion of additional capital proved justified: the picture turned out to be the seventh highest ranking domestic theatre rental musical of the seventies.
Casablanca ST. CBS/Fox VC.

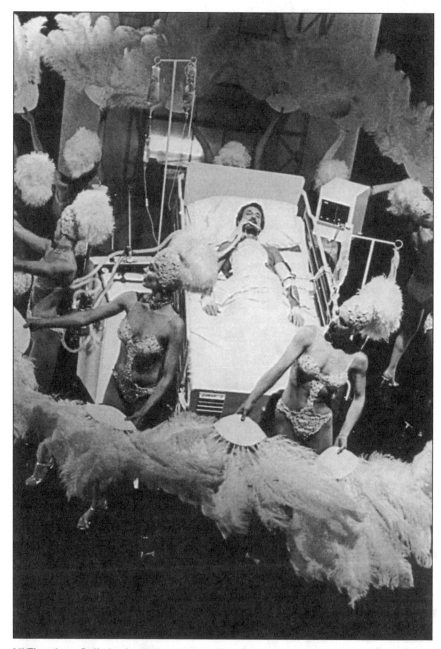

All That Jazz. Suffering from a heart attack, Roy Scheider creates an oneiric production number.

COAL MINER'S DAUGHTER

Music & lyrics: Loretta Lynn, etc.
Screenplay: Tom Rickman
Produced by: Bernard Schwartz for Universal
Directed by: Michael Apted
Photography: Ralf D. Bode (Technicolor; Panavision)
Cast: Sissy Spacek, Tommy Lee Jones, Beverly D'Angelo, Levon Helm
Songs: "Honky-Tonk Girl"; "Sweet Dreams of You" (Don Gibson); "You're Lookin' at Country"; "Coal Miner's Daughter"; "One's on the Way" (Shel Silverstein)
Released: February 1980; 125 minutes

Only five years after Ronee Blakley had portrayed a Loretta Lynn-type singer in *Nashville*, Sissy Spacek portrayed the singer herself in a full screen biography (it was the fifth highest ranking musical of the seventies in domestic theatre rental fees). The movie begins with the not quite 14-year-old Loretta Webb (played when the totally convincing Miss Spacek was 29) living with her impoverished family in the coal mining town of Butcher Holler, Kentucky, and her sudden marriage to a local war veteran, Mooney Lynn (Tommy Lee Jones). The Lynns move to the state of Washington where Mooney gets the idea of promoting his wife as a singer. After a rapid rise, Loretta is a headliner at Nashville's Grand Ole Opry, but she soon must face up to assorted marital, professional, and emotional problems, including the death of her friend, Patsy Cline (Beverly D'Angelo). Loretta even has a nervous breakdown on stage (recalling both *Nashville* and *The Rose*), before the film comes to its relatively happy ending.
MCA ST. MCA VC.

FAME

Music: Michael Gore, etc.
Lyrics: Dean Pitchford, etc.
Screenplay: Christopher Gore
Produced by: David DeSilva & Alan Marshall for MGM
Directed by: Alan Parker
Choreography: Louis Falco
Photography: Michael Seresin (Metrocolor; Panavision)
Cast: Irene Cara, Lee Curreri, Laura Dean, Antonia Franceschi, Albert Hague, Paul McCrane, Anne Meara, Barry Miller, Gene Anthony Ray, Maureen Teefy, Debbie Allen
Songs: "Red Light"; "Fame"; "Out Here on My Own" (lyric: Lesley Gore); "Is It Okay If I Call You Mine?" (Paul McCrane); "I Sing the Body Electric"
Released: April 1980; 133 minutes

Most of *Fame* was filmed in and around New York's High School of the Performing Arts when it was located at 120 West 46th Street (the school has since moved to another location and the building itself was destroyed by fire in 1988). The story covers a four-year time period, from auditions to graduation, and concentrates—in episodic fragments—on a cross-section of the students: the mousy, late-blooming would-be actress (Maureen Teefy), the loudmouthed but sensitive would-be comic (Barry Miller), the belligerent black would-be dancer (Gene Anthony Ray), the insecure homosexual would-be actor (Paul McCrane), the dedicated would-be composer (Lee Curreri), the pushy but gullible would-be singer (Irene Cara), and the uppity would-be ballerina (Antonia Franceschi). For the most part, the characters come across as self-indulgent, tiresomely foul-mouthed, and immature—and ever-ready to burst into an exuberant, unprovoked dance whether in the school's dining hall or on the traffic-snarled street outside. The movie sparked the successful CBS television series of the same name in which Albert Hague (a composer in his own right) repeated his role of the music teacher, and in which Debbie Allen (who had a bit role in the film) first won her own fame.
RSO ST. MGM/UA VC.

Pennies from Heaven. "Love Is Good for Anything That Ails You" performed by Bernadette Peters and a schoolchildren's band in a dream sequence.

PENNIES FROM HEAVEN

Screenplay: Dennis Potter
Produced by: Nora Kaye & Herbert Ross for MGM
Directed by: Herbert Ross
Choreography: Danny Daniels
Photography: Gordon Willis (Metrocolor; Panavision)
Cast: Steve Martin, Bernadette Peters, Jessica Harper, Vernel Bagneris, John McMartin, Christopher Walken, Jay Garner, Tommy Rall, Robert Fitch
Songs: "The Clouds Will Soon Roll By" (Harry Woods-Billy Hill); "Yes, Yes" (Con Conrad-Cliff Friend); "Did You Ever See a Dream Walking?" (Harry Revel-Mack Gordon); "Pennies from Heaven" (Arthur Johnston-Johnny Burke); "Love Is Good for Anything That Ails You" (Friend-Matty Malneck); "I Want to Be Bad" (Ray Henderson-B. G. DeSylva, Lew Brown); "Let's Misbehave" (Cole Porter); "Life Is Just a Bowl of Cherries" (Henderson-Brown); "Let's Face the Music and Dance" (Irving Berlin)
Released: December 1981; 107 minutes

Set in Chicago in 1934, this unsavory, neo-Brechtian tale of a frustrated but ever hopeful sheet-music salesman named Arthur (Steve Martin), his degraded wife (Jessica Harper), and his pathetic mistress (Bernadette Peters), is punctuated throughout by contrasting musical sequences using recordings of the period played on the soundtrack. These include Arthur's routine with a crusty bank manager (Jay Garner) to the tune of "Yes, Yes," with Busby Berkeley-type girls prancing all over the art-deco bank; a sinister bum (Vernel Bagneris) dancing to Arthur Tracy's version of the title song as the rain turns into a shower of pennies; and Arthur and his mistress, in a grubby movie house watching *Follow the Fleet*, suddenly replacing Astaire and Rogers on the screen during the "Let's Face the Music and Dance" sequence. The movie, which could never be mistaken for a remake of the 1936 release of the same name starring Bing Crosby, was adapted by Dennis Potter from his BBC television play.
Warner ST. MGM/UA VC.

Victor/Victoria. Robert Preston and Julie Andrews singing "You and Me" in a gay Parisian nightclub.

VICTOR / VICTORIA

Music: Henry Mancini
Lyrics: Leslie Bricusse
Screenplay: Blake Edwards
Produced by: Blake Edwards & Tony Adams for MGM
Directed by: Blake Edwards
Choreography: Paddy Stone
Photography: Dick Bush (Metrocolor; Panavision)
Cast: Julie Andrews, James Garner, Robert Preston, Lesley Ann Warren, Alex Karras
Songs: "You and Me"; "The Shady Dame from Seville"; "Le Jazz Hot"; "Crazy World"; "Chicago, Illinois", "Gay Paree"
Released: March 1982; 133 minutes

Described by some critics as sophisticated and hilarious and others as crude and moldy, *Victor/Victoria,* set in Paris in 1934, is about Vicki Adams (Julie Andrews), a singer so down on her luck that she tries to cadge a free meal in a restaurant by claiming there is a cockroach in her food (a bit a flimflammery previously practiced by Billy DeWolfe in Bing Crosby's 1942 movie *Dixie*). Urged by a homosexual nightclub entertainer (Robert Preston), Vicki passes herself off as a man (named Victor) in order to get work as a female impersonator in a cabaret. She succeeds so well in this deception that a Chicago gangster (James Garner) becomes totally confused as to whether he is falling in love with a woman or a man, and even the gangster's peroxided mistress (Lesley Ann Warren) makes a play for Victor. The farcical tale had a number of cinematic antecedents: Reinhold Schunzel's 1933 German film *Viktor und Viktoria* (also Schünzel's French-language version *Georges et Georgette,* plus the 1959 German remake under the original title), and Victor Saville's 1935 English film *First a Girl,* starring Jessie Matthews.
Polygram ST. MGM/UA VC.

ANNIE

Music: Charles Strouse
Lyrics: Martin Charnin
Screenplay: Carol Sobieski
Produced by: Ray Stark for Columbia
Directed by: John Huston
Choreography: Arlene Phillips
Photography: Richard Moore (Metrocolor; Panavision)
Cast: Albert Finney, Carol Burnett, Bernadette Peters, Ann Reinking, Tim
   Curry, Geoffrey Holder, Edward Herrmann, Aileen Quinn, Roger
   Minami, Peter Marshall, Loni Ackerman
Songs: "Tomorrow"; "It's the Hard-Knock Life"; "Maybe"; "I Think I'm
   Gonna Like It Here"; "Little Girls"; "We Got Annie"; "Let's Go
   to the Movies"; "You're Never Fully Dressed Without a Smile";
   "Easy Street"; "I Don't Need Anything but You"
Released: April 1982; 128 minutes

Thomas Meehan's libretto for the 1977 Broadway musical, *Annie,* put the two main characters of Harold Gray's comic strip, "Little Orphan Annie," into an original story, set in New York in December 1933, about a female Oliver Twist (Andrea McArdle) who escapes from an orphanage by being adopted by billionaire Oliver "Daddy" Warbucks (Reid Shelton). Its screen transformation, however, took a number of liberties. Annie's initial invitation to visit Warbucks no longer takes place at Christmas; a scene in Hooverville was cut and a scene at Radio City Music Hall was added; Warbucks decision to adopt Annie is now only to please his secretary (with whom he is in love); two characters, Punjab and Asp, who were in the comic strip, were written into the screenplay; a new climax has Annie escape death on a drawbridge by being rescued by Punjab in an autogiro; and the greedy, besoned orphanage director, Miss Hannigan, gets a last-minute change of heart.

Columbia paid a record $9.5 million for the screen rights and spent some $52 million on the production, the second highest domestic theatre rental musical of the 1980s. Just before shooting began, director Randall Kleiser was replaced by John Huston, who had never before worked on a musical. Six of the 14 songs in the original score were dropped and five new ones were added. Previous non-musical versions of the comic strip, both titled *Little Orphan Annie,* were made in 1932 (with Mitzi Green) and in 1938 (with Ann Gillis). *Columbia ST. RCA/Columbia VC.*

Annie. At the White House, Annie (Aileen Quinn) teaches "Tomorrow" to Eleanor Roosevelt (Lois DeBanzie), Daddy Warbucks (Albert Finney) and President Roosevelt (Edward Herrmann).

FLASHDANCE

Screenplay: Tom Hedley & Joe Eszterhas
Produced by: Don Simpson & Jerry Bruckheimer for Paramount
Directed by: Adrian Lyne
Choreography: Jeffrey Hornaday
Photography: Don Peterman (Movielab Color; Panavision)
Cast: Jennifer Beals, Michael Nouri, Sunny Johnson, Kyle T. Heffner, Lilla Skala, Belinda Bauer, Cynthia Rhodes, Marine Jahan
Songs: "Flashdance. . .What a Feeling" (Giorgio Moroder-Keith Forsey, Irene Cara); "I Love Rock 'n' Roll" (Jake Hooker, Alan Merrill); "Manhunt" (Doug Cotler, Richard Gilbert); "Gloria" (Giancarlo Bigazzi, Trevor Veitch, Umberto Tozzi); "Lady, Lady, Lady" (Moroder-Forsey); "Seduce Me Tonight" (Moroder-Forsey)
Released: April 1983; 95 minutes

Set in Pittsburgh, this modern-day Cinderella fable offers a heroine (Jennifer Beals) who is a welder by day and a go-go dancer by night (though she never strips completely), and whose dearest wish is to become a dancer with the Pittsburgh Ballet. Her boss at the construction company (Michael Nouri) plays both Prince Charming and Fairy Godfather by smoothing the way for her audition, which so totally captivates the myopic judges they cannot see that her carefully edited dance is performed by a double, Marine Jahan. The script (which seems to have been created as a distaff variation on *Saturday Night Fever)* makes sure that the lady is well acquainted with all the four-letter words, but we know she is really a good girl because she regularly goes to confession. *Flashdance* was the third highest ranking musical of the 1980s in domestic theatre rental fees.
Casablanca ST. Paramount VC.

YENTL

Music: Michel Legrand
Lyrics: Alan Bergman & Marilyn Bergman
Screenplay: Jack Rosenthal & Barbra Streisand
Producer-director: Barbra Streisand for MGM/UA
Photography: David Watkin (Metrocolor, Panavision)
Cast: Barbra Streisand, Mandy Patinkin, Amy Irving, Nehemiah Persoff, Steven Hill
Songs: "A Piece of Sky"; "Papa, Can You Hear Me?"; "No Wonder"; "The Way He Makes Me Feel"; "Will Someone Ever Look at Me That Way?"; "This Is One of Those Moments"; "Where Is It Written?"
Released: October 1983; 134 minutes

With *Yentl* Barbra Streisand became the first woman to produce, co-author, direct, and star in her own film. Set in Eastern Europe in 1904, the movie has much the same atmosphere as *Fiddler on the Roof* (set a year later in Czarist Russia) as it tells of a Jewish teenage girl (Streisand) who disguises herself as a man in order to be allowed to study the Talmud at the yeshiva. Through a farfetched series of events, she marries the fiancee (Amy Irving) of the young male scholar (Mandy Patinkin) she also fancies. After the truth is revealed (literally), Yentl packs her bags and—in an ending all too reminiscent of the "Don't Rain on My Parade" staging in *Funny Girl*—stands bravely on the deck of a crowded ship transporting immigrants to America. The movie was derived from Isaac Bashevis Singer's short story, "Yentl, the Yeshiva Boy" (set in Poland in 1873), which, in 1974, Singer adapted into a play in collaboration with Leah Napolin. Virtually all the film's songs are sung by Miss Streisand as soundtrack soliloquies.
CBS ST. MGM/UA VC.

Yentl. Newlyweds Amy Irving and Barbra Streisand in an awkward situation.

FOOTLOOSE

Lyrics & screenplay: Dean Pitchford
Producers: Lewis Rachmil & Craig Zadan for IndieProd (released by Paramount)
Directed by: Herbert Ross
Choreography: Lynne Taylor-Corbett
Photography: Ric Waite (Movielab Color; Panavision)
Cast: Kevin Bacon, Lori Singer, Dianne Wiest, John Lithgow, Christopher
Penn, Sarah Jessica Parker, Elizabeth Gorcey
Songs: "Footloose" (Kenny Loggins); "Let's Hear It for the Boy" (Tom Snow);
"Almost Paradise" (Eric Carmen); "Holding Out for a Hero" (Jim
Steinman); "Dancing in the Sheets" (Bill Wolfer); "I'm Free" (Loggins);
"Somebody's Eyes" (Tom Sow); "The Girl Gets Around" (Sammy Hagar);
"Never" (Michael Gore)
Released: February 1984; 107 minutes

Featuring what one critic has called "high gloss junk-food songs," *Footloose,* like
Paramount's *Flashdance* before it, won success because its music was so geared to the
pop market that the sale of soundtrack albums and music video had a profound influence
on the sale of tickets at the box office. (It was the fourth highest ranking musical of the 1980s
in Variety's list of "All-Time Film Rental Champs.") Filmed in Payson, Utah, the picture is
set in a small midwestern town where youngsters must do battle against the religious
authorities over their right to dance which, to no one's surprise, they win. Two unusual
aspects of the film's score is that all the songs had lyrics by the movie's author, Dean
Pitchford, and all but the title song were written after *Footloose* had been shot and edited.
Columbia ST. Paramount VC.

The Cotton Club. Diane Lane and Richard Gere.

THE COTTON CLUB

Screenplay: William Kennedy, Francis Coppola, Mario Puzo
Produced by: Robert Evans for Orion
Directed by: Francis Coppola
Choreography: Michael Smuin, Henry LeTang, Gregory Hines
Photography: Stephen Goldblatt (Technicolor; Panavision)
Cast: Richard Gere, Gregory Hines, Diane Lane, Lonette McKee, Bob
Hoskins, James Remar, Nicolas Cage, Allen Garfield, Fred Gwynne,
Gwen Verdon, Maurice Hines, Julian Beck, Novella Nelson, Tom
Waits, Thelma Carpenter, Charles "Honi" Coles, Larry Marshall,
Diane Venora
Songs: "Creole Love Call" (Duke Ellington); "Am I Blue?" (Harry Akst-
Grant Clarke); "Crazy Rhythm" (Joseph Meyer, Roger Wolfe Kahn-
Irving Caesar); "Doin' the New Low-Down" (Jimmy McHugh-
Dorothy Fields); "Minnie the Moocher" (Cab Calloway-Clarence
Gaskill); "Copper-Colored Gal" (J. Fred Coots-Benny Davis)
Released: November 1984; 127 minutes

Because of many production problems—resulting in a cost of $47 million—*The Cotton Club* was a financial disaster, even though it was one of the most highly touted productions of the 1980s. The musical melodrama centers around Harlem's Cotton Club between 1928 and 1931 at a time when it offered floor shows featuring top black entertainers while maintaining a "whites only" policy for the audience. Director Francis Coppola captures the atmosphere of the club, both backstage and onstage (though none of the numbers is filmed in its entirety) through a frequently violent story involving real rival gangsters Owney Madden (Bob Hoskins) and Dutch Schultz (James Remar), a fictitious white cornet player (Richard Gere) who becomes a movie star, and a black dancer (Gregory Hines) who becomes a Broadway headliner.
Geffen ST. Nelson VC.

A CHORUS LINE

Music: Marvin Hamlisch
Lyrics: Edward Kleban
Screenplay: Arnold Schulman
Produced by: Cy Feuer & Ernest H. Martin for Embassy & PolyGram
Directed by: Richard Attenborough
Choreography: Jeffrey Hornaday
Photography: Ronnie Taylor (Technicolor; Panavision)
Cast: Gregg Burge, Michael Douglas, Vicki Frederick, Michelle Johnston, Pam Klinger, Terrence Mann, Alyson Reed, Justin Reed, Matt West
Songs: "I Hope I Get It"; "I Can Do That"; "At the Ballet"; "Surprise, Surprise"; "Nothing"; "Let Me Dance for You"; "Dance: Ten, Looks: Three"; "One"; "What I Did for Love"
Released: December 1985; 118 minutes

The longest running show in Broadway history, *A Chorus Line,* which opened in 1975 and closed 15 years later, presented two main problems for its screen adaptation—it tells a nonlinear story (by James Kirkwood and Nicholas Dante) in which 17 finalists auditioning for a chorus line of eight reveal their backgrounds and personalities through a series of songs and monologues, and its action is confined to the bare stage of a darkened theatre. Filming the property, which Universal bought for $5.5 million and subsequently sold to PolyGram for $7.8, proved too much of a hurdle for such directors and/or writers as Michael Bennett (who conceived and directed the stage production), Mike Nichols, Bo Goldman, Sidney Lumet, and James Bridges, and it was finally put together by director Richard Attenborough and writer Arnold Schulman. The movie still limits most of the action to the theatre (it was filmed at the Mark Hellinger in New York), visually opening up only for brief outdoor scenes and flashbacks involving the show's explosive director (Michael Douglas) and his former flame (Alyson Reed), who unexpectedly shows up as an auditioning dancer.

The score was kept mostly intact except for the elimination of three songs, two of which were replaced by "Surprise, Surprise" and "Let Me Dance for You." Four of the principals—Vicki Frederick, Pam Klinger, Justin Ross, and Matt West— had previously appeared in *A Chorus Line* on Broadway.
Casablanca ST. Nelson VC.

A Chorus Line.

LITTLE SHOP OF HORRORS

Music: Alan Menken
Lyrics & screenplay: Howard Ashman
Produced by: David Geffen for The Geffen Co.
Directed by: Frank Oz
Choreography: Pat Garrett
Photography: Robert Paynter (Technicolor; Panavision)
Cast: Rick Moranis, Ellen Greene, Vincent Gardenia, Steve Martin,
Tichina Arnold, Tisha Campbell, Michelle Weeks, James Belushi,
John Candy, Christopher Guest, Bill Murray
Songs: "Little Shop of Horrors"; "Skid Row (Downtown)"; "Grow for Me";
"Somewhere That's Green"; "Dentist"; "Feed Me"; "Suddenly
Seymour"; "Suppertime"; "Mean Green Mother from Outer Space"
Released: December 1986; 94 minutes

Based on the 1982 Off Broadway hit (which had been based on Roger Corman's 1960 quickie film), *Little Shop of Horrors* was adapted to the screen by its stage librettist, Howard Ashman. Wimpish Seymour (Rick Moranis), a clerk in a skid row flower shop, takes special care of a ravenous Venus's-flytrap he has named after his inamorata Audrey (Ellen Greene, who had been in the original production), only to have the monster mutant get out of hand by demanding more and more human meat. One memorable comic bit was the encounter between Steve Martin as a sadistic dentist and Bill Murray as his masochistic patient. Well suited to this spoof on sci-fi genetic-mutation pictures was the score by Ashman and Alan Menken, who added a new song, "Mean Green Mother from Outer Space," for the movie. *Geffen ST. Warner VC.*

LA BAMBA

Screenplay: Luis Valdez
Produced by: Taylor Hackford & Bill Borden for Columbia
Directed by: Luis Valdez
Photography: Adam Greenberg (Technicolor; Panavision)
Cast: Lou Diamond Phillips, Esai Morales, Rosana DeSoto, Elizabeth
Peña, Danielle Von Zerneck, Rick Dees, Joe Pantoliano, Los Lobos,
Marshall Crenshaw
Songs: "Saturday Night"; "Who Do You Love?"; "Rock All Night"; "You're
Mine"; "All My Love, All My Kisses"; "Baby, Baby"; "Donna" (Ritchie
Valens); "La Bamba" (William Clauson); "Little Darlin'"; "Come on,
Let's Go"; "Summertime Blues"
Released: July 1987; 103 minutes

Capitalizing on the burgeoning Hispanic film market, *La Bamba,* based on the life of rocker Ritchie Valens, was released in both English and Spanish versions. Something of a companion piece to *The Buddy Holly Story,* the movie traces the rapid rise of the Chicano teenage singer (né Ricardo Valenzuela) whose meteoric eight-month career was tragically ended at the age of 17 when he was killed in the same plane crash that also cost the life of Holly. In the movie, Valens (portrayed by Lou Diamond Phillips with the voice of David Hidalgo of the Los Lobos group) is discovered by a savvy manager while still in high school in southern California, and before long he has three hits on the best-selling charts, including the movie's title song. (Ironically, Valens, who could not speak Spanish, sang a gibberish rock version of the Mexican folk tune.) The film's main area of conflict is the singer's sometimes aggressive relationship with his under-achieving half-brother. *Warner/Slash ST. RCA/Columbia VC.*

Dirty Dancing. Patrick Swayze and Jennifer Grey.

DIRTY DANCING

Screenplay: Eleanor Bergstein
Produced by: Linda Gottlieb for Vestron
Director: Emile Ardolino
Choreographer: Kenneth Ortega
Photography: Jeff Jur (Technicolor; Panavision)
Cast: Patrick Swayze, Jennifer Grey, Jerry Orbach, Cynthia Rhodes, Kelly
        Bishop, Jack Weston, Charles "Honi" Coles, Lonny Price
Songs: "(I've Had) The Time of My Life" (Franke Previte-John DeNicola -
        Donald Markowitz); "Be My Baby"; "She's Like the Wind" (Patrick
        Swayze); "Hungry Eyes"; "Stay"; "Yes" (Merry Clayton); "You Don't
        Own Me"; "Hey, Baby"; "Overload"; "Love Is Strange"
Released: August 1987; 97 minutes

Like *Flashdance* and *Footloose*, *Dirty Dancing* offered a simpleminded story closely linked to frenetic dancing accompanied by an unremitting musical soundtrack (whose popularity as a record album also helped at the box office). The first feature film of Vestron Pictures, the home video company, it also catered to moviegoers' nostalgia for the early sixties (though many numbers have a more contemporary sound). The mix worked well enough to make the release the seventh highest ranking musical of the eighties in domestic theatre rentals. The locale is a Catskills resort where a shy teenager known as Baby (Jennifer Grey) has gone with her family. There she comes of age first by experiencing the elicit pleasures of uninhibited dancing (no one calls it dirty in the film), then by bedding with the resort's star dancer (Patrick Swayze), and finally by winning family approval after performing in an interminable wish-fulfilling production number.
RCA ST.   Vestron VC.

BIRD

Music: Charlie Parker, etc.
Screenplay: Charlie Parker, etc.
Producer-director: Clint Eastwood for Warner Bros.
Photography: Jack N. Green (Technicolor; Panavision)
Cast: Forest Whitaker, Diane Venora, Michael Zelniker, Samuel E. Wright,
        Keith David, Michael McGuire, Damon Whitaker
Music: "Lester Leaps In" (Lester Young); "I Can't Believe That You're in Love
        With Me" (Jimmy McHugh); "Laura" (David Raskin); "All of Me"
        (Gerald Marks); "This Time the Dream's on Me" (Harold Arlen); "Ko
        Ko"; "Cool Blues"; "April in Paris" (Vernon Duke); "Now's the Time";
        "Ornithology"; "Parker's Mood"
Released: September 1988; 161 minutes

When alto saxophonist Charie Parker (known as "Bird" or "Yardbird") died in 1955 at the age of 34, he was instantly anointed one of jazz's authentic legends. He was also, in common with many jazz greats, a self-destructive junkie and alcoholic, and the somber, uncompromising film that Clint Eastwood has made of his last years—with Forest Whitaker in the title role that had once been intended for Richard Pryor—reveals the man's personal weaknesses as well as his seminal influence as a towering figure in the avant-garde bebop movement. For the soundtrack, the movie reproduces Parker's own solos from recordings and air checks, which are skillfully blended with newly recorded performances by some of today's outstanding jazzmen (though it's Charles McPherson who doubles for Parker in the ensemble passages).
Columbia ST. Warner VC.

Bird. Samuel E. Wright as Dizzy Gillespie and Forest Whitaker
as Charlie Parker.

THE LITTLE MERMAID

Music: Alan Menken
Lyrics: Howard Ashman
Screenplay: John Musker & Ron Clements
Producers: Howard Ashman & John Musker for Walt Disney
Directors: John Musker & Ron Clements (Technicolor)
Voices: Jodi Benson, Pat Carroll, Samuel E. Wright, Kenneth Mars, Buddy
Hackett, Rene Auberjonais, Ben Wright
Songs: "Daughters of Triton"; "Part of Your World"; "Poor Unfortunate
Souls"; "Under the Sea"; "Kiss the Girl"; "Les Poissons"
Released: November 1989; 82 minutes

The 28th feature-length animated film released by the Disney studio was its first cartoon based on a fairy tale since *Sleeping Beauty* in 1959. Inspired by the Hans Christian Andersen fable, the Disneyfied version tells of a spunky bra-wearing mermaid princess named Ariel who lives with her father, the sea lord Triton, in his underwater kingdom. Restless Ariel so wants to be a human that she makes a pact with Ursula, the nasty but campy sea witch, in return for a pair of legs. Unlike the Andersen original, however, in which the mermaid dissolves into sea foam because her love for a young man is unrequited, the film ends happily with Ariel getting a kiss from the charming fish-eating prince she had rescued from drowning. The movie was the fifth highest ranking musical of the 1980s in domestic theatre rental fees. A previous screen version was made in the Soviet Union in 1976, and a 17-minute ballet version was a feature of the 1952 movie, *Hans Christian Andersen*.
Disney ST. Disney VC.

The Little Mermaid. Sea princess Ariel making the pact with the scheming sea witch Ursula.

The Doors. Meg Ryan and Val Kilmer.

THE DOORS

Music and Lyrics: The Doors and others
Screenplay: J. Randal Johnson, Oliver Stone
Produced by: Bill Graham, Sasha Harari, A. Kitman Ho
Directed by: Oliver Stone for Tri-Star Pictures
Photography: Robert Richardson (Panavision)
Cast: Val Kilmer, Meg Ryan, Kathleen Quinlan, Frank Whaley, Kevin Dillon, Kyle MacLachlan, Billy Idol, Dennis Burkley, Josh Evans, Michael Madsen, Michael Wincott
Songs: "Light My Fire"; "The End"; "When the Music Is Over"; "Not to Touch"; "Touch Me"; "(The) Soft Parade"; "Five to One" (The Doors); "Back Door Man" (Willie Dixon); and many others
Released: March 1991; 134 minutes.

Part faux documentary and part head-film in approach, *The Doors* might have been titled *Jim Morrison*. From sepia-toned childhood memories, to an untimely but unsurprising death at age 27, the film is clearly about the troubled rock star, not the band. Val Kilmer creates a believably brooding, volatile Morrison, opposite a perky Meg Ryan. The Doors' recordings provide a sonic backdrop to the film, along with a large number of other 1960s hits. Kilmer adds vocals to recordings used in concert scenes. His odd resemblance to Morrison and a deft mix of original recordings and added vocals give the film an uncanny realism. The story of Morrison's self-destructive descent into a morass of sex, drugs and alcohol has become so common in the history of rock and roll that the story risks being a cliché. Off-stage scenes, complete with saturated colors and dizzying combinations of sound and image, give a lengthy, tour of Morrison's addled perception of the world. Director Oliver Stone, who once approached Morrison with the idea of a film biography, makes a cameo appearance as a film-school professor.
Elektra ST. Avid Home Entertainment VC.

THE COMMITMENTS
Music and Lyrics: Various
Screenplay: Dick Clement, Ian La Frenais, Marc Abraham, based on the novel by Roddy Doyle
Produced by: Brian Morris
Directed by: Alan Parker for Twentieth Century-Fox
Photography: Gale Tattersall (Technicolor)
Cast: Robert Arkins, Michael Aherne, Angeline Ball, Maria Doyle, Dave Finnegan, Bronagh Gallagher, Félim Gormley, Glen Hansard, Dick Massey, Johnny Murphy, Kenneth McCluskey, Andrew Strong, Colm Meaney
Songs: "Mustang Sally"; "Too Many Fish in the Sea"; "Mr. Pitiful"; "Show Me"; "Bye Bye Baby"; "Take Me to the River"; "The Dark End of the Street"; "Hard to Handle"; "Chain of Fools"; "I Never Loved a Man (The Way I Love You)"; "Try a Little Tenderness"; "In the Midnight Hour", and many others
Released: August 1991; 118 minutes

Director Alan Parker (*Fame*, *Bugsy Malone* and *Evita*) takes an unflinching look at working-class life in Dublin with The Commitments. Jimmy Rabbitte, a young huckster and born promoter, delights in interviewing himself as though on screen. Explaining that "The Irish are the blacks of Europe, and Dubliners are the blacks of Ireland, and the Northsiders are the blacks of Dublin. So, say it once, say it loud, 'I'm black and I'm proud.'" Thus, he makes his case for forming an Irish soul band. Shot in dilapidated Dublin neighborhoods, the film's gritty, yet humorous depiction of working-class life is as much a part of the story as the fate of band and the lives of its members. Following a brilliant audition montage, which helped earn the film an Academy Award Nomination for editing, a rag-tag group of misfits form the band. As relationships begin to sour, the group degenerates into shouting, brawling mayhem before disbanding. More than 40 songs are heard in the film, some sung by a remarkable cast of predominantly novice actors.
Uni/MCA ST. Fox VC

For the Boys. Bette Midler as Dixie Leonard.

FOR THE BOYS

Music and Lyrics: Various
Screenplay: Marshall Brickman, Neil Jemenez, Lindy Laub
Produced by: Assheton GortonFor Twentieth Century-Fox
Directed by: Mark Rydell for Twentieth Century-Fox
Photography: Stephen Goldblatt (Panavision; color by DeLuxe).
Cast: Bette Midler, James Caan, George Segal, Patrick O'Neal, Christopher Rydell, Arye Gross, Norman Fell, Rosemary Murphy, Bud Yorke.
Songs: "Billy-A-Dick" (Haogy Carmichael, Paul Francis Webster); "Stuff Like That There: (Jay Livingston, Ray Evans); "P.S. I Love You" (Johnny Mercer, Gordon Jenkins); "The Girlfriend of the Whirling Dervish" (Al Dubin, Johnny Mercer, Harry Warren); "I Remember" (Johnny Mercer, Victor Schertizinger); "Baby It's Cold Outside" (Frank Loesser); "Dreamland" (Dave Grusin, Alan & Marilyn Bergman); "For All We Know" (J. Fred Coots and Sam M. Lewis); "Come Rain or Come Shine" (Johnny Mercer, Harold Arlen); "In My Life" (John Lennon, Paul McCartney); "I Remember You" (Johnny Mercer, Victor Schertzinger); "Every Road Leads Back to You" (Diane Warren); and many others
Released: November 1991; 145 minutes

For the Boys, a melodramatic tale spanning some 50 years, was largely a vehicle for Bette Midler, who received an Academy Award nomination for her performance. The film follows the life of singer Dixie Leonard (Midler) and her tempestuous relationship with fellow entertainer Eddie Sparks (James Caan). Told in a series of flashbacks, the film is peppered with subplots that appear and disappear. Dixie and Eddie are bitter and angry after their relationship until their reunion in the last moments of the film. Although poorly received by critics, *For the Boys* did well enough at the box office. Its strongest scenes are those in which Midler belts classic pop tunes from the stage, especially the jumping USO number "Stuff Like That There."
Wea/Atlantic ST. Fox Video VC.

BEAUTY AND THE BEAST

Music and Lyrics: Alan Menken, Howard Ashman
Screenplay: Linda Woolverton
Produced by: Don Hahn for Buena Vista/ Walt Disney
Directed by: Gary Trousdale, Kirk Wise
Voices: Paige O'Hara, Robby Benson, Richard White, Jerry Orbach, David Ogden Stiers, Angela Lansbury, Bradley Michael Pierce, Jesse Corti, Rex Everhart, Jo Anne Worley
Songs: "Belle"; "Gaston"; "Be Our Guest"; "Something There"; "The Mob Song"; "Beauty and the Beast"
Released: November 1991; 84 minutes

Credited with setting a new standard in feature-length, animated films, Disney's *Beauty and the Beast* is a spectacle in the tradition of lavish Hollywood musicals, and was nominated for an Academy Award for best picture. This is old-style Disney exemplified and heightened, complete with a touching tale of youthful self-discovery, true love and the requisite happy ending. But the story is so masterfully told, the score so strong, and the animation so artful that it becomes believable, about two very real, star-crossed young people. The familiar tale is expanded to give Belle a bookish, inquisitive nature. She fends off the advances of the arrogant, handsome Gaston, who has decided he will marry her. Belle's father, a gentle and absent-minded inventor, gets himself lost in the woods, turns up at the Beast's dismal castle, and is soon imprisoned there. Belle sets off to rescue him, eventually trading her own freedom for her father's.

Viewers know from the outset of the film that the Beast is actually a handsome young prince under a spell. The spell, a punishment for cruelty, states that he must find someone to love him before the last petal falls from a magical rose, or he will remain a beast for the rest of his life. Just when it looks as though all hope is lost, Belle's love saves the hideous Beast and he is once again turned into a handsome young prince – one who has given up his cruel ways.

While the story hinges on a few central characters, it is the retinue of ancillary characters that adds richness. When the prince was transformed into a beast, his entire household staff was also caught in the spell and turned into such things as a clock, a teapot, a candlestick, a broom, etc. They all speak, sing, and dance, of course. "Be Our Guest," an ensemble number featuring the Beast's household companions, is a production number rivaling Hollywood's grandest musicals.

The song "Beauty and the Beast" won an Academy Award, while the songs "Belle" and "Be Our Guest" received nominations. *Beauty and the Beast* was followed by *Beauty and the Beast: The Enchanted Christmas* and *Belle's Magical World*, both released in 1997 on video. *Beauty and the Beast* was the first animated musical to be adapted for Broadway, opening at the Palace Theater in 1994.

Walt Disney ST. Walt Disney Home Video VC.

Beauty and the Beast. Lumiere and friends perform "Be Our Guest."

Belle looks beyond the Beast's outward appearance and finds true love.

NEWSIES

Music: Alan Menken
Lyrics: Jack Feldman
Screenplay: Bob Tzudiker, Noni White
Produced by: Michael Finnell
Directed by: Kenny Ortega for Warner/Walt Disney
Photography: Andrew Laszlo (Technicolor)
Cast: Christian Bale, David Moscow, Bill Pullman, Gabriel Damon, Luke Edwards, Maz Casella, Ann-Margaret, Robert Duvall
Songs: "Carrying the Banner"; "Escape from Snyder"; "Fightin' Irish"; "Strike Action"; "High Times, Hard Times"; "King of New York"; "My Lovey-Dovey Baby"; "Once and for All"; "Rooftop"; "Santa Fe"; "Seize the Day"; "The World Will Know"
Released: April 1992, 121 minutes

A Hollywood back-lot set and an enormous cast of singing, dancing children give *Newsies* the feel of a bygone era of Hollywood musicals. Set in 1890s New York, the film tells the true story of a group of newsboys standing up against the greed of newspaper publisher Joseph Pulizter (Robert Duvall). When Pulitzer raises the paper prices he is charging the newsies, they band together and begin a strike. Eventually the entire child labor force of New York is involved. A strong group of young actors keep the film light, despite its Dickensian setting in New York's lower east side. Though an honest attempt at an old-fashioned musical, *Newsies* didn't create much stir at the box office.
Walt Disney ST. Walt Disney VC.

Sister Act. Whoopi Goldberg.

SISTER ACT

Music and Lyrics: Marc Shaiman
Screenplay: Joseph Howard
Produced by: Jackson DeGovia.
Directed by: Emile Ardolino for Buena Vista
Photography: Adam Greenberg (Technicolor)
Cast: Whoopi Goldberg, Maggie Smith, Kathy Najimy, Wendy Makkena, Mary Wickes, Harvey Keitel, Bill Nunn, Robert Miranda, Richard Portnow.
Songs: "Shout" (Ronald Isley, Rudolph Isley, O'Kelly Isley); "My Guy" (William Robinson Jr.); "Heat Wave" (Brian Holland, Lamont Dozier, Edward Holland); "Bar Nun" (Jimmy Vivino); "Homalone" (Tom Malone); "I Will Follow Him" (Norman Gimbel, Arthur Altman, J.W. Stole, Del Roma)
Released: November, 1992, 100 minutes

Sister Act was an enormous success (despite a spate of bad reviews), scoring number four in 1992 box office receipts. Whoopi Goldberg plays a Reno lounge singer who sees her mob boyfriend and his henchmen murder a man. Fearing for her life, she goes to the police, who agree to protect her in exchange for her testimony. They hide her in a convent, where no one but the Monsignor and Mother Superior know her story. A fish out of water in the cloistered environment, her misfit ways create constant visual and verbal humor. She ends up directing the convent choir, transforming it from a bland, mousy outfit into an energized, up-beat band of hip, rockin' sisters. When the mob finds her and takes her to Reno, the nuns descend upon the city to rescue her. Sister Act was followed by Sister Act 2: Back in the Habit (1993).
Hollywood Records ST. Touchstone Home Video VC.

The Bodyguard. Kevin Costner and Whitney Houston

THE BODYGUARD

Music and Lyrics: Various
Screenplay: Lawrence Kasdan
Produced by: Lawrence Kasdan, Jim Wilson, Kevin Costner
Directed by: Mick Jackson for Warner/Tig/Kasdan Pictures
Photography: Andrew Dunn (Technicolor)
Cast: Kevin Costner, Whitney Houston, Gary Kemp, Bill Cobbs, Ralph Waite,
Tomas Arana, Michele Lamar Richards, Mike Starr
Songs: "I Will Always Love You" (Dolly Parton); "I Have Nothing" (David Foster, Jud
Friedman, Allan Dennis Rich, Linda Thompson); "I'm Every Woman" (Nickolas
Ashford, Valerie Simpson); "Run to You" (Allan Rich, Jud Friedman); "Queen of
the Night" (Whitney Houston, La Reid, Babyface, Daryl Simmons); "Someday
(I'm Coming Back)" (Lisa Stansfield, Andy Morris, Ian Devaney); and others
Released: November 1992; 129 minutes

Dolly Parton's poignant song "I Will Always Love You," was a country hit for the singer/
songwriter in 1974, and was re-released as a single in 1982. Parton also sang it as a theme
song on her TV variety show of the 1980s. But it hadn't become a song that everyone just
seems to know by osmosis. Then came *The Bodyguard* and Whitney Houston's recording
of the song, and "I Will Always Love You" became one of the most succesful singles in pop
music history, staying at #1 for 14 weeks. The script for the film was originally written in the
1970s for Steve McQueen. Kevin Costner plays a former Secret Service agent, now working as a private security guard hired to protect a famous singer (Houston) who has been
receiving death threats. Romance, suspense and action are loosely stitched together to
create a movie intended to appeal to the widest possible audience. It worked. Opening
scenes feature an uncredited appearance by Sean Connery.
BMG Arista ST. Warner Home Video VC.

The Bodyguard. Kevin Costner

ALADDIN

Music: Alan Menken
Lyrics: Howard Ashman; Tim Rice
Screenplay: John Musker, Ron Clements, Ted Elliott, Terry Rossio
Produced by: R.S. Vander Wende For Walt Disney
Directed by: John Musker, Ron Clements, Ted Elliott, Terry Rossio
Voices: Scott Weinger, Brad Kane, Robin Williams, Linda Larkin, Lea Salonga, Jonathon Freeman, Frank Welker, Gilbert Gottfried, Douglas Seale
Songs: "Arabian Nights" (lyric by Howard Ashman); "Friend Like Me" (lyric by Howard Ashman); "Prince Ali"; (lyric by Howard Ashman, reprise lyric by Tim Rice); "One Jump Ahead" (lyric by Tim Rice); "A Whole New World" (lyric by Tim Rice)
Released: November 1992, 90 minutes

After creating magic with the music and lyrics for *The Little Mermaid* and *Beauty and the Beast*, Alan Menken and Howard Ashman teamed up once again to work on *Aladdin*. The pair completed only three songs for the film before Ashman's untimely death. Lyricist Tim Rice stepped in to complete the project, winning an Academy Award with Menken for the song "A Whole New World." Menken also took home the Oscar for best score. The real showstopper in this film is Robin Williams' over-the-top, improvisatory characterization of the Genie. Willams' rapid-fire, turn-on-dime style of monologue was perfect for animated characterization. Like *The Little Mermaid* and *Beauty and the Beast*, *Aladdin* is a standard fairytale with young characters maturing, to find both themselves and love. The film, which placed twenty-first on the 1998 Variety listing of "Top 50 Grossing Domestic Films, was followed by *Aladdin: King of Thieves*, released on video in 1996.
Disney ST. Walt Disney Home Video VC.

Aladdin poses as Prince Ali Ababwa.

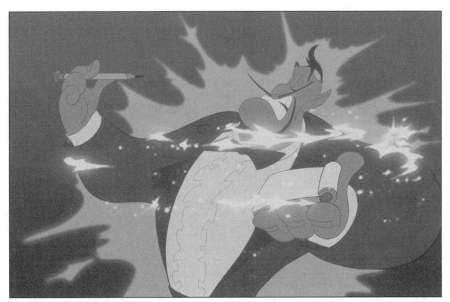

Aladdin. The Genie puts on a show.

Aladdin. Jasmine and Aladdin live happily ever after.

THE NIGHTMARE BEFORE CHRISTMAS

Music and Lyrics: Danny Elfman
Screenplay: Tim Burton (poem), and Michael McDowell (adaptation),
    Caroline Thompson (screenplay)
Produced by: Tim Burton, Denise Di Novi, Kathleen Gavin
Directed by: Henry Selick for Touchstone Pictures
Cinematography: Pete Kozachik (Technicolor)
Cast: Danny Elfman, Chris Sarandon, Catherine O'Hara, William Hickey, Glenn Shadix,
    Paul Reubens, Ken Page, Ed Ivory
Songs: "This Is Halloween"; "Jack's Lament"; "Doctor Finklestein/In the Forest";
    "What's This?"; "Town Meeting Song"; "Jack's Obsession"; "Kidnap the Sandy
    Claws"; "Making Christmas"; "Nabbed"; "Oogie Boogie's Song"; "Sally's Song";
    "Poor Jack"
Released: October 1993; 76 minutes

With *The Nightmare Before Christmas*, Tim Burton created an on-screen world and characters that are both completely unreal and startlingly real. Once an animator for Disney, Burton uses clay figures and a stop-action filming process, "claymation," that brings them to life. Even subtle facial expressions are executed by this method. This remarkably realistic motion is applied to inventive, ghostly figures and placed on equally creative sets. In Burton's world, towns exist solely to execute holiday preparations. Jack, one of the ghostly denizens of the appropriately lifeless Halloweentown, stumbles into the vivid, bustling burg of Christmastown. He falls in love with Christmas, and a nightmare of holiday intrigue ensues, complete with singing and dancing. It's a children's art film. Most viewers probably come away uncomfortably wondering if it's a Christmas movie about Halloween, or a Halloween movie about Christmas.
Disney ST. Touchstone Home Video VC.

The Nightmare Before Christmas. Jack in Halloweentown.

The Swan Princess

THE SWAN PRINCESS
Music: Lex de Azevedo
Lyrics: David Zippel
Screenplay: Richard Rich, Brian Nissen
Produced by: Richard Rich, Tom Tobin, Terry Noss for New Line Cinema.
Directed by: Richard Rich (Technicolor)
Voices: Michelle Nicastro, Jack Palance, Sandy Duncan, Steven Wright, John Cleese, Steve Vinovich
Songs: "Far Longer Than Forever"; "No More Mr. Nice Guy"; "This Is My Idea"; "Practice, Practice, Practice"; "No Fear"; "Princesses on Parade"; "Eternity – Dreams Come True"
Released: November 1994, 90 minutes

Relying on pre-computer techniques of hand-painting animation cells, writer/director Richard Rich, a defector from Disney, took over four years to complete *The Swan Princess*. A young princess and prince, heirs to separate kingdoms, are pushed toward a romance by their parents, who hope to merge their kingdoms. The children grow up and fall in love, only to be torn apart by an evil sorcerer. The sorcerer turns the princess into a swan and imprisons her on his castle lake. Love prevails in time for a happy ending, but not before three animals befriend the imprisoned swan. Bright spots include Jack Palance's hard-bitten characterization of Rothbart, Steve Wright's deadpan delivery of Speed, and John Cleese's wonderfully overdone Jean-Bob. The film was followed by video sequels *The Swan Princess II* (Escape from Castle Mountain) in 1997, and *The Swan Princess III* in 1998.
Sony ST. Turner VC.

THE LION KING

Music and Lyrics: Elton John and Tim Rice
Screenplay: Irene Mecchi, Jonathan Roberts, Linda Woolverton
Produced by: Chris Sanders for Walt Disney
Directed by: Roger Allers and Rob Minkoff (Technicolor)
Voices: Matthew Broderick, Rowan Atkinson, Niketa Calame, Jim Cummings, Whoopi
Goldberg, Jeremy Irons, Robert Guillaume, James Earl Jones, Cheech Marin,
Jonathan Taylor Thomas
Songs: "Circle of Life"; "I Just Can't Wait to Be King"; Be Prepared"; "Hakuna Matata";
"Can You Feel the Love Tonight"; incidentally "The Lion Sleeps Tonight" (Hugo
Peretti, George Weiss, Luigi Creatore, based on a song by Solomon Linda and
Paul Campbell); "It's a Small World" (Robert Sherman and Richard Sherman)
Released: June, 1994, 88 minutes

The Lion King, which received reviews criticizing its "lack of fun," topped the list of U.S. box office receipts in 1994. The film brought home $298.9 million dollars that year, and at this writing, it is number seven on Variety's All-Time Top Film Rentals list. The Lion King was a new twist in a long-successful formula for Disney, and certainly the most serious venture since The Black Cauldron. The plot (which bears a strong resemblance to the 1960s, Japanese, animated series "Jungle Emperor"), faces the topics of death, guilt and betrayal. This is the first of the Disney animated films to use an original story. Simba, a cuddly, playful lion cub, is the son of Mufasa, the king of the lions. Simba knows that someday he will inherit the throne. He thinks all the world loves him, which proves to painfully untrue. His uncle Scar (Jeremy Irons), Mufasa's brother, arranges for Mufasa's death, leaving young Simba to bear the blame. Simba flees into exhile. Mufasa's death is depicted in a startlingly graphic scene which prompted some reviewers to caution parents against letting young children see the film.

Unlike Disney's previous animated features, The Lion King placed a love story as a sub-plot to the more important themes of self-discovery and responsibility. Simba's love interest, a lioness named Nala, convinces him to return to the Pride of Lions and take his place on the throne. Computer assisted animation helped to provide sweeping backdrops that give a sense of endless wilderness to the film. With the booming voice of James Earl Jones in the role of Mufasa, Jeremy Irons as a cold, dry Scar, Jonathan Taylor Thomas as young Simba and Matthew Broderick as the more mature Simba, the dialogue is a feast for the ears. Comic relief arrives via such voices as Whoopi Goldberg and the inimitable Nathan Lane.

The music for The Lion King is another departure from traditional Disney fare. Tim Rice suggested Elton John to Disney brass to collaborate on the songs, and, though all thought he'd probably turn the project down, John jumped at the chance. There was a pop hit before the movie was even released. Hans Zimmer's lush musical score won an Academy Award, as did the song "Can You feel the Love Tonight" (Elton John and Tim Rice). The staged version of the film created a sensation when it opened on Broadway in November of 1997. The Lion King was followed by The Lion King II: Simba's Pride, released direct to video in the U.S., in 1998.
Disney ST. Walt Disney Home Video VC.

The Lion King. Mufasa and Zazu.

The Lion King. Simba, Pumbaa and Timon.

Pocahontas. Pocahontas and John Smith.

POCAHONTAS
Music and Lyrics: Alan Menken and Stephen Schwartz
Screenplay: Carl Binder, Susannah Grant, Philip LaZebnik (Andrew Chapman, uncredited)
Produced by: James Pentecost for Walt Disney
Directed by: Mike Gabriel and Eric Goldberg
Voices: Irene Bedard, Mel Gibson, David Ogden Stiers, John Kassir, Russell Means, Christian Bale, Linda Hunt, Danny Mann, Billy Connolly, Joe Baker, Judy Kuhn, John Pomeroy
Songs: "The Virginia Company"; "Steady As the Beating Drum"; "Just Around the Riverbend"; Listen With Your Heart"; "Mine, Mine, Mine"; "Savages"; "Colors of the Wind"
Released: June 1995, 81 minutes

Pocahontas, which premiered on a huge outdoor screen in New York City's Central Park, tells a sweet tale of fictionalized history in early America. The twenty-something Pocahontas of this animated film was actually about eleven years old when John Smith arrived in her world. In history she did marry an Englishman, John Rolfe, and traveled to England with him. She died there while in her early twenties. The film reverses the long-standing screen images of native Americans as savages and early explorers as dignified gentlemen – in the extreme. The script has the explorers as greedy savages, while the Native Americans are noble, wise folk, living in blissful harmony with the natural world. Alan Menken won an Academy Award for the score and, with Stephen Schwartz, a Golden Globe for "Colors of the Wind." Pocahontas was followed in 1998 by the video sequel Pocahontas II: Journey to a New World.
Disney ST. Disney Home Video VC.

Toy Story. Buzz Lightyear and Woody.

TOY STORY

Music and Lyrics: Randy Newman
Screenplay: Joss Wheden, Andrew Stanton Joel Cohen and Alec Skolow. Based on a story
by John Lasseter, Andrew Stanton, Pete Docter and Joe Ranft.
Produced by: Ralph Guggenheim, Bonnie Arnold for Walt Disney
Directed by: John Lasseter (Technicolor)
Voices: Tom Hanks, Tim Allen, Don Rockels, Jim Varney, Wallace Shawn,
John Ratzenberger, Annie Potts, John Morris, Penn Jillette, Erik von Detten,
Laurie Metcalf, R. Lee Ermey, Sarah Freeman
Songs: "You've Got a Friend in Me," "Strange Things," "I Will Go Sailing No More"
Released: November 1995; 81 minutes

Toy Story was the first feature film created entirely by computer. A child's collection of toys comes to life when no one is looking. They walk and talk and display intricate layers of toy-room politics. Woody (Tom Hanks) is a simple cowboy doll that is the young owner's favorite toy. He reigns as king of the toy hill until a high-tech Buzz Lightyear doll (Tim Allen) arrives as a gift. With the appearance of Buzz, the politics change and Woody is displaced as the favorite. Buzz however, doesn't realize that he is a toy and works with dogged determination to repair his spaceship (actually the cardboard box in which he was packaged), intending to complete his mission. When the family moves to a new house, Buzz and Woody are marooned at a filling station. They work together to reunite with the family, forging a friendship in the process. Shifting perspectives and toy antics that are unhampered by the laws of physics are all executed in groundbreaking animation. It's just barely a musical, with three fairly incidental songs.
Disney ST. Disney Home Video VC.

Mr. Holland's Opus. Richard Dreyfuss.

MR. HOLLAND'S OPUS
Music: Michael Kamen, various
Screenplay: Patrick Sheane Duncan
Produced by: Robert W. Cort, Ted Field, Michael Nolin
Directed by: Stephen Herek for Buena Vista/Hollywood Pictures
Photography: Oliver Wood (Technicolor)
Cast: Richard Dreyfuss, Glenne Headly, Jay Thomas, Olympia Dukakis, W. H. Macy, Alicia Witt, Terrence Howard, Damon Whitaker, Jean Louisa Kelly, Alexandra Boyd
Songs: "Cole's Song" (Michael Kanes, Julien Lennon and Justin Clayton "Beautiful Boy" (John Lennon); "An American Symphony (Mr. Holland's Opus)"; "Louie Louie" (Richard Berry); "Someone to Watch Over Me" (George and Ira Gershwin)
Released: January 1996; 143 minutes

In telling the story of a high school music teacher's thirty-year career, *Mr. Holland's Opus* became a manifesto for the continuation of arts programs in American public schools. Holland (Richard Dreyfuss) has reluctantly given up a life on the road and aspirations to be a composer for marrying and settling down. A surprise pregnancy seals his fate. Holland blossoms as a teacher, but is dealt an ironic blow by having a deaf son. As the decades pass, complete with occasional evening-news clips, Holland's various students leave. One seeks a stage career in New York, one dies in Viet Nam and another becomes governor of the state. After thirty years, but still too soon for his retirement, the school district eliminates the music program for budgetary reasons, throwing Holland out of a job. On the day he packs to leave the school he is given a tribute before an cheering auditorium filled with his former students. (With all that support, especially with the governor there, you would think it would have saved the music budget and Holland's job; but then it would lose the Hollywood melodrama.) Many of the former high-school musicians take the stage and miraculously, without rehearsal, perform the piece he has been composing for several years, "Mr. Holland's Opus."
Polygram ST. Hollywood Pictures VC.

The Hunchback of Notre Dame.

THE HUNCHBACK OF NOTRE DAME

Music and Lyrics: Alan Menken, Stephen Schwartz
Screenplay: Irene Mecchi, after the novel by Victor Hugo
Produced by: Roy Conti, Don Hahn
Directed by: Gary Trousdale, Kirk Wise for Walt Disney
Cast: Tom Hulce, Demi Moore, Tony Jay, Kevin Kline, Paul Kandel, Jason Alexander, Charles Kimbrough, Mary Wickes, David Ogden Stiers, Heidi Mollenhauer
Songs: "The Bells of Notre Dame"; "Out There"; "God Help the Outcasts"; "Heaven's Light"; "Hellfire"; "A Guy Like You"; "The Court of Miracles"; "Someday"; "Topsy Turvy"
Released: June 1996; 91 minutes

Disney both followed and broke its own model for animated success with *The Hunchback of Notre Dame*. A plucky heroine appears in the form of the gypsy Esmerelda (Demi Moore), and she finds love and happiness before the end of the tale. But in this story the young woman rescues her man, Phoebus (Kevin Kline), and breaks the heart of the suffering hunchback Quasimodo (Tom Hulce), who also has fallen in love with her. Also in love with her, and hating himself for loving a gypsy, is the evil Judge Frollo (Tony Jay). There is happy ending, but a qualified one, as the poor, disfigured Quasimodo finds affection but not romantic love. The darkness and layers of this story are beautifully set in a cathedral that is as much a character in the story as a backdrop to it. Director Gary Trousdale appears as the voice of the Old Heretic. Bette Midlers sings the final reprise of "God Help the Outcasts." The pop vocal group All-4-One had a hit single with "Someday."
Walt Disney ST. Walt Disney Home Video VC.

THAT THING YOU DO!

Music and Lyrics: Adam Schlesinger, others (songs), Howard Shore (score)
Screenplay: Tom Hanks
Produced by: Jonathan Demme, Gary Goetsman, Edward Saxon
Directed by: Tom Hanks (Twentieth Century Fox)
Photography: Tak Fujimoto
Cast: Tom Everett Scott, Liv Tyler, Jonathon Schaech, Steve Zahn, Ethan Embry, Tom Hanks, Bill Cobbs, Rita Wilson
Songs: "That Thing You Do!"; "Sad Sad Boy"; "Back Together" (Adam Schlesinger); "Lovin' You Lots and Lots"; "It's Not Fair"; "La Señora de dos Costas" (Tom Hanks); "Mr. Dowtown"; "Voyage Around the Moon"; "Hold My Hand, Hold My Heart"; "Will You Marry Me" (Tom Hanks, Gary Goetzman, Mike Piccirillo); "All My Only Dreams"; "Dance with Me Tonight"; "Drive Faster"; "She Knows It"; (Scott Rogness, Rick Elias); "I Need You (That Thing You Do)" (Scott Rogness, Rick Elias, Linda Elias); "Little Wild One" (David Gibbs, Steve Hurley, Phil Hurley, Fred Elringham); "Spartacus" (Tom Hanks, arranged by Wayne Jones); "Time to Blow" (Steve Tyrell, Robert Mann); "Blue Spot" (Alphonse Mouzon); "All My World Is Over"; "Shrimp Shack"; "Twangin'"; "Cock 'n' Bull"; "Watch Your Money" (Mike Piccirillo)
Released: October 1996; 110 minutes

Tom Hanks' first foray into writing/directing resulted in this feel-good film about a 1960s, one-hit wonder rock group, aptly named the Wonders. An Erie, Pennsylvania, band gets their break on the strength of one good song, and is swept into the machinery of pop music. Nice-guy drummer (Tom Everett Scott) is dragged into the group moments before their first taste of success, after the regular drummer breaks his arm. Hanks plays a good-hearted Playtone Records executive who gives the band a teen-idol image and milks the popularity of their hit single. The band melts down after one summer tour, and we are left with the hero finding his own career as a jazz drummer, and riding off into the sunset with the lead singer's jilted sweetheart (Liv Tyler). The group's song, "That Thing You Do!," is a catchy little toe-tapper – and mercifully so, given the number of times it's heard in the film. It received both Academy Award and Golden Globe nominations as best song.
Sony ST. Fox VC.

That Thing You Do!

The Preacher's Wife. Whitney Houston.

THE PREACHER'S WIFE

Music and Lyrics: Various
Screenplay: Allan Scott, Nat Mauldin and Todd Graff (uncredited). Based on
The Bishop's Wife by Leonardo Bercovici and Robert E. Sherwood.
Produced by: Samuel Goldwyn Jr. for Touchstone Pictures and the
Samuel Goldwyn Company.
Directed by: Penny Marshall
Photography: Miroslav Ondricek (Technicolor)
Cast: Whitney Houston, Denzel Washington, Courtney B. Vance, Gregory Hines, Jenifer
Lewis, Loretta Devine, Lionel Richie, Paul Bates, Justin Pierre Edmund, Lex
Monson, Darvel Davis Jr., William James Stiggers Jr., Marcella Lowery, Cissy
Houston, Aaron A. McConnaughey
Songs: "Somebody Bigger Than You and I" (Johnny Lange, Hy Heath and Sonny Burke);
"Lay Aside Every Weight" (Glenn Burleigh); Hold On, Help Is in the Way" (Rev.
Kenneth Paden); "You Were Loved" (Diane Warren); "Who Would Imagine a
King" (Mervyn Warren, Hallerin Hilton Hill); "My Heart Is Calling" (Kenneth
"Babyface" Edwards); "I Believe in You and Me" (David Wolfert, Sandy Linzer); "I
Love the Lord" (Richard Smallwood); "Step by Step" (Annie Lennox)
Released: December 1996, 124 minutes

The Preacher's Wife, a light, Merry Christmas comedy, is a remake of the 1947 *The
Bishop's Wife*, which starred Gary Grant, David Niven and Loretta Young. A preacher
(Courtney B. Vance) struggles to hold together both the souls and aging building of his
inner city church. In the process he overlooks the needs of his wife (Whitney Houston) and
son. An angel named Dudley (Denzel Washington) drops in to put things right. The film toys
with a possible romance between the preacher's wife and the angel, as the angel rediscov-
ers the physical world he has left behind. In the end he does his job, setting the preacher
and his wife back on the right track. A sub-plot of the film makes Houston a former nightclub singer who now sings only in church. That seemingly minor plot point allows for some
fine gospel singing from Houston, backed by a rousing gospel choir, and one scene in a
nightclub where she sings "I Believe in You and Me." That song became the movie's big
hit.
BMG/Arista ST. Touchstone Home Video ST.

EVITA

Music and Lyrics: Andrew Lloyd Webber and Tim Rice
Screenplay: Alan Parker and Oliver Stone, based on the musical by Andrew Lloyd
  Webber and Tim Rice
Produced by: Robert Stigwood, Alan Parker, Andrew G. Vajna FOR Hollywood Pictures
Directed by: Alan Parker
Photography: Darius Khondji (Technicolor)
Cast: Madonna, Antonio Banderas, Jonathan Pryce, Jimmy Nail, Victoria Sus,
  Julian Littman
Songs: "Don't Cry For Me Argentina"; "Rainbow High"; "Oh What a Circus"; "On This
  Night of a Thousand Stars"; "Another Suitcase in the Hall"; "High Flying,
  Adored"; "You Must Love Me"; and others
Released: December 1996, 134 minutes

It took some twenty years and several false starts before *Evita* made the move from stage to film. (It had actually started as an album in 1976.) Francis Ford Coppola, Richard Attenborough and Oliver Stone each took a shot at the project. In fact, Stone's writing credit stems not from any work on the eventual film, but Writer's Guild regulations regarding receiving credit for his earlier treatment of the musical. In the end it took director Alan Parker, with a list of Hollywood musical credits that includes *Fame*, *The Commitments*, *Bugsy Malone* and *Pink Floyd-The Wall*, to pull it off.

Madonna, no one's first choice for the title role, lobbied long and hard to win the part. (Argentinians protested profusely over her casting as their national heroine.) She brought physical and temperamental resemblance to Eva, and a fragility to the role. Madonna worked with a voice teacher to prepare for the demands of the score. Playing a Che that is less a stereotype than the corresponding Che Guevera role in the stage musical, Antonio Banderas is a smoldering, sardonic narrator/commentator, something of a one-man Greek chorus.

With few lines of spoken of dialogue, the film, like the original stage version, is highly operatic in construction. Andrew Lloyd Webber and Tim Rice had long since abandoned their collaboration when the film version of Evita went into production, but they joined forces to add one song to the film, "You Must Love Me," which won an Oscar for best song.

Evita tells the story of Eva Duarte Peron, who rises from a life of poverty and prostitution and a mildly successful acting career to become the wife of soon-to-be Argentine president, General Juan Peron. A visually rich film, filled with stylish period costumes and sepia-toned scenes of Buenos Aires (many of which were shot in Budapest), the movie races through the story of her rise to fame and power to her death from cancer at age 26. "Don't Cry for Me Argentina," the showstopping number for Elaine Paige in London and Patti LuPone on Broadway, is treated MTV style, with a collage of edits inserted into Madonna's singing on the balcony of the Casa Rosada.

WEA/Warner ST. Hollywood Pictures Home Video VC.

Evita. Jonathan Pryce and Madonna.

Evita. Madonna

EVERYONE SAYS I LOVE YOU
Music and Lyrics: Various
Screenplay: Woody Allen.
Produced by: Robert Greenhut for Sweetland Films (Miramax)
Directed by: Woody Allen
Photography: Carlo Di Palma, A.I.C. (Technicolor)
Cast: Alan Alda, Woody Allen, Drew Barrymore, Goldie Hawn, Edward Norton, Julia Roberts, Tim Roth, Lukas Haas, Gaby Hoffman, Natalie Portman, Natasha Lyonne, David Ogden Stiers
Songs: "Everyone Says 'I Love You'" (Bert Kalmar, Harry Ruby); "Makin' Whoopee"; "My Baby Just Cares for Me" (Walter Donaldson, Gus Kahn); "Looking at You" (Cole Porter); "Just You, Just Me" (Jesse Greer, Raymond Klages); "I'm a Dreamer (Aren't We All)" (Ray Henderson, B.G. DeSylva, Lew Brown)
Released: January 1997; 101 minutes

Everyone Says I Love You is a movie musical in the old-fashioned sense of the word, particularly modeled on the movies of the 1930s. People break into song at the slightest provocation, with nannies, hospital patients, ghosts and a panhandler joining in, usually with a witty or romantic intent and result. The film tells a multi-layered tale of an upper-crust New York family and their special brand of angst. Between the painfully self-obsessed dialogues for which Woody Allen is famous are sprinkled grandiose song-and-dance numbers. The final package is something that teeters somewhere between *Annie Hall* and *Swing Time*. Most of Allen's cast members, himself included, are intentially non-singers (or, at best, infrequent singers), Goldie Hawn being the pleasant exception. On the up side of that casting choice, the film offers some unpretentious, honest deliveries of tunes. Appearing in a curious cameo, Itzhak Perlman and his daughter, pianist Navah Perlman, entertain at a fund-raising party.
BMG/RCA Victor ST. Miramax VC.

HERCULES
Music and Lyrics: Alan Menken, David Zippel
Screenplay: Ron Clements, Donald McEnery, Bob Shaw, Irene Mecchi.
Produced by: Alice Dewey, John Musker, Ron Clements
Directed by: John Musker, Ron Clements
Cast: Tate Donovan, Joshua Keaton, Roger Bart, Danny DeVito, James Woods, Susan Eagan, Bob Goldthwaite, Matt Frewer, Rip Torn, Samantha Eggar, Barbara Barrie, Hal Holbrook
Songs: "One Last Hope"; "Go the Distance"; "The Gospel Truth"; "A Star Is Born"; "I Won't Say (I'm in Love)"; "Zero to Hero"
Released: June 1997 92 minutes

With *Hercules*, Disney made a return to the lighter musical comedy fare of its earlier animated musicals. Gone are the serious tones of *Pocahontas*, *The Hunchback of Notre Dame* and *The Lion King*. *Hercules* is a happy, snappy Disney romp through Greek mythology. Yes, the young Hercules grows up and finds love in very Disney fashion, but he does it with the help of a doting Pegasus and a diminutive satyr named Phil (Danny DeVito). Hercules (Tate Donovan) is half man/half deity and all teenager, tripping over his too-big feet and trashing entire structures in the process with his unbridled strength. He learns that he is the son of Zeus (Rip Torn) and must prove himself a true hero to regain his place among the other deities. "Herc" performs a laundry list of heroic feats, but it is in risking his own life to save Meg (Susan Eagan) that he wins back his birthright. He then gives it up to remain on earth with her as a mortal. Charlton Heston is also heard on the soundtrack. Singer Michael Bolton scored a hit with "Go the Distance."
Disney ST. Disney Home Video VC.

Hercules.

Anastasia.

ANASTASIA

Music: Stephen Flaherty (songs), David Newman (score)
Lyrics: Lynn Ahrens
Screenplay: Susan Gauthier, Bruce Graham, Bob Tzudiker and Noni White.
Also Arthur Laurents (1956 screenplay), based on the play by Marcelle
Maurette, as adapted by Guy Bolton
Produced by: Don Bluth & Gary Goldman for Fox Animation Studios
Directed by: Don Bluth & Gary Goldman (Technicolor)
Voices: Meg Ryan, John Cusack, Kelsey Grammer, Christopher Lloyd, Hank Azaria,
Bernadette Peters, Kirsten Dunst, Angela Lansbury, Liz Calloway (Anastasia
singing), Lacey Chabert, Jim Cummings, Jonathan Dokuchitz (Dmitri singing),
Rick Jones, Andrea Martin, Glenn Walker Harris Jr., Debra Mooney, Arthur
Malet, Charity James
Songs: "Once Upon a December"; "A Rumor in St. Petersburg"; "Journey to the Past";
"Viaje Tiempo Atras" (spanish version of "Journey to the Past"); "In the Dark of
the Night"; "Learn to Do It"; "Paris Holds the Key (To Your Heart)"; "At the
Beginning"
Released: November 1997, 94 minutes

Anastasia was Fox's maiden voyage into the Disney-dominated sea of animated, feature-length films. It pits a spunky female lead against forces of evil, sending her off accompanied by a cute animal companion, and providing her with a happily-ever-after romance. Based in the 1956 Ingrid Bergman film, the story whisks past the death of Czar's family and the entire Russian Revolution in one quick scene. Anastasia and her grandmother escape execution, only to be separated. The princess suffers amnesia and grows up in an orphanage, unaware of her royal roots. Turned out to live on her own, she runs into two men who want to find someone to pass off as the missing Anastasia, in hopes of collecting a handsome reward. The irony is that they discover they are grooming the real thing. The film is given spice by the villainous portrayal of Rasputan (voice of Christopher Lloyd) and several chase sequences.
WEA Atlantic Records ST. Fox VC.

Mulan.

MULAN

Music: Matthew Wilder, score by Jerry Goldsmith
Lyrics: David Zippel
Screenplay: Robert D. San Souci based on an anonymous poem.
Produced by: Pam Coats
Directed by: Barry Cook, Tony Bancroft
Cast: Ming-Na Wen, Lea Salonga (Mulan singing), Eddie Murphy, B.D. Wong, Donny Osmond (Shang singing), Harvey Fierstein, Jerry S. Tondo, Gedde Watanabe, James Hong, Miguel Ferrer, Soon-Tek Oh, Freda Foh Shen, Pat Morita, June Foray, George Takei
Songs: "Reflection"; "Honor to Us All"; "I'll Make a Man Out of You"; "A Girl Worth Fighting For"; "True to Your Heart"
Released: June 1998, 88 minutes

Disney's thirty-sixth animated full-length film, *Mulan*, like so many of the previous films, centers on a plucky heroine and provides a lovable animal sidekick. The story is taken from an ancient Chinese folk legend. The Emperor decrees that one man from each family must step forward to fight against the Huns. In order to spare her aged, ailing father from the hardships and dangers of war, Mulan steals the family sword, disguises herself as a boy and runs off to join the army. The film balances feminist ideals and romance as Mulan flies in the face of societyís conventions and expectations. She is joined in her adventures by a tiny, street-smart dragon named Mushu (Eddie Murphy). Over 700 people were involved in creating the striking animation and artwork. Pop legend Stevie Wonder was brought in to sing "True to Your Heart" over the end credits.
Disney ST. Disney Home Video VC.

THE PRINCE OF EGPYT

Music & Lyrics: Stephen Schwartz
Score: Hans Zimmer
Screenplay: Philip LaZebnik, Nicholas Meyer
Produced by: Penney Finkelman Cox, Sandra Rabins, Jeffrey Katzenberg (executive producer), Ron Rocha (associate producer)
Directed by: Brenda Chapman, Steve Hickner and Simon Wells
Voices: Val Kilmer, Ralph Fiennes, Sandra Bullock, Helen Mirren, Jeff Goldblum, Michelle Pfeiffer, Patrick Stewart, Danny Glover, Martin Short, Steve Martin
Songs: "Deliver Us"; "All I Ever Wanted"; "Through Heaven's Eyes"; "Playing with the Big Boys"; "The Plagues"; "When You Believe"; "I Will Get There"
Released: December 1998

With *The Prince of Egypt* DreamWorks Pictures combined two winning Hollywood traditions, a Disney-style animated musical with a Cecille B. DeMille-like Biblical epic story. Stephen Schwartz, successful in his twenties as the composer/lyricist for *Godspell* and *Pippin*, was signed to write the songs. The result is the most serious-minded of animated musicals despite some added comic characters – and it may have lost some small children in the process. In the familiar story Moses is placed in a basket by his troubled Hebrew slave mother and sent down the Nile, believing that some generous free woman will adopt her infant boy, saving him from Egyptian capture. That someone turns out to be the Queen of Egypt, and Moses is brought up as a prince. Through a happenstance that part Bible and part Hollywood, Moses encounters his Hebrew siblings, Miriam and Aaron, and learns his true identity. He is greatly changed by the realization, and flees his royal life to finds Tzipporah, a Bedouin woman he was once given as a gift but who escaped. The two fall in love and for some years leads a simple life as shepherds. Out of the blue the burning bush appears to him along with the voice of God calling him to return to Egypt and release the Hebrews from their enslavement. He finds that his father has died and his brother, Rameses, has become Pharoah. Moses tries in vain to plead his cause to Rameses, who refuses to comply, even in the face of plagues and widespread famine. Moses warns his brother of one last oncoming plague that God has revealed to him, and again Rameses is deaf to his pleas. After his young son dies, Rameses angrily tells his brother to take the Hebrews and leave Egypt. At the Red Sea the Hebrews encounter the Egyptian army, but God sends a huge fire to block the soldiers. The waters of the Red Sea part, leaving an escape route for Moses and the Hebrews. When the Egyptian army attempts to follow, the waters crash on them, drowning out all danger for the Hebrews. Moses and his people safely travel to a new homeland, and the movie ends with him on Mount Sinai receiving the Ten Commandments. The song "When You Believe" became a hit single in a version by pop divas Whitney Houston and Mariah Carey.

The Prince of Egypt.

TARZAN

Music & Lyrics: Phil Collins
Screenplay: Tab Murphy, adapted from the novel by Edgar Rice Burroughs
Directed by: Chris Buck, Kevin Lima
Voices: Tony Goldwyn, Wayne Knight, Brian Blessed, Nigel Hawthorne, Glenn Close, Minnie Driver, Lance Henriksen, Rosie O'Donnell
Songs: "Son of Man"; "Strangers Like Me"; "Trashin' the Camp"; "Two Worlds"; "You'll Be in My Heart"
Released: June 1999

Tarzan and Hollywood. The tradition of film renderings of Edgar Rice Burroughs's famous jungle character, first introduced in the 1912 novel *Tarzan of the Apes*, goes back to the silent era. Besides over two dozen novels, many comic books, and radio and television programs, there have been 43 film adaptations of Tarzan in various guises. The story is basic, familiar to everyone who has seen the timeless films of the 1930s starring Johnny Weismuller and Maureen O'Hara. Tarzan is an orphan boy, left in the African jungle, adopted by a gorilla family. He grows up happy and unselfconscious, until one day a human expedition intrudes, including a zoologist, Professor Porter, his beautiful daughter, Jane, and their greedy jungle guide, Clayton. Tarzan learns his true nature when he meets the humans, and is torn by where his allegiance should lie. This is complicated by falling in love with Jane. Through the villianous Clayton the humans show their mean side, threatening the apes with capture. Tarzan instinctively defends his ape family, pledging his loyalty to them. Jane stays in the jungle with him, of course. Unlike other Disney musicals, most of songs are sung by Phil Collins on the soundtrack, rather than emanating from the characters themselves, and become like animated MTV music video numbers. Disney's animators continued to push the technological envelope in *Tarzan*, employing the computer-generated illusion of a three dimensional background.

THE KING AND I

Music: Richard Rodgers
Lyrics: Oscar Hammerstein II
Screenplay: Peter Bakalian, Jacqueline Feather, David Seidler. Conceived and adapted for animation by Arthur Rankin
Produced by: James G. Robinson, Arthur Rankin, Peter Bakalian
Directed by: Richard Rich
Voices: Miranda Richardson, Christiane Noll, Martin Vidnovic, Ian Richardson, Darrell Hammond, Allen D. Hong, David Burnham, Armi Arabe, Tracy Venner Warren, Adam Wylie
Songs: "I Whistle a Happy Tune"; "Hello, Young Lovers"; "The March of the Siamese Children"; "Getting to Know You"; "Shall I Tell You What I Think of You?"; "A Puzzlement"; "I Have Dreamed"; "Shall We Dance"
Released: March 1999; 89 minutes. Warner Bros. Rated G

Something akin to watching an episode of *Scooby-Doo, Where Are You?* with some of the best songs of the musical theatre interspersed throughout, this cartoon remake of *The King and I* was the brainchild of animation specialist Arthur Rankin. Eight songs from Richard Rodgers and Oscar Hammerstein II's classic 1951 Broadway show were performed in mostly truncated versions, while the screenplay took extreme liberties with the original storyline, simplifying things considerably. Adding slapstick, cutesy animals, and kickboxing, and turning the Kralahome into a wicked sorcerer, suggested a desperate attempt to appeal to members of a younger demographic who were unlikely to take a shine to the sophisticated songs anyway.

Two numbers cut from the 1956 live-action version, "I Have Dreamed" and "Shall I Tell You What I Think of You?," were included this time, while the undisputed musical highlight was Barbra Streisand's medley that encompassed the former tune, along with "We Kiss in a Shadow" and "Something Wonderful," taken from her 1987 *Broadway Album* and played during the closing credits. Martin Vidnovic, who provided the voice of the King, had played Lun Tha in the 1977 Broadway revival of the show.

SOUTH PARK: BIGGER LONGER & UNCUT

Music & lyrics: Trey Parker, Marc Shaiman
Screenplay/producers: Trey Parker, Matt Stone, Pat Brady
Directed by: Trey Parker
Cast: Trey Parker, Matt Stone, Mary Kay Bergman, Isaac Hayes, George Clooney, Brent Spiner, Eric Idle, Minnie Driver, Dave Foley
Songs: "Mountain Town"; "Uncle Fucka"; "Wendy's Song"; "It's Easy, Mmmkay"; "Hell Isn't Good"; "Blame Canada"; "Kyle's Mom's a Bitch"; "What Would Brian Boitano Do?"; Up There"; "La Resistance"; "I Can Change"; "I'm Super"; "The Mole's Reprise"; "Eyes of a Child"
Released: June 1999; 82 minutes. Paramount. Rated R

A musical made by people who clearly find nothing funnier than to see characters break into song, this extension of the hit Comedy Central series was created by Trey Parker and Matt Stone. With its deliberately crude animation and nihilistic outlook, *South Park: Bigger Longer & Uncut* satirized censorship by having war escalate between the United States and Canada because of a foul-mouthed movie the parents of South Park believe has corrupted their children. Most of the tunes were throwaways, the joke being that they couldn't be further lyrically from the sort of songs sung in your traditional Hollywood musical, so packed with expletives were they. One of the less provocative (and more tuneful) numbers, "Blame Canada," a rallying cry performed by the angered adults, ended up with an Oscar nomination.

South Park. Ike, Kyle, and Cartman.

LOVE'S LABOUR'S LOST

Screenplay by & directed by: Kenneth Branagh
Produced by: David Barron, Kenneth Branagh
Choreography: Stuart Hopps
Cast: Kenneth Branagh, Richard Briers, Richard Clifford, Carmen Ejogo, Nathan Lane, Adrian Lester, Matthew Lillard, Natascha McElhone, Gerald McEwan, Emily Mortimer, Alessandro Nivola, Stefania Rocca, Alicia Silverstone, Timothy Spall
Songs: "I'd Rather Charleston" (George Gershwin, Desmond Carter); "I Won't Dance" (Jerome Kern, Jimmy McHugh, Dorothy Fields, Oscar Hammerstein II, Otto Harbach); "I Get a Kick Out of You" (Cole Porter); "No Strings" (Irving Berlin); "The Way You Look Tonight" (Kern, Fields); "I've Got a Crush on You" (George and Ira Gershwin); "Cheek to Cheek" (Berlin); "Let's Face the Music and Dance" (Berlin); "There's No Business Like Show Business" (Berlin); "They Can't Take That Away from Me" (The Gershwins)
Released: June 2000; 94 minutes. Miramax. Rated PG

Credited with bringing a fresh cinematic perspective to Shakespeare, Kenneth Branagh, serving as director, adapter, and actor, found critical favor and appreciative audiences for his takes on *Henry V* (1989), *Much Ado about Nothing* (1993), and the full-length, four-hour-plus *Hamlet* (1996). His decision to film one of the Bard's works that hadn't been translated to the big screen since the silent era, *Love's Labour's Lost,* was enhanced by the added gimmick of weaving classic songs of the 1930s into the verse. (Approximately 70 percent of the original text was discarded to make way.) Updating the storyline to 1939, Branagh was in effect hoping to mimic the gaiety of that era's musicals, particularly the Astaire–Rogers vehicles, six of his 10 chosen numbers coming from their films.

A cast mostly not known for singing or dancing gave it a game try, notably in a sexed-up rendition of "Let's Face the Music and Dance," while the West End's Adrian Lester showed, during "I've Got a Crush on You," that he was the only ensemble member with genuine terpsichorean skills. It was Nathan Lane, however, who walked off with the musical-comedy honors, leading the company through "There's No Business Like Show Business." Filming mostly on soundstages (at Shepperton Studios) made Tim Harvey's set designs look that much lovelier, Branagh once again proved himself a superb interpreter of Shakespeare's verse, and nobody seemed to pay any attention whatsoever to this rather sweet, occasionally arch, and often audacious attempt to do something off the beaten track.

Love's Labour's Lost. Emily Mortimer, Carmen Ejogo, Natascha McEllhone, and Alicia Silverstone.

DANCER IN THE DARK

Music: Björk
Lyrics: Lars von Trier, Sjón Sigurdsson
Directed by & screenplay by: Lars von Trier
Produced by: Vibeke Windeløv
Choreography: Vincent Paterson
Cast: Björk, Catherine Deneuve, David Morse, Peter Stormare, Joel Grey, Vincent Paterson, Cara Seymour, Jean-Marc Barr, Vladica Kostic, Siobhan Fallon, Zeljko Ivanek
Songs: "Cvalda"; "I've Seen It All"; "Smith & Wesson"; "In the Musicals"; "107 Steps"; "Next to Last Song"; "New World (Overture)"
Released: September 2000; 141 minutes. Fine Line Features. Rated R

Dogma 95, a guerilla-style filmmaking technique championing handheld cameras and realism, and the artifice of the musical genre made for an unhappy combination in Danish director Lars von Trier's grim *Dancer in the Dark*. Icelandic cult singer Björk portrayed a simple, musical-worshipping Czech émigré working a dead-end job at a tool factory in Washington State (circa 1964) to pay for the eye operation her son will need; the young boy is in certain danger of inheriting his mother's debilitating condition, which is causing her to go blind. Set in the United States but filmed in Trollhattan, Sweden, with an ever-moving, nausea-inducing camera, *Dancer* stacked the deck against its hapless heroine, crossing the line from stark drama to an almost morose level of cinéma vérité cruelty.

In addition to snatches of three *The Sound of Music* songs and an old-fashioned pre-title overture, the film paid homage to the genre with the inclusion of *The Umbrellas of Cherbourg*'s Catherine Deneuve as Björk's compassionate co-worker and *Cabaret*'s Joel Grey performing an aborted dance in a courtroom. Using multiple cameras to capture Björk's musical fantasies, the numbers were choppy, failing to relieve the ever-present gloom. Björk's songs (one of which, "I've Seen It All," brought her and her lyricists, von Trier and Sjón Sigursson, an Oscar nomination) scrupulously avoided tradition, being more akin to wailing chants with an aversion to melody. The movie's comparisons to the far superior *Pennies from Heaven* in theme only emphasized its failure to make a potent statement about the need for escapism from a bleak existence.

Dancer In the Dark. David Morse and Björk.

THE FANTASTICKS

Music: Tom Jones
Lyrics: Harvey Schmidt
Screenplay: Tom Jones, Harvey Schmidt
Directed by: Michael Ritchie
Produced by: Michael Ritchie, Linne Radmin
Choreography: Michael Smuin
Cast: Joel Gray, Barnard Hughes, Jean Louisa Kelly, Joe McIntyre, Jonathon Morris, Brad Sullivan, Teller
Songs: "Much More"; "Never Say No"; "Metaphor"; "The Abduction Song"; "Soon It's Gonna Rain"; "Happy Ending"; "This Plum Is Too Ripe"; "I Can See It"; "'Round and 'Round"; "They Were You"; "Try to Remember"
Released: September 2000; 86 minutes. United Artists. Rated PG

A jewel box of a musical, Tom Jones and Harvey Schmidt's *The Fantasticks* (which opened at the Sullivan Street Theater in May of 1960) represented the best Off-Broadway had to offer, a combination of witty observations on love, poetically melodic songs, and a deeper examination of relationships than most works in or out of its genre were willing to offer. So "small" was it in everyone's mind, so blatantly theatrical in approach, that there didn't seem to be any viable reason to turn it into a motion picture, despite the fact that it became, by a wide margin, the longest-running show in Off-Broadway history (it finally closed in 2002 after 17,162 performances). Director Michael Ritchie, however, had a special fondness for the property and managed to convince Jones and Schmidt to write a screenplay, opening it up visually but pretty much retaining all of the text and numbers. United Artists agreed to back the project provided the budget was kept low. Filming in San Rafael Valley, Arizona, Ritchie managed to capture the gentle spirit of the piece, a meditation on the difficult steps from youthful infatuation to disillusionment to the acceptance of an imperfect love. The film was ready for distribution in 1995, only to come up against a roadblock that represented a lamentable step backward for the genre.

Despite the filmmakers having in no way disgraced what had become a highly revered work, test-screening audiences weren't crazy about the musical, causing UA and MGM to shelve it for a reputation-destroying five-year stretch. Before they unleashed it (in token engagements), they handed it over to Francis Ford Coppola for reshaping. The 110-minute film was shaved down by 24 minutes, losing several bits of dialogue, along with, most unfortunately, the opening rendition of the show's most enduring song, "Try to Remember," and a delightful duet for Grey and Brad Sullivan, "Plant a Radish." Although these cuts did not cause irreparable harm to the film, they were *not* in any way improvements. All of these excisions, including the original "rape-heavy" version of "It Depends on What You Pay" (replaced by the less incendiary "The Abduction Song"), were available as extras on the DVD. Unjustly, the most famous of all Off-Broadway shows became one of the least well-known of all movie musicals of recent years.

The Fantasticks. Jean Louisa Kelly and Joe McIntyre.

The Fantasticks. Joe McIntyre and Jean Louisa Kelly.

MOULIN ROUGE!

Screenplay: Baz Luhrmann, Craig Pearce
Produced by: Martin Brown, Baz Luhrmann, Fred Baron
Directed by: Baz Luhrmann
Choreography: John O'Connell
Cast: Nicole Kidman, Ewan McGregor, John Leguizamo, Jim Broadbent, Richard Roxburgh, Garry McDonald, Jacek Koman, Matthew Whitter, Kerry Walker, Caroline O'Connor, David Wenham, Christine Anu, Kylie Minogue, Linal Haft
Songs: "Nature Boy" (Eden Ahbez); "The Sound of Music" (Richard Rodgers, Oscar Hammerstein II); "Children of the Revolution" (Marc Bolan); "Zidler's Rap" (Baz Luhrmann, Craig Pearce, Marius de Vries); "Lady Marmalade" (Bob Crewe, Kenny Nolan); "Diamonds Are a Girl's Best Friend" (Jule Styne, Leo Robin); "Material Girl" (Peter H. Brown, Robert S. Rans); "Rhythm of the Night" (Diane Warren); "Your Song" (Elton John, Bernie Taupin); "The Pitch/The Can Can" (Jacques Offenbach, Luhrmann, Pearce); "One Day I'll Fly Away" (Will Jennings, Joe Sample); "Elephant Love Medley" (various); "Come What May" (David Baerwald); "Like a Virgin" (Billy Steinberg, Tom Kelly); "Roxanne" (Sting); "Le Tango du Moulin Rouge" (Marianito Mores, Luhrmann, Pearce); "Fool to Believe" (Luhrmann, Pearce, de Vries, Craig Armstrong); "The Show Must Go On" (Freddie Mercury, Brian May, Roger Taylor, John Deacon); "Chamma Chamma" (Sameer); "The Hindi" (Steve Sharples)
Released: May 18, 2001; 128 minutes. 20th Century Fox. PG-13

Despite the presence of Toulouse-Lautrec, Australian filmmaker Baz Luhrmann's kinetic, often maddening *Moulin Rouge!* was in no way a remake of the 1952 film of the same name, which starred José Ferrer as the diminutive French painter. A pastiche of stunning visuals, rapid-fire editing, and pop standards that ran the gamut from full performances to sound bites to the equivalent of dance mixes, Luhrmann's film was busy, busy, busy to be sure. Set in 1899 Paris, cheekily referred to here as "the summer of love," *Moulin* told the tragic tale of naive writer Christian's love for the Moulin Rouge's star entertainer and courtesan Satine, who has been promised to a powerful duke.

Combining computer-generated visuals, mattes, jittery jumps, and a frequently sweeping camera, *Moulin's* look (it was filmed entirely on the soundstages of Sydney's Fox Studios Australia) was that of a fantasy never-world, as Montmartre might have appeared in the imagination of those submerged in its decadence and chaotic high life. The film came most breathtakingly to life with Ewan McGregor's rendition of Elton John's "Your Song," revealing a highly impressive set of pipes, making this one film actor whose busy schedule should also consist of recording an occasional CD on the side. It was McGregor who was the heart and soul of the movie, despite it being his leading lady, Nicole Kidman, who rated an Oscar nomination. The film earned eight nominations total, including that for Best Picture, solidifying its commendable box office performance. It was, in fact, credited with revitalizing the genre, proving that there was an audience in the new millennium for what had too often been deemed a dead art form, as long as modern editing could be used to hold viewers' attention.

Moulin Rouge! Nicole Kidman and Ewan McGregor.

Moulin Rouge! Nicole Kidman.

HEDWIG AND THE ANGRY INCH

Music & lyrics: Stephen Trask
Directed by & screenplay by: John Cameron Mitchell
Produced by: Christine Vachon, Katie Roumel, Pamela Koffler
Choreography: Jerry Mitchell
Cast: John Cameron Mitchell, Miriam Shor, Stephen Trask, Theodore Liscinski, Rob Campbell, Michael Aronov, Andrea Martin, Michael Pitt, Maurice Dean Wint, Ben Mayer-Goodman, Alberta Watson
Songs: "Tear Me Down"; "The Origin of Love"; "Sugar Daddy"; "Angry Inch"; "Wig in a Box"; "Wicked Little Town"; "Hedwig's Lament/Exquisite Corpse"; "Midnite Radio"
Released: July 2001; 92 minutes. Fine Line Features. Rated R

Part musical theatre, part concert, *Hedwig and the Angry Inch* was the bracingly original collaboration of actor John Cameron Mitchell and musician Stephen Trask. Their idea was to present the life of a fictional, semi-transsexual, would-be-punk-rocker East Berlin émigré, as told through a connecting narrative between songs performed onstage by Hedwig and his/her backup band. Having agreed to a sex-change operation in order to marry a U.S. soldier and get out of communist Germany, Hansel-turned-Hedwig was instead left with mutilated genitals, hence the "angry inch" that gave his band its name. Abandoned by his army lover and then again by aspiring musician Tommy Gnosis, whose career he nurtured, the embittered Hedwig embarks on a tatty concert tour in the shadow of Tommy's tremendously successful career, performing before mostly bewildered diners at a chain restaurant called Bilgewaters.

Initially workshopped in a gay punk club before ending up Off-Broadway in February of 1998 in a theatre converted from a hotel ballroom, *Hedwig* became a downtown sensation. It ran more than two years for a total of 857 performances, in the process and bridging the gap between theatre and club music. Although its very theatrical nature might have precluded any thought of a movie adaptation, Mitchell himself had firm ideas of how to reimagine his work in a cinematic sense and served as both screenwriter and director.

Keeping most of the concert numbers intact (two, "The Long Grift" and "Random Generation Number," were relegated to the background), enhancing the storyline by making the Gnosis character visible and adding a part for Hedwig's determined manager Phyllis Stein (Andrea Martin), *Hedwig* was just as clever and exciting to behold onscreen, belying its theatrical origins. (Its musical highlight was its one traditionally presented production number, the catchy "Wig in a Box.") Its rather specialized subject matter and its bold approach to questioning sexual identity (Hedwig, a gay man living as a woman, shares his bed with bandmate Itzhak, a gay man played by an actress hiding behind a beard) made it miles above the average mall fare in hipness and intelligence, thereby limiting its appeal. Instead, Mitchell had made the perfect midnight cult movie for the decade.

Hedwig and the Angry Inch. (Clockwise from center) John Cameron Mitchell, Rob Campbell, Stephen Trask, Miriam Shor, Michael Aronov, and Theodore Liscinski.

8 MILE

Screenplay: Scott Silver
Produced by: Curtis Hanson, Brian Grazer, Jimmy Iovine
Directed by: Curtis Hanson
Songs include: "Lose Yourself" (Eminem, Jeff Bass, Luis Resto)
Cast: Eminem, Kim Basinger, Mekhi Phifer, Brittany Murphy, Evan Jones, Omar Benson Miller, De'Angelo Wilson, Eugene Byrd, Taryn Manning, Anthony Mackie, Michael Shannon, Nashawn Breedlove
Released: November 2002; 111 minutes. Universal. Rated R

A semi-autobiographical depiction of rapper Eminem's (real name Marshall Mathers) breakthrough from aimless denizen of Detroit's poverty-stricken 313 District to hip-hop champion, *8 Mile* took its title from a reference to one of the city's sociological dividing points. Directed by Curtis Hanson with a fierce degree of realism and written by Scott Silver to sound almost improvisational with its expletive-ridden street talk, the film was the best endorsement for the hip-hop movement that motion pictures has yet to offer.

So far away in style and tone from the MacDonald–Eddy operettas of the 1930s it might as well be taking place on another planet, *8 Mile* was still very much a "musical," reflecting the dominant soundtrack of the day, with rap "battles" taking the place of staged numbers. Hurling rhyming insults back and forth as an expression of hostility, these riffs had the effect of winning a girl's heart the way a traditional love ballad would, as shown in the lunch truck scene where Eminem's pointed dissection of a homophobic fellow employee convinces Brittany Murphy that he might be the one for her.

Few films have depicted the devastation of urban blight as vividly as this one, most strikingly in the conversion of the city's once-grand Michigan Theater movie palace into a shabby parking garage. After many years of failing to acknowledge contemporary sounds, the Motion Picture Academy made a stab at "street cred" by awarding the movie's major song "Lose Yourself" the coveted Oscar. The fact that nobody bothered to sing it at the year's ceremony could be interpreted by its fans and detractors in a variety of ways.

8 Mile. Brittany Murphy and Eminem.

CHICAGO

Music: John Kander
Lyrics: Fred Ebb
Screenplay: Bill Condon
Produced by: Martin Richards
Director/Choreographer: Rob Marshall
Cast: Renée Zellweger, Catherine Zeta-Jones, Richard Gere, Queen Latifah, John C. Reilly, Lucy Liu, Taye Diggs, Colm Feore, Christine Baranski, Dominic West, Mýa Harrison, Deirdre Goodwin, Denise Faye, Ekaterina Chtchelkanova, Susan Misner
Songs: "And All That Jazz"; "Funny Honey"; "When You're Good to Mama"; "Cell Block Tango"; "All I Care About"; "We Both Reached for the Gun"; "Roxie"; "I Can't Do It Alone"; "Mister Cellophane"; "Razzle Dazzle"; "Nowadays"; "I Move On"
Released: December 2002; 113 minutes. Miramax. Rated PG-13

First there was the announcement that after more than 25 years of proposals, plans, and promises, a movie of Bob Fosse, John Kander, and Fred Ebb's sizzling Broadway triumph *Chicago* (opening in June of 1975, it ran for 936 performances) would at last be made, with choreographer Rob Marshall at the helm. Next there was the advance buzz that Marshall had actually come up with a winner, followed by critical support once the movie finally opened and then audience enthusiasm that kept building and building. When the film chalked up 13 Oscar nominations, fans held their breath in disbelief and anticipation. And then it happened: a musical, the first to do so in 34 years, won the coveted Academy Award for Best Picture. Box office receipts ultimately soared to $170 million in the United States alone. Was this really happening in the new millennium? Had musicals finally made it back to the degree that they were again deemed worthy of respect in an industry that had pretty much given up on the genre?

The incentive for getting this long-dormant project off the ground was a scaled-down 1996 Broadway revival of the show, which turned into such a profitable and long-running venture (still going as of this printing) that Hollywood figured something about it had to be adaptable. A pungent, often cynical satire on the fleeting nature of flash-in-the-pan celebrity and those who crave it, the story, based on a 1926 straight play by Maurine Dallas Watkins, centered on a show business wannabe, Roxie Hart, who kills her lover and becomes a media darling while awaiting trial.

Believing that modern movie audiences had trouble accepting characters breaking into song (a concern no doubt centered on those who don't like musicals, as opposed to true fans), Marshall's approach was to take Fosse's "musical vaudeville" and stage the numbers as if they were happening in the minds of its characters. Therefore, Roxie's introduction to her greedy lawyer Billy Flynn was presented like a burlesque striptease; their bogus press conference like a ventriloquist sideshow; the trial itself a circus. In the film's most brilliant number, "Cellblock Tango," the sounds of a lonely prison at night turn into Roxie's introduction to her fellow killers, each one enacting the crime that put her behind bars.

Marshall's direction was thrillingly cinematic (edited for maximum impact) while remaining faithful in tone and spirit to the original work. Across-the-board brilliant performances were brought forth from the cast, four of whom (Zellweger, Zeta-Jones, Reilly, Latifah) earned Oscar nominations, with Catherine Zeta-Jones as the foxy, unrepentant Velma Kelly going home the winner. Five songs from John Kander and Fred Ebb's outstanding stage score were dropped altogether, while a sixth, "Class," was filmed and then discarded from the theatrical print, to be offered only as an extra on the DVD packaging. One new song, "I Move On," was heard over the end credits and earned an Oscar nod as well.

Chicago. Catherine Zeta-Jones.

A MIGHTY WIND

Screenplay: Christopher Guest, Eugene Levy
Produced by: Karen Murphy
Directed by: Christopher Guest
Cast: Bob Balaban, Ed Begley Jr., Jennifer Coolidge, Paul Dooley, Christopher Guest, John Michael Higgins, Michael Hitchcock, Don Lake, Eugene Levy, Jane Lynch, Michael McKean, Larry Miller, Christopher Moynihan, Catherine O'Hara, Jim Piddock, Parker Posey, Harry Shearer, Deborah Theaker, Fred Willard
Songs: "Old Joe's Place" (Christopher Guest, Michael McKean, Harry Shearer); "The Good Book Song" (McKean, Shearer); "When You're Next to Me" (Eugene Levy); "A Kiss at the End of the Rainbow" (McKean, Annette O'Toole); "Just That Kinda Day" (Guest, McKean); "One More Time" (Catherine O'Hara, Levy); "Never Did No Wanderin'"(McKean, Shearer); "Main Street Rag" (John Michael Higgins); "Skeletons of Quinto" (Guest); "Loco Man" (Shearer); "Fare Away" (CJ Vanston, McKean, O'Toole); "Potato's in the Paddy Wagon" (McKean, O'Toole); "Barnyard Symphony" (Guest); "A Mighty Wind" (Levy, Guest, McKean); "The Sure-Flo Song" (O'Hara)
Released: April 2003; 92 minutes. Warner Bros. Rated PG-13

Actor-writer-director Christopher Guest's style of deadpan mockumentary had gained a cult following through such comedies as *Waiting for Guffman* and *Best in Show,* though the template for all of these, *This Is Spinal Tap,* was in fact directed by his friend Rob Reiner. This time the faux band embodied by *Tap* members Guest, Michael McKean, and Harry Shearer was the Folksmen, a 1960s-style folk group. Also along for the ride were Guest regulars Eugene Levy (the film's co-writer) and Catherine O'Hara as Mitch and Mickey, whose partnership once extended beyond the stage, and the sappily Christian-influenced New Main Street Singers. All came together for a tribute to late folk icon Irving Steinbloom, to be produced by his son (Bob Balaban) at New York's Town Hall (the interiors were actually shot at LA's Orpheum Theater).

Using his customary interview format, Guest left it up to his cast to improvise their way to laughs, with Fred Willard as a blowhard manager and former TV star with an inappropriate joke for every occasion; Ed Begley Jr. as a public broadcasting executive given to Yiddish phrasing; and Jennifer Coolidge as a crass, pinheaded press agent coming off best. Some spot-on folk parodies were heard mostly in fragments, though the accompanying album covers and poster art often got the joke across just as well. Mitch and Mickey's signature ballad, "A Kiss at the End of the Rainbow," earned an Oscar nomination for McKean and his collaborator, wife Annette O'Toole, though the snappy title song was the real gem on hand.

A Mighty Wind. Harry Shearer, Michael McKean, and Christopher Guest.

FROM JUSTIN TO KELLY

Screenplay: Kim Fuller
Produced by: Gayla Aspinall, John Steven Agoglia
Directed by: Robert Iscove
Choreography: Travis Payne
Cast: Kelly Clarkson, Justin Guarini, Katherine Bailess, Anika Noni Rose, Greg Siff, Brian Dietzen, Jason Yribar, Theresa San Nicholas
Songs: "I Won't Stand in Line" (Randy Sharp, Steve Diamond); "The Luv (The Bounce)" (Tommy Sims, Kim Fuller); "Brandon's Rap" (Greg Siff); "Forever Part of Me" (Lucie Silvas, Matt Prime); "It's Meant to Be" (Michael Wandmacher, Robert Iscove, Jonathan Sanchez); "Timeless" (Karen Poole, Henrik Norberg, Oscar Merner, Peer Astrom, Anders Bagge); "Wish upon a Star" (Silvas, Ben Chapman, Martin Harrington); "Madness" (Sims); "Anytime" (Sam Watters, Louis Biancaniello); "That's the Way I Like It" (Harry Casey, Richard Finch)
Released: June 2003; 81 minutes. 20th Century Fox. Rated PG

American Idol, the new millennium's update of *Ted Mack's Amateur Hour,* became such a television phenomenon within its first season on the air (2001–2) that someone had the seemingly foolproof idea of reuniting the series's first winner, Kelly Clarkson, with her runner-up, Justin Guarini, on the big screen. What they concocted, however, was not simply an extension of the TV show's sing-into-a-microphone presentation but an actual traditional-style musical, in which the two young vocalists broke into songs in the midst of the storyline. That storyline, alas, turned out to be about as sophisticated as the 1960s *Beach Party* series it resembled, and just as devoid of wit or anything to do with the lives of real teenagers.

The skimpy plot had Kelly and Justin meet while on spring break in Miami, as they gyrated along with their pals and fellow vacationers to a collection of sound-alike tunes, going through the motions of a pin-headed romantic plot that was mercifully over in 81 minutes. Neither performer showed any ease in the acting department, Travis Payne's choreography resembled the robotic techno movements that had become the unfortunate norm in music videos, and the closest thing to a memorable song was the sole oldie, "That's the Way I Like It," made famous in the 1970s by K.C. and the Sunshine Band and saved for the big dance finale. *From Justin to Kelly* bombed so colossally at the box office that it was sent to the video shelves within a month of its release, proving that what fans of *Idol* enjoyed about the show was the competition, and not the thought of seeing their "idols" paired up to sing within a plotline.

From Justin to Kelly. Kelly Clarkson and Justin Guarini.

CAMP

Screenplay/Directed by: Todd Graff
Produced by: Katie Roumel, Christine Vachon, Pamela Keffler, Danny DeVito, Michael Shamberg, Stacey Sher, Jonathan Weisgal
Choreographers: Michele Lynch, Jerry Mitchell
Cast: Daniel Letterle, Joanna Chilocoat, Robin DeJesus, Steven Cutts, Vince Rimoldi, Kahiry Bess, Tiffany Taylor, Sasha Allen, Alana Allen, Anna Kendrick, Don Dixon, Stephen DiMenna, Stephen Sondheim
Songs: "How Shall I See You through My Tears" (Robert Telson, Lee Breuer); "Losing My Mind" (Stephen Sondheim); "Wild Horses" (Mick Jagger, Keith Richards); "I'm Still Here" (Sondheim); "Turkey Lurkey Time" (Burt Bacharach, Hal David); "And I Am Telling You I'm Not Going" (Tom Eyen, Henry Krieger); "The Ladies Who Lunch" (Sondheim); "I Sing for You" (Michael Gore, Lynn Ahrens); "Century Plant" (Victoria Williams); "Here's Where I Stand" (Gore, Ahrens); "The Want of a Nail" (Todd Rundgren)
Released: July 2003; 110 minutes. IFC Films. Rated PG-13

Actor Todd Graff wrote and directed this comedy inspired by his teen years as a student at Stagedoor Manor, a training ground for aspiring show business youngsters. The *Camp* roster included Vlad, a knockout handsome golden boy so straight he doesn't even appreciate show music; awkward Ellen, who develops a crush on him; and part-time drag queen Michael, who also pines for Vlad. Filmed on location at the real Stagedoor Manor (here called Camp Ovation) in Loch Sheldrake, in the Catskills, the film's humor comes from the inappropriate casting required for the junior league productions, such as a white girl belting out "And I Am Telling You I'm Not Going" from *Dreamgirls,* and two black boys asked to look as Jewish as possible for a production of *Fiddler on the Roof.* Despite addressing the predominance of gay youths at the camp, the film clearly had an eye on the mainstream box office by allowing the heterosexual characters to have all the physical intimacy.

Combining established songs with new tunes meant to represent the work of an embittered composer forced to make a living at the camp, the movie's best moments were its musical ones, including the gospel-like opening number "How Shall I See You Through My Tears"; Tiffany Taylor's defiant rendition of "Here's Where I Stand"; and a delightful re-creation of Michael Bennett's choreography for the "Turkey Lurkey Time" number from *Promises, Promises.* There were also no less than three Stephen Sondheim numbers on hand, which was fitting, insomuch as the revered songwriter actually put in a brief appearance as a show of support.

Camp. Robin DeJesus and Joanna Chilocoat.

DE-LOVELY

Music & lyrics: Cole Porter
Screenplay: Jay Cocks
Produced by: Irwin Winkler, Rob Cowan, Charles Winkler
Directed by: Irwin Winkler
Choreography: Francesca Jaynes
Cast: Kevin Kline, Ashley Judd, Jonathan Pryce, Kevin McNally, Sandra Nelson, Allan Corduner, John Barrowman, Keith Allen, James Wilby, Kevin McKidd, Richard Dillane, Edward Baker-Duly, and Robbie Williams, Lemar, Elvis Costello, Alanis Morissette, Caroline O'Connor, Sheryl Crow, Mick Hucknall, Diana Krall, Vivian Green, Lara Fabian, Mario Frangoulis, and Natalie Cole
Songs: "In the Still of the Night"; "Anything Goes"; "Weren't We Fools?"; "Well Did You Evah?"; "Easy to Love"; "It's De-Lovely"; "What Is This Thing Called Love?"; "Let's Misbehave"; "Let's Do It, Let's Fall in Love" "True Love"; "Night and Day"; "Begin the Beguine"; "Be a Clown"; "Just One of Those Things"; "Experiment"; "I Get a Kick Out of You"; "Love for Sale"; "It's Alright with Me"; "Why Shouldn't I?"; "Another Openin', Another Show"; "So in Love"; "Ev'ry Time We Say Goodbye"; "You're the Top"; "Get Out of Town"; "Goodbye, Little Dream, Goodbye"; "Blow, Gabriel, Blow"
Released: July 2004; 125 minutes. MGM. Rated PG-13

It would appear that Hollywood's *second* movie biopic of the immortal songwriter Cole Porter (1891–1964) was meant to atone somewhat for the flagrant disregard for accuracy seen in *Night and Day,* Warner Bros.' 1946 take on his life. Not only was that movie full of fabrications for the sake of drama, as was the norm in such projects, but the puritanical code of the era required the omission of Porter's homosexual inclinations altogether. Times having changed, it being the 21st century, after all, director Irwin Winkler and writer Jay Cocks managed to work men into Porter's bed for their version, even including a male–male kiss, but they let it be known that, according to their thesis, the composer's socialite wife, Linda Thomas (whom he actually married more for position and convenience than desire), was the real love of his life. While Kline resembled the actual Porter no more than Cary Grant did in the earlier film, it was nice to hear this always welcome actor sing onscreen again, although he deliberately weakened his voice in an effort to reproduce Cole's lack of prowess in this department.

As chock full of clichés in its own way as the first biopic, *De-Lovely* didn't exactly stick to the truth, either, presenting Linda as a beauty some 20 years Cole's junior (she was, in fact, eight years his senior); handing the immortal "Night and Day" to another cast member of *Gay Divorce* (portrayed by John Barrowman) rather than star Fred Astaire, who had debuted it in real life; and giving the impression that "I Love You" was knocked off for a Nelson Eddy film, rather than the Broadway show *Mexican Hayride.* To give this blatantly old-fashioned film a contemporary slant, Winkler included onscreen performances from such singers as Diana Krall, Elvis Costello, Robbie Williams, and, best of the lot, Vivian Green doing a sultry rendition of "Love for Sale" as Kline samples the wares in a gay club. Jack L. Warner was probably spinning in his grave.

RAY

Screenplay: James. L. White
Story: Taylor Hackford, James L. White
Produced by: Taylor Hackford, Stuart Benjamin, Howard Baldwin
Directed by: Taylor Hackford
Cast: Jamie Foxx, Kerry Washington, Regina King, Clifton Powell, Joe Adams, Bokeem Woodbine, Aunjanue Ellis, C. J. Sanders, Curtis Armstrong, Richard Schiff, Larenz Tate, Sharon Warren
Songs: "Route 66" (Bobby Troup); "Straighten Up and Fly Right (Nat King Cole, Irving Mills); "Rock This House" (Lowell Fulson); "Everyday I Have the Blues" (Peter Chatman); "Baby Let Me Hold Your Hand" (Ray Charles); "Roll with My Baby" (Sam Sweet); "The Midnight Hour" (Sweet); "Mess Around" (Ahmet Ertegun); "I Got a Woman" (Charles); "Hallelujah I Love Her So" (Charles); "Drown in My Own Tears" (Henry Glover); "Mary Ann" (Charles); "Leave My Woman Alone" (Charles); "What Kind of Man Are You?" (Charles); "Night Time Is the Right Time" (Lew Herman, Samuel Mathews); "What'd I Say?" (Charles); "I Believe to My Soul" (Charles); "Georgia on My Mind" (Hoagy Carmichael, Stuart Gorrell); "Hit the Road Jack" (Percy Mayfield); "Unchain My Heart" (Bobby Sharp, Teddy Powell); "You Don't Know Me" (Eddy Arnold, Cindy Walker); "I Can't Stop Loving You" (Don Gibson); "Bye Bye Love" (Boudleaux Bryant, Felice Bryant); "Born to Lose" (Ted Daffan); "Hard Times (No One Knows Better Than I)" (Charles)
Released: October 2004; 153 minutes. Universal. Rated PG-13

In one sense very much a traditional biopic, *Ray* charted the turbulent career of singer-songwriter Ray Charles (real name Ray Charles Robinson), in a warts-and-all portrait that dwelled heavily on his drug addiction, his philandering, ugly confrontations with racism, bad parenting, the traumatic memory of his younger brother's death, and his struggle with losing his sight at the age of seven. On the other hand, Taylor Hackford's lengthy drama forsook the biopic structure of yore by making sure that this depiction of a musician's life was very much thought of first and foremost as a drama and *not* a musical, insomuch as each and every performance of a song was either truncated or interrupted at some point by dialogue or jumps in the narrative to other scenes altogether.

The hits were all there in some form or another, however, including Charles's breakthrough on the Atlantic record label, the jiving, sexually fused "What'd I Say?," as well as his number-one ABC records best-sellers "Georgia on My Mind," "Hit the Road Jack," and "I Can't Stop Loving You." While Jamie Foxx was asked to mime to Charles's actual vocals and piano playing, his performance was nevertheless a remarkably rich one, earning him a well-deserved Oscar. No less superb was Sharon Warren as Ray's resilient and inspiring, no-nonsense mother.

Although Charles himself worked on the film (shot mostly in and near New Orleans), he was not around to bask in its box office success, as well as its impressive showing at the Oscars, where it ended up one of the year's Best Picture nominees. He died on June 10, 2004, at the age of 73.

BEYOND THE SEA

Screenplay: Kevin Spacey, Lewis Colick
Produced by: Arthur Friedman, Andy Paterson, Jan Fantl, Kevin Spacey
Directed by: Kevin Spacey
Choreography: Rob Ashford
Cast: Kevin Spacey, Kate Bosworth, John Goodman, Bob Hoskins, Brenda Blethyn, Greta Scacchi, Caroline Aaron, Peter Cincotti, William Ullrich
Songs: "Mack the Knife" (Marc Blitzstein, Kurt Weill); "Lazy River" (Hoagy Carmichael, Sidney Arodin); "Jump Down, Spin Around" (Harry Belafonte, Norman Luboff, William A. Attaway); "Rock Island Line" (Lonnie Donegan); "Splish Splash" (Bobby Darin, Jean Murray); "Artificial Flowers" (Jerry Bock, Sheldon Harnick); "Beyond the Sea" (Charles Trenet, Albert Lasry, Jack Lawrence); "Dream Lover" (Darin); "Once upon a Time" (Lee Adams, Charles Strouse); "Hello, Young Lovers" (Richard Rodgers, Oscar Hammerstein II); "That's All" (Bob Haymes, Alan Brandt); "Fabulous Places" (Leslie Bricusse); "Charade" (Henry Mancini, Johnny Mercer); "Change" (Darin); "Simple Song of Freedom" (Darin); "Ain't Got No Mama (Ain't Got No Papa)" (Kevin Spacey); "The Curtain Falls" (Sol Weinstein); "As Long as I'm Singing" (Darin); "Some of These Days" (Sheldon Brooks)
Released: December 2004; 119 minutes. Lionsgate. Rated PG-13

Kevin Spacey was so set on realizing his dream of portraying dynamic entertainer Bobby Darin that he decided to take control of the entire project himself, serving as director, co-writer, and co-producer on the biopic *Beyond the Sea*. A framing device of Darin putting together a self-portrait on film was a surreal touch intended to ease folks into the fact that 44-year-old Spacey was going to be portraying Darin from his early twenties until his death at the age of 37. While the physical resemblance became more pronounced when Darin reached his mustached, thinning-hair stage, there was no denying that Spacey did an ace job of mimicking the entertainer's swinging vocals.

Emphasizing the sometimes blissful, sometimes stressful relationship between Darin and his wife, actress Sandra Dee, *Sea* followed the predictable path of many such films and was therefore strongest in its numbers, intent on packing in pretty much every famous Darin tune and then some. While most were done on nightclub stages, Spacey wanted his biopic to be a genuine musical as well, allowing "Lazy River," the title song, and "As Long as I'm Singing" to segue into unapologetically old-fashioned production numbers. This approach made for a highly entertaining show and a respectful portrait of the artist, but it was considered commercially dicey and frightened away Hollywood. Because of this, Spacey was obliged to find backing from the UK and Germany, filming the movie in the latter country.

Beyond the Sea. Kevin Spacey.

THE PHANTOM OF THE OPERA

Music/produced by: Andrew Lloyd Webber
Lyrics: Richard Stilgoe, Charles Hart
Screenplay: Andrew Lloyd Webber, Joel Schumacher.
Directed by: Joel Schumacher
Choreography: Peter Darling.
Cast: Gerard Butler, Emmy Rossum, Patrick Wilson, Miranda Richardson, Minnie Driver, Ciaran Hinds, Simon Callow, Jennifer Ellison
Songs: "Auction at the Opera Populaire, 1919 (Prologue)"; "Think of Me"; "Angel of Music"; "Little Lotte"; "The Mirror"; "The Phantom of the Opera"; "The Music of the Night"; "I Remember/Stranger Than You Dreamt It"; "Magical Lasso"; "Notes"; "Prima Donna"; "Poor Fool, He Makes Me Laugh"; "Il Muto"; "Why Have You Brought Me Here?"; "Raoul I've Been There"; "All I Ask of You"; "Masquerade"; "Why So Silent/Ultimatums"; "Wishing You Were Somehow Here Again"; "Wandering Child"; "We Have All Been Blind"; "Twisted Every Way"; "Don Juan"; "The Point of No Return"; "Down Once More"; "Track Down This Murderer"; "Learn to Be Lonely"
Released: December 2004; 141 minutes. Warner Bros. Rated PG-13

Already the West End's most successful composer, Andrew Lloyd Webber clearly hit all the right notes where the general public was concerned by turning Gaston Leroux's 1912 novel *The Phantom of the Opera* into a stage musical. When the show opened in London in 1986 and then two years later in New York, its blend of gothic terror and romance struck such a nerve that it became nothing less than a worldwide phenomenon, racking up sales figures above $5 billion and becoming Broadway's longest-running show ever (and still running, as of the publication of this book). Despite the sensation, a movie adaptation was a long time arriving, the first such plans having been derailed a few years after the American premiere, that version to have featured both the original stage stars, Michael Crawford and Sarah Brightman. Tired of waiting and rich enough to do it independently, Lloyd Webber eventually took a hands-on approach to the project, serving as co-writer and producer for a no-expense-spared adaptation shot at Pinewood Studios that made few alterations to his work. A new song, "No One Would Listen," was written for the Phantom, only to have its lyrics changed and the revision given to Minnie Driver (who was otherwise dubbed throughout the movie, by Margaret Preece) to sing during the end credits, as "Learn to Be Lonely."

Director Joel Schumacher, always good at visual stylization, certainly made the movie look great (it earned Oscar nominations for art direction and cinematography) but erred in the casting of Gerard Butler, whose growling, rock-star-like vocals and lack of vulnerability made one wish the project had been done before Crawford got too old. The score never sounded so lush, and the nicest number, "All I Ask of You," was as lovely in its presentation onscreen as it had been onstage. Lloyd Webber's dependency on recitative and his frequent repetition of themes throughout did not always play as well, these being very much the stuff of live theatre. People who always hated the show (and its huge success guaranteed plenty of those) dismissed the film as well, but admirers had little to complain about, since it was pretty much a faithful transfer. The $51 million that the *Phantom* movie grossed in the United States, however, in no way matched the work's stunning theatrical success (overseas figures, however, were more substantial), suggesting that this old-fashioned combination of song and melodrama worked best for those witnessing it in person.

The Phantom of the Opera. Emmy Rossum and Gerard Butler.

The Phantom of the Opera. Patrick Wilson.

BRIDE & PREJUDICE

Music & lyrics: Anu Malik (music); Zoya Akhtar, Farham Akhtar, Chaman Lal Chaman, PaulMayeda Berges, Dev Kholi
Screenplay: Paul Mayeda Berges, Gurinder Chadha
Produced by: Deepak Nayar, Gurinder Chadha
Directed by: Gurinder Chadha
Choreography: Seoj Khan
Cast: Aishwarya Rai, Martin Henderson, Nadir Babbar, Anupam Kher, Naveen Andrews, Namrata Shirodkar, Daniel Gillies, Indira Varma, Sonali Kulkarni, Nitin Chandra Ganatra, Peeya Rai Choudhouri, Alexis Bledel, Marsha Mason
Songs: "Punjabi Wedding Song"; "A Marriage Has Come to Town"; "My Lips Are Waiting (a.k.a. Goa Groove)"; "No Life without Wife"; "Dola Dola"; "Take Me to Love"
Released: February 2005; 111 minutes. Miramax. Rated PG-13

In the wake of several adaptations of the novels of Jane Austen, director Gurinder Chadha (*Bend It Like Beckham*) figured audiences could stand to see another take on arguably the writer's most famous work, *Pride and Prejudice,* by modernizing it, moving the location from England to India, and, best of all, tossing in some musical numbers. The individualistic Elizabeth Bennett therefore became Lalita Bakshi, of a middle-class family living in Amritsarj, while Darcy retained his name but became an American hotelier of enormous wealth. While still commenting to some degree on class and position, the new angle of presenting an interracial couple raised an eyebrow or two from their mothers but was hardly presented as a serious issue or looked upon as an obstacle, which would no doubt have given the progressive-thinking Austen a great deal of pleasure.

Although Bollywood musicals continued to circulate in ever-wider markets, there had been little in the way of crossover appeal to the more mainstream, Caucasian audiences this *Bride & Prejudice* hoped to rectify, honoring the Indian motion picture traditions while mingling them with a touch of Hollywood. Songs like "Punjabi Wedding Song" and "Dola Dola" were sung in Hindi, while the others had English lyrics. The highlights were "A Marriage Has Come to Town," with a marketplace erupting in a swirl of colors around the Bakshi sisters, and the sprightly "No Life without Wife," which had the four siblings cavorting around their home in their pajamas like something out of *Grease.* Although a straightforward adaptation of the story would come along that same year and prove more popular, this film was clearly the more inventive and enjoyable of the two.

Bride & Prejudice. Aishwarya Rai and Martin Henderson.

TIM BURTON'S CORPSE BRIDE

Music & lyrics: Danny Elfman; additional lyrics: John August
Screenplay: John August, Caroline Thompson, Pamela Pettler. Based on characters created by Carlos Grangel and Tim Burton
Produced by: Tim Burton, Allison Abbate
Directors: Mike Johnson, Tim Burton
Cast: Johnny Depp, Helena Bonham Carter, Emily Watson, Tracey Ullman, Paul Whitehouse, Joanna Lumley, Albert Finney, Richard E. Grant, Christopher Lee, Michael Gough, Jane Horrocks, Enn Reitel
Songs: "According to Plan"; Remains of the Day" (w/August); "Tears to Shed" (w/ August); "The Wedding Song"
Released: September 2005; 77 minutes. Warner Bros. Rated PG

As a delightful respite from the increasing preponderance of CGI, *Tim Burton's Corpse Bride* presented its ghoulish story through the dying art of stop-motion animation. Burton had previously ventured into this field with his 1993 cult classic *The Nightmare Before Christmas,* on which he had served as producer and creator of the story and characters. This time he shared the directorial credit with Mike Johnson, but the characters he created along with Carlos Grangel were the real accomplishment, a combination of the grotesque and the adorable, including the money-hungry Everglots, she a reed-thin tower of sharp lines and beehive hair, he a roly-poly ball of grimace; a maggot with the voice of Peter Lorre; and an imposing, hunchbacked pastor. The story of a timid lad who, on the eve of his arranged wedding, finds himself accidentally wed to a walking corpse, *Corpse Bride* was short and sweet, visually stunning, and very slight. Danny Elfman provided four songs that were in no way memorable, the best presented of the quartet being "Remains of the Day," sung by the undead (the lead vocal was by Elfman himself) in a barroom as they welcome Victor to the after-life. Its splash of bright colors and merriment, contrasted to the muted color scheme in the fairly lifeless real world, made for an amusing irony.

Tim Burton's Corpse Bride. Victor Van Dort and Corpse Bride.

WALK THE LINE

Screenplay: Gill Dennis, James Mangold
Produced by: James Keach, Cathy Konrad
Directed by: James Mangold
Cast: Joaquin Phoenix, Reese Witherspoon, Ginnifer Goodwin, Robert Patrick, Dallas Roberts, Dan John Miller, Larry Bagby, Shelby Lynne, Tyler Hilton, Waylon Malloy Payne, Shooter Jennings, Sandra Ellis Lafferty, Dan Beene
Songs: "Folsom Prison Blues" (John R. Cash); "Milk Cow Blues" (Kokomo Arnold); "I Was There When It Happened" (Fern Jones); "Lewis Boogie" (Jerry Lee Lewis); "Get Rhythm" (Cash); "You're My Baby" (Cash); "Juke Box Blues" (Helen Carter, Maybelle Carter); "Rock 'n Roll Ruby" (Cash); "That's All Right" (Arthur Crudup); "Home of the Blues (Cash, Lillie McAlpin, Glenn Douglas); "Time's a-Wastin'"; "Candy Man Blues" (John S. Hurt); "I Walk the Line" (Cash); "Wildwood Flower" (A. P. Carter); "It Ain't Me Babe" (Bob Dylan); "Jackson" (Jerry Lieber, Billy Edd Wheeler); "I Got Stripes" (Cash, Charlie Williams); "I'm a Long Way from Home" (Hank Cochran); "Cocaine Blues" (T. J. Arnall); "Ring of Fire" (June Carter, Merle Kilgore); "Long Legged Guitar Pickin' Man" (Marshall Grant)
Released: November 2005; 136 minutes. 20th Century Fox. Rated PG-13

Since country music legend Johnny Cash went down a particularly colorful path of drug addiction, philandering, paternal disapproval, and guilt over his brother's death, he was a natural for a film musical biopic. He also had one of the great frustrating "courtships" in the history of show business, wooing and pursuing fellow artist June Carter, who drove him to the brink of self-destruction with her resistance, until she finally relented to an onstage proposal (in 1968), dramatized here as the finale. Using the triumphant recording of Cash's live album at California's Folsom State Prison as the starting point, James Mangold's film had the singer look back upon his life, starting in 1944 with the devastating loss of his much-admired older brother, following him to his success on the charts with such tunes as "Folsom Prison Blues," "I Walk the Line," and "Ring of Fire," the last, alas, performed only in a truncated manner, as was the custom of too many modern musical biographies. There were also samplings of performances from some of the other icons with whom Cash interacted, such as Jerry Lee Lewis, Elvis Presley, and Waylon Jennings (here played by his son, Shooter).

Doing their own singing, Joaquin Phoenix and Reese Witherspoon gave excellent accounts of the off- and onstage behavior of two of country music's most revered performers, earning Oscar nominations, with Witherspoon becoming the year's winner. Having been sanctioned by Cash and Carter shortly before their deaths (they passed away within months of each other in 2003), *Walk the Line* blended all the expected elements with few surprises and nearly lost track of the joy of music, so much did it wallow in Cash's demons, but for audiences it really clicked. The box office take shot past the $100 million mark, meaning that Johnny and June, or perhaps Joaquin and Reese, meant a lot more to the paying customers than anyone could have imagined.

RENT

Music & lyrics: Jonathan Larson
Screenplay: Stephen Chbosky
Produced by: Jane Rosenthal, Robert De Niro, Chris Columbus, Mark Radcliffe, Michael Barnathan
Directed by: Chris Columbus
Choreography: Keith Young
Cast: Anthony Rapp, Adam Pascal, Rosario Dawson, Jesse L. Martin, Wilson Jermaine Heredia, Idina Menzel, Tracie Thoms, Taye Diggs
Songs: "Seasons of Love"; "Rent"; "You'll See"; "One Song Glory"; "Light My Candle"; Today 4 U"; "Tango Maureen"; "Life Support"; "Another Day"; "Out Tonight"; "No Day but Today"; "Will I?"; "Santa Fe"; "I'll Cover You"; "Over the Moon"; "La Vie Boheme"; "I Should Tell You"; "Take Me or Leave Me"; "Without You"; "Goodbye Love"; "What You Own"; "Your Eyes"
Released: November 2005; 135 minutes. Columbia. Rated PG-13

Although most of his résumé hardly suggested Chris Columbus was the right director to bring Jonathan Larson's seminal stage musical *Rent* to the screen, the filmmaker seemed to do everything right in retaining the integrity and exhilaration of a work that had become nothing less than a cultural touchstone for a generation. Larson's intention to create a rock musical that would introduce a younger demographic to the world of live theatre wound up making an impact beyond his wildest dreams. The tragedy, however, was that he would not live to see it, dying on the eve of the show's Off-Broadway launch in January 1996. The raves and sold-out crowds guaranteed a Broadway transfer and a 5,123 performance, 12-year run, with a Tony Award for Best Musical and a Pulitzer Prize along the way. A modern-day variation on *La bohème,* Larson's version followed the lives of eight struggling twenty-somethings in Manhattan's Lower East Side as they face a future of financial uncertainty, AIDS, and societal indifference. The message to savor life's small rewards and keep an open heart and mind to your fellow human being was never more potent in light of the irony of its creator's untimely passing.

Honoring the work, Columbus surprised everyone by engaging six of the eight cast originals (Rosario Dawson replaced Daphne Ruben-Vega, and Tracie Toms filled in for Fredi Walker) and opening up the piece in ways that were both imaginative and sensible. "Tango Maureen" led into a dazzling dance fantasy; "Santa Fe" had its cast cavorting through a subway car; the title song (staged on the Warner Bros. backlot) literally set the street ablaze; a roving camera caught the "Take Me or Leave Me" standoff between Maureen and Joanne brilliantly; and the simple opening of having the principals sing "Seasons of Love" on a bare stage paid homage to *Rent*'s origins. Several recitative pieces were changed into dialogue or dropped ("Halloween," "Contact," Christmas Bells," etc.), but these omissions in no way diluted the emotional power. Despite having done its source proud, the film caused barely a stir at the box office, just another maddening example of modern audiences' failure to support superior entertainment.

MRS HENDERSON PRESENTS

Screenplay: Martin Sherman
Produced by: Norma Heyman
Directed by: Stephen Frears
Choreography: Eleanor Fazan, Debbie Astell
Cast: Judi Dench, Bob Hoskins, Will Young, Christopher Guest, Kelly Reilly, Thelma Barlow, Anna Brewster, Rosalind Halstead, Sarah Solemani, Natalia Tena, Camille O'Sullivan, Thomas Allen, Samuel Barnett
Songs: "(You May Not Be an Angel but) I'll String Along with You" (Harry Warren, Al Dubin); "Letting in the Sunshine" (Noel Gay); "Inspiration" (P. Boyle, R. Bristow, C. Rose, George Fenton, Simon Chamberlain); "Goody Goody" (Matty Malneck, Johnny Mercer); "Girl in the Little Green Hat" (Jack Scholl, Bradford Browne, Max Rich); "Marseillaise" (traditional); "The Grecian Frieze" (Boyle, Bristow, Rose, Fenton, Chamberlain); "Babies of the Blitz" (D. Barnes, R. Burrows, Fenton, Chamberlain); "Blue Nightfall" (Burton Lane, Frank Loesser); "All the Things You Are" (Jerome Kern, Oscar Hammerstein II); "Sails of the Windmill" (Hyslop/Rose, Fenton, Chamberlain)
Released: December 2005; 103 minutes. Weinstein Co. Rated R

Like the Rita Hayworth vehicle *Tonight and Every Night* (Columbia, 1945), *Mrs Henderson Presents* paid tribute to London's resilient Windmill Theatre, which defiantly stayed open during the Blitz, but the newer film did so with far more wit, poignancy, naughtiness, and complexity. It was also a more intentional attempt to tell the theatre's real story, covering the period before and during World War II and making a potent comment on the necessity of entertainment, the destructive nature of war, and the pointlessness of prurience in the face of far more serious matters. Overall, a wonderful film, though not a full-scale musical in the sense of the earlier version. Instead, *Henderson* featured onstage numbers (both old and newly penned) that often were interrupted or that segued into offstage events or montages. The fragments that are there perfectly captured the tacky yet spirited vaudeville feel the creators were aiming for. Carrying the bulk of the songs were British TV performer Will Young and Camille O'Sullivan, while the plotline was handed over to Judi Dench (in a magnificent, Oscar-nominated turn), as a frivolous British widow who purchases the shuttered Windmill in an effort to give herself something to do, and Bob Hoskins (also serving as executive producer), as the dignified manager who butts heads with her at every turn. It made for a terrific showcase for both actors, and Stephen Frears's assured direction and Martin Sherman's crackling script actually captured the tone of a smart comedy of the era in which the picture was set. Among the new tunes written in the style of the period, the exhilarating "Babies of the Blitz" was the standout.

Mrs Henderson Presents. Kelly Reilly.

THE PRODUCERS

Music & lyrics: Mel Brooks
Screenplay: Mel Brooks, Thomas Meehan
Produced by: Mel Brooks, Jonathan Sanger
Director/Choreographer: Susan Stroman
Cast: Nathan Lane, Matthew Broderick, Uma Thurman, Will Ferrell, Gary Beach, Roger Bart, Eileen Essell, Jon Lovitz, John Barrowman
Songs: "Opening Night"; "We Can Do It"; "I Wanna Be a Producer"; "Der Guten Tag Hop Clop"; "Keep It Gay"; "When You Got it, Flaunt It"; "Along Came Bialy"; "That Face"; "Haben Sie Gehört das Deutsche Band?"; "You Never Say Good Luck on Opening Night"; "Springtime for Hitler"; "Heil Myself"; "You'll Find Your Happiness in Rio"; "Betrayed"; "'Til Him"; "Prisoners of Love"; "There's Nothing Like a Show on Broadway"; "The Hop-Clop Goes On"; "Goodbye!"
Released: December 2005; 135 minutes. Universal/Columbia. Rated PG-13

So thoroughly did the critics and theatre community love Mel Brooks's 2001 musicalization of his off-the-wall 1968 comedy classic *The Producers* that the show wound up with sellout crowds (it ran six years for a total of 2,502 performances) and a record 12 Tony Awards, making a movie adaptation pretty much a sure thing. What Brooks and company had in mind was simply to let the show's stars Nathan Lane and Matthew Broderick, as well as director/choreographer Susan Stroman, repeat their duties onscreen, keeping the performances and staging pretty much intact. It wasn't so much an "opening up" as it was a record of the production, and it thereby looked very studio-bound and old-fashioned in the commercial 2005 motion picture market, which might have been one reason for its box office failure.

Curiously, the show's big opening set piece, "The King of Broadway," was cut prior to the picture's release, though it was crucial in setting the nutty tone of the musical. Instead, Lane and Broderick were asked to bombastically enact the plot setup of a desperate showman concocting a scheme of how to bilk his backers by deliberately putting on a flop show. What had been played to perfection in 1968 by Zero Mostel and Gene Wilder now established a rather shrill and off-putting feel to much of the movie. Also cut from the show's mostly perfunctory score was a brief song for Nazi playwright Franz Liebkind, "In Old Bavaria," and "Where Did We Go Right?" Brooks added two new songs, "You'll Find Your Happiness in Rio" and "There's Nothing Like a Show on Broadway," the latter for the closing credits, but the standout tunes remained "Prisoners of Love" and the unforgettably tasteless showstopper "Springtime for Hitler," both of which came from the original movie.

The Producers. Matthew Broderick.

A PRAIRIE HOME COMPANION

Screenplay: Garrison Keillor
Produced by: Robert Altman, Wren Arthur, Joshua Astrachan, Tony Judge, David
Levy
Directed by: Robert Altman
Cast: Marylouise Burke, Woody Harrelson, L. Q. Jones, Tommy Lee Jones, Garrison Keillor, Kevin Kline, Lindsay Lohan, Virginia Madsen, John C. Reilly, Maya Rudolph, Tim Russell, Sue Scott, Meryl Streep, Lily Tomlin
Songs: "Tishomingo Blues" (Spencer Williams); "Slow Days of Summer" (Garrison Keillor); "Softly and Tenderly" (Will Thompson); "Old Plank Road" (Robin and Linda Williams); "My Minnesota Home (from *The Old Folks at Home;* Stephen Foster, Keillor); "You Have Been a Friend to Me" (A.P. Carter); "Whoop-I-Ti-Yi-Yo" (traditional; Keillor); "Gold Watch & Chain" (Carter); "Let Your Light Shine on Me" (traditional); "The Day Is Short" (Keillor, Richard A. Dworsky); "Goodbye to My Mama" (Keillor); "Bad Jokes" (Keillor); "Frankie & Johnny" (traditional; Keillor); "Red River Valley" (traditional); "While Ye May" (Kevin Kline, Robert Herrick); "In the Sweet By and By" (Sanford Bennett, Joseph Phillbrick Webster)
Released: June 2006; 96 minutes. Picturehouse. Rated PG-13

Garrison Keillor's long-running radio show *A Prairie Home Companion* (it debuted in 1974) bucked modern tradition by being very much in the style of what radio *used* to be, a combination of songs, sketches, jokes, and sound effects (many executed by the marvelous Tom Keith), performed before a live audience. Keillor's hope of somehow transferring this into a motion picture that would mingle his supporting cast of favorites with A-list stars was realized when maverick director Robert Altman came along. Altman figured the best way to adapt *Prairie* to film was simply to reenact a broadcast and then surround the onstage performances with crisscrossing stories of its participants as they presented their last program before the corporate gluttons move in and destroy a form of entertainment considered passé and financially impractical.

This sometimes melancholy meditation on the end of an era and the anticipation of death itself (ironically, Altman died within the year of the movie's release, on November 20, 2006) was chock full of songs, some tossed off like ad libs in the dressing rooms, others spoofing commercial ditties (sometimes incorporating traditional melodies), and some of them full-out numbers. This being a busy Altman ensemble, most of those songs were interrupted by offstage chatter (the picture was shot in the Fitzgerald Theater in St. Paul, Minnesota), or even by other songs, adhering to the filmmaker's signature style of overlapping voices and keeping the audience on its toes, never telegraphing what important details might fly by in the background. Cowboys Woody Harrelson and John C. Reilly had the undisputed musical highlight with their racy "Bad Jokes," while Meryl Streep once again proved herself as fine a singer as she was an actress, notably on "My Mississippi Home." As always, the camps were divided between the Altman devotees and the mainstream, most of whom had given up on the colorfully offbeat director years before.

IDLEWILD

Director/screenplay: Bryan Barber
Produced by: Charles Roven, Robert Guralnick
Choreography: Hinton Battle
Cast: André Benjamin, Antwan A. Patton, Paula Patton, Terrence Howard, Faizon Love, Malinda Williams, Cicely Tyson, Macy Gray, Ben Vereen, Paula Jai Parker, Bobb'e J. Thompson, Patti LaBelle, Ving Rhames
Songs: "Greatest Show on Earth" (André Benjamin); "Makes No Sense" (Benjamin); "Bowtie" (Antwan "Big Boi" Patton, Patrick Brown, Phalon Alexander); "Chronomentrophobia" (Benjamin, Patton); "The Rooster" (Carlton Mahone, Patton, Donny Mathis); "Movin' Cool (The After Party)" (Benjamin, Patton, Joi Gilliam, David Sheats); "Take Off Your Cool" (Benjamin); "Church" (Benjamin, Patton, Kevin Kendrick, Patrick Brown, Myrna Brown); "She Slowly Lives in My Lap" (Benjamin); "Vibrate" (Benjamin); "When I Look in Your Eyes" (Kendrick); "PJ & Rooster" (Benjamin, Patton); "Morris Brown" (Benjamin, Patton)
Released: August 25, 2006; 121 minutes. Universal. Rated R

Hip-hop performers André "André 3000" Benjamin and Antwan A. "Big Boi" Patton, who went under the combined name of OutKast, enlisted their frequent music video collaborator, Bryan Barber, to come up with a motion picture vehicle they hoped would be as unpredictable as their recording output. What they unleashed on the public, *Idlewild,* certainly got points for not playing it safe, but this messy combination of Prohibition-era melodrama, modern sounds grafted onto1930s-style production numbers, and overdone camera tricks turned out more puzzling than satisfying. The story of a straitlaced undertaker who earns extra cash playing piano in a wild Georgia nightspot known as Church, where his irresponsible childhood friend (and part-time bootlegger) Rooster performs, *Idlewild* had some jumpy musical numbers often enhanced by down-and-dirty choreography, punctuating a fairly mundane gangster subplot. Offstage, Benjamin was seen singing with his cuckoo clocks in "Chronomentrophobia" and Patton mumbled a few lyrics while indulging in a shootout/car chase on "Church," but most of the tunes were kept to a stage setting. Songs were often badly sound-balanced, as they uncomfortably wove hip-hop with more traditional music; Benjamin crooning "She Slowly Lives in My Lap" while tending to his lover's corpse was simply cringe-inducing; and neither Ben Vereen nor Patti LaBelle was asked to sing. The best song, "PJ & Rooster"—staged like a lavish MGM production number complete with chorus girls on a gleaming white staircase and Benjamin hopping about his piano—unfortunately had the end credits plastered over it.

Idlewild. Antwan A. Patton.

DREAMGIRLS

Music: Henry Krieger
Lyrics: Tom Eyen (additional lyrics: Siedah Garrett, Willie Reale, Scott Cutler, Beyoncé Knowles, Anne Preven)
Director/screenplay: Bill Condon
Produced by: Laurence Mark
Choreography: Fatima Robinson
Cast: Jamie Foxx, Beyoncé Knowles, Eddie Murphy, Jennifer Hudson, Danny Glover, Anika Noni Rose, Keith Robinson, Sharon Leal, Hinton Battle
Songs: (Lyrics by Eyen unless otherwise stated.) "I'm Looking for Something"; "Goin' Downtown"; "Takin' the Long Way Home"; "Move"; "Fake Your Way to the Top"; "Cadillac Car"; "Steppin' to the Bad Side"; "Love You I Do" (Garrett); "I Want You Baby"; "Family"; "Dreamgirls"; "Heavy"; "It's All Over"; "And I Am Telling You I'm Not Going"; "Love Love Me"; "I'm Somebody"; "When I First Saw You"; "Patience" (Reale); "I Am Changing"; "Perfect World" (Garrett); "I Meant You No Harm"; "Jimmy's Rap"; "Lorrell Loves Jimmy"; "Step on Over"; "I Miss You Old Friend"; "One Night Only"; "Listen" (Cutler, Knowles, Preven); "Hard to Say Goodbye"
Released: December 2006; 130 minutes. DreamWorks/Paramount. Rated PG-13

Insomuch as Michael Bennett's direction of the 1981 Broadway smash *Dreamgirls* (it ran until 1985 for 1,521 performances) was frequently praised for its fluidity, likening it to cinema, it is ironic that it took a full 25 years for this exciting, accessible, and highly popular stage piece to make it to the movies. So good, however, did the transfer turn out to be that it is unimaginable that any earlier adaptation might have been superior in casting, direction, production values, and emotional impact. In the highly capable hands of director-writer Bill Condon (*Chicago's* scenarist), *Dreamgirls* pulsated with music and energy, zipping from one song to the next, easily making the transition from stage-set numbers to songs that sprang forth during dialogue scenes. Charting the rise of a Detroit girl group called the Dreams (clearly patterned on Diana Ross and the Supremes in spirit, though not in incident), the film, like the stage play, lost some momentum along the way once so much attention shifted from its most fascinating character, the headstrong and dazzlingly talented Effie White. Condon's choice of *American Idol* runner-up Jennifer Hudson for this part could not have paid off better, as her gut-wrenching rendition of the show's famous showstopper, "And I Am Telling You I'm Not Going," was every bit as thrilling here as it had been when original cast member Jennifer Holliday performed it to Tony Award glory. Repeating this triumph, Hudson ended up with the Academy Award.

Earning himself a nomination was comedian Eddie Murphy as the womanizing, self-destructive Jimmy Early, showing an amazing ease at singing in the tradition of such soulful pioneers as Jackie Wilson and James Brown. Condon wisely dispensed with several recitative numbers from the stage show, including "Press Conference" and Lorrell's "Ain't It So?," while four new songs were added to the mix. "Patience," a protest number for the Dreams and Early, "Listen" a solo for pop sensation Beyoncé Knowles, and the best of the lot, an Effie number, "Love You I Do," all ended up with Oscar nominations. A great addition to the film year in every respect, *Dreamgirls* scored big at the box office, taking in more than $100 million.

Dreamgirls. Sharon Leal, Beyoncé Knowles, and Anika Noni Rose.

Dreamgirls. Beyoncé Knowles, Anika Noni Rose, and Jennifer Hudson.

ONCE

Director/screenplay: John Carney
Produced by: Martina Niland
Cast: Glen Hansard, Markéta Irglová, Bill Hodnett, Danuse Ktrestova, Alastair Foley, Gerry Hendrick, Hugh Walsh, Kate Haugh, Geoff Minogue
Songs: "And the Healing Has Begun" (Van Morrison); "Say It to Me Now" (Glen Hansard); "All the Way Down" (Hansard); "Falling Slowly" (Hansard, Markéta Irglová); "Leave" (Hansard); "If You Want Me" (Irglová); "Lies" (Hansard, Irglová); "Gold" (Fergus O'Farrell); "Trying to Pull Myself Away" (Hansard); "When Your Mind's Made Up" (Hansard); "Fallen from the Sky" (Hansard); "The Hill" (Irglová); "Once" (Hansard)
Released: May 2007; 87 minutes. Fox Searchlight. Rated R

A movie that ended up getting on the good side of pretty much everybody by its sheer lack of pretentions, *Once* was shot in and around Dublin with a handheld camera and the most miniscule of budgets. The simple story of a part-time street singer and vacuum cleaner repairman who is goaded into realizing his potential as a professional musician by an immigrant who assists him in cutting a demo, the film, refreshingly, gave over a good degree of its brief running time to its songs. Rather than offer mere samplings of numbers, or draw attention away from them by dialogue or concurrent action, as was too often the norm in the modern musical, director-writer John Carney pretty much let the music play, reminding audiences that this is, after all, the very center of the life of his chief protagonist and should therefore dominate the screen.

Having once been a member of the Irish band The Frames, Carney contacted its leader, Glen Hansard, to write him some songs for the film he was developing and ended up realizing that only Hansard himself could bring authenticity to the part, casting him, along with pianist and songwriter Markéta Irglová, to carry the picture. Although most of the numbers consisted of performances of Hansard on guitar or in the recording studio, Irglova did get to sing a composition of her own, "If You Want Me," while walking through the streets of Dublin at night, listening to the tune in her headphones, the closest concession to a traditional musical moment. Her big duet with Hansard, "Falling Slowly," sung in a music shop and representing their bonding moment, was the standout, however, and ended up the year's Oscar winner for Best Song.

Once. Markéta Irglová and Glen Hansard.

HAIRSPRAY

Music: Marc Shaiman
Lyrics: Marc Shaiman, Scott Wittman
Screenplay: Leslie Dixon. Based on the screenplay by John Waters and the musical play by Thomas Meehan and Mark O'Donnell
Produced by: Neil Meron, Craig Zaidan
Director/choreographer: Adam Shankman
Cast: John Travolta, Michelle Pfeiffer, Christopher Walken, Amanda Bynes, James Marsden, Queen Latifah, Brittany Snow, Zac Efron, Elijah Kelley, Allison Janney, Nikki Blonsky, Taylor Parks, Paul Dooley, Jerry Stiller
Songs: "Good Morning Baltimore"; "The Nicest Kids in Town"; "It Takes Two"; "(The Legend of) Miss Baltimore Crabs"; "Breakout"; "I Can Hear the Bells"; "Ladies' Choice"; "The New Girl in Town"; "Welcome to the 60s"; "Run and Tell That"; "Big, Blonde and Beautiful"; "Boink Boink"; "Trouble on the Line"; "(You're) Timeless to Me"; "I Know Where I've Been"; "Tied Up in the Knots of Sin"; "Without Love"; "(It's) Hairspray"; "You Can't Stop the Beat"; "Come So Far (Got So Far to Go)"; "Mama, I'm a Big Girl Now"; "Cooties"
Released: July 2007; 117 minutes. New Line Cinema. Rated PG

A celebration of local teen dance shows of the early 1960s, John Waters's 1988 comedy (and hands down his best movie) *Hairspray* was so tuneful in spirit that it cried out for the full musical treatment, which it got in a big way. With a glorious score by Marc Shaiman and Scott Wittman, and just the right balance of heart, social commentary, and the Waters trademark celebration of all things tacky, the 2002 Broadway version of *Hairspray* turned into one of the highpoints of the decade. It earned eight Tony Awards (including that for Best Musical) and totaling 2,642 performances in its six-and-a-half-year run. The story of how chubby teen Tracy Turnblad's determined efforts to become a regular dancer on Baltimore's *The Corny Collins Show* leads to her helping to end discrimination against the black community, *Hairspray* offered an affectionate glimpse of a bygone era of teased hair and more innocent values, while also criticizing the backward traditions that maintained segregation both on the airwaves and in urban living. Carrying on the original movie's novelty of having Tracy's mom be played by a man (after Waters's favorite, Divine, in his last role), gravel-voiced Harvey Fierstein made an indelible impression onstage. Although there was much dissension over him not getting to repeat his role onscreen, his replacement, John Travolta, found his own degree of pathos and hilarity and made the part very much his own triumph.

Working closely with Shaiman and Wittman, director Adam Shankman turned out to be ideal to guide the project to the big screen, having been a former dancer and choreographer. Therefore, the dynamic vibe that had kept the show exploding with energy was successfully reimagined onscreen, as the spirit never flagged, with one highlight after another, from Tracy's joyful opening ode "Good Morning Baltimore" (actually filmed on the streets of Toronto), to the dizzy sendup of romantic ballads "I Can Hear the Bells" (complete with its heroine gliding out of a bathroom stall with a train of toilet paper), to the smashing "Welcome to the 60s," which was capped off by Travolta and newcomer Nikki Blonsky joining the happy celebrants of Baltimore as they danced in the streets, the sort of moment that reminded us all of why we love musicals. Of the original stage score, a jailhouse number, "The Big Dollhouse," was omitted, while "It Takes Two" was trimmed away to a few lines, and both "I'm a Big Girl Now" (featuring three Tracys: Ricki Lake from the original film; Marisa Jarret Winokur from the show; and Blonsky) and "Cooties" were saved for the end credits. Those credits also featured one of several new tunes, the upbeat "Come So Far (Got So Far to Go)," which was so good it was hard to comprehend why the Oscar committee did not include it among that year's Best Song nominees.

Hairspray. Christopher Walken and John Travolta.

Hairspray. Jerry Stiller, John Travolta, and Nikki Blonsky.

ROMANCE & CIGARETTES

Director/screenplay: John Turturro
Produced by: John Penotti, John Turturro
Choreography: Tricia Brouk
Cast: James Gandolfini, Susan Sarandon, Kate Winslet, Steve Buscemi, Bobby Cannavale, Mandy Moore, Mary-Louise Parker, Aida Turturro, Christopher Walken, Barbara Sukowa, Elaine Stritch, Eddie Izzard, Amy Sedaris
Songs: "A Man without Love" (John Barry Mason, Daniele Pace, Mario Panzeri, Roberto Livraghi); "When the Savior Reached Down for Me" (traditional); "Piece of My Heart" (Bert Berns, Jerry Ragavoy); "Hot Pants" (James Brown, Fred Wesley); "Prisoner of Love" (Russ Columbo, Clarence Gaskill, Leo Robin); "Delilah" (Les Reed, Barry Mason); "I Want Candy" (Bert Berns, Robert Feldman, Gerald Goldstein, Richard Gottehrer); "Scapricciatiello (Do You Love Me Like You Kiss Me)" (Vento, Albano, Manning, Hoffman); "Red Headed Woman" (Bruce Springsteen); "Little Water Song" (Nick Cave, Bruno Pisek); "It Must Be Him" (Maurice Vidalin, Gilbert Becaud, Mack David); "The Girl That I Marry" (Irving Berlin); "Ten Commandments of Love" (Marshall Paul)
Released: September 2007; 106 minutes. Boroturro. Not rated

Actor John Turturro's third film as a director-writer, *Romance & Cigarettes* might best be described as a "karaoke musical." In it, the cast members broke into song, competing with the actual recordings, as opposed to the *Pennies from Heaven* style of mouthing the songs without their own vocals being audible. This gimmick was patched onto a plot about a construction worker whose infidelity with a trash-talking lingerie saleswoman causes a bitter resentment in his wife. It made for one strange movie, albeit one with some pointedly funny commentary on the never-ending battle of the sexes. Because it sure didn't resemble anything else around, it earned points simply for being so bravely "out there." In a prime example of its quirkiness, Cyndi Lauper's recording of "Prisoner of Love" played as James Gandolfini sang along while preparing for his circumcision. Meanwhile, Susan Sarandon and Christopher Walken musically cavorted with umbrellas, and a street-full of pregnant ladies danced. Not MGM's Freed Unit, to be sure.

Despite favorable mention at film festivals, UA/MGM let the finished movie languish on the shelf for two years, until Turturro himself distributed it in a few select venues. While it was difficult to judge the vocal prowess of the stars, it was great fun seeing them throw themselves into this oddball project with such abandon, with especially good work from Kate Winslet, as Gandolfini's proudly vulgar lover; the ever-dependably weird Walken, as an Elvis obsessive relative; and Elaine Stritch, not allotted a song but stealing the show in her single scene as Gandolfini's truculent mom.

Romance & Cigarettes. Susan Sarandon.

ACROSS THE UNIVERSE

Screenplay: Dick Clement, Ian La Frenais
Story: Julie Taymor, Clement La Frenais
Produced by: Suzanne Todd, Jennifer Todd, Matthew Gross
Directed by: Julie Taymor
Choreography: Daniel Ezralow
Cast: Evan Rachel Wood, Jim Sturgess, Joe Anderson, Dana Fuchs, Martin Luther McCoy, T. V. Carpio, Joe Cocker, Bono, Eddie Izzard, Salma Hayek
Songs: By John Lennon and Paul McCartney: "Girl"; "Helter Skelter"; "Hold Me Tight"; "All My Loving"; "I Want to Hold Your Hand"; "With a Little Help from My Friends"; "It Won't Be Long"; "I've Just Seen a Face"; "Let It Be"; "Come Together"; "Why Don't We Do It in the Road?"; "If I Fell"; "I Want You (She's So Heavy)"; "Dear Prudence"; "I Am the Walrus"; "Being for the Benefit of Mr. Kite"; "Because"; "Oh! Darling"; "Strawberry Fields Forever"; "Revolution"; "Across the Universe"; "Happiness Is a Warm Gun"; "Blackbird"; "Hey Jude"; "Don't Let Me Down"; "All You Need Is Love"; "Lucy in the Sky with Diamonds." By George Harrison: "Blue Jay Way"; "Something"; "While My Guitar Gently Weeps." By Lennon, McCartney, Harrison, and Ringo Starr: "Flying"
Released: September 2007; 133 minutes. Columbia. Rated PG-13

Beatles fans with grim memories of the 1978 film of *Sgt. Pepper's Lonely Hearts Club Band* had reason to be especially leery of director Julie Taymor's proposal to comment on the turbulent changes of the 1960s by stringing a storyline together consisting of songs by the Fab Four. Luckily, while it contained neither much of a plot to get excited over, nor anything akin to the final statement on what the decade and its social uprisings were all about, *Across the Universe* did no disservice to the most influential pop group of the century. The story involved a Liverpool shipyard worker who comes to America to find his absent dad and ends up falling in love with a young girl from an affluent family as their lives are torn apart by upheaval and war. *Across the Universe* found room for no less than 31 Beatles tunes throughout the plot, managing for the most part not to have to stretch in order to accommodate lyrics that were never intended to comment on this particular screenplay.

With the exception of comedian Eddie Izzard's croaky vocals on "Being for the Benefit of Mr. Kite"; the cast was up to the challenge and sang the tunes quite well, especially leading man Jim Sturgess, who bore more than a passing resemblance to Paul McCartney, no doubt a deliberate intention. Taymor's inventive visuals, which often reminded one of the madness of director Ken Russell, was a fusion of color and near-chaos, lively and surreal but never off-putting. There was a psychedelic drug trip via Bono's striking version of "I Am the Walrus," a mind-bending induction-center nightmare to the tune of "I Want You (She's So Heavy)," a trio of Joe Cockers wailing "Come Together," Dana Fuchs's potently Janis Joplin–like "Helter Skelter," and some plaintive renditions of "Something" and "Strawberry Fields Forever" by Sturgess. The film was packaged and sold like a big deal but ended up being treated like something for the cult category.

WALK HARD: THE DEWEY COX STORY

Screenplay: Judd Apatow, Jake Kasdan
Produced by: Judd Apatow, Jake Kasdan, Clayton Townsend
Directed by: Jake Kasdan
Cast: John C. Reilly, Jenna Fischer, Raymond J. Barry, Margo Martindale, Kristen Wiig, Chip Hormess, Conner Rayburn, Tim Meadows, Chris Parnell, Matt Besser, David Krumholtz
Songs: "Gamblin' Man" (David Honeyboy Edwards); "Cut My Brother in Half Blues" (Michael Andrews, Judd Apatow, Jake Kasdan); "Take My Hand" (Antonio Ortiz, Apatow, Kasdan); "Jump Little Children" (Robert Shad); "(Mama) You Got to Love Your Negro Man" (Andrews, John C. Reilly, Robert Walker, Apatow, Kasdan); "That's Amore" (Harry Warren, Jack Brooks); "Walk Hard" (Marshall Crenshaw, Reilly, Apatow, Kasdan); "A Life without You (Is No Life at All)" (Mike Viola); "Let's Duet" (Charlie Wadhams, Benji Hughes); "Darling" (Viola, Reilly); "Guilty as Charged" (Wadhams, Gus Seyffert); "Royal Jelly" (Dan Bern); "Let Me Hold You (Little Man)" (Bern, Viola, Manish Raval); "Black Sheep" (Andrews, Van Dyke Parks); "There's a Change a'Happening (I Can Feel It)" (Bern, Andrews, Apatow, Kasdan); "Starman" (David Bowie); "Weeping on the Inside" (Bern, Viola, Reilly); "Beautiful Ride" (Bern, Viola); "(I Hate You) Big Daddy" (Viola); "(Have You Heard the News) Dewey Cox Died" (Bern); "Farmer Glickstein" (Bern)
Released: December 2007; 96 minutes. Columbia. Rated R

The music star biopic—most specifically such recent entries as *Ray* and *Walk the Line*—came in for a satirical roasting in *Walk Hard: The Dewey Cox Story.* Tracing the rise and fall and comeback of the fictional Dewey Cox, who is haunted by a childhood accident in which he accidentally cut his brother in half with a machete, Jake Kasdan and Judd Apatow tapped into myriad musical (not to mention hair and clothing) styles from rock 'n' roll to folk to protest to disco. They even mocked the crossover of certain rock performers into an orchestral, more complicated method of production, here with Cox's "Black Sheep," which includes a goat and African Bushmen on the track.

The film called for an actor adept at parody who could actually sing, and John C. Reilly was the ideal choice (he even contributed to the writing of some tunes), capturing Dewey's dopey sincerity and show-business selfishness (sinking into the requisite clichés of womanizing and drugs) with the right degree of winking sendup. If things weren't always consistently on the mark, there were some glorious bits, ribbing the Beatles (cleverest of all being Paul Rudd as a very Liverpudlian John Lennon) and 1970s variety shows. The innuendo-ridden "Let's Duet" and the Bob Dylan spoof "Royal Jelly" were among the funniest of the parody numbers, as was the catchy title song, which Jackson Browne, Jewel, Lyle Lovett, and Ghostface Killah joined in on near the finale. Perhaps not sure what was being lampooned, or embracing the clichés too affectionately to see them skewered, audiences skipped it.

Walk Hard: The Dewey Cox Story. Jack Black, Paul Rudd, Jason Schwartzman, and Justin Long.

Sweeney Todd: The Demon Barber of Fleet Street. Johnny Depp and Helena Bonham Carter.

SWEENEY TODD:
THE DEMON BARBER OF FLEET STREET

Music & lyrics: Stephen Sondheim
Screenplay: John Logan; based on the musical by Stephen Sondheim and Hugh Wheeler, from an adaptation of *Sweeney Todd* by Christopher Bond
Produced by: Richard D. Zanuck, Walter Parkes, Laurie MacDonald, John Logan
Directed by: Tim Burton
Cast: Johnny Depp, Helena Bonham Carter, Alan Rickman, Timothy Spall, Sacha Baron Cohen, Jamie Campbell Bower, Laura Michelle Kelly, Jayne Wisener, Edward Sanders
Songs: "No Place Like London"; "The Worst Pies in London"; "Poor Thing"; "My Friends"; "Green Finch and Linnet Bird"; "Alms! Alms!"; "Johanna"; "Pirelli's Miracle Elixir"; "The Contest"; "Wait"; "Ladies in Their Sensitivities"; "Pretty Women"; "Epiphany"; "A Little Priest"; "Johanna (Act II)"; "God, That's Good!"; "By the Sea"; "Not While I'm Around"
Released: December 2007; 116 minutes. DreamWorks/Warner Bros. Rated R

Another long-dormant stage property benefited from the movies' "musical renaissance" of the 2000s, there being few of this genre that suggested such dazzling cinematic possibilities as Stephen Sondheim's masterpiece, *Sweeney Todd: The Demon Barber of Fleet Street*. The fog-swirling, gas-lit cobblestone streets of Victorian London that provided the setting for this particular gothic story were realized to the fullest (the Oscar-winning sets, built at Britain's Pinewood Studios, were by Dante Ferretti) by one of the movies' masters of the macabre, Tim Burton, who also rose to the occasion when it came to producing both the chills and the emotional punch. Sondheim's 1979 Broadway tuner had its origins in a straightforward version of the Todd legend, a play by Christopher Bond in which unjustly imprisoned barber Benjamin Barker returns to London seeking vengeance on the corrupt judge who stole away his wife and child. His unholy alliance with pie-shop proprietor Mrs. Lovett results in a gleeful rampage of cannibalism as Barker, masquerading as Sweeney Todd, offs his tonsorial customers so that they can provide the filling for Lovett's meat pies. (Burton made sure blood was in abundance, often spurting it right into the camera lens.)

Keeping things close-up and intimate, rather than emphasizing the "grand" in this Grand Guignol, Burton chose to eliminate the lyrics from the show's ever-present "The Ballad of Sweeney Todd," a driving and exciting piece of music sung by the chorus, which had commented on the action at hand. Gone, too, from the original score were sailor Anthony's duet with Johanna, "Kiss Me"; Judge Turpin's perverse rendition of "Johanna" (ultimately chopped from most stage versions as well); "Wigmaker Sequence," and "The Letter," while only the lead-in to "Ladies in Their Sensitivities" remained, and "God, That's Good" dropped the choral parts, which included the song's title phrase. While Bonham Carter was a weak singer, she certainly looked the part of the crazed Mrs. Lovett; Depp (in an Oscar-nominated performance), also not a trained vocalist, was frighteningly unsettling as the brooding Todd; Rickman and Spall made for chillingly sleazy villains; and the real singing was left to unknowns Bower, Wisener, and young Sanders. Despite the compromises, *Sweeney Todd* was a deeply satisfying, unforgettable experience overall.

MAMMA MIA!

Music & lyrics: Benny Andersson, Björn Ulvaeus; some songs with Stig Anderson
Screenplay: Catherine Johnson
Produced by: Judy Craymer, Gary Goetzman
Directed by: Phyllida Lloyd
Choreography: Anthony van Laast
Cast: Meryl Streep, Pierce Brosnan, Colin Firth, Stellan Skarsgaard, Julie Walters, Dominic Cooper, Amanda Seyfried, Christine Baranski
Songs: "I Have a Dream"; "Honey, Honey"; "Money, Money, Money"; "Mamma Mia"; "Chiquitita"; "Dancing Queen"; "Our Last Summer"; "Lay All Your Love on Me"; "Super Trouper"; "Gimme! Gimme! Gimme! (A Man after Midnight)"; "Voulez-Vous"; "SOS"; "Does You Mother Know"; "Slipping through My Fingers"; "The Winner Takes It All"; "I Do, I Do, I Do, I Do, I Do"; "When All Is Said and Done"; "Take a Chance on Me"; "Waterloo"; "Thank You for the Music"
Released: July 2008; 108 minutes. Universal. Rated PG-13

Pilfering a plotline from the 1968 Gina Lollobrigida comedy *Buona Sera, Mrs. Campbell* and embellishing it with nearly two dozen ABBA pop hits resulted, unexpectedly, in one of the most commercially successful endeavors in theatre history. Opening in the West End in 1999 and then on Broadway two years later (and still running as of the publication of this book), *Mamma Mia!* defied all criticism (of which there was plenty) to become the sort of audience sensation of which others can only dream. Despite her uninspired staging, Phyllida Law was enlisted to bring the property to the big screen and botched up more than once with her overly busy camerawork that frequently pulled focus away from or interrupted the numbers. "Gimme! Gimme! Gimme" kept getting relegated to the background; "Lay All Your Love on Me" was a promising set piece left unfulfilled despite the appearance of flippered beach boys; and the most exciting dance number onstage, "Voulez-Vous," was butchered beyond coherence.

The perfunctory plot involved young Sophie Sheridan inviting to her upcoming Greek wedding the three men she suspects might be the father she never knew, putting her mother on the spot. The already established pop lyrics did not always coincide with what was happening onscreen, but it was a constant relief to get away from the threadbare script and back to the undeniably infectious tunes that had always been such fun to hear on the radio. Four songs from the stage version, "The Name of the Game," "Under Attack," "One of Us," and "Knowing Me, Knowing You," were dropped, while another ABBA song, "When All Is Said and Done," was added for a wedding-reception toast. Colin Firth had a nice moment strumming the guitar and warbling "Our Last Summer"; the undisputed highlight was Meryl Streep's smashing rendition of "The Winner Takes It All," performed on a windswept hilltop; and there were bursts of bright energy throughout, including the lady islanders hopping about a pier to "Dancing Queen." The box office take was enormous, showing that *Mamma Mia!*'s hold on the public was unstoppable.

HIGH SCHOOL MUSICAL 3: SENIOR YEAR

Screenplay: Peter Barsocchini
Produced by: Bill Borden, Barry Rosenbush
Directed by: Kenny Ortega
Choreography: Kenny Ortega, Bonnie Story, Charles Kaplow
Cast: Zac Efron, Vanessa Hudgens, Ashley Tisdale, Lucas Grabeel, Corbin Bleu, Monique Coleman, Olesya Rulin, Alyson Reed, Matt Prokop, Jemma McKenzie-Brown
Songs: "Now or Never" (Matthew Gerrard, Robbie Nevill); "Right Here Right Now" (Jamie Houston); "I Want It All" (Gerrard, Nevill); "Can I Have This Dance" (Adam Anders, Nikki Hassman); "A Night to Remember" (Gerrard, Nevill); "Just Wanna Be with You" (Andy Dodd, Adam Watts); "The Boys Are Back" (Gerrard, Nevill); "Walk Away" (Houston); "Scream" (Houston); "Last Chance" (Randy Petersen, Kevin Quinn); "We're All in This Together" (Gerrard, Nevill); "High School Musical" (Gerrard, Nevill); "Just Getting Started" (Houston)
Released: October 2008; 109 minutes. Walt Disney Pictures. Rated G

Vapid and mechanical as it was, the Disney Channel's *High School Musical* (2006) became nothing less than a cultural phenomenon, introducing a younger generation to the whole concept of telling a story through song and dance and thereby making it acceptable to view other such strange and wonderful creatures. An imaginatively titled sequel, *High School Musical 2* (2007), was quickly rolled off the assembly line to further huge audiences, and then the Disney studio made the curious decision to let part 3 be unleashed to theatres instead of cable TV. *High School Musical 3: Senior Year* therefore had a bigger budget and was something of an improvement over its predecessors, although like them, it was stitched together by Peter Barsocchini's by-the-numbers script, which involved teen lovers Troy and Gabriella's uncertainty about their future spent at different colleges. (*HSM3* was shot in Salt Lake City.) The more important plotline centered around the school's big "musicale" and bitchy Sharpay Evans's efforts to take center stage in the show, choreographed by her presumably gay brother, Ryan—although this being a Disney fantasy for the family trade, no sexual revelations were made. The exuberant dancing (ranging from Sharpay and Ryan's dream sequence "I Want It All" to the junkyard pas de deux "The Boys Are Back") was far more impressive than the generic tunes, although the title song (done at graduation to a swirl of gowns) was pretty catchy. The standout cast member remained the series's breakout star, Zac Efron; the movie made lots of money; and the Disney people stayed happy.

High School Musical 3: Senior Year. Zac Efron and Vanessa Hudgens.

REPO! THE GENETIC OPERA

Music & lyrics/screenplay: Darren Smith, Terrance Zdunich
Produced by: Daniel Jason Heffner, Carl Mazzocone, Oren Koules, Mark Burg
Directed by: Darren Lynn Bousman
Cast: Alex Vega, Paul Sorvino, Anthony Stewart Head, Sarah Brightman, Paris Hilton, Bill Moseley, Ogre, Terrance Zdunich
Songs: (partial list) "Vuk-R" (Yoshiki); "Repo Man" (Smith, Zdunich, Yoshiki); "Aching Hour" (Smith, Zdunich)
Released: November 2008; 98 minutes. Lionsgate. Rated R

First performed in miniature in LA rock clubs and coffeehouses before being expanded for fringe theatre and Off-Broadway, *Repo! The Genetic Opera* was then turned into a midnight cult-wannabe motion picture shot in Toronto, with deliberately garish photography, bits of animation, and comic book panels setting the tone for yet another nightmarish look into the not-so-distant-future. Here, a powerful corporation called GeneCo makes its fortune in donor transplants, only to send out a rampaging repo man to extract the organs in question when payments are not made. It was grotesque in the extreme, with body parts and blood galore on display (i.e., following her big onstage performance, Sarah Brightman gouged her eyes out). Writers Darren Smith and Terrance Zdunich unfortunately steered clear of both melody and wit, instead having their cast sing one recitative after another describing the situations on hand, giving little sense of variation to the proceedings. With the exception of three titles, none of the tunes, which seemed to bear such names as "Infected," "It's a Thankless Job," "Graverobber," and "Seventeen," were listed in the end credits. This monumentally annoying movie was dumped quickly on the market in a few select venues, garnering some of the year's worst reviews.

Repo! The Genetic Opera. Kevin Ogilvie and Anthony Head.

CADILLAC RECORDS

Director/screenplay: Darnell Martin
Produced by: Andrew Lack, Sofia Sondervan
Cast: Adrien Brody, Jeffrey Wright, Gabrielle Union, Columbus Short, Cedric the Entertainer, Emmanuelle Chriqui, Eamonn Walker, Mos Def, Beyoncé Knowles
Songs: "I'm a Man" (Ellas McDaniel); "Country Blues" (Robert Leroy Johnson, McKinley Morganfield); "I Can't Be Satisfied" (Morganfield); "Forty Days and Forty Nights" (Bernhard Roth); "Juke" (Walter Jacobs); "I'm Your Hoochie Coochie Man" (Willie Dixon); "My Babe" (Dixon); "Smokestack Lightnin'" (Chester Burnett); "Maybellene" (Chuck Berry); "No Particular Place to Go" (Berry); "Promised Land" (Berry); "All I Could Do Was Cry" (Berry Gordy, Roquel Davis, Gwen Gordy Fuqua); "At Last" (Harry Warren, Mack Gordon); "Trust in Me" (Milton Ager, Jean Schwartz); "I'd Rather Go Blind" (Billy Foster, Ellington Jordan); "Last Night" (Jacobs); "Evolution of Man" (McDaniel, A. Bailey, Steve Jordan); "Once in a Lifetime" (Beyoncé Knowles, Amanda Ghost, Scott McFarnon, Ian Dench, James Dring, Jody Street)
Released: December 2008; 109 minutes. TriStar. Rated R

Dramatizing the history of Chess Records (1950–69) allowed director-writer Darnell Martin to pay tribute not only to cofounder Leonard Chess (Leonard's brother, Philip, was pretty much relegated to the background), but to five of its most influential artists: Muddy Waters, Little Walter, Howlin' Wolf, Chuck Berry, and Etta James. Therefore, audiences got a half-dozen mini-biopics in one. Fortunately, not only were all of the actors playing these singers outstanding in their performances, but they were required to mimic the vocalizing style of the artists they were embodying, which they did equally well. *Cadillac Records* was a look at the fleeting and corruptive nature of fame, as all the performers find themselves being pushed from the limelight for the next up-and-comer, most of them stumbling into the expected biopic pitfalls of alcohol, multiple sex partners, and spendthrift ways (only Howlin' Wolf was depicted as having the good sense to look after his money). The film was also potent in showing the unfortunate effect that racism had on their lives, as their skin color still negated their artistic accomplishments in the eyes of so many.

While Martin let too much of the music get interrupted by dialogue and quick montages, there was still plenty to savor, with a frighteningly imposing Eammon Walker as the practical Wolf; a playful Mos Def as the label's biggest attraction, Chuck Berry; and an amazingly good Beyoncé Knowles (the film's executive producer) as the tough but vulnerable Etta James. Knowles was allotted the most onscreen performing time, with top-notch renditions of "At Last" and "All I Could Do Was Cry," plus an original composition by herself and several others, "Once in a Lifetime," sung over the closing credits.

Cadillac Records. Cedric the Entertainer, Adrien Brody, and Jeffrey Wright.

HANNAH MONTANA—THE MOVIE

Screenplay: Dan Berendsen
Produced by: Miles Millar, Alfred Gough
Directed by: Peter Chelsom
Cast: Miley Cyrus, Billy Ray Cyrus, Emily Osment, Jason Earles, Mitchel Tate Musso, Moises Arias, Lucas Till, Vanessa Williams, Margo Martindale, Peter Gunn
Songs: "The Best of Both Worlds" (Matthew Gerrard, Robbie Nevil); "The Good Life" (Gerrard, Bridget Benenate); "Let's Get Crazy" (Coleen Fitzpatrick, Michael Kotch, Dave Derby, Michael Smith, Stefanie Ridel, Mim Nervo, Liv Nervo); "Backwards" (Marcel and Tony Mullins); "Bless the Broken Road" (Bobby Boyd, Jeff Hanna, Marcus Hummon); "Don't Walk Away" (Miley Cyrus, John Shanks, Hillary Lindsey); "Dream" (Shanks, Kara DioGuardi); "Back to Tennessee" (Billy Ray Cyrus, Tamara Dunn, Matthew Wilder); "Crazier" (Taylor Swift, Robert Ellis Orrall); "Hoedown Throwdown" (Adam Anders, Nikki Hassman); "Butterfly Fly Away" (Alan Silvestri, Glen Ballard); "Rockstar" (Aristeois Archontis, Jeannie Lurie, Chen Neeman); "The Climb" (Jessi Alexander, Jon Mabe); "You'll Always Find Your Way Back" (Swift, Martin Johnson); "Let's Do This" (Derek George, Tim Owens, Adam Tefteller, Ali Theodore); "Spotlight" (Scott Culler, Anne Preven)
Released: April 2009; 102 minutes. Walt Disney. Rated G

Average high school student by day, singing sensation by night: *Hannah Montana* was one of the Disney Channel's biggest draws with the preteen female demographic, turning its star, Miley Cyrus, into a pop culture icon of the moment. The further success of a 3-D concert film, *Hannah Montana/Miley Cyrus: Best of Both Worlds* (2008), guaranteed a big-screen spin-off for the series with Cyrus and the rest of the cast principals on hand, including her real-life father, country singer Billy Ray Cyrus, portraying her widowed dad. Keeping things very chaste and unsophisticated for the intended audience, *Hannah Montana—The Movie* was just more of what unfolded on weekly TV, combining fairly forgettable pop numbers with a predictable plot that has Miley Stewart forced to return to her Tennessee roots when her fame (as Hannah Montana) becomes too much for her father to endure. Keeping up her masquerade while falling for a too-cute-to-be-true ranch hand (Lucas Till), Miley/Hannah ends up doing a fund-raiser to thwart an evil real estate developer. Too many songs were cut into fragments or merely shunted to the soundtrack, but there was a sweet duet for the Cyruses, "Butterfly Fly Away," and a lively line dance to "Hoedown Throwdown," reprised by most of the cast during the end credits.

Hannah Montana—The Movie. Miley Cyrus and company.

PASSING STRANGE

Music: Stew, Heidi Rodewald
Lyrics & book: Stew
Directed by: Spike Lee (from Annie Dorsen's staging)
Produced by: Spike Lee, Steve Klein
Choreography: Karole Armitage
Cast: Stew, Daniel Breaker, De'Adre Aziza, Eisa Davis, Colman Domingo, Chad Goodridge, Rebecca Naomi Jones, Christian Casan, Christian Gibbs, Heidi Rodewald
Songs: "Prologue (We Might Play All Night)"; "Baptist Fashion Show"; "Church Blues Revelation/Freight Train"; "Arlington Hill"; "Sole Brother"; "Must Have Been High"; "Mom Songs"; "Merci Beaucoup, M. Godard"; "Amsterdam"; "Keys (Marianna), "Keys (It's Alright), "We Just Had Sex"; "Stoned"; "Berlin: A Black Hole with Taxis"; "May Day (There's a Riot Going On)"; "What's Inside Is Just a Lie/And Now I'm Ready to Explode"; "Identity"; "The Black One"; "Come Down Now"; "Youth's Unfinished Song"; "Work the Wound"; "Passing Phase"; "Cue Music"; "Love Like That"
Released: August 2009; 136 minutes. Sundance Selects. Not rated

A startlingly different concept in musical theatre, musician Stew's *Passing Strange* presented his autobiographical quest for identity during his trips to Amsterdam and Berlin, through narration and song. As a cast of six enacted and sang his story, Stew (real name Mark Stewart) remained onstage with his guitar, providing the connecting narrative thread while his musicians performed in miniature orchestra pits allowing them to be visible to the audience. Partially a concert, the show's strength came from its thought-provoking, emotionally charged book about the elusive quest for authenticity and from its energetic cast, chief among them Daniel Breaker, in a smashing, star-making turn as Stew's younger self.

Following a 2006 run at Berkeley Rep, and then its Off-Broadway debut in 2007 at New York's Public Theatre, *Passing Strange* opened on Broadway at the Belasco Theatre on February 28, 2008, to raves, eventually earning a Tony Award for Stew's script. Rather than put his very distinctive cinematic touch to the work by opening it up into an actual film, director Spike Lee instead chose to simply shoot the piece (on video) during its July 20, 2008, closing performance, allowing for close-ups and emphasis on certain minutiae, but letting the work speak for itself. The movie was given a handful of token playdates in movie theatres on top of being made available on-demand on cable television.

Passing Strange. Daniel Breaker and Stew.

FAME

Screenplay: Allison Burnett
Produced by: Tom Rosenberg, Gary Lucchesi, Richard Wright, Mark Canton
Directed by: Kevin Tancharoen
Choreography: Marguerite Derricks
Cast: Asher Book, Kristy Flores, Paul Iacono, Paul McGill, Naturi Naughton, Kay Panabaker, Kherington Payne, Collins Pennié, Walter Perez, Anna Maria Perez de Tagle, Debbie Allen, Charles S. Dutton, Kelsey Grammer, Megan Mullally, Bebe Neuwirth
Songs: "Habanera" (Georges Bizet), "All That Jazz" (Fred Ebb, John Kander), "This is My Life" (Damon Elliott), "Someone to Watch Over Me" (George and Ira Gershwin), "Out Here on My Own" (Lesley Gore, Michael Gore), "Can't Hide from Love" (James Poyser, Phonte Coleman), "The-Boyz-in-the-Hood" (O'Shea Jackson, Andre Young, Eric Wright), "Try" (Alon Levitan), "What a Mighty God We Serve" (traditional), "Straight Up" (Elliot Wolff), "Tubthumping" (Judith Abbott, Bruce Duncan, Paul Greco, Darren Hamer, Alice Nutter, Nigel Hunter, Louise Watts, Allen Whalley), "One Week" (Ed Robertson), "You Took Advantage of Me" (Richard Rodgers, Lorenz Hart), "You Made Me Love You" (James V. Monaco, Joseph McCarthy), "Get on the Floor" (James Poyser, Phone Coleman, Carlitta Durand), "Hold Your Dream" (Matthew James Murphy), "Fame" (Michael Gore, Dean Pitchford)
Released: September 2009; 105 minutes. MGM. Rated PG-13

Encouraged no doubt by the success of the *High School Musical* franchise, MGM figured the time was right to update Alan Parker's *Fame,* which had become a recognizable name in itself, the original 1980 movie being quite influential in its way of mixing music and drama, inspiring a TV series, a stage adaptation, and a reality show. Dispensing with the grit and unpleasantness that had helped make the original movie stand out and have resonance in its time, the new *Fame* instead was a much sunnier, blander (no pregnancies, no molestations, no nudity, no confessions of homosexual feelings) glimpse into four years in the lives of a group of aspiring youngsters at Manhattan Performing Arts High School. The script found room for the Oscar-winning title tune from the first version (used as a curtain call), as well as "Out There on My Own," giving the best of the newcomers, Naturi Naughton, her big moment to shine as she played it plaintively on the piano in an empty auditorium. In contrast, she was shown earning her stripes among her fellow students singing hip-hop on a recording and in a live performance, both of which only diminished her vocal strengths beneath a lot of techno-overproduction. Such were the times. There was a reprisal of the famous lunch jam scene from three decades past, and sprinklings of dramatic moments and dialogue echoed the earlier picture, but otherwise it was pretty much a revision, not a direct copy. Debbie Allen, featured briefly in the original and a guiding force behind the TV show, popped up here as the school principal.

Fame. Anna Maria Perez de Tagle, Paul McGill, and Paul Iacono.

THE PRINCESS AND THE FROG

Music & lyrics: Randy Newman
Directed by: John Musker, Ron Clements
Screenplay: Ron Clements, John Musker, Rob Edwards
Story: Ron Clements, John Musker, Greg Erb, inspired in part by *The Frog Princess* by E. D. Baker
Cast: Anika Noni Rose, Keith David, Bruno Campos, Michael-Leon Wooley, Jennifer Cody, Jim Cummings, Jenifer Lewis, Oprah Winfrey, Terrence Howard, John Goodman, Peter Bartlett
Songs: "Down in New Orleans"; "Almost There"; "Friends on the Other Side"; "When We're Human"; "Gonna Take You There"; "Ma Belle Evangeline"; "Dig a Little Deeper." Additional song by Ne-Yo: "Never Knew I Needed"
Released: November 2009; 95 minutes. Walt Disney Studios. Rated G

Supervised by Pixar's creative force, John Lasseter, Walt Disney Studios' 49th animated feature, *The Princess and the Frog,* was a welcome addition to the company's output, simply because it was a return to form, being the first hand-drawn project in five years, during which time computer-generated imagery had become the norm. Also working in its favor was the decision to make it a musical with a brand-new score, something animators in the new millennium had forsaken in favor of an occasional background tune or established pop hit. Randy Newman supplied some flavorful songs to complement the beautifully illustrated New Orleans setting, including "When We're Human," performed in the bayou by a gleeful gator and the two amphibian leads, and the requisite "be yourself" number, "Dig a Little Deeper." The real highlight, however, was "Almost There," presented in an animation style unlike the rest of the film, one that resembled the simple but hipper, sharper-edged drawings from the studio's experimental era of the mid-1950s.

The storyline, a variation on E. D. Baker's *The Frog Princess,* had its leading lady kiss a frog in hopes of breaking the spell that has turned him from human to amphibian, but added a humorous twist to the original plot by having the well-meaning heroine end up a frog as well.

Much was made of the fact that *Princess*'s central character, Tiana (voiced by *Dreamgirls'* Anika Noni Rose), was the studio's very first black heroine, although this being a safe, family entertainment out to amuse rather than tackle controversial themes, racial issues were avoided. Instead, the Disney folks simply wanted modern audiences to realize that women of color had as much right to aspire to a "happily ever after" ending as anyone. The public response was good rather than sensational, suggesting that in the CGI era it had now become difficult for some to look at animation the way it *used* to be.

The Princess and the Frog. Tiana and Prince Naveen.

NINE

Music & lyrics: Maury Yeston
Directed by: Rob Marshall
Choreography: Rob Marshall, John DeLuca
Screenplay: Michael Tolkin, Anthony Minghella; based on the musical with book
by Arthur L. Kopit, adaptation from the Italian by Mario Fratti
Cast: Daniel Day-Lewis, Marion Cotillard, Penélope Cruz, Judi Dench, Fergie,
Kate Hudson, Nicole Kidman, Sophia Loren
Songs: "Overture Delle Donne"; "Guido's Song"; "A Call from the Vatican"; "Folies
Bergère"; "Be Italian"; "My Husband Makes Movies"; "Cinema Italiano";
"Guarda la Luna"; "Unusual Way"; "Take It All"; "I Can't Make This Movie"
Released: December 2009; 118 minutes. Weinstein Co. Rated PG-13

Revered by critics and fellow filmmakers far more than by the general public, Federico Fellini's highly personal, often maddening glimpse into his own troubled creative process, *8 ½* (1963), added half a digit and became the 1982 Broadway musical *Nine*. Under Tommy Tune's ever-inventive direction, *Nine* received its share of raves and won the coveted Tony Award for Best Musical but was *not,* despite its origins, obvious film material.

Following a successful 2003 revival/revision, Hollywood's newfound interest in adapting Broadway musicals for the big screen allowed Rob Marshall, the man who had turned *Chicago* into an Oscar-laden hit, the opportunity to see if he could work similar magic with *Nine*. Unfortunately, Marshall jettisoned a good deal of the music, giving over far too much footage to the drama, some sequences echoing those from the original movie. Gone from the stage score were "Not Since Chaplin," "The Germans at the Spa" (already dropped from the revival), "Only with You," "Nine," "The Bells of St. Sebastian," "A Man Like You," the entire "Grand Canal" medley, "Simple," and, most curiously, "Getting Tall," the pivotal summing up of the whole piece, sung to Guido by his nine-year-old self. Yeston added "Cinema Italiano," to comment on the story's mid-1960s time frame; "Guarda la Luna," based on an instrumental theme from the show; and "Take It All," which was an inferior version of the show's more potent "Be on Your Own."

Although the cast was quite impressive both vocally and in their performances, especially Marion Cotillard as Guido's neglected wife, *Nine* lost a lot of its eccentric charm and emotional power on the way to the screen. It came off more like a noncommercial curio with momentary spurts of visual and audio excitement, too often curtailed by Marshall's bad habit of overlapping the dramatic scenes with the musical ones, rather than letting the latter dominate.

Nine. Kate Hudson and Daniel Day-Lewis.

INDEXES

MOVIE INDEX

COMPOSER/LYRICIST INDEX

Burnett, Chester
Cadillac Records, 353

Burrows, R.
Mrs Henderson Presents, 336

Cahn, Sammy
Anchors Aweigh, 132
Court Jester, The, 203
Road to Hong Kong, 226
Robin and the 7 Hoods, 230

Carmichael, Hoagy
Beyond the Sea, 329
Gentlemen Prefer Blondes, 177
Ray, 328

Carter, A.P.
Prairie Home Companion, A, 338
Walk the Line, 334

Carter, Desmond
Love's Labour's Lost, 314

Carter, Helen
Walk the Line, 334

Carter, June
Walk the Line, 334

Carter, Maybelle
Walk the Line, 334

Casey, Harry
From Justin to Kelly, 325

Casey, Warren
Grease, 266

Cash, John R.
Walk the Line, 334

Cave, Nick
Romance & Cigarettes, 345

Chaman, Chaman Lal
Bride & Prejudice, 332

Chamberlain, Simon
Mrs Henderson Presents, 336

Chapman, Ben
From Justin to Kelly, 325

Charles, Ray
Ray, 328

Charnin, Martin
Annie, 274

Chatman, Peter
Ray, 328

Child, Desmond
Moulin Rouge!, 318

Churchill, Frank
Snow White and the Seven Dwarfs, 76

Clarke, Grant
On With the Show, 6

Cochran, Hank
Walk the Line, 334

Cohan, George M.
Yankee Doodle Dandy, 111

Cole, Nat King
Ray, 328

Coleman, Cy
Sweet Charity, 249

Collins, Phil
Moulin Rouge!, 318
Tarzan, 311

Columbo, Russ
Romance & Cigarettes, 345

Comden, Betty
Bells Are Ringing, 222
It's Always Fair Weather, 197
On The Town, 157
Take Me Out to the Ball Game, 151

Crenshaw, Marshall
Walk Hard: The Dewey Cox Story, 347

Crewe, Bob
Moulin Rouge!, 318

Crudup, Arthur
Walk the Line, 334

Cutler, Scott
Dreamgirls, 340
Hannah Montana the Movie, 354

Cyrus, Billy Ray
Hannah Montana the Movie, 354

Cyrus, Miley
Hannah Montana the Movie, 354

Daffan, Ted
Ray, 328

Darin, Bobby
Beyond the Sea, 329

David, Hal
Camp, 326

David, Mack
Cinderella, 155
Romance & Cigarettes, 345

Davis, Roquel
Cadillac Records, 353

Deacon, Roger
Moulin Rouge!, 318

Dench, Ian
Cadillac Records, 353

dePaul, Gene
Seven Brides for Seven Brothers, 184

Derby, Dave
Hannah Montana the Movie, 354

DeSylva, B. G.
Good News, 144
Singing Fool, The, 4
Sunny Side Up, 8

deVries, Marius
Moulin Rouge!, 318

Diamond, Steve
From Justin to Kelly, 325

Dietz, Howard
Bandwagon, The, 179

DioGuardi, Kara
Hannah Montana the Movie, 354

Friml, Rudolf
Firefly, The, 74
Rose Marie (1936), 51
Rose Marie (1954), 183

Fry, Christopher
Beggar's Opera, The, 180

Fuller, Kim
From Justin to Kelly, 325

Fulson, Lowell
Ray, 328

Fuqua, Gwen Gordy
Cadillac Records, 353

Gamble, Kenneth
Moulin Rouge!, 318

Garrett, Siedah
Dreamgirls, 340

Gaskill, Clarence
Romance & Cigarettes, 345

Gay, John
Beggar's Opera, The, 180

Gay, Noel
Mrs Henderson Presents, 336

George, Derek
Hannah Montana the Movie, 354

Gerrard, Matthew
Hannah Montana the Movie, 354
High School Musical 3: Senior Year, 351

Gershe, Leonard
Funny Face, 208

Gershwin, George
American in Paris, An, 166
Damsel in Distress, A, 75
Funny Face, 208
Girl Crazy, 125
Goldwyn Follies, The, 79
Love's Labour's Lost, 314
Porgy and Bess, 220
Rhapsody in Blue, 131
Shall We Dance, 69
Shocking Miss Pilgrim, The, 142

Gershwin, Ira
American in Paris, An, 166
Barkleys of Broadway, The, 152
Country Girl, The, 190
Cover Girl, 128
Damsel in Distress, A, 75
Funny Face, 208
Girl Crazy, 125
Give a Girl a Break, 182
Goldwyn Follies, The, 79
Love's Labour's Lost, 314
Porgy and Bess, 220
Rhapsody in Blue, 131
Shall We Dance, 69
Shocking Miss Pilgrim, The, 142
Star is Born, A (1954), 188

Ghost, Amanda
Cadillac Records, 353

Gibb, Barry, Robin and Maurice
Saturday Night Fever, 265

Gibson, Don
Ray, 328

Gilbert, Cary
Moulin Rouge!, 318

Gilliam, Joi
Idlewild, 339

Glover, Henry
Ray, 328

Goldstein, Gerald
Romance & Cigarettes, 345

Goodwin, Joe
Hollywood Revue of 1929, The, 7

Gordon, Mack
Cadillac Records, 353
Down Argentine Way, 97
Mother Wore Tights, 143
Orchestra Wives, 113
Poor Little Rich Girl, 58
Springtime in the Rockies, 114
Summer Stock, 161
Sun Valley Serenade, 104
Sweet Rosie O'Grady, 123
That Night in Rio, 101
Three Little Girls in Blue, 138
Wake Up and Live, 67
Week-End in Havana, 105
We're Not Dressing, 30

Gordy, Berry
Cadillac Records, 353

Gore, Michael
Camp, 326
Fame, 271

Gorrell, Stuart
Ray, 328

Gottehrer, Richard
Romance & Cigarettes, 345

Grant, Marshall
Walk the Line, 334

Green, Adolph
Bells Are Ringing, 222
It's Always Fair Weather, 197
On The Town, 157
Take Me Out to the Ball Game, 151

Grey, Clifford
Hit the Deck, 193
Love Parade, The, 10
Smiling Lieutenant, The, 15

Guest, Christopher
Mighty Wind, A, 324

Hamlisch, Marvin
Chorus Line, A, 278

Hammerstein, Oscar II
Beyond the Sea, 329
Carmen Jones, 189
Carousel, 203
Deep in My Heart, 191
Flower Drum Song, 224
Great Waltz, The, 85
High, Wide and Handsome, 70
King and I, The, 205,

Composer/Lyricist Index

Livingston, Jerry
Cinderella, 155

Livraghi, Roberto
Romance & Cigarettes, 345

Lloyd Webber, Andrew
Evita, 304
Phantom of the Opera, The, 330

Loesser, Frank
Guys and Dolls, 200
Hans Christian Andersen, 175
How to Succeed in Business Without Really
Trying, 239
Neptune's Daughter, 153
Thank Your Lucky Stars, 123
Where's Charley?, 173

Loewe, Frederick
Brigadoon, 187
Camelot, 241
Gigi, 219
My Fair Lady, 234
Paint Your Wagon, 251

Luboff, Norman
Beyond the Sea, 329

Luhrmann, Baz
Moulin Rouge!, 318

Lurie, Jeannie
Hannah Montana the Movie, 354

Lynn, Loretta
Coal Miner's Daughter, 271

Mabe, Jon
Hannah Montana the Movie, 354

MacDermot, Galt
Hair, 267

Mahone, Carlton
Idlewild, 339

Malik, Anu
Bride & Prejudice, 332

Malneck, Matty
Mrs Henderson Presents, 336

Mancini, Henry
Beyond the Sea, 329
Darling Lili, 254
Victor/Victoria, 273

Martin, Hugh
Best Foot Forward, 124
Meet Me In St. Louis, 130

Mason, (John) Barry
Romance & Cigarettes, 345

Mathis, Donny
Idlewild, 339

Mathews, Samuel
Ray, 328

May, Brian
Moulin Rouge!, 318

Mayfield, Percy
Ray, 328

McAlpin, Lillie
Walk the Line, 334

McCarthy, Joseph
Rio Rita, 9

McCartney, Paul
Across the Universe, 346
Hard Day's Night, A, 231
Help!, 238
Yellow Submarine, 246

McDaniel, Ellas
Cadillac Records, 353

McFarnon, Scott
Cadillac Records, 353

McHugh, Jimmy
Dancing Lady, 26
King of Burlesque, 50
Love's Labour's Lost, 314

McKean, Michael
Mighty Wind, A, 324

Menken, Alan
Aladdin, 292
Beauty and the Beast, 286
Hercules, 306
Hunchback of Notre Dame, The, 301
Little Mermaid, 282
Little Shop of Horrors, 279
Newsies, 288
Pocahontas, 298

Mercer, Johnny
Belle of New York, The, 169
Beyond the Sea, 329
Blues In the Night, 107
Daddy Long Legs, 194
Darling Lili, 254
Fleet's In, The, 109
Harvey Girls, The, 136
Hollywood Hotel, 78
Mrs Henderson Presents, 336
Seven Brides For Seven Brothers, 184
Star Spangled Rhythm, 117
Varsity Show, 72
You Were Never Lovelier, 115

Mercury, Freddie
Moulin Rouge!, 318

Merner, Oscar
From Justin to Kelly, 325

Merrill, Bob
Funny Girl, 244

Meskill, Jack
Folies Bergere de Paris, 41

Mills, Irving
Ray, 328

Mitchell, Sidney
One in a Million, 64

Monaco, James
Road to Singapore, 95
Sing You Sinners, 84

Mores, Marianito
Moulin Rouge!, 318

Morey, Larry
Snow White and the Seven Dwarfs, 76

SCREENWRITER INDEX

DIRECTOR INDEX

Director Index

CHOREOGRAPHERS INDEX

PRODUCER INDEX

Producer Index

Iovine, Jimmy
8 Mile, 321

Jackson, Felix
Can't Help Singing, 129

Jacobs, Arthur P.
Doctor Dolittle, 242
Goodbye, Mr. Chips, 250

Jessel, George
Dolly Sisters, The, 134

Jewison, Norman
Fiddler on the Roof, 257

Jones, Paul
Fleet's In, The, 109
Road to Morocco, 116
Road to Utopia, 134
Road to Zanzibar, 101

Judge, Tony
Prairie Home Companion, A, 338

Kasdan, Jake
Walk Hard: The Dewey Cox Story, 347

Kasdan, Lawrence
Bodyguard, The, 291

Katzenberg, Jeffrey
Prince of Egypt, The, 310

Kaufman, Albert S.
Paramount on Parade, 12

Kaye, Nora
Pennies from Heaven, 272

Keach, James
Walk the Line, 334

Klein, Steve
Passing Strange, 355

Koch, Howard W.
On a Clear Day You Can See Forever, 255

Koffler, Pamela
Camp, 326
Hedwig and the Angry Inch, 320

Kohlmar, Fred
Bye Bye Birdie, 228
Pal Joey, 214
That Night in Rio, 101

Konrad, Cathy
Walk the Line, 334

Koules, Oren
Repo! The Genetic Opera, 352

Lack, Andrew
Cadillac Records, 353

Laemmle, Carl Jr.
King of Jazz, 11
Show Boat (1936), 57

Landon, Joseph
Finian's Rainbow, 243

Lang, Walter
There's No Business Like Show Business, 192

Lasky, Jesse L.
Rhapsody in Blue, 131

LeBaron, William
Gang's All Here, The, 126
Orchestra Wives, 113
Rio Rita, 9
She Done Him Wrong, 22
Springtime in the Rockies, 114
Stormy Weather, 121
Week-End in Havana, 105

Lee, Spike
Passing Strange, 355

Lehman, Ernest
Hello, Dolly!, 253

Lerner, Alan Jay
Paint Your Wagon, 251

LeRoy, Mervyn
Gypsy, 226
Rose Marie (1954), 183
Wizard of Oz, The, 88

Levy, David
Prairie Home Companion, A, 338

Lloyd Webber, Andrew
Phantom of the Opera, The, 330

Logan, John
Sweeney Todd: The Demon Barber of Fleet Street, 349

Lord, Robert
Gold Diggers of 1935, 42
Wonder Bar, 30

Lubitsch, Ernst
Love Parade, The, 10
Monte Carlo, 13
One Hour With You, 15
Smiling Lieutenant, The, 15

Lucchesi, Gary
Fame (2009), 356

Luft, Sidney
Star Is Born, A (1954), 188

Luhrmann, Baz
Moulin Rouge!, 318

MacDonald, Laurie
Sweeney Todd: The Demon Barber of Fleet Street, 349

MacGowan, Kenneth
King of Burlesque, 50
Tin Pan Alley, 100
Wake Up and Live, 67

Mamoulian, Rouben
Love Me Tonight, 17

Mark, Lawrence
Dreamgirls, 340

Markey, Gene
Lillian Russell, 96
On the Avenue, 65
Second Fiddle, 87

Marshall, Alan
Fame, 271

Martin, Ernest H.
Chorus Line, A, 278

CAST INDEX

Almeida, Laurindo
Star is Born, A (1954), 188

Alvarado, Don
Rio Rita, 9

Ameche, Don
Alexander's Ragtime Band, 83
Down Argentine Way, 97
Lillian Russell, 96
Moon Over Miami, 103
One in a Million, 64
That Night in Rio, 101

Ames, Joyce
Hello, Dolly!, 253

Ames, Leon
Anchors Aweigh, 132
Meet Me in St. Louis, 130

Amos 'n Andy
Big Broadcast of 1936, The, 48

Anderson, Daphne
Beggar's Opera, The, 180

Anderson, Eddie "Rochester"
Birth of the Blues, 104
Cabin in the Sky, 119
Show Boat (1936), 57
Star Spangled Rhythm, 117
Wake Up and Live, 67

Anderson, Ivie
Day at the Races, A, 70

Anderson, Joe
Across the Universe, 346

Anderson, Robert
Give a Girl a Break, 182

Andrews, Dana
State Fair, 133
Up In Arms, 127

Andrews, Julie
Darling Lili, 254
Mary Poppins, 233
Sound of Music, The, 237
Star!, 246
Thoroughly Modern Millie, 240
Victor/Victoria, 273

Andrews, Naveen
Bride & Prejudice, 332

Andrews Sisters
Road to Rio, 144

Angelus, Paul
Yellow Submarine, 246

Ann-Margret
Bye Bye Birdie, 228
Newsies, 288
Viva Las Vegas, 229

Anthony, Ray
Daddy Long Legs, 194

Anu, Christine
Moulin Rouge!, 318

Arabe, Armi
King and I, The (1999), 312

Arana, Tomas
Bodyguard, The, 291

Arden, Eve
Cover Girl, 128
Dancing Lady, 26
Grease, 266
Night and Day, 137
Ziegfeld Girl, 102

Arias, Moises
Hannah Montana the Movie, 354

Arkins, Robert
Commitments, The, 284

Arlen, Richard
Paramount on Parade, 12

Arlen, Roxanne
Gypsy, 226

Armen, Kay
Hit the Deck, 193

Armetta, Henry
Anchors Aweigh, 132
Merry Widow, The, 34
One Night of Love, 32
Poor Little Rich Girl, 58
Thank Your Lucky Stars, 123

Armstrong, Curtis
Ray, 328

Armstrong, Louis
Cabin in the Sky, 119
Glenn Miller Story, The, 183
Hello, Dolly!, 253
High Society, 207

Arnaz, Desi
Too Many Girls, 99

Arnold, Edward
Annie Get Your Gun, 159
Lillian Russell, 96
Roman Scandals, 27
Take Me Out to the Ball Game, 151
Ziegfeld Follies, 135

Arnold, Tichina
Little Shop of Horrors, 279

Aronov, Michael
Hedwig and the Angry Inch, 320

Arthur, Jean
Paramount on Parade, 12

Arthur, Maureen
How to Succeed in Business Without Really
Trying, 239

Arthur, Robert
Mother Wore Tights, 143

Astaire, Fred
Band Wagon, The, 179
Barkleys of Broadway, The, 152
Belle of New York, The, 169
Blue Skies, 140
Broadway Melody of 1940, 92
Carefree, 84
Daddy Long Legs, 194
Damsel in Distress, A, 75

Berle, Milton
  Muppet Movie, The, 268
  Sun Valley Serenade, 104

Berlin, Irving
  This Is the Army, 122

Bernie, Ben
  Wake Up and Live, 67

Bess, Kahiry
  Camp, 326

Besser, Matt
  Walk Hard: The Dewey Cox Story, 347

Besserer, Eugenie
  Jazz Singer, The, 3

Bessy, Claude
  Invitation to the Dance, 206

Best, Willie
  Cabin in the Sky, 119

Beymer, Richard
  West Side Story, 223

Bickford, Charles
  High, Wide and Handsome, 70
  Star Is Born, A (1954), 188

Bikel, Theodore
  My Fair Lady, 234

Bil Baird Marionettes
  Sound of Music, The, 237

Biltmore Trio
  Broadway Melody, The, 5

Bing, Herman
  Broadway Melody of 1940, 92
  Footlight Parade, 25
  Great Waltz, The, 85
  Great Ziegfeld, The, 54
  Maytime, 66
  Merry Widow, The, 34
  Night and Day, 137
  One Night of Love, 32
  Rose Marie (1936), 51
  Sweethearts, 86

Bishop, Julie
  Rhapsody in Blue, 131

Bishop, Kelly
  Dirty Dancing, 280

Bisoglio, Val
  Saturday Night Fever, 265

Björk
  Dancer in the Dark, 315

Black, Karen
  Nashville, 262

Blackburn Twins
  Take Me Out to the Ball Game, 151
  Words and Music, 150

Blackmer, Sidney
  High Society, 207

Blaine, Vivian
  Guys and Dolls, 200
  State Fair, 133
  Three Little Girls in Blue, 138

Blair, Nicky
  Viva Las Vegas, 229

Blake, Amanda
  Star Is Born, A (1954), 188

Blakley, Ronee
  Nashville, 262

Blanc, Mel
  Neptune's Daughter, 153

Blandick, Clara
  Wizard of Oz, The, 88

Blane, Sally
  Show of Shows, The, 11

Bledel, Alexis
  Bride & Prejudice, 332

Blessed, Brian
  Tarzan, 311

Blethyn, Brenda
  Beyond the Sea, 329

Bleu, Corbin
  High School Musical 3: Senior Year, 351

Bliss, Lucille
  Cinderella, 155

Block, Jesse
  Kid Millions, 37

Blondell, Joan
  Dames, 33
  Footlight Parade, 25
  Gold Diggers of 1933, 23
  Gold Diggers of 1937, 64
  Grease, 266

Blonsky, Nikki
  Hairspray, 343

Blore, Eric
  Flying Down to Rio, 28
  Folies Bergere de Paris, 41
  Gay Divorcee, The, 36
  Joy of Living, 81
  Road to Zanzibar, 101
  Shall We Dance, 69
  Swing Time, 61
  Top Hat, 47

Blue, Ben
  Big Broadcast of 1938, The, 80
  For Me and My Gal, 116
  High, Wide and Handsome, 70
  Two Girls and a Sailor, 129

Blyden, Larry
  On a Clear Day You Can See Forever, 255

Blyth, Ann
  Great Caruso, The, 163
  Kismet, 202
  Rose Marie (1954), 183
  Student Prince, The, 186

Bogart, Humphrey
  Thank Your Lucky Stars, 123

Bois, Curt
  Cover Girl, 128
  Great Waltz, The, 85

Carle, Richard
Anything Goes, 52
Merry Widow, The, 34
One Hour With You, 15
One Night in the Tropics, 98
San Francisco, 59

Carlisle, Mary
Double or Nothing, 72

Carlson, Richard
Too Many Girls, 99

Carmichael, Hoagy
Young Man With a Horn, 158

Carminati, Tullio
One Night of Love, 32

Carnovsky, Morris
Rhapsody in Blue, 131

Caron, Leslie
American in Paris, An, 166
Daddy Long Legs, 194
Gigi, 219

Carpenter, Carleton
Summer Stock, 161
Three Little Words, 160

Carpenter, Ken
Road to Zanzibar, 101

Carpenter, Thelma
Cotton Club, The, 277

Carpentier, Georges
Show of Shows, The, 11

Carpio, T.V.
Across the Universe, 346

Carr, Charmian
Sound of Music, The, 237

Carradine, John
Alexander's Ragtime Band, 83
Court Jester, The, 203

Carradine, Keith
Nashville, 262

Carrillo, Leo
Lillian Russell, 96
One Night in the Tropics, 98

Carroll, Diahann
Carmen Jones, 189
Porgy and Bess, 220

Carroll, Georgia
Girl Crazy, 125
Yankee Doodle Dandy, 111
Ziegfeld Girl, 102

Carroll, Joan
Meet Me in St. Louis, 130

Carroll, John
Monte Carlo, 13

Carroll, Madeleine
On the Avenue, 65

Carroll, Nancy
Paramount on Parade, 12

Carroll, Pat
Little Mermaid, The, 282

Carson, Jack
Blues in the Night, 107
Carefree, 84
Star Is Born, A (1954), 188
Thank Your Lucky Stars, 123

Carter, Benny
Stormy Weather, 121
American in Paris, An, 166

Carter, Jack
Viva Las Vegas, 229

Carter, Nell
Hair, 267

Carver, Lynne
Broadway Melody of 1940, 92
Maytime, 66

Casan, Christian
Passing Strange, 355

Casella, Max
Newsies, 288

Caselotti, Andrianna
Snow White and the Seven Dwarfs, 76

Castro, Fidel
You Were Never Lovelier, 115

Catlett, Walter
My Gal Sal, 110
On the Avenue, 65
Pinocchio, 91
Star Spangled Rhythm, 117
Up In Arms, 127
Varsity Show, 72
Wake Up and Live, 67
Yankee Doodle Dandy, 111

Caulfield, Joan
Jolson Story, The, 140

Caupolican, Chief
Whoopee!, 14

Cavanaugh, Hobart
Footlight Parade, 25
Wonder Bar, 130

Cavanaugh, Paul
Night and Day, 137

Cawthorn, Joseph
Gold Diggers of 1935, 42
Great Ziegfeld, The, 54
Lillian Russell, 96
Love Me Tonight, 17
Music In the Air, 39
Naughty Marietta, 44
Sweet Adeline, 39

Cedric the Entertainer
Cadillac Records, 353

Chabert, Lacey
Anastasia, 308

Chakiris, George
Gentlemen Prefer Blondes, 177
West Side Story, 223
White Christmas, 186

Cast Index

Cast Index

Cast Index

Cast Index

Cast Index

Cast Index

Cast Index

STUDIO INDEX